D0249626

To 'Joy My Freedom

To 'Joy My Freedom

SOUTHERN BLACK WOMEN'S LIVES AND LABORS AFTER THE CIVIL WAR

Tera W. Hunter

HARVARD UNIVERSITY PRESS

CAMBRIDGE, MASSACHUSETTS

LONDON, ENGLAND

To my parents and in memory of my grandparents

Copyright © 1997 by Tera W. Hunter
All rights reserved
Printed in the United States of America
Third printing, 1998

First Harvard University Press paperback edition, 1998

Library of Congress Cataloging-in-Publication Data
Hunter, Tera W.
To 'joy my freedom: Southern Black women's lives and labors after
the Civil War / Tera W. Hunter.
p.   cm.
Includes bibliographical references and index.
ISBN 0-674-89309-3 (cloth)
ISBN 0-674-89308-5 (pbk.)
1. Afro-American women—Employment—Georgia—Atlanta—
History—19th century. 2. Afro-American women—Employment—
Georgia—Atlanta—History—20th century. 3. Afro-American women—
Georgia—Atlanta—History—19th century. 4. Afro-American women—
Georgia—Atlanta—History—20th century. I. Title.
HD6057.5.U52G45   1997
331.4′089′960730758231—dc21
96-51473

Contents

Illustrations follow page 144

Preface

his book began with a few newspaper articles on the 1881
Atlanta washerwomen's strike. This one event engaged my interest
enough to inspire a full-length study and taught me some fundamental
lessons about how to research and write a history of black women. The
strike piqued my curiosity because it challenged conventional wisdom
about the limited capacity of working-class women's protests. What I
discovered about the strikers and the astute political strategies they
adopted to make their voices heard left me eager to know more about
the women and their city. A central tension that would be clear in the
bigger story I would eventually piece together was readily apparent in
this early event. Here was a group of black women, a decade and a half
removed from slavery, striving to achieve freedom, equality, and a
living wage against tremendous odds.

The limitations of the extant evidence for this strike cautioned me
about the difficulties of finding primary sources covering a broader
scope. Just as the strike had yielded limited first-hand accounts by the
women, finding direct testimony of black women would be my biggest
challenge. The process of researching the strike also taught me how to
make the most of sources that are typically used to study ordinary
people but have been less frequently applied specifically to black
women workers. By thinking expansively about how to find and interpret historical sources and scavenging for clues in whatever evidence
was at hand, I was able to discover a great deal of relevant material
about the broad dimensions of black and Southern lives. This book

draws from a large variety of primary documents, including diaries, household account books, newspapers, census data, municipal records, city directories, personal correspondence, oral interviews, government reports, business records, photographs, political cartoons, and organizational records.

This is a study of the black female majority in the urban South: women who worked for wages and who were primarily confined to domestic labor. The women worked as cooks, maids, child-nurses, laundresses, and other specialized servants. These laborers and their experiences in the workplace form the core of this book. The women were also mothers, lovers, fraternal members, religious devotees, consumers, political activists, and partygoers, and these experiences are treated in depth as well.

My analysis of black women's struggles covers the period from the final days of slavery during the Civil War through another momentous watershed, the Great Migration during World War I. Their strategies to achieve self-sufficiency and to counter the deleterious effects of subjugation took many forms: they developed an arsenal of everyday tactics of resistance; they built institutions; they developed informal neighborhood networks of support. But as black women struggled to overcome conditions of abject poverty and servitude, employers and public authorities worked even harder to repress and contain them through every means at their disposal. Although this contest often took place behind closed doors, much of it was also fought out in public view. African-American women were central to public discourse about race, gender, and labor in the South. The public airing of presumably private disputes highlighted the broader ramifications of domestic work. Clearly, African-American women were outpowered and outnumbered. They fought for dignity and self-respect and won small gains, moments of reprieve, and symbolic political victories. But their lives involved more than struggle and pain. They found pleasure in their neighborhoods, families, churches, mutual aid organizations, dance halls, and vaudeville theaters.

Atlanta, Georgia, the heart of the burgeoning New South, is the landscape in which these rich and complex stories unfold. In many ways, Atlanta was representative of urban centers throughout the South in the period following the Civil War. But in other ways it was distinctive—in its youth, vitality, and ambition to lead the South into the modern industrial world. For African Americans, however, Atlanta was a paradox. It fostered a great sense of hope but also despair about the realization of full citizenship rights. Although Atlanta was a self-consciously forward-looking city, it was retrogressive in its race, gender, and labor relations. As the book opens during the last days of the Civil War, we witness the energy and optimism that blacks would carry with them to the city once the war was over. But by the time of World War I, despite the gains they had made, African Americans would find it necessary to take drastic measures to escape mounting repression. As the book ends, the narrative is brought full circle as blacks once again were on the move, emigrating in large numbers out of Atlanta and out of the South.

Prologue

*I*n the spring of 1866, Julie Tillory journeyed by foot to Atlanta with her two young children in tow. Like the thousands of other newly free people pouring into the city during Reconstruction, they had no earthly belongings except the tattered clothes on their backs. Tillory had been sent word that her brother Paul and his wife and children had relocated to Atlanta recently. Unlike most other freedpeople who arrived without kin, Tillory was fortunate to have her brother's family and could share their cramped quarters and food.

One of Tillory's first concerns upon her arrival was to visit the office of the Freedmen's Bureau. She wanted assistance in locating her husband, John Robinson, who had been separated from her during the war. Robinson and Tillory had been owned by two different masters and lived separately on neighboring plantations. When the war broke out and slaveholders began fleeing for safe territory to escape invasion by the Union Army, Robinson refused to accompany his master and fled. For a while, Tillory would hear occasional news about her husband— that he was hiding out in their county, waiting for the right opportunity to retrieve her and the children. But no such opportunity ever came. The news gradually petered out and Tillory lost contact. She had no idea if Robinson was alive or dead.

When Tillory found the Freedmen's Bureau office, she encountered Northern missionaries and Union Army officials busily tending to the business of helping destitute families find shelter, food, clothing, and work. Her eyes fixed on a missionary woman who was herself overwhelmed by the tasks before her and the gravity of her responsibilities. Apparently in awe of the seeming contradiction of destitution and determination surrounding her, the missionary pondered the state of affairs. She asked Tillory a question that had been burning in her mind ever since her arrival in the South and her first-hand observation of the monumental changes brought about by Union victory. Why would you want to leave the certainties and comforts of your master's plantation, where subsistence was guaranteed, for the uncertainties before you? she asked. Without a moment's pause, Tillory replied: "to 'joy my freedom."[1] To enjoy the splendid fruits of freedom at last! Here was her opportunity to protect her dignity, to preserve the integrity of her family, and to secure fair terms for her labor. Tillory's resolve and endurance typified the spirit of ex-slaves determined to be truly free, despite the absence of material comforts.

The atmosphere inside the Freedmen's Bureau office was solemn and intense, but a different mood prevailed on the streets downtown. Amid the hustle and bustle of Saturday business there were clusters of freedpeople frolicking around and jostling one another, stopping occasionally to buy food from vendors or listen to street musicians. Susie Pride, Minnie Freeman, and Savannah Bruce walked through the crowds. Their multicolored dresses and decorative parasols held above their heads to filter the bright sunlight were striking. They carried fans to cool themselves in the summer heat, and they wiped their brows with embroidered handkerchiefs. A white woman, Abbie Brooks, encountered the trio on the sidewalk and was taken aback by what appeared to her to be "uppity" Negro women enjoying their freedom with just a little too much panache! Brooks would write in her diary: "Their appearance is unmistakably African." The way the women walked with a "swaggering air," and the vivid colors of their dresses sewn together in seemingly incongruent patterns, were for Brooks an eyesore. These sights would "inspire the most casual observer with a feeling of contempt and rebellion," Brooks wrote. "We are in a manner ruled by the typical wooly haired sons of Ham—whose superiority has never been acknowledged by any enlightened race in the world."[2]

Clearly the joy of freedom signified many things to black women, the full dimensions of which neither sympathetic Northerners nor erstwhile slaveholders fully understood or appreciated. These black women strolling the streets of Atlanta were playfully constructing new identities that overturned notions of racial inferiority and that could only be interpreted by many white Southerners as signs of African aesthetics run amok. Black women were determined to make freedom mean the opportunity to find pleasure and relaxation with friends, family, and neighbors. Their lives as field and house slaves on plantations and in antebellum cities had been governed by rules and regulations over which they had no control. As freedpeople, however, they were committed to balancing the need to earn a living with needs for emotional sustenance, personal growth, and collective cultural expressions. Despite the topsy-turvy world that Brooks feared, in which sartorial style symbolized the threat of black domination, these women were neither carefree nor almighty. Come Monday morning the parasols, fans, and handkerchiefs would be put aside, as they engaged in washing, cooking, cleaning, scrubbing, and mopping in exchange for a wage.

Racial caste and the demands of the Southern political economy dictated that black women work, and in Southern cities their options were confined to household labor. Their experiences as laborers would determine how meaningful freedom would be. But for ex-slave women, whose social value had long resided in the labor power they could expend to benefit their masters and in the prospective laborers they could reproduce, work was a means to self-sufficiency, not an end in itself. Black women would encounter, however, employers with attitudes like that of Abbie Brooks, resentful of their new status and resolved to prevent the extension of democracy. The tumultuous struggle that ensued between worker and employer would not be easily resolved.

CHAPTER ONE

"Answering Bells Is Played Out": Slavery and the Civil War

llen, a house slave in Atlanta, violated a long-established code of racial etiquette by wearing her mistress's toiletries during the early years of the Civil War. Imagine Ellen standing in the master bedroom of the Big House, playfully staring at her likeness reflected in a looking-glass mounted on a Victorian vanity. She primps her hair, rearranges her clothing, and shifts the view of her profile from front to side. Taking her pick among an array of dainty crystal bottles, she sniffs earthy and then floral fragrances and carefully applies one of the perfumes. While reveling in the crisp, cool feel of amber-tinted drops of liquid against her skin, she dreams about a life far away from the drudgery of her circumscribed existence—a life she believes could soon be within her reach.

Ellen audaciously indulged these vicarious pleasures repeatedly, even after being reprimanded by her owner, Samuel P. Richards, and eventually whipped. In pampering and adorning her body with the magical elixir, Ellen transgressed feminine beauty rituals intended to enhance white bodies only. She laid claim to a measure of possession of her own person—and a womanly person at that. The Civil War, as Ellen perceived, could erode the rituals of daily life in the South. Bondwomen like Ellen notified slaveowners that they could neither take servile obedience for granted nor be assured that chattel slaves would cook, clean, wash, mend, or greet arriving visitors as they had before. As another slave woman abruptly replied in response to her owner's command to attend to her duties: "answering bells is played out."[1]

Such incidents expose the increasingly pronounced clash of expectations between masters and slaves during the Civil War. Ellen waged her bets on the destruction of slavery, which strengthened her resolve to take risks in testing the limits of bondage as she awaited its official demise. Samuel P. Richards, by contrast, believed the war was a temporary annoyance and inconvenience; he predicted that "when we come to a successful end to the war" slavery would continue. Despite Richards's disinclination to concede to the winds of change, Ellen's defiance and similar acts by other slaves exasperated him as he struggled to protect his diminishing authority. Richards complained: "I am disgusted with negroes and feel inclined to sell what I have. I wish they were all back in Africa,—or—Yankee Land. To think too that this 'cruel war' should be waged for them."[2] The war of nerves conducted by slaves taxed Richards's patience more severely than any actions on the battlefields and served as a harbinger of future difficulties in Southern labor relations long after the Confederacy's defeat. However small and symbolic this friction may appear, conflicts and renegotiations over the meaning of slavery and freedom increased as the war progressed, with prolonged consequences for all Southerners.

SIMILAR vignettes of contestation between slaves and masters were repeated throughout the region. As the Union and Confederate troops faced off at Fort Sumter, African Americans were poised to intervene in this revolutionary moment to influence the outcome of the war in their favor.[3] A slave mistress in Savannah summed up the changed dispositions of slaves who were testing the limits of the institution: the Negroes "show a very different face from what they have had heretofore."[4] Slave resistance was not unique to the Civil War, but black countenances evinced new meanings not readily discernible to masters under normal conditions in the antebellum era. African Americans articulated objections against the system of human bondage more consciously and openly than ever before.

Slaveholders formerly secure in their privileged positions and confident in the docility and loyalty of their most prized slaves in the Big House showed new faces as well—the faces of disillusion and betrayal. Slaves, the critics most cognizant of the constraints of human bondage, rejected the long-held beliefs of masters. Planters learned of "the perfect impossibility of placing the least confidence in any Negro" very early in the war, as one Savannah patrician noted. "In too many numerous instances those we esteemed the most have been the first to desert us."[5] And those who stayed were no more reliable inasmuch as they ceased to labor on former terms. "I was sorely tried with Fanny, my cook a very dull, obstinate servant," remarked another Georgian. "I make our coffee every morning and then find great difficulty in getting her to get our simple breakfast."[6] Masters had not yet discerned that the worrisome, but seemingly innocuous, concessions they reluctantly made, such as making coffee or cajoling the cook to prepare the morning meal, would hasten the collapse of slavery.

As the certainty of slavery became more tenuous during the War, latent tensions and sharply contrasting world views and ambitions of various groups surfaced. The internecine battles between slaves and masters, North and South, slaveholding and nonslaveholding whites prefigured conflicts that would continue to plague the region for many years. In cities like Atlanta, where urban conditions made slavery precarious long before the war began, the sudden and dramatic population growth and commercial expansion during the war helped to secure slavery's demise.

IN THE antebellum period, Atlanta was barely a blip on the map. In the 1820s, it served as a railroad depot in the foothills of north Georgia for neighboring farmers. By the 1850s, a fusion of Northern entrepreneurs along with the native-born yeomen inaugurated the business of city building. The expansion of railroad lines enabled swifter commerce west, further south, north, and to the Atlantic coast, enhancing the city's strategic geography by the eve of the Civil War.[7]

Atlanta's growth was fostered by the Civil War and by the railroad. Its dramatic rise countered an emblematic feature of Southern economic development. The South lagged behind the North in urbanization and industrialization, a tribute to the overwhelming predominance of plantation slavery and agriculture. Cities of any significance in the antebellum era, such as Savannah, New Orleans, and Charleston, catered to the needs of the planter elite.[8] The Southern states seceded to conserve plantation slavery and its urban subordinates, but secession produced unexpected consequences: the war destroyed slavery, and it transformed several inauspicious towns into developing metropolises. By the end of the war, New South cities like Atlanta began eclipsing the eminence of Old South cities.

Atlanta was conspicuous within the region from its inception. The predominance of merchants and manufacturers and the absence of planters within the city's economic elite invited early comparisons to the commercial ambitions of cities in the North. Even at this incipient stage of urban development, some Atlantans took pride in an entrepreneurial spirit that attracted young, upwardly mobile white men dedicated to commerce and industry, and this foreshadowed events and accolades to come. Upstarts were welcomed to the city to help build the railroads that stood at the center of the economy, and to develop related industries, like foundries and rolling mills. Other businesses included hotels, a brewery, a saw mill, a flour mill, a shoe factory, wagon builders, furniture shops, cigar factories, leather tanneries, a whiskey distillery, and agricultural implement manufacturers.[9] This diversity of businesses offered opportunities for consumers and workers, slave and free, not typical of the region. But even as Atlanta self-consciously touted itself as a progressive divergence from the South's dependence on one-crop agriculture, it also resisted social and political change.

Atlanta's distinctive economy presented conflicting interests for the city's power brokers as the Civil War approached. Most businessmen initially opposed secession out of fear that alienation from the Union would obstruct interregional trade, though they relented in due course.[10] Their apprehension regarding the adverse consequences of military invasion and Confederate government policies was well-founded. Farmers and traders fearful of impressment refrained from bringing their wares to city markets, which led to a shortage of foodstuffs and dry goods. Acute class conflict among whites surfaced as deprived consumers rioted, looted provision houses, and stole from wealthy residents in protest over spiraling prices, greedy speculation, and government impressment. Poverty led destitute patriots to turn against their allies. In March 1863, starving wives of Confederate soldiers rioted and pilfered provision houses in the central business district on Whitehall Street. The wives of artisans, factory workers, and Confederate soldiers displayed similar disenchantment in boisterous crowds in other towns. An Atlanta newspaper castigated these "women seizures" as a movement of "very wicked and ignorant women, generally instigated thereto and led by rascally individuals."[11]

Though commerce plummeted as predicted, no one could have foreseen the salutary impact of the war on the growth and development of manufacturing and urban expansion. The centrality of cities as distribution centers for the rebel forces boosted the importance of Atlanta as a strategic location, second only to Richmond. The military demand for ordnance and the fabrication of other items for civilian and military use, such as boots, buckles, buttons, saddles, uniforms, revolvers, and railroad cars, encouraged the building of new factories and the retooling of old operations. The influx of slaves, soldiers, runaways, military laborers, military officials, and refugee slaveholders generated a tremendous population expansion. In 1860, Atlanta's population had stood at less than ten thousand; two years later it had nearly doubled.

This sudden expansion of inhabitants presented an immediate problem of social control. In its earlier frontier days, Atlanta had a reputation as a "crossroads village" that attracted rowdies, vagabonds, bootleggers, and prostitutes. These "disreputable" sorts congregated in Snake Nation, along Peter's Street, and Murrell's Row, near Decatur Street, the beginnings of red-light districts and a thriving "underworld." Early city officials had a difficult time enforcing laws against prostitution, cockfighting, discharging firearms in the streets, and rolling live hogs in hogsheads down hills. Murder, larceny, gambling, insobriety, disorderly conduct, and indecent exposure filled the pages of the court dockets in the antebellum period—an inclination only heightened by the chaos of the war.[12]

Ramblers and roughnecks did not present the most formidable challenge to the city unless they also happened to be black. Slavery, as it was known in most of the plantation South, did not take root in Atlanta in the same way, where commerce and a complementary "urban promotive creed" prevailed. In the rural South, slavery ordered labor relations and plantation life; in the urban South, slavery was only one source of labor and was merely incidental to a city's character. In 1860 there were only 1900 blacks in Atlanta, 20 percent of the population, and all but twenty-five persons were slaves. Individual slaves performed important labor in a wide variety of occupations, including brakemen, blacksmiths, boilermakers, and paper mill workers. Yet most African Americans were concentrated in domestic work, as in other antebellum cities, mainly in hotels and boardinghouses.[13] Even with such a relatively small number of slaves in the city, however, they were difficult to control, since the usual mechanisms were simply not as effective. Slaves were freer to roam about in the larger society among a denser populace, rather than being quarantined on isolated farms. The kind of labor they performed in small workshops or hotel establishments did not lend itself as easily to direct and constant supervision as did gang labor in the fields.

The economic and political priorities of Atlanta as a relatively young city were different from those of more established Southern cities where slaves were more numerous, but they did not deter slavery altogether. Samuel P. Richards, a British-born merchant, bought slaves for his farm in the countryside, hired the slaves of other owners, and purchased servants specifically to work in his Atlanta home. In December 1862, he purchased thirteen-year-old Ellen after two years of hiring her: "I have committed the unpardonable sin of the Abolitionists in buying a negro. I am tired of the trouble of getting a servant every Christmas and we have found Ellen a pretty good girl."[14] A few months later he purchased a family of three slaves: Joe, Caroline, and their three-year-old child. Richards sent the husband to work on the farm in the country and the wife and child to the city residence. Though somewhat skeptical at first about the outcome of his investment, Richards was soon optimistic about high returns. He purchased Ellen for $1,225, several hundred dollars below her former owner's asking price, and within five months he estimated that her value had risen to $2,000. Gloating over the appreciation of his property, despite the exigencies of an economy spun out of control, Richards predicted a Confederate victory and the continuance of slavery. He believed that "negroes will command very high prices as there will be so much demand for labor to raise cotton and a great many will have been taken by the Yankees."[15]

In reality, Ellen's price rose because of wartime inflation as well as the scarcity of household slaves. As one slaveholder wrote to another about the prospects of finding experienced domestics in the city: "Many desirable negroes are daily offered by people who are obliged to sell— but the kind most offered are field hands—men[,] boys and young women."[16] The relatively lower prices for field hands advertised by slave dealers lends credence to this observation.[17] The influx of refugee whites into the city may have contributed to the market for domestic slaves. But the urgent need for able-bodied field workers to sustain the plantation system and to raise crops for the subsistence of civilians and soldiers alike made it more difficult to find slaves hired expressly for domestic labor.[18]

The impressment of slaves by the Confederacy was a further drain on waning supplies. Samuel Stout, the head surgeon for the Army of Tennessee, headquartered in Atlanta, wrote to patrons in Florida for help for one of the Confederacy's largest hospitals. "In nothing can you aid us more than by sending us fruits and vegetables. Labor is also very much in demand. Every negro hired to the hospital, enables us to send an able-bodied soldier to the field."[19] Domestic servants were especially in demand—men as nurses, women as laundresses, and both as cooks.[20]

The hire-out system alleviated some of the inconveniences of scarcity by permitting slaves or owners to make short-term arrangements for daily, monthly, or yearly work. Given the diverse and fluctuating needs of urban economies, whites in cities relied on the hiring system to balance the demands for labor with the legal constraints that slavery imposed on bound workers. Many owners hired out their chattel property to friends as favors. Some sought to lighten their financial hardships by relieving themselves of the daily care of slaves, or to rid themselves of the burdens of managing unruly and willful slaves.[21] Ellen Campbell, an Augusta ex-slave, described the circumstances leading to her working for hire at age fifteen: "My young missus wus fixin' to git married, but she couldn't on account de war, so she brought me to town and rented me out to a lady runnin' a boarding house." But the arrangement was short-lived. Campbell dropped a serving tray, and the boardinghouse keeper stabbed her in the head with a butcher's knife in punishment. Campbell's enraged mistress revoked the contract immediately.[22] Slaveholders, however, were often willing to bear the risks of abuse when the profits reaped from hire contracts provided their sole income.[23]

The hire-out system democratized access to slaves by enabling white wage-earners to benefit from the system, even as some white workers were forced to compete with slaves. If they could not afford to buy a slave outright, some could afford to hire slaves as helpers as their needs demanded them. Thus, the proportion of the white population that owned slaves in the cities was higher than in the rural areas, even though individual holdings were smaller.[24] Jennie Akehurst Lines, the wife of a union printer in Atlanta, wrote letters to her sister detailing a dilemma of white workers' hiring practices. The spiraling costs of living and the insecurity of her husband's trade during a period marked by workplace strife and uncertain wages limited the Lineses' family income. Yet Jennie Lines remained steadfast in her opinion of the necessity of hiring domestic labor. "I presume you think I ought not to keep help," she wrote. "If I did not I should have to pay out the same amount for washing. True we should save the food and clothing but I do not believe we should save one dime more."[25] Aside from the economic rationale, the drudgery and quantity of the work also provided a motivation, which the printer's wife described as her lack of "taste" for certain kinds of work.[26] "Besides I could never look nice myself, keep my baby or my house clean. Sylvanus dont want me to do kitchen drudgery in this country—says he will break up house keeping if I insist on doing without help."[27] Slaves for hire raised the standard of living for a segment of the white working class and gave some nonslaveowners a direct investment in preserving the institution. The effect of such white racial unity and the contradictory relations between blacks and whites of similar economic circumstances would become more apparent in later years—especially in the strained relations between household workers and poor white employers.

Some aspects of urban slavery were similar to those of rural slavery. The sexual exploitation of women was equally onerous whether it occurred on plantations or in urban households. Black women were subjected to sexual abuse by slaveowners, overseers, and drivers. They were assaulted by individual men and gangs. Though most women were helpless in the face of violations of their persons, some fought their assailants directly at great risk. Others devised strategies to evade molestation without open confrontation. Louisa, a Georgia house slave, avoided the clutches of her master by sleeping in the room with his children or nailing up the windows of her own house. He persisted and found a way into her room, however, and she turned up the light of lamps to distract and dissuade him. Still undaunted, he made efforts to cajole and coerce Louisa by offering "two dollars to feel her titties," which she also refused. Afforded little protection against unwanted sexual advances and exploitation of their reproductive capabilities, many black women who resisted were beaten, mutilated, sold, or killed.[28] During the Civil War, Union and Confederate soldiers took advantage of their positions of power and authority to rape slave women, sometimes in the presence of the women's parents, husbands, children, and grandchildren who were forced to stand by, helpless and horrified.[29]

In other ways, urban slavery had distinct advantages and disadvantages compared to rural slavery. The small slaveholding units in urban areas almost inevitably meant that slave families were torn apart. As we saw, when Samuel P. Richards purchased a family consisting of parents and child, he split the group by sending the father to the country and the mother and child to the city. Urban house slaves often suffered double isolation: they were cut off from their families as well as from other slaves.[30] The small holdings of individual owners also put greater burdens on slaves to perform labor beyond their capability. With few or no other slaves to share the work load, slave exertion could be pushed to the limits, which was especially burdensome for domestic servants expected to perform on constant call.[31] A former slave from Nashville recounted the onerous labor that she endured when she was hired out. "They hired me to nurse, but I had to nurse, cook, chop in the fields, chop wood, bring water, wash, iron and in general just do everything," she recalled as an adult.[32] She awoke before the sun rose, made the fire, and commenced both house and field work, which was remarkable because she was only six years old at that time.

Children were especially vulnerable to exploitation in isolation from their parents or other adult slaves. Jennie Lines summed up the logic of hiring girls: "We have a negro girl sixteen years old. She is large enough and strong enough to do everything, and I mean she shall if I keep her. We pay $4 a month for her besides clothes; that you know is cheap for a grown woman."[33] After some complaints about twelve-year-old Beckie's master raising her rate, despite her poor performance, Lines wrote with increased confidence: "She improves. Perhaps she will in a few months be just the help I need. I can make her do my work just as I want it done, which I can not do with an older one."[34] Lines expected the young ones to perform with the same degree of skill and perseverance as women twice their age—cooking, washing, cleaning, and caring for an infant.

Despite the hardships of urban bondage, the system could not enforce the same degree of coercion as rural bondage did. Slaves living in

cities were afforded many opportunities for living a relatively autonomous life. Anonymity within a dense population and customary practices that permitted slaves of absent owners to find their own shelter in
sheds, attics, basements, single rooms, or small houses encouraged
independence. In addition, urban slavery permitted casual contact between unfree and free people, black and white. Pass systems, curfews,
and other laws were designed to limit the mobility of slaves while away
from their official workplaces without the permission of owners, but in
reality, these mechanisms were usually not strictly enforced. Thread-
bare municipal infrastructures and minuscule resources did not allow
for controlling any segment of the population, slave or free. Though
some owners tried to limit interactions among blacks by spreading slave
housing all over the city, they did not have the wherewithal to keep
close watch over slaves. Slaves took advantage of the lax patrol to move
around the city, to participate in a rich, if still limited, communal life
almost as if they were free. They gathered to socialize in markets,
grocery stores, grogshops, street corners, churches, and the homes of
friends—clandestinely during the day and openly at night.[35]

Slaves living independent of their masters' constant supervision
posed a persistent threat to the system and tested the capability of the
municipal government to act as a surrogate for the owners. The demands of the Civil War and the conditions it created frustrated antebellum mechanisms of control. In 1863, the Atlanta City Council made
an extra effort to enforce a pass system to regulate the large influx of
slave military laborers. But overlapping civilian and military authority
blurred the chain of command, hindering the city from implementing
unilateral decisions. The city council made another futile attempt in the
same year to limit black mobility by requiring all blacks, except body
servants, to "be kept in some negro yard or house, and not [be] permitted to go at large through the city" after work hours.[36]

During the war, a number of factors contributed to the growing
number of slaves who were living and working independently. The
unanticipated growth of the black population made any attempts to
control slaves impractical. The inflated costs and shortages of housing
for everyone, regardless of race or status, made it difficult to govern
who should live where. The increasing demand for black labor in a
broad range of enterprises made it beneficial for slaveowners to defy the
laws and allow their slaves to earn their own living. Many whites

suffered the psychological effects of the loss of bound labor, but many were still eager to reap its profits. Other slaveowners facing privation abandoned slaves in cities, forcing more blacks into the self-hire system to avoid destitution. The city's futile attempts to control all of these unforeseen forces created a general atmosphere of lax regulation of the conventional constraints of slavery and even greater tolerance of blacks who committed petty crimes.[37]

As city officials and masters in Atlanta lost their grip on bound labor, fear of outright slave rebellion troubled the white residents. In 1863, this anxiety increased when two female slaves were arrested for setting a boardinghouse on fire. In addition, slaves organized "Negro balls" in local hotels, ostensibly to raise money for Confederate soldiers and their body servants. Though the city initially approved these seemingly innocent amusements, people came to see them as public disturbances with the potential to stir up rebellion. But these "Negro balls," no matter how annoying, prompted only occasional cause for concern. The city's bigger problem was the more pervasive and less dramatic daily struggle between slaves and masters that undermined the changing institution as the war lingered on.[38] African Americans seized the moment to pursue their aspirations and in the process revealed latent contending notions of freedom that shook the confidence and ideology of slaveholders. The conspicuous defiance of house slaves shattered illusory assumptions, and their behavior exposed the conflicts that would continue once slaves were free.

The arrival in Atlanta of refugee slaveholders with their slaves who were fleeing embattled areas of the Confederacy multiplied the city's problems of social control. Refugee slaves and oldtimers used the occasion of social disarray to flee. The Lineses' young slave who had been denied extended contact with her mother ran away. Beckie, her replacement, also deserted, though she was caught and beaten before she completed her escape. Undaunted, she left again a few months later on a professed trip to pick blackberries and never returned.[39]

Slaves took greater liberties through the hire system in their quest for freedom during the war. "Old Clarissa" was sent to Savannah with the understanding that she would remit a certain portion of her wages to her master on a regular basis. But upon her arrival she repudiated the agreement by sending a smaller portion of her earnings. Her perplexed master weighed the merits of acquiescence versus punishment, knowing that an alienating gesture could risk forfeiting his property and lone source of income.[40] Once exposed to urban life, slaves were not easily coerced into returning to plantations. Another slave, Rachel, grew accustomed to the independent life afforded by renting a room and working as a washerwoman in Atlanta. No amount of persuasion from her mistress could convince Rachel to avoid the imminent dangers of the approaching Union Army and return to her owner's protective care. As Rachel stated, she "preferred to await the coming of Sherman in her present quarters."[41]

The majority of slaves remained on plantations or in white urban households until the war's end. The heavily armed white civilian populace, the power of the Confederate troops, and the rough terrain of north Georgia made it difficult for slaves to escape. Some, no doubt, conformed to their masters' expectations of ideal servants—in outward appearance if nothing else. But outward compliance could be deceptive as slaves harbored deeper resentments that would resurface after they were free and subjected to conditions reminiscent of slavery. At least a few slaves may have shown genuine concern toward their masters who were in dire straits or faced plundering Yankees. Some slaves bought Confederate bonds, raised money to help Confederate soldiers, buried valuables or sewed silverware into mattresses to escape detection by Union invaders, or even donated their savings to cash-poor slaveowners.[42]

Acts of generosity clearly required slaves to go beyond the call of duty, but they did not dampen the yearning for freedom. Phyllis, a much beloved slave of Grace Elmore, gently tried to articulate this lesson to her owner. Elmore professed regard for Phyllis and spoke of her in this way: "She is very intelligent, reads, writes, [is] half white and was brought up like a white child by her former mistress." But Elmore did not appreciate Phyllis's answer to an important question: "I asked Phyllis if she liked the thought of being free." Phyllis replied that yes, she wanted to be free, "tho' she'd always been treated with perfect kindness, and could complain of nothing in her lot." Despite her good treatment Phyllis insisted that she "wanted the power to do as she liked." Disappointed by the reply from an "intelligent" slave, Elmore mocked Phyllis's and other slaves' views about freedom which in her estimation failed to comprehend the magnitude of the responsibilities.[43]

   Masters increasingly, if begrudgingly, recognized that kind gestures and appearances of orderly behavior could be feigned as many slaves demonstrated their contempt for bound labor, overtly or covertly, when opportunities arose. Slaves who helped to hide their owners' heirlooms and valuables one day might lead the Yankees directly to the loot the next day.[44] Some house slaves directly attacked the most visible signs of their oppression by claiming the products of their uncompensated labor, such as cash, clothing, jewelry, household items, or food from the table or pantry. Others defaced the ostentatious mansions that stood in marked contrast to their own sparse shanties.[45] While many refused to work at all, others changed their work pace and the quality of their output, provoking typical complaints like the following: "Fanny as usual cooked miserably: the worst turkey dressing I have seen in my life."[46] As the mistress Lines reported of the infamous Beckie: she "makes me a great trouble ironing days. She is so careless and stupid."[47] In sheer exasperation, another mistress complained: "I think O, if I had a good cook; it would be a pleasure to keep house." This slaveholder's highest aspiration at that moment was to find just "one who would take care or even do what they are told to do."[48]

   Some slaves who remained in their masters' households used the mobility and independence afforded by urban bondage to fight against the system. A slave woman in Richmond spent her earnings from washing the clothing of rebel soldiers on baking bread for Union prisoners of war. According to one account: "she got in to the prisoners through a hole under the jail-yard fence; knowing all the while she'd be shot, if caught at it."[49] Aggie Crawford, an Athens cook, defied prohibitions against slave literacy designed to keep blacks ignorant of current affairs. She stole newspapers to keep fellow slaves abreast of the war and sold whiskey, probably to save money for a planned escape.[50] Similarly, Tiny, the "last and *dearest* girl" of Samuel P. Richards's brother Jabez, made preparations for fleeing to freedom. She stole "first, about $150 from him and receiving no punishment she next stole about the same amount from Dr Doyle!" In another case, "Patience (who had been especially petted) managed to steal enough coffee, sugar, and flour to live on for many weeks."[51]

   The resilience exhibited by house slaves in their increased shows of defiance during the war meant that work that had been performed by slaves exclusively might not get done at all, which translated into more physical labor for white women. "John, Sarah and Rose have left and I did the washing for six weeks," a Natchez, Mississippi, slaveowner remarked. I "came near ruining myself for life as I was too delicately raised for such hard work," she stated.[52] Others noted the added encumbrances of physical labor imposed on other whites beyond their own households. "For the first time in my life, I saw & had white people to wait on me," noted a mistress during a stopover at a boardinghouse outside Atlanta. "The lady where we boarded waited on the table & cooked sometimes. She was kind hearted & very obliging but I could not bear for her to wait on us."[53] Other white women encountered dire privation that forced them to do what they had always considered unthinkable for women of their race—sell their own labor. "Many who were well supplied for months and some for a year, have been compelled to come to town and perform day work for a living, the man making $30. & $35. per month and the woman 5 cents or 10 cents a piece for washing," observed a Georgia slaveholder.[54] These excursions by whites into paid or unpaid labor dramatize the topsy-turvy world produced by the war, but they were temporary inconveniences. Few white women in the South, no matter how poor, worked as domestics either during or after the war.

White soldiers in the trenches echoed the sentiments of the women they left behind to maintain the home front as the men suddenly discovered the arduousness of housework. An army veteran and planter wrote sympathetically to Jefferson Davis, the President of the Confederacy, with a plan to send domestic help to the soldiers' camps. "The *hardest,* and *most painful duty* of the *young Volunteers,* is to *learn how* to *Cook,* and *wash.*" Emphasizing the novelty of this ordeal, he stated: "At *home,* the *young* Soldier, has his *Food Cooked* for *him,* by his *Mother, Sister's or* by *our Slaves*—but not *so* in the *Field* of *Battle.*"[55] A Union soldier in Georgia suffered similar agony. "I spend the afternoon in washing, mending and baking. I was very tired at night and wondered how women gets through with as much work as they do. Washing, etc. is the hardest work I have to do."[56]

Not all slaveholders acquiesced to the changing conditions of slavery. Many extolled slave loyalty at the same time that they took extra measures to subjugate their slaves further. The fears and bitterness that slaveowners harbored in the years immediately before the war in anticipation of its arrival induced some to exercise brutal force once the war began. If some slaves became more unruly during the war, they were responding not only to new opportunities for freedom but also to increased violence from their masters. Many owners, even some who were mild-mannered under normal circumstances, became more abusive or more neglectful as they realized they would eventually lose their investment in human chattel.[57]

THE MUCH anticipated arrival of the Union Army in northwest Georgia occurred in May 1864. Sherman's march toward the Gate City en route to the sea, more than any other single event heretofore, inspired songs of jubilee among slaves and excited fears of rebellion among whites. Sherman plotted the invasion of Atlanta, a strategic interior city in Dixie, to destroy its key military resources and asphyxiate the network feeding supplies to Robert E. Lee's forces in Virginia. Sherman's arrival shattered the last remnants of slaveholders' authority and control.

White women on the home front were bearing more responsibility for slave management than they were accustomed to doing. In the absence of fathers and husbands they quickly had to learn new skills in negotiation to deal with recalcitrant slaves not apt to respect their authority. After Sherman's arrival, a group of almost one hundred white women from Jonesboro, near Atlanta, submitted a petition to Governor Joseph E. Brown, in haste: "There are no men left here scarcely and the few who are, are almost impotent to afford any protection to us the females and our children." They requested an exemption of military service for the town marshal because the slaves in the vicinity "have been taught by long experience to regard [him] with awe & fear."[58] But despite such efforts to inculcate trepidation, slaveholders had to face another contingent of willful slaves. Runaways trailed the Northern liberators into Atlanta for the chance to participate directly in the destruction of slavery and the Confederacy. African Americans deserted their masters en masse—about nineteen thousand followed the General as he moved through the state. One planter captured the overwhelming feeling of betrayal this scene evinced: "Every servant gone to Sherman in Atlanta . . . We thought there was a strong bond of affection on their side as well as ours!"[59] The sight of blacks and whites looting and destroying fortifications and private property bore out the worst fears of many white Atlantans.[60]

As the Union Army approached Atlanta, slaveholders were reminded once again that outward appearances could mask the true feelings of their slaves. House slaves considered to be the most faithful and diligent were the first to refuse to work or to desert to the rear of Sherman's troops. Slaveowners voiced both surprise and dismay in recalling the characteristics of runaway slaves like Tiny and Patience—the "dearest" and the "most petted" slaves of Jabez Richards, mentioned previously. Other examples were plentiful: Mary, a "faithful girl" was "near free & did as she pleased—but waited on her [mistress] & like a dog—was by her side constantly." But when the Yankees arrived, a different Mary emerged as she helped her mistress's family prepare the carriage for escape and refused to climb aboard herself. "To her [mistress's] surprise, she held back & said I am not going—an officer (Yank) will come to take me; after awhile & he did."[61]

Some slaveholders dismayed by the acts of betrayal as they evacuated the city sought revenge. The Union Army arrived at one Georgia plantation to discover that the owners had chained down a house slave before vacating to avoid the indignity of her defection. When the slaves began running away, "her master swore she should stay and cook for him and his family. He 'would fix her'; so he had heavy iron shackles put on her feet so she could not run off."[62] While some slaves were left behind in dire straits, others were taken away with little regard for the impact on black families. When Emma Prescott departed she took along Patience, a child-nurse, ignoring the needs of Patience, who had recently married Allen Slayton of Columbus. Prescott justified splitting up the black family by emphasizing her own suffering: "I had to be separated from my husband too." By acting in her own best interest, Prescott shattered any illusion of reciprocal relations between slaves and masters.[63]

Sherman besieged the city of Atlanta on September 1, 1864, as the civilian evacuation was well under way. Confederate officers admitted defeat and surrendered the next day. They began to demolish military ordnance and machinery, including the Atlanta Rolling Mill and locomotives filled with ammunition, to deprive enemy invaders of their benefits. In November, the Union Army systematically destroyed all remaining manufacturing plants, torching four to five thousand buildings and the entire business district. Renegade soldiers, without the authority of their commanding officers, added to the damage by pillaging private residences. Few edifices outlasted the demolition.

Black residents in the city were not left unscathed by General Sherman, whose contempt for them was well known. Sherman's troops raped black women and destroyed black-owned property, including a church. En route to Savannah at the end of the year, Sherman's men caused the death of hundreds of blacks trailing in the rear by removing a pontoon bridge before the refugees could cross over a river, leaving them at the mercy of advancing Confederates.[64] But Sherman's abuse of African Americans did not dissipate white anxieties as slaveholders returned to Atlanta during the winter months.[65] As one woman stated: "Several old men are left & they go from one plantation to another with guns in their hands trying to keep [slaves] down." She continued, "we fear the negroes now more than anything else."[66]

As the Battle of Atlanta ended, it was undeniable that Ellen, the recalcitrant slave playing with her mistress's toiletries in front of the vanity, had calculated the bleak prospects for slavery more accurately than her master. The destruction of slavery was accomplished with the participation of slaves themselves, not just by military maneuvers or decisions promulgated in the White House or the halls of Congress. The slaves who ran away to join the Union Army; those who scraped and saved funds to rescue captured Union soldiers; those who cooked, washed, and spied for the federal troops; and those who remained in the custody of plantations and urban households and refused to accept preexisting terms for their uncompensated labor—all in their own way helped to erode human bondage. As African Americans asserted themselves during the heat of the war, they set the stage for the renegotiation of labor and social relations for many years to come.

CHAPTER TWO

Reconstruction and the Meanings of Freedom

$\mathcal{T}$he Union victory at Appomattox in the spring of 1865 marked the official end of the war and inspired somber reflection, foot-stomping church meetings, and joyous street parades among the newly free. African Americans eagerly rushed into Atlanta in even greater numbers than before. Between 1860 and 1870, blacks in Atlanta increased from a mere nineteen hundred to ten thousand, more than doubling their proportion in the city's population, from 20 to 46 percent.

Women made up the majority of this burgeoning population. Kate Bowie, who had spent her early years in Atlanta until she was sold away to Alabama at age fourteen, returned to the city with her husband after the war, hoping to find relatives still in place. The Bowie family and others journeyed to the city by foot from rural areas in the state or from more distant parts where their masters had relocated to escape the Union Army. Vria Mickens, a widow and mother, left the countryside to escape from the hardships of a depressed agricultural economy and from the limited economic opportunities for unattached women; planters preferred to negotiate with male heads of households. Retaliations by ex-Confederates and repression by the Ku Klux Klan drove women as well as men to cities to find relief.[1]

Wherever they came from, virtually all black women were compelled to find jobs as household workers once they arrived in the city. Some had acquired experience in such jobs as house slaves; others had worked in the fields or combined field and domestic chores. Whether or not they were working as domestics for the first time, black women had to struggle to assert new terms for their labor. The Civil War had exposed the parallel contests occurring in white households as the conflict on the battlefield, in the marketplace, and in the political arena unfolded. The war continued on the home front during Reconstruction after the Confederacy's military defeat. Ex-slaves declared their rights to enjoy the fruits of their labor and to reconstitute their lives as autonomous human beings. Owners-turned-employers showed their determination to mold a subservient black female work force and marshaled legal and extralegal measures to that end. Neither workers nor employers would be satisfied with piecemeal victories. Both were challenged by the vicissitudes of life in a city destroyed during the war but on the brink of new developments.

JUST AS black women and men in Atlanta had to reconstitute their lives as free people and build from the ground up, the city was faced with similar challenges. The legacy of physical desecration left by Sherman's invasion was everywhere. Tons of debris, twisted rails, dislodged roofs, crumbled chimneys, discharged cannon balls, and charred frame dwellings cluttered the streets.[2] Visitors to the city swapped remarks on the distinctive spirit of industry exemplified in the repair and rebuilding. "The citizens are very enterprising," a Northern missionary commented. "The whole town presents a business air, *not* peculiar to Southern towns generally." Another awed traveler noted, "what is more remarkable, the men who are bringing a city out of this desert of shattered brick—raising warehouses from ruins, and hastily establishing stores in houses half furnished and unroofed—were not Yankees, but pure Southerners." These insightful remarks revealed that Atlanta aspired to construct a city in the New South in the image of established cities above the Mason-Dixon line.[3]

The capitalist zeal that impressed outsiders offered few benefits to the average person, however. Overwhelmed contractors could not keep up with demands, which added to housing shortages that sent prices for rents soaring beyond the means of most residents. Housing was scarce for everyone, yet the Democrat-controlled city government, true to its nascent commercial credo, placed its highest priorities on re-erecting office buildings for private businesses.[4] Some builders took advantage of the shortage to offer makeshift huts and shanties to freedpeople at exorbitant prices.[5] Ex-slaves in more dire straits assembled scanty lodging that consisted of tents, cabins, and shanties made of tin, line, and cloth on rented parcels of land.[6] These "abodes of wretchedness," as one missionary described them, had "doors . . . so small I have to stoop very low, and when in, can scarcely stand up without bumping my head against the apology for a roof."[7] The cost of food and other consumer goods likewise followed the pattern of scarcity, poor quality, and deliberate price gouging.[8]

The abrupt population growth and the inability of private charities or public coffers to relieve the migrants of want exacerbated postwar privation. Almost everyone in the city, regardless of race, shared the status of newcomer. It was not just African Americans who were migrating to the city in large numbers; so did many whites. In 1860, there were 7,600 whites living in Atlanta, ten years later there were 11,900.[9] White yeoman farmers fled to the city to find wage labor in the wake of the elimination of their rural self-sufficiency. White Northern and foreign industrial workers followed the prosperity promised by the railroad and construction boom.

Women and children, black and white, were particularly noticeable among the destitute sprawled over the desolate urban landscape. The indigent included elderly, single women, widows of soldiers, and wives of unemployed or underemployed men. White women seamstresses who numbered in the thousands during the war were reduced to poverty with the collapse of military uniform manufacturers.[10] Labor agents egregiously contributed to the disproportionate sex ratio among urban blacks by taking away men to distant agricultural fields, leaving the women and children deserted.[11] Those abandoned wandered the streets and scavenged for food, often walking between ten and forty miles per day. "Sometimes I gits along tolerable," stated a widow washerwoman with six children. "Sometimes right slim; but dat's de way wid everybody—times is powerful hard right now."[12]

The municipal government showed neither the capability nor the ambition to meet the needs of the poor. It allocated few resources for basic human services. Yet the Freedmen's Bureau, which was established by the federal government in 1865 to distribute rations and relief to ex-slaves, to monitor the transition to a free labor system, and to protect black rights, proved inadequate also. The bureau was preoccupied with stemming migration, establishing order, and restoring the economy, which led it to force blacks into accepting contracts without sufficient regard for the fairness of the terms. The federals evicted ex-slaves from contraband camps or pushed them further from the center of town to the edges—out of sight and out of mind.[13] Bureau officials urged their agents: "You must not issue rations or afford shelter to any person who can, and will not labor for his or her own support." Labor agents, sometimes working on behalf of planters or the Freedmen's Bureau, targeted contraband camps to recruit farm hands. Those unwilling to accept the labor contracts offered them were thrown out of the camps. And those who "[had] no visible means of support, but live from day to day, by such jobs as they pick up, but have no permanent contract" were held liable for prosecution under vagrancy laws.[14]

Ex-slaves who were evicted from the camps by the end of 1865 were more fortunate than they could appreciate initially. They escaped a smallpox epidemic in the city that devastated the enclaves. One missionary reported a horrifying scene she witnessed in the camps: "Men, women, and children lying on the damp ground suffering in every degree from the mildest symptoms to the most violent. The tents crowded, no fire to make them comfortable, and worse all the poor creatures were almost destitute of wearing apparel."[15] The dead who lay around the sick and suffering were buried in the ground half-naked or without clothes at all.

African Americans survived the epidemic, postwar poverty generally, and other hardships wrought by war and reconstruction by pooling their meager resources. They organized mutual aid societies, gave fund-raising fairs, and built a hospital.[16] Northern missionaries also donated money and goods, though charity, like self-help, encountered overwhelming odds.[17] While watching "the sick, Aged women and children not half clad and almost nothing to eat huddled away," one missionary recognized the shortcomings inherent in her assignment. "Kind words make but little impression when they are shivering with cold and hunger and we have nothing to give to make them more comfortable."[18] When all other tactics failed to meet subsistence needs, some among the poverty-stricken resorted to appropriating the food they needed from the backyard vegetable gardens of better-off residents.[19]

African-American women and men were willing to endure the adversities of food shortages, natural disasters, dilapidated housing, and inadequate clothing in postwar Atlanta because what they left behind in the countryside, by comparison, was much worse. In the city at least there were reasons to be optimistic that their strength in numbers and their collective strategies of empowerment could be effective. In rural areas, however, their dispersion and separation by miles of uninhabited backwoods left them more vulnerable to elements intent on depriving them of life, liberty, and happiness. Abram Colby, a Republican legislator from Greene County, summed up the motivations for migration by stating that blacks went to Atlanta "for protection." He explained further: "The military is here and nobody interferes with us here . . . we cannot stop anywhere else so safely."[20]

African Americans moved to the city not only in search of safety, but also in search of economic self-sufficiency. Though most ex-slaves held dreams of owning farm land, many preferred to set up households in a city with a more diverse urban economy. In Atlanta they encountered an economy that was quickly recovering from the war and continuing to grow in the direction propelled by military demands and the promise of modernization. The railroad maintained its preeminence in the city, as did related industries, enabling the transport of people and goods. Locally produced consumer items such as hosiery, clothing, cornmeal, furniture, cabinetry, baked goods, straw hats, and patent medicines— including the headache tonic progenitor of the world-renowned Coca-Cola—filled the rails.[21]

Though the kaleidoscope of industry appeared to offer vast possibilities for workers, African Americans were slotted into unskilled and service labor. Black men filled positions with the railroads; as day workers, they groomed roads, distributed ballast, and shoveled snow off the tracks. As brakemen, they coupled and uncoupled stationary cars and ran along the roof of moving trains to apply the brakes, risking life and limb. Many others worked in rolling and lumber mills, mostly in the lowest-paid positions as helpers to white men. Hotels employed black men as cooks, waiters, porters, bellhops, and barroom workers. A few ex-slaves worked in bakeries, small foundries, the paper mill, and candy factories. Slave artisans were high in number in the antebellum South, but in the postbellum era black men were rarely hired in skilled positions. They were able to benefit from the aggressive physical rebuilding of Atlanta, however, in the construction trades, as painters, carpenters, and brickmasons. Between 1870 and 1880, the proportion of black male shoemakers tripled to constitute the majority of the entire trade. A select few owned small businesses such as barber shops and grocery stores or worked in the professions as teachers and ministers.[22]

The range of job opportunities for black women was more narrow than for men. Black women were excluded from small manufacturing plants that hired white women, such as those that made candy, clothing, textiles, paper boxes, bookbinding, and straw goods. They were confined primarily to domestic labor in private homes as cooks, maids, and child-nurses. A few black women found related jobs in local hotels—a step above the same work performed in private households. Large numbers worked in their own homes in a relatively autonomous craft as laundresses, which had the advantage of accommodating family and community obligations. More desirable, yet less accessible, were skilled jobs outside domestic service as seamstresses or dressmakers. The most typical job in the needle trades was piece-rate work subcontracted out, which had the same home-bound advantages as laundry work, but not the creative license of dressmakers. Only a few black women were able to escape common labor and enter the professions as teachers.[23]

Reconstruction of the post-slavery South occurred on many levels. Just as the city's infrastructure had to be rebuilt for daily life to reach a new normalcy, so blacks had to rebuild their lives as free people by earning an independent living. Women's success or frustrations in influencing the character of domestic labor would define how meaningful freedom would be. Slave women had already demonstrated fundamental disagreements with masters over the principles and practices of free labor during the war. This conflict continued as workers and employers negotiated new terms. Even the most mundane and minute details of organizing a free labor system required rethinking assumptions about work that had previously relied on physical coercion. An employer acknowledged the trial-and-error nature of this process: "I had no idea what was considered a task in washing so I gave her all the small things belonging to the children taking out all the table cloths sheets counterpanes & c." The novice employer then decided in the same haphazard manner to pay the laundry worker 30 cents a day. But the laborer asserted her own understanding of fair work. "She was through by dinner time [and] appeared to work steady. I gave her dinner and afterwards told her that I had a few more clothes I wished washed out," the employer explained. "Her reply was that she was tired." The worker and employer held different expectations about the length of the work day and the quantity of the output of labor.[24]

African Americans labored according to their own sense of equity, with the guiding assumption that wage labor should not emulate slavery—especially in the arbitrariness of time and tasks. The experience of an ex-slave named Nancy illustrates this point. As some ex-slaves departed from their former masters' households, the burden of the work shifted to those who remained. Consequently, when the regular cook departed, Nancy's employer added cooking and washing to her previous child-care job, without her consent. Nancy faked illness on ironing days and eventually quit in protest against the extra encumbrance.[25]

If workers and employers disagreed on the assignment of specific tasks, they also disagreed on how to execute them. Workers held to their own methods and preferences; employers held to theirs. Margaret, a cook, was scornful of her employer's practice of washing dishes in the sitting room, rather than in the detached kitchen. "Gwine to wash dishes in dis ere room; dis ar the gemman's sittin'-room, and ye gwine to turn it into de kitchen?" In the South, the kitchen of many houses was a self-contained building in the backyard. Etta Stearns, on the other hand, was a recent migrant from New England, where the kitchen was an integral part of the main house. These regional architectural differences also exposed cultural values. The stand-alone Southern kitchen symbolized elite white women's alienation from the labor that they had relegated to slaves, which Stearns was unaccustomed to. She and Margaret continued to clash over similar issues, until Margaret "threw down the gauntlet" and laid down the law. "[I am] gwine to be cook ob dis ere house, and I'se want no white woman to trouble me," she stated. Margaret summoned her many years of experience to her defense, refusing to grant a superior knowledge on the basis of race. "We done claned dishes all our days, long before ye Yankees hearn tell of us, and now does ye suppose I gwine to give up all my rights to ye, just cause youse a Yankee white woman?" She concluded with another rhetorical query: "Does ye know missus that we's free now? Yas, free we is, and us ant gwine to get down to *ye*, any more than to them ar rebs."[26]

If Margaret's frustrations reached an intolerable level, she could exercise a new privilege as a free worker to register the ultimate complaint: she could quit and seek better terms for her work. Ex-slaves committed themselves to this precept of free labor with a firmness that vexed employers. "We daily hear of people who are in want of servants, and who have had in their employ in the last three or four months, a dozen different ones," stated a familiar news report. "The common experience of all is that the servants of the 'African-persuasion' can't be retained," it continued. "They are fond of change and since it is their privilege to come and go at pleasure, they make full use of the large liberty they enjoy."[27] One employer hired a worker for every day in one month, hoping to beat the statistical odds by having at least one who would show up to cook breakfast. Within a six-month time period, at least ten different workers departed Samuel P. Richards's household. Gertrude Thomas hired six different workers who quit within one month.[28]

African-American women decided to quit work over such grievances as low wages, long hours, ill treatment, and unpleasant tasks. Quitting could not guarantee a higher standard of living or a more pleasant work environment for workers, but it was an effective strategy to deprive employers of complete power over their labor. Conditions of work per se were not the only motivating factors of brief tenure, however. Black women sometimes created short-term assignments as they moved about from city to city.[29] In the absence of formal time off, women used their mobility within the labor market to juggle income-earning for their families along with their other responsibilities as mothers and wives. "All their *colored gentry* have taken their departure and set up for themselves, some *six* of them! Lou is her own cook and manager now," Richards complained.[30] Lou and her peers compelled employers to acknowledge that black women had families of their own to consider in the decisions they made about their wage work. Black women creatively maneuvered their gainful labor patterns, demonstrating an acute awareness of the limits of continuous, grossly underpaid labor. Occasional refusals to sell their labor or self-imposed limits enabled working-class women to conduct their own family and community affairs in ways that mitigated the demands of white supremacy and the market economy.

Employers did not share the same interpretations of labor mobility, however. They blamed the subversive influence of Yankees and "pernicious" Negroes for inciting "bad" work habits, or they explained quitting as a scientifically proven racial deficiency.[31] Whereas recently freed slaves often worked as much as they needed to survive and no more, white Southerners believed that if they refused to work as hard as slaves driven by fear they were mendicants and vagrants. "When a wench gets very hungry and ragged, she is ready to do the cooking for any sized family," a news report exclaimed. "But after she gets her belly well filled with provender, she begins to don't see the use of working all day and every day, and goes out to enjoy her freedom."[32]

Although many white Southerners resented the presence of the Freedmen's Bureau as the Northern overseer of Reconstruction, they readily sought its assistance to stem the revolving door of domestic workers. "What are persons to do when a 'freedman' that you hire as a nurse goes out at any time & against your direct orders?" one former master queried the bureau. "What must be done when they are hired and do only just what they please? orders being disregarded in every instance," he asked further. A bureau agent responded with an answer to alleviate the employer's frustrations and to teach him a lesson about the precepts of free labor. "Discharge her and tell her she dont suit you," the agent stated simply. "If you have a written contract with them and they quit you without good and sufficient cause—I will use all my power to have them comply," he reassured. But if these words provided comfort, the bureau agent made clear that the operative words were "without good and sufficient cause." He reiterated the employers' obligations and responsibilities to respect the liberties of workers: "You are expected to deal with them as Freemen and Freewomen. Individual exceptions there may be but as a whole where they are well treated they are faithful and work well."[33]

The federal government refused to return to white employers unilateral power to prohibit the mobility of black workers, leading employers to elicit the support of local laws. Quitting work became defined as "idleness" and "vagrancy"—prosecutable offenses. Southern state legislatures began passing repressive Black Codes in 1865 to obstruct black laborers' full participation in the marketplace and political arena. In 1866, the Atlanta City Council responded in a similar vein to stop the movement of household workers: it passed a law requiring employers to solicit recommendations from previous jobs in order to distinguish "worthy" from "worthless" laborers and to make it more difficult for workers to change jobs. Complaints continued long after the law took effect, which suggests its ineffectiveness.[34]

Implicit in legal efforts to preempt black labor mobility was the idea that employers would cooperate with one another to make the restrictions effective. Just as state Black Codes prohibited planters and employers from competing for black labor and driving up their wages, the advocates of local statutory restrictions expected similar class solidarity to prevail. But employers sometimes held contradictory opinions about the emergent free enterprise system. The ethics of class unity clashed with individual initiative. When Gertrude Thomas could not find a laborer willing to accept her terms for employment, Leah arrived at a propitious moment in search of a job as a cook. "That night and the next morning I ate two biscuits which she baked . . . At dinner the next day she baked one of the best plum pies I ever tasted," Thomas reported. She gave Leah high marks, but her husband objected to hiring an ex-slave who probably did not arrive with her previous employers' blessings. When Mr. Thomas requested written proof of good standing, Leah left and never returned, much to the chagrin of Mrs. Thomas. "I certainly sacrificed a good deal to principle for I lost an opportunity to get an excellent cook at 5 dollars per month," she stated. "Dr. Dennings family [Leah's former employers] will not be benefited," Thomas added.[35]

Not all privileged Southerners were as committed to the etiquette of class cooperation as Gertrude Thomas's husband. A woman named Harriet was hired for a mutual probationary period, "to see if she would like to live with us permanently, & if we would like to keep her permanently," her new employer explained. But before such an agreement could be consummated, Harriet's former employers appealed for her to return to complete a spinning project. "The truth was, they had some company," the new employer conjectured. "This girl could under the excuse of [spinning] the cloth be there, & help them one half or two thirds of the time at the house keeping & cooking, & cost them nothing but her board." Gertrude Thomas apparently resented the intense competition that thwarted implicit collective goals: "It suited well for them to deprive us of her just at the time we most needed her."[36]

Black women used the marginal leverage they could exercise in the face of conflict between employers to enhance their wages and to improve the conditions of work. When Hannah, "a cook & washer of the first character," was approached by Virginia Shelton in search of domestic help, she bargained for an agreement to match her needs.

Hannah wanted to bring along her husband, a general laborer, and expected good wages for both of them. Shelton made an initial offer of $5 per month to Hannah and $10 per month to her husband. But the couple demanded $8 and $15, to which Shelton acceded. Shelton realized that it was worth making compromises with a servant she had traveled a long distance to recruit.[37]

Not all negotiations ended so pleasantly or in the workers' favor, however. Mary Long refused to cook for her employer, Mrs. Montell, in an attempt to receive a holiday one Sunday, and an argument ensued. Long also refused to accede to her boss's command to keep quiet, which angered Mr. Montell. He stepped in and struck the cook twenty-five times with a hickory stick, remarking that "he didnt allow any nigger to sass his wife."[38] Domestic workers often complained of physical abuse by employers following disputes about wages, hours of work, or other work-related matters. Sometimes family members were left to seek redress on a worker's behalf after fatal incidents. Samuel Ellison explained the argument that led to the death of his wife, Eliza Jane. Mrs. Ellison had argued with her employer, Mrs. L. B. Walton, about washing clothes. According to Ellison's husband, "My wife asked Mrs. Walton who would pay her for her washing extra clothes and which she was not bound to do by her contract." Walton's husband intervened and "abused" the laundress for "insulting" his wife. He left the house, returned and began another argument, insisting to Ellison, "shut up you God damn bitch." The fight ended when Walton shot Eliza Jane Ellison to death.[39]

African-American women like Ellison undoubtedly paid a high price for the simple desire to be treated like human beings. Incidents like this one made it apparent that freedom could not be secured through wage labor alone. The material survival of African Americans was critical, but they also needed to exercise their political rights to safeguard it. The political system had to undergo dramatic transformation to advance their interests, but here too they faced many obstacles.

The Ku Klux Klan, an anti-black terrorist organization founded by former Confederate soldiers in 1866, mounted the most bitter opposition to black rights. The KKK quickly became dominated by Democratic Party officials bent on preempting black participation in the electoral arena. The Klan sought to wrest economic and political power from the governing Republicans in order to restore it to the antebellum

planter elite and to the Democrats. KKK members victimized Republican politicians like Abram Colby, whom they stripped and beat for
hours in the woods. They harassed registered voters and independent
landholders, ransacked churches and schools, intimidated common laborers who refused to bow obsequiously to planters, and tormented
white Republicans sympathetic to any or all of the foregoing.[40]

African Americans' recalcitrance in commonplace disagreements
with employers routinely provoked the vigilantes. Alfred Richardson, a
legislator from Clarke County, suggested how labor relations continued to have strong political ramifications. The KKK assisted employers
in securing the upper hand in conflicts with wage household workers.
"Many times, you know, a white lady has a colored lady for cook or
waiting in the house, or something of that sort," Richardson explained.
"They have some quarrel, and sometimes probably the colored woman
gives the lady a little jaw. In a night or two a crowd will come in and
take her out and whip her." The Klan stripped and beat African Americans with sticks, straps, or pistol barrels when all else failed to elicit their
compliance.[41]

If the KKK was determined to halt the reconstruction of a free labor
system, it was most insistent about eliminating black political power.
Though women were denied the right to vote in the dominant political
system, they actively engaged in a grass-roots political culture that
valued the participation of the entire community. Black women and
children attended parades, rallies, and conventions; they voiced their
opinions and cast their votes on resolutions passed at mass meetings.
In the 1860s and 1870s, women organized their own political organizations, such as the Rising Daughters of Liberty Society, and stood
guard at political meetings organized by men to allow them to meet
without fear of enemy raids. They boldly tacked buttons on the clothing they wore to work in support of favorite candidates. They took
time off from work to attend to their political duties, such as traveling
to the polls to make sure men cast the right ballots. White housekeepers were as troubled by the dramatic absences of domestic workers on
election day or during political conventions as were the planters and
urban employers of men.[42] During an election riot in nearby Macon, a
newspaper reported: "The Negro women, if possible, were wilder than
the men. They were seen everywhere, talking in an excited manner,
and urging the men on. Some of them were almost furious, showing it

to be part of their religion to keep their husbands and brothers straight in politics."[43]

Whether they gave political advice and support to the men in their families and communities or carried out more directly subversive activities, black women showed courage in the face of political violence. Hannah Flournoy, a cook and laundress, ran a boardinghouse in Columbus well known as a gathering place for Republicans. When George Ashburn, a white party leader stalked by the KKK, looked to her for shelter she complied, unlike his other supporters in the town. Flournoy promised him, "You are a republican, and I am willing to die for you. I am a republican, tooth and toe-nail."[44] But neither Flournoy nor Ashburn could stop the Klan in its determination to take the life of freedom fighters. After Klansmen killed Ashburn, Flournoy escaped to Atlanta, leaving behind valuable property.

Republican activists like Ashburn and Flournoy were not the only victims of KKK violence. The Klan also targeted bystanders who happened to witness their misdeeds. In White County, Joe Brown's entire family was subjected to sadistic and brutal harassment because Brown had observed a murder committed by the Klan. "They just stripped me stark naked, and fell to beating us," Brown reported later. "They got a great big trace-chain, swung me up from the ground, and swung [my wife] up until she fainted; and they beat us all over the yard with great big sticks." The Klan continued its torture against his mother-in-law and sister-in-law. "They made all the women show their nakedness; they made them lie down, and they jabbed them with sticks." Indiscriminate in violating adults and children, the KKK lined up Brown's young daughters and sons "and went to playing with their backsides with a piece of fishing-pole."[45]

Organized sexual-assault raids against black women were especially common in rural areas where terrorist groups like the KKK thrived. Rhoda Ann Childs of Henry County was snatched from her house by eight white men in her husband's absence. After she was beaten and thrown to the ground, she reported: "One of the two men Stood upon my breast, while two others took hold of my feet and stretched My limbs as far apart as they could, while the man Standing upon my breast applied the Strap to my private parts until fatigued into stopping, and I was more dead than alive." An ex-Confederate soldier, she continued, "fell upon me and ravished me. During the whipping one of the men had run his pistol into me, and Said he had a hell of a mind to pull the trigger."[46]

Migrating to Atlanta certainly improved the personal safety of ex-slaves escaping the KKK and sexual assaults, but it did not ensure foolproof protection against bodily harm. Black women risked sexual abuse no matter where they lived. Domestics in white homes were the most susceptible to attacks. A year after the war ended, Henry McNeal Turner and other black men mounted the podium and wrote petitions to demand the cessation of sexual assaults upon black women. Freedom, they insisted, was meaningless without ownership and control over one's own body. Black men took great offense at the fact that while they were falsely accused of raping white women, white men granted themselves total immunity in the exploitation of black women. *"All we ask of the white man is to let our ladies alone,* and they need not fear us," Turner warned. "The difficulty has heretofore been *our ladies were not always at our disposal."*[47] In Savannah, black men mobilized the Sons of Benevolence "for the protection of female virtue" in 1865.[48] In Richmond, African Americans complained to military authorities that women were being "gobbled up" off the streets, thrown into the jail, and ravished by the guards. In Mobile, black men organized the National Lincoln Association and petitioned the Alabama State Constitutional Convention to enact laws to protect black women from assault by white civilians and the police.[49]

Most whites refused to acknowledge the culpability of white men in abusing black women. "Rape" and "black women" were words that were never uttered in the same breath by white Southerners. Any sexual relations that developed between black women and white men were considered consensual, even coerced by the seductions of black women's lascivious nature. Rape was a crime defined exclusively, in theory and in practice, as perceived or actual threats against white female virtue by black men, which resulted in lynchings and castrations of numbers of innocent black men. But Z. B. Hargrove, a white attorney, admitted with rare candor that the obsession with black men raping white women was misplaced. "It is all on the other foot," as he put it. The "colored women have a great deal more to fear from white men."[50]

Black Atlantans during Reconstruction were subjected to other kinds of physical violence, especially at the hands of white civilians and police.

Black soldiers, the most visible symbols of black freedom during the immediate postwar years, were frequent targets of angry whites. One black soldier was shot dead in cold blood, and the white man who murdered him was heralded for killing a "damned nigger." Fourth of July celebrations and parades were also occasions for racial violence, especially against the dignified black militias and individuals marching in the processions.[51] Police officers not only condoned these acts during holidays, they also repeatedly disregarded the rights of freedpeople every day. When Mary Price objected to being called a "damned bitch" by a white neighbor, Mr. Hoyt, he brought police officer C. M. Barry to her door to reprimand her. Price's mother, Barbara, pregnant at the time, intervened and spoke to the police: "I replied that I would protect my daughter in my own house, whereupon he pulled me out of the house into the street. Here he called another man and the two jerked and pulled me along [the street] to the guard house and throwed me in there." When a Freedmen's Bureau agent complained to the mayor and city council on the Prices' behalf, the complaint was rebuffed by a unanimous vote acquitting the policeman of all charges against him. Meanwhile, mother and daughter were arrested, convicted for using profane language, and forced to pay $350 each in fines and court costs. Only after it became clear that the Bureau would persist in its efforts to get justice for the Price women did the mayor have a change of heart and fine the offending policeman. Barry was one of the worst officers on the force, and the Freedmen's Bureau eventually forced the city council to fire him, though he was rehired a year later.[52]

AFRICAN AMERICANS not only had to ward off physical threats; they were also challenged by the existence of perfectly legal abuses that diminished the meaning of freedom. Ex-slaves defined the reconstruction of their families torn asunder by slavery and war as an important aspect of the realization of the full exercise of their civil rights. But former masters seized upon the misery of African Americans, with the assistance of the law, to prolong the conditions of slavery and deny them the prerogative of reuniting their families. The Georgia legislature passed an Apprentice Act in 1866, ostensibly to protect black orphans by providing them with guardianship and "good" homes until they reached the age of consent at twenty-one. Planters used the law to reinstate bondage through uncompensated child labor.[53] Aunts, uncles, parents, and grandparents inundated the Freedmen's Bureau with requests for assistance in rescuing their children, though this same agency also assisted in apprenticing black minors. Martin Lee, for example, a former slave living in Florence, Alabama, wrote to the chief of the Georgia bureau for help in releasing his nephew from bondage. He had successfully reunited part of his extended family, but could not gain the release of his nephew despite the fact that he and the child's mother, Lee's sister, were both willing and able to take custody.[54]

If admitted enemies of black freedom recklessly disregarded the unity of black families through apprenticeships, some of their friends operated just as wantonly. The American Missionary Association (AMA) sometimes impeded parents and relatives who wished to reclaim their children. In 1866, the AMA started an orphanage that operated out of a tent. Soon afterward they opened the Washburn Orphanage in a building to accommodate the large number of homeless black children who were surviving on the streets on scant diets of saltpork and hardtack. But the asylum functioned as a temporary way station for children before apprenticing them out as domestic help to white sponsors. "I succeeded in getting a little girl from the orphans asylum by the name of Mary Jane Peirce," one eager patron of the orphanage exclaimed. "Her father and mother are both dead. She has a step mother and a little step brother." Peirce's new guardian minced no words in disclosing reckless disregard for the reunion of the child's family. "I am glad she will have no outside influence exherted upon her," the guardian admitted.[55]

Rebecca Craighead, the matron of the asylum, shared this disregard toward "outside influence." She considered even temporary institutional custody tantamount to the abrogation of all parental rights and zealously sent the children away to white guardians in Ohio and Michigan. "My idea is that *they* have no further claim upon them, and that we have a right to find homes for such, just as much as though they had no relatives," Craighead argued. Her behavior forced parents and other relatives to kidnap their own kin. "An aunt took one of our girls away yesterday, I allowed her to go to the c[e]lebration, and she took her from there," the asylum matron complained.[56] Though Craighead was eventually reprimanded by AMA officials for her attitude, the asylum's overall efforts in meeting demands for child servants were so successful that when financial considerations closed the doors of the orphanage within three years, homelessness among black children in Atlanta had been virtually wiped out.[57]

African Americans persisted in pursuing the reconstitution of family ties, despite the obstacles put in their way. Craighead recognized the persistence of these ex-slaves, yet she showed neither respect nor sensitivity toward the virtues of their ambition. "Somehow these black people have the faculty of finding out where their children are," she acknowledged.[58] Both the uncle, Martin Lee, who used official channels to retrieve his nephew, and the anonymous aunt, who relied on her own resources to "steal" her niece, displayed no small measure of resourcefulness in achieving their aims. Men no less than women, non-kin as well as kin, sought to recreate the family bonds that had been strained or severed by slavery and the Civil War.

Not all missionaries were as insensitive as Craighead; there were others, like Frederick Ayers, who fully appreciated the significance of family to ex-slaves. "The idea of 'freedom' of independence, of calling their wives and their children, and little hut their *own*, was a soul animating one, that buoyed up their spirits," he observed. It also "inspired strong hopes and influenced them to persistent efforts of self-preservation, and human elevation," he continued.[59] At the sight of several families sharing the same abode, another missionary in Augusta similarly took note: "Some were bound together by no ties of kindred."[60] As a people historically deprived of fundamental knowledge of blood relatives, African Americans customarily transformed the strict definition of kinship. Slavery as well as freedom produced the conditions that tested these principles daily.

Broad understandings of kinship encouraged black women to assume responsibility for needy children other than their natural offspring. Silvey, for example, could hardly survive on the minimal subsistence she earned, yet she extended compassion to the youngsters lost or deserted by other ex-slaves. "She was hard put to it, to work for them all," observed her former owner, Emma Prescott. But "of course, as our means were all limited, we could not supply her enough to feed them. Her life, was anything but ease & it was a pitiful sight."[61]

The sentiment that permitted the expansion of family relationships was not limited to bonds between children and adults. When the Freedman's Bank opened an office in Atlanta in 1870, Epsey Jones, a domestic worker, not only opened an account for herself, but also for her stepmother, Alice Jones. Since Jones's natural mother had died when she was quite young, her stepmother had guided her through the formative years of development. The death of Epsey Jones's father may have encouraged her to take steps to ensure her stepmother's future. Similarly, marriages built bridges between individuals that expanded kin in other directions. Eleanor Williams, a cook, opened a bank account for her mother-in-law, Rebecca Williams.[62]

The significance of family was also demonstrated in the naming of offspring for beloved kin—a continuation of a practice dating to slavery.[63] Aurena Edwards, a cook, gave her three sons the names of her father and brothers. Caroline Riley, a washerwoman, named her daughter in her mother's honor. Family reunions were major motivations for migration and, to some extent, settlement within the city. Caroline Gaston and her daughter Missouri Howard moved to Atlanta from Merriweather County, and both lived on the same street and worked as washerwomen. Although the act of bringing families together in one locality assumed an important priority, attachments with known relatives who lived outside the city were also maintained. Ann Dougherty, a dressmaker in Atlanta, opened a bank account for her mother, Philis Grant, although Grant lived in Augusta, which had its own bank branch.[64]

The most complicated family issues involved romantic relationships between women and men. For generations slaves had married one another and passed on the importance of conjugal obligations, despite the absence of legal protection. Marriages between slaves were long-term commitments, usually only disrupted by forcible separation or the death of a spouse. Emancipation offered new opportunities to reaffirm marital vows and to reunite couples who had previously lived "abroad" in the households of different masters. Even before the last shots of gunfire ending the Civil War, thousands of husbands and wives sought the help of Union officers and Northern missionaries to register their nuptials and to conduct wedding ceremonies.[65] The significance of formalizing these ties was articulated by a black soldier: "*I praise God for this day!* The Marriage Covenant is at the foundation of all our rights."[66] Putting marriages on a legal footing bolstered the ability of ex-slaves to keep their families together, to make decisions about labor and education, and to stay out of the unscrupulous grasp of erstwhile masters.

The hardships of slavery and war that disrupted families, however, meant that in the postwar period spouses were not always reunited without problems and tensions. Slaves traveled long distances to reunite with spouses from whom they had been separated for years. They wrote love letters and mailed them to churches and to the Freedmen's Bureau, and retraced the routes of labor agents who had taken their partners away.[67] Emotional bonds were sometimes so intense that spouses would choose to suffer indefinitely if they could not be reunited with their lost loved ones. But affections undernourished by hundreds of miles and many years might be supplanted by other relationships. Many ex-slaves faced awkward dilemmas when spouses presumed to be dead or long-lost suddenly reappeared. Ex-slaves created novel solutions for the vexing moral, legal, and practical concerns in resolving marital relations disrupted by forces beyond their control. One woman lived with each of her two husbands for a two-week trial before making a decision. Some men felt obligated to two wives and stayed married to one wife while providing support to the other. In one case, perhaps unique, a wife resumed her relationship with her first husband, while the second husband, a much older man, was brought into the family as a "poor relation."[68]

The presence of children complicated marriages even further. Some spouses registered their marriages with the Freedmen's Bureau or local courts even when their spouses were dead or missing, in order to give legal recognition to their children. When both parents were present and unable to reconcile their differences, child custody became a point of contention. Madison Day and Maria Richardson reached a mutual agreement to separate after emancipation. The love between husband and wife may have changed, but the love that each displayed for their children did not. The Richardsons put the Freedmen's Bureau agent in a quandary in determining who should receive custody. "Neither husband nor wife seem to be in a condition to provide for the children in a manner better than is usual with the freedpeople," the agent noted. "Still both appear to have an affectionate regard for the children and each loudly demands them."[69]

Aside from confronting the thorny problem of child custody when marriages dissolved, estranged couples also had to reconcile disputes about the marriage itself and the rights and obligations it entailed. Individuals sometimes brought expectations to their intimate relationships that were different from those of the other partner; or mutually agreed upon goals and responsibilities may have changed over time. Ex-slaves sometimes faced the choice between exercising personal freedom, which emancipation offered for the first time, and acting in the interests of the collective, which their life conditions had always demanded.

Rosa and David Freeman apparently struggled over these issues to neither person's satisfaction. When the couple lived in Florida, Rosa Freeman filed many complaints with federal officials about her husband's physical abuse. But the beatings continued, even after they moved to Georgia. Differing interpretations of marital rights and responsibilities are evident in Rosa Freeman's efforts not only to stop the violence, but also to redress unfulfilled obligations. "He has abused me & refuses to pay for the rent of my room & has not furnished me with any money, food or clothing," she reported. David Freeman was apparently not pleased with the power of the law invested in his wife as a result of their marriage. "He told me he would rather Keep a woman than be married—because she could not carry him to law & I could," the wife explained. Weary of Mr. Freeman's antics, Mrs. Freeman insisted on a bona fide divorce. Her husband, however, would agree to a legal separation only if it would not cost him any money. If David Freeman would not satisfy his obligations in wedlock, Rosa Freeman gave him an ultimatum: "I said if you want to leave me; leave me like a man!"[70]

SHEER survival and the reconstruction of family, despite all the difficulties, were the highest priorities of ex-slaves in the postwar period. But the desire for literacy and education was closely related to their strategies for achieving economic self-sufficiency, political autonomy, and personal enrichment. By 1860, 5 percent of the slave population had defied the laws and learned to read and write. Some were taught by their masters, but many learned to read in clandestine sessions taught by other blacks. African Americans all over the South organized secret schools long before the arrival of Northern missionaries. When a New England teacher arrived in Atlanta in 1865, he discovered an ex-slave already running a school in a church basement.[71]

African Americans welcomed the support of New England teachers and the federal government in their education movement. But centuries of slavery had stirred the longing for self-reliance in operating schools and filling teaching staffs, with assistance, but without white control. Ex-slaves enthusiastically raised funds and donated in-kind labor for building, repairing, and maintaining school houses. They opened their spartan quarters to house teachers and shared vegetables from their gardens to feed them. Ex-slaves in Georgia ranked highest in the South in the amount of financial assistance donated to their own education.[72]

The education movement among African Americans in Georgia went hand in hand with the demand for political rights. In January 1865, black ministers formed the Savannah Education Association, which operated schools staffed entirely with black teachers. Despite the efforts of General Davis Tillson, the conservative head of the Freedmen's Bureau, to keep politics out of the organization, African Americans and more liberal white allies infused the group with political objectives. The name was changed to the Georgia Equal Rights and Education Association, explicitly linking equal rights in the political arena with the pursuit of education. The organization became an important training ground for black politicians and laypersons at the grass-roots level and functioned as the state's predecessor to the Republican Party.[73]

The impact of black-elected officials on public education and other issues, however, was thwarted not only by KKK vigilantes and Democratic opposition, but also by conservatives within their own Republican Party. There were chameleon politicians like the Civil War Governor Brown, who switched his party affiliation to Republican but retained his Democratic commitments to abrogating black rights. When the legislature voted to expel black members in September 1868, just a few months after the first meeting of the Republican-controlled body, Brown along with most white Republicans supported the ouster of their black allies. Congress restored the legislators in 1869 under the Reorganization Act, but the Democratic Party victory the following year terminated the Radical program.[74]

African Americans' advocacy of universal public education did not fare better at the city level, because the municipal government was firmly controlled by Democrats and businessmen. William Finch, elected in 1870 as one of Atlanta's first black city councilmen, made universal education a hallmark of his election campaign. Finch attempted, but failed, to galvanize the support of the white working class on this issue. City hall's cold reception shifted the burden of basic

education for blacks to private foundations. Finch did succeed in getting the council to absorb two primary schools run by the AMA. After
his short term in office and unsuccessful bid for reelection in December
1871, he continued to be a strong advocate of public education and
helped to negotiate a deal in 1872 whereby the city would pay nominal
costs for some blacks to receive secondary training at Atlanta University. No publicly funded high school for blacks would be created until
a half-century later, however.[75]

Former slaves of all ages were undeterred in their goals to achieve
literacy, regardless of the obstacles imposed by municipal and state
governments. "It is quite amusing to see little girls eight or ten years
old lead up full-grown women, as well as children, to have their names
enrolled," remarked a missionary. "Men, women, and children are daily
inquiring when the 'Free School' is to commence, and whether all can
come[.] There is a large class of married women who wish to attend, if
the schools are not too crowded."[76] Household workers figured prominently among this group of older, eager scholars. Their eagerness to
learn was not diminished, although often interrupted, by the pressing
demands of gainful labor. In fact, these obstacles may have increased
the value of education in the eyes of the ex-slaves. Sabbath schools
operated by black churches and evening classes sponsored by the Freedmen's Bureau and Northern missionaries afforded alternatives for those
who could not sacrifice time during the day. But black women also
inventively stole time away from work by carrying their books along
and studying during spare moments—even fastening textbooks to backyard fences to glimpse their lessons as they washed clothes.[77]

As parents, working-class adults were especially committed to the
education of their children. The story of Sarah J. Thomas, a young
woman from Macon, whose mother was a cook and washerwoman, is a
poignant illustration. Thomas wrote Edmund Asa Ware, president of
Atlanta University, to gain his support in her plans to enroll in the
secondary school. "I exspected to come to Atlanta to morrow but I am
dissappointed. The reason I can not come to morrow is this. You know
how mothers are! I guess about their youngest children *girls* especially,"
she wrote. Mother Thomas was protective of her daughter and reluctant to send her away alone. "In order that I may *come* Mr. Ware!
mother says can she get a place to work there in the family?" she asked.
The younger Thomas boasted of her mother's fine skills and reputation

and slipped in her salary history. She assured the president, surely swamped by requests for financial aid, that her matriculation depended upon parental supervision, not the need for money. "Mother says she dont mean *not* the *least* to work to pay for *my schooling?* father pays for that him self she dont have any thing to do with it she only want to be where she can see me."[78] The young scholar's astute strategizing swayed both her mother and the school's president; she entered Atlanta University and achieved a successful teaching career after graduation in 1875.

Clandestine antebellum activities and values had bolstered the exemplary efforts of African Americans to seek literacy and to build and sustain educational institutions after the war. Ex-slaves took mutual obligations seriously. Their belief in personal development was aided rather than hampered by ideals that emphasized broad definitions of kinship and community. Freedom meant the reestablishment of lost family connections, the achievement of literacy, the exercise of political rights, and the security of a decent livelihood without the sacrifice of human dignity or self-determination. Ex-slave women migrated to Atlanta, where they hoped they would have a better chance of fulfilling these expectations. They were faced with many challenges; uppermost among them were the white residents who were resentful of the abolition of slavery and persisted in thwarting the realization of the true meaning of freedom. Black women continued to struggle, resilient and creative, in pursuing their goals for dignity and autonomy. The character of the contest had already been cast, but the many guises of domination and resistance had yet to be exhausted as life in the New South unfolded.

Working-Class Neighborhoods and Everyday Life

frican-American women who moved to Atlanta in the 1870s and early 1880s encountered a city still in its formative stages of development. The most dire postwar privation dissipated as the economy recovered from depressions and physical desecration. African-American efforts to make freedom meaningful were coming to fruition, even as circumstances beyond their control continued to infringe upon their life chances. In the post-Reconstruction era, as city leaders moved away from the economic ideals of the planter aristocracy and the erstwhile Confederacy, it became increasingly obvious that the capitalist dreams of the elites exploited black and poor people. Investments pouring into the city from financiers in the northeast and abroad were allocated to the benefit of those citizens who were already the most advantaged. This pattern of inequitable distribution of resources was nowhere more apparent than in the physical and social geography of the city. Jim Crow was already on the horizon, ordering separate and unequal black and white worlds. Black women would have to negotiate the literal rough terrain of Atlanta and the social consequences it imposed on their everyday lives as they struggled to earn a living for their families and searched for peace of mind.

THE RAILROAD, one of the most modern symbols of the era, played a prominent role not only in Atlanta's economy, as it had since the city's establishment, but also in the geography of the city as urbanism expanded. Rail lines formed intersections through the center of town, like spokes in a wheel, and streets were laid out at right angles to these projections within a grid pattern. Not only did this layout facilitate ground mobility, it accentuated the controlling influence of commerce and the railroad itself.

Unlike some modern metropolises in the northeast, where most black and poor people were housed in the inner city, Atlanta's Central Business District (CBD) and wealthy whites dominated the triangular core where intersecting railroad lines met. Residential development also differed from the antebellum "marble-caking" or "backyard" pattern of cities such as Charleston and New Orleans, where blacks were scattered behind the homes of whites. In Atlanta, African Americans lived in more sizable clusters throughout the city; large numbers of each race lived in every ward, and neither group significantly outnumbered the other. The short radius of the city limits in 1880 made it likely that residents would live in close proximity to one another and would walk to places of business or work. Rigid segregation was virtually impossible to achieve in the aftermath of the Civil War, as the massive influx of migrants compounded the scarcity of housing and forced everyone to find accommodations wherever they could; but this would soon change.[1]

The physical conditions of city life in this period were rugged at best, despite the best efforts of boosters to paint a pretty picture of Atlanta. A still primitive water system forced all except privileged residents to obtain their water from private wells and springs, which were vulnerable to contamination from many sources. Inadequate drainage and sewerage systems not only tainted the water supply but also subjected houses built on unevenly graded terrain to flooding. Unpaved streets were the norm, especially on low ground, because of the difficulty of maintaining roads with soil permeated with the outflow of thousands of individual privies. Malodorous and unsanitary debris generated from hog pens, slaughter houses, and guano plants, as well as household garbage and dead animals disposed of in streets and gullies, were typical.[2]

Despite the relative heterogeneity of residential patterns and rudimentary urban development that challenged the maintenance of optimal health and sanitation, not everyone suffered alike. There were already signs of the beginnings of Jim Crow by 1870, and this became more noticeable over the next decade. Poor people were thrust to the outskirts in row houses, tenements, and shanties where unkempt streets prevailed. They were forced to live nearest the contaminated and unsightly areas on the lowest elevations of the city. Wealthier whites lived in houses located on the higher streets, which not only shielded them from natural disasters but also drained waste onto less fortunate residents living in the valleys.[3] As city officials began to address some of the needs for a clean and healthy environment, they implemented policies to benefit the most privileged citizens while willfully neglecting or exacerbating the burdens of the least powerful. In the late 1870s and 1880s, sanitary laws authorized the collection of garbage within the CBD to be dumped into outlying black and poor neighborhoods.[4] When the city began to build water and gas lines during Reconstruction, it purposely constructed them to begin and end at the city's commercial district and at the residential doorsteps of the elite. Wealthier residents had enough water to sprinkle their lawns and could also afford to purchase mineral water from secluded springs. Meanwhile, most others lacked potable water for drinking and bathing. Though wage-earners protested class-biased regulations, the majority of the population would continue to lug water from hydrants and wells until just prior to the First World War. The lack of convenient water supplies not only impaired the health of blacks, but it also encumbered the labor process for household workers reliant on water to do their jobs.[5]

Real estate promoters and street railway entrepreneurs, in many instances one and the same, were among the leading engineers of race- and class-driven urban development. In the 1870s, George W. Adair and Richard Peters introduced horse-drawn trolleys to extend the construction of fashionable Victorian mansions outside of the CBD. Adair and Peters shrewdly built the trolley lines to stretch from downtown to the southwest, conveniently passing through the new West End suburb, past their own private residences. Mass transportation encouraged like-minded professionals to purchase stately houses in the upper-class retreat.[6] From the beginning of its incorporation as a town in 1868, the West End took steps to secure the area as an exclusive suburb. Much of the town's early business was devoted to regulating saloons and driving out the "lower orders."[7]

Other street car lines were constructed in the 1870s to encourage affluent communities. The Peachtree Street line facilitated growth of what would become Atlanta's preeminent neighborhood in the 1880s in the north, and the Ponce de Leon line provided access to a resort and mineral springs in the northeast. Two trolley lines also began and ended at principal industrial areas, enabling access to working-class whites who could afford the fee. The Marrietta Street line pulled white workers northwest, close to the Atlanta Rolling Mill, foundries, and railroad shops. The Decatur Street line, which extended east toward the

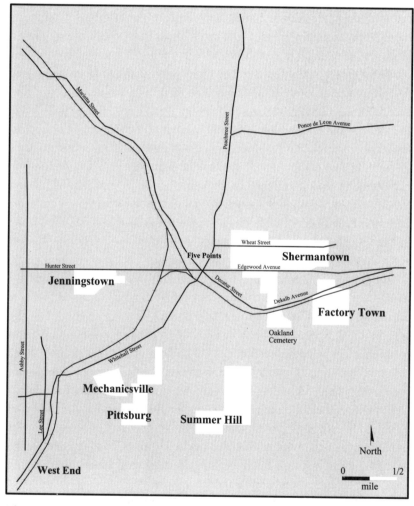

African-American and white working-class neighborhoods in Atlanta, 1880. Copyright © 1996 by Georgia State University, Department of Geography, Cartography Research Laboratory.

Oakland Cemetery in the vicinity of Factory Lot, was initiated in the 1860s as poor whites were driven from the center of town. The Atlanta and Charlotte Air-Line Railway built shops there by 1878, and the Fulton Cotton Spinning Company opened in 1881. The small rural village in this area grew into an urban slum that became known as Factory Town.[8]

The horse-drawn trolley system had the smallest effect on black settlement in the city, since most blacks could only afford to ride occasionally on Sundays for recreation. But real estate agents still influenced the residence patterns of African Americans by directing them toward certain areas in the city—those least desirable to whites. William Jennings, a Republican lawyer, owned a tract of land in the southeast quadrant of town in the third ward that had been plundered by Sherman's troops. By 1866, unable to induce whites to move into this section, Jennings turned to African Americans. But it was blacks themselves and white New England missionaries who built the institutions that fostered the development of cohesive enclaves and stimulated growth. In 1867, the African Methodist Episcopal (AME) denomination founded Wood's Chapel in the home of congregant Mary Hill, and the American Missionary Association built the Ayer School. Two years later, the Freedmen's Aid Society bought the school and renamed it the Summer Hill School. The Northern Methodists built Clarke's Chapel and Clarke University (later Clarke College).[9]

Due north of Summer Hill stood Shermantown in the fourth ward— named for the general of the liberating forces who occupied the area during the Civil War. From the perspective of a white tourist in the area in 1879, Shermantown consisted of "a random collection of huts forming a dense negro settlement." The lithograph that accompanied this description in *Harper's Weekly*, however, depicts a more consciously arranged village. Wooden shacks are set up in a circle surrounding a well, with clotheslines stretched across the middle, and a thatched roof held up by wooden poles stands right at the center, covering the implements of the washerwoman's trade. Women and men are shown working, lounging, and moving along in their daily activities, dodging a pig and chickens strutting in their pathways.[10]

Shermantown continued as the most vibrant and largest black settlement until the early twentieth century, when west side areas began to eclipse its prominence. Big Bethel AME Church was the first black church in Atlanta, dating back to the 1840s. It was destroyed by the Union Army in 1864 and rebuilt in this area after the Civil War. James Tate, a grocer and former slave, started the first school for blacks in the church in 1865, which was then taken over by the American Missionary Association a year later and renamed the Storrs School. Bethel played a prolific role in community building since it was also the first home of Morris Brown College in 1881. Wheat Street Baptist Church and the First Congregational Church were also located in this area. The black business district on Wheat Street (later Auburn Avenue) would develop here by the end of the century.

Just opposite Shermantown on the west side of town, Jenningstown began growing in 1867, named after the real estate promoter of Summer Hill. This subdivision was one of the few areas on hilly land available to black residents, and it acquired the appellation Diamond Hill. Land was priced to sell to people with few means. Congregants of New Hope Presbyterian Church, the Second Colored Methodist Church, and Friendship Baptist Church worshipped on this ground. The Haynes Street school was opened in a vacant building of Friendship Church, which was also the first site for the Atlanta Baptist Seminary (later Morehouse College) in 1879 and the Atlanta Baptist Female Seminary (later Spelman College) in 1881. Atlanta University also acquired land in Diamond Hill in 1869.[11]

Three major enclaves were in place by 1870, and within just a few years Pittsburg and Mechanicsville grew next to each other in the southwest adjacent to the posh West End. The repair shops and clouds of smoke that gushed out from trains made the area resemble the industrial Pennsylvania city that inspired its name. The large number of black male common laborers employed nearby likewise accounted for the designation Mechanicsville. By 1880, more than a third of the African-American population was concentrated within these largely black enclaves.[12] Though segregation was not yet complete, these distinctive African-American neighborhoods showed marked signs of community life as their residents struggled to counter the deprivations produced by the exploitive physical and social geography of the city.

The women who constituted the majority of the black residents, and half of the black wage-earners, bore a large share of the responsibility for sustaining family and community within these neighborhoods.[13] In the 1880s, 70 percent of black families consisted of two parents. In contrast to most white households of a similar type, most black women shared the burden of wage earning with their male spouses.[14] Black men were paid relatively higher wages than women, but even the combination of both spouses' incomes was sometimes insufficient for establishing a comfortable standard of living. Nor was marriage a guarantee of two steady incomes. Unemployment was a common experience for male common laborers—not to mention separation or the death of a husband, which could reduce a family's resources unexpectedly. As one widowed washerwoman recalled later: "I married a good man and we lived together seventeen years and had six children. He died and left me with all of these children to raise. He was a good husband and father and provided for his family as best he could." She remembered one of her most distressing days after her spouse's death when her children cried for food. "I hated to borrow. I scraped up enough meal to make a little hoe-cake of bread. I broke it among them and went back to my ironing, crying."[15]

Disproportionately high mortality among African Americans could take its emotional and financial toll on surviving relatives and friends. But the existence of relatively small urban families, on average six or fewer people living in the same household, had its benefits. Small family size permitted the pooling of resources, such as two families sharing one dwelling. This practice was evident in Shermantown where houses tended to be larger, though not as apparent in other areas. In Jennings-town, however, African-American families shared their living quarters with individual boarders at a higher rate than they did elsewhere in the city. The presence of several adults in a household increased the chances that families could survive on scant wages, as the one-third of black women living in Atlanta and other cities who carried the burden of raising families alone could attest.[16]

NEARLY all the women wage-earners who contributed to the coffers of black families were household workers, regardless of marital status or age. By 1880, at least 98 percent of all black female wage-earners in Atlanta were domestics. The average woman could expect to enter the occupation between the ages of ten and sixteen and remain in it until the age of sixty-five or longer.[17] Although domestic labor was a virtual prerequisite for black survival, age, marriage, and childbirth affected the decisions women made about wage labor. Younger and single women tended to become general housemaids and child-nurses. Many girls were hired at a young age to perform tasks from rocking cradles to the full range of caretaking responsibilities for charges not much younger than themselves.

Pre-adolescent Dorothy Bolden acquired jobs washing baby diapers and babysitting when she and her brother helped her mother by picking up and delivering the laundry. Older and married women, especially those with children, chose cooking and washing. As Sarah Hill explained her employment history: "I'se been workin' ever since I knowed what work was. 'Fo' I got married I maided and cooked . . . Fust, I maided awhile, and then I cooked awhile, I never was no more good at workin' out after I got married and started havin' chillun, so I just stayed at home and tuk in washin'."[18] Younger women concentrated in general service positions and contributed to their parents' income. But once they married or began giving birth to children of their own, they made occupational choices that gave them more time and flexibility for their new responsibilities. Employers did not always appreciate these decisions, especially when they became attached to workers they liked. Georgia Telfair had worked for one family from age fourteen until age twenty: "My wite folkes begged me not to leave 'em, when I told 'em I wuz gwine to marry Joe Telfair."[19]

Married women like Georgia Telfair made decisions about wage work in conjunction with spouses who often preferred to assume the major responsibility for breadwinning themselves, if their incomes permitted. Some women expressed with pride their husband's desires to keep them out of wage housework, as Carrie Nancy Fryer exclaimed: "Dat was a good husband! I had six chillun. He say: Honey, no! I workin' makin' enough to support you. All I want you to do is keep dis house clean and me and my chillun." Mr. Fryer promised to pay Mrs. Fryer the money every week she would have normally earned from wage work, if she would stay home and take care of their family.[20] Fryer appreciated the gesture, but she would sneak out occasionally and do wage work.

AFRICAN-AMERICAN women and men were seeking to achieve economic independence and well-being, minimizing women's exposure to white employers' impositions and sexual exploitation, despite the protestations of employers, who derided these efforts as "playing the lady" or displays of false pretension.[21] Moreover, black men, like women, valued the work that women did for their own families, as Edward Bacon, a brickmason, suggested. "During my first wife's lifetime she never worked out for no other family, for she didn't have to do it. I was making plenty to support her, and the only work she did was her own housework." During his second marriage, however, his unemployment made it necessary for his wife Susie to take in washing, which he also respected: "that dollar a week she gets for it comes in mighty handy when I'm out of work. A dollar's worth of flour or meal will keep you from going hungry a long time when you're out hunting for a job."[22]

African-American women established their own preferences within domestic labor, but these sometimes clashed with the expectations of employers. Initial negotiations occurred during the hiring process. Most household workers were hired by word of mouth, some by newspaper advertisements or employment agencies. Workers exchanged information among themselves about the availability of jobs and the reputations of employers seeking help. Women leaving good situations took special care to pass on the jobs to younger relatives or friends. Employers likewise communicated with each other to secure workers. The death of an employer or changed family circumstances prompted employers to place their favorite workers in the homes of other family members.[23] The average white wage-earner's family in the South engaged the services of at least a washerwoman. A middle-class home employed a general domestic in addition or perhaps a cook, full or part time. An upper-middle-class family most likely added a child-nurse. And the most elite white families enlarged their staff to include representatives from all of these positions, as well as specialized cooks, chambermaids, lady's maids, waiters, kitchen sculleries, butlers, and valets.[24] Although in theory workers were usually hired to fill specific occupations, in practice they were usually required to assume many roles.

Most workers labored from sunup to sundown seven days a week, though laundresses usually worked only six days. Their wages ranged on average from $4 to $8 a month; though in a few cases, some women earned as much as $10 to $12. The remarkable characteristic of these rates was that they changed so little over time and across occupations. When variations existed, cooks tended to command the highest wages per hour and kitchen sculleries the lowest. Laundresses could increase their earnings by adding on clients and seeking help from family members. These were low wages compared to those of most other workers at the time.[25]

Low wages made it difficult to survive, but no wages were even worse. Some employers cheated their workers by contriving spurious grounds for denying them their rightful earnings. Or sometimes employers would substitute perishables or durable goods in lieu of cash for remuneration, without the workers' consent. Daphne, a domestic worker, normally received between $3 and $8 a month in wages, according to her employer's record. Though the circumstances prompting a change in this pattern during one month are not clear, Daphne received okra and rice valued at $6.50 and $.50 in cash in lieu of her usual compensation.[26] Women could also face deductions for behavioral infractions such as lost time and impudence, or for breaking or misplacing objects.[27]

Bona fide agreements between workers and employers could lead to the use of nonmonetary compensation. But since domestic labor did not rank high in the priorities of the employers' budgets, changes in finances could prompt nonpayment or false promises to pay later. The low value that employers placed on domestic labor is strikingly apparent when one compares the outlays for wages to other expenditures: the yearly sum of wages for several workers usually constituted a mere fraction of the total yearly budgets of middle-class households.[28] Employers often spent considerably more money on their most trivial or inconsequential expenses—such as chewing gum, liquor, or donations to street beggars.[29]

There were distinct, if overlapping, skills and talents involved in household labor, and all of it was arduous. Even as the expectations of good housekeeping dovetailed with changes in the economy and family life, very little changed in the actual labor processes of housework in the nineteenth century. Technological advances hardly ever reached individual homes, and the few that did made limited improvements.[30]

The specific duties and work conditions of general domestics varied according to the economic means of employers and the number of other servants hired. Hauling water and tending fires consumed a large part of the daily routine. The work of servants in wealthy families was facilitated by their access to gas and indoor plumbing. This advantage, however, was offset by the ostentatious surroundings and lavish objects that required extra care. Servants working in more modest homes might have fewer articles to maintain, but the work was harder if they lacked amenities such as piped-in water.

Any number of a dizzying array of chores were required of general domestics. They changed the bed and table linen, counted and separated the wash to prepare for the washerwoman, dusted furniture and staircases, scrubbed floors, emptied and cleaned chamber pots, polished silver, brushed carpets, and watered indoor plants. Sometimes they went on errands, fed and watered pets, helped with garden and yard work. Their bosses might also require cooking, helping with preserving and preparing foodstuffs, or washing dishes and cleaning the kitchen. Women hired to perform general duties would sometimes do the laundry, ironing, mending, and caring for children.[31] General maids were considered to be not only household workers, but also servants who performed a ceremonial role. In greeting arriving guests at the door, they signaled entry into households of high regard and social status. But work indeed it was, not only to perform the arduous physical labor, but also to respond to employers' constant beckoning to satisfy their wants. The relatively few servants who lived with employers faced the added encumbrance of having to respond to unpredictable intrusions that diminished time off for themselves.

Child-nurses would arrive early in the day to keep children occupied and protected while their parents engaged in other remunerative and social activities. One nurse described her duties as follows: "I not only have to nurse a little white child, now eleven months old, but I have to act as playmate or 'handy-andy,' not to say governess, to three other children in the home, the oldest of whom is only nine years of age." She washed and fed the children and put them to bed, which required around-the-clock work according to the infant's and children's needs. But even when the children demanded little attention, the work did not end there. "It's 'Mammy, do this,' or 'Mammy, do that,' or 'Mammy, do the other,' from my mistress, all the time. So it is not strange to see 'Mammy' watering the lawn in front with the garden hose, sweeping the sidewalk, mopping the porch and halls, dusting around the house, helping the cook, or darning the socks."[32] These child-care providers

were often the primary caretakers of white children, yet their subordination imparted early lessons of power and privilege to their charges.
Adolescent white Southerners witnessed and participated in the rituals
eliciting servility and deference very early in life, learning the concrete
meaning of their racial and class position vis-à-vis black servants.

Dorothy Bolden recalled the complicated relationships between
nurse-maids and the children they cared for. Bolden loved taking care
of children from the time she started babysitting for her mother's
laundry patrons. She continued to take care of children as part of her
duties as a general household worker when she became an adult. "You
gave as much love to their children that you would give to yours
almost," she acknowledged. "You respected the child and you protected
the child in that home while you was working," she continued. Bolden
stressed the emotional work expected of domestics and especially child-
nurses, and she lamented the lack of regard that she suffered in return.
She explained that white parents "would teach their children that they
was better than you was. She dark, she ignorant," Bolden explained. She
puzzled over the contradiction in this hostility: "'Cause when their
mother would leave them and you had to take care of them, if they
stumped their toe, you had to kiss it and comfort that child, pet him
and let him know somebody cared." Bolden also suggested that white
children behaved ambivalently toward her. A child might treat her with
respect out of the parents' sight, but "he would turn around when his
mother get there and spit on you. Call you black, call you nigger."[33]

If taking care of children was the most emotionally draining work,
cooking required the most skill and creativity. Cooking was the only
household chore to benefit from technological advances in this period.[34] The cast iron stove, common by the late nineteenth century, was
the most important improvement, replacing the open fireplaces that
had reigned in earlier kitchens. Cast iron stoves required less fuel,
worked more efficiently and safely, and were built high enough off the
ground to prevent constant bending by the cook. But the lack of built-in
thermostats forced cooks to gauge the level of heat through trial and
error—arranging dampers and drafts or placing foods in strategic spots
according to estimates of the time and degree of heat required. In other
respects, food preparation remained virtually the same in the 1880s as
it had been in 1800. Most black cooks developed improvisational styles
of food preparation that defied the notion of scientific housewifery.

They measured and added ingredients according to previous experience and the impulses of their imaginations. Black women recognized the intelligence required for the craft. As one cook described her work: "Everything I does, I does by my head; its all brain work."[35] In addition to the creative labor, cooks also washed dishes, mopped floors, cleaned and maintained the stoves, pots, pans, and utensils. The degree of autonomy they enjoyed varied, but they generally planned the meals and marketed for groceries.[36]

The comfort evoked by the warmth of kitchens and their pleasant smells made them a prime social space, especially for children of the employing household in search of company and treats. In this way, cooks also contributed to raising white children who sought refuge in their work areas. A white family without a cook was such an anomaly in one Georgia town that a visitor asked: "But who do the children talk to?"[37] If some employers were preoccupied with satisfying the needs of their children, cooks were concerned about their own families. Cooks sometimes had flexible workdays that allowed them to go home in between meals or leave following the afternoon supper.[38]

Cooking may have required the most inventiveness, but laundry work was the most difficult job. Unlike cooking, which benefited from technological advances in stoves, laundry work became more dreadful as a result of industrialization. Manufactured cloth not only increased the amount of clothing people obtained, but the production of washable fabric such as cotton increased the need for washing. Laundry work was the single most onerous chore in the life of a nineteenth-century woman, and the first chore she would hire someone else to perform whenever the slightest bit of discretionary income was available. Even poor urban women might send out at least some of their wash. In the North, this meant that women, especially those living in tenements lacking the proper equipment, might send their dirty clothes to commercial laundries.[39] In the South, however, where the adoption of technological advances lagged and manual laborers predominated, many poor whites sent out part or all of their wash to black women.[40]

A few washerwomen may have been too poor to afford the proper equipment, or too isolated from other women who could share their equipment, so that they ended up working in the homes of their employers.[41] But normally, most laundresses worked in their own homes and neighborhoods. The work of the washerwoman began on

Monday mornings and continued throughout the week until she delivered clean clothes on Saturday. The sight of "tall, straight negro girls marching through the street carrying enormous bundles of soiled clothes upon their heads," from the homes of patrons to their own homes, was common every week.[42]

Gallons of water had to be toted from wells, pumps, or hydrants for washing, boiling, and rinsing clothes. Washerwomen made their own soap from lye, starch from wheat bran, and wash tubs from beer barrels cut in half. They supplied washboards, batting blocks or sticks, work benches, fuel, and cast iron pots for boiling. Different fabrics required varying degrees of scrubbing and then soaking in separate tubs with appropriate water temperatures. When weather permitted, work was often performed outdoors under shaded trees. The saturated garments were hung on clotheslines, plum bushes, or barbed wire fences—marked by the telltale signs of three-pronged snags on the finished products. But inclement conditions moved the work inside, and clotheslines were hung across the main room. Once the clothes were dry, several heavy irons were heated on the stove and used alternately. After each use, the irons were rubbed with beeswax and wiped clean to minimize the buildup of residue. One by one items were sprayed or dampened with water or starch and pressed into crisp form.[43]

Flexibility marked the main advantage of laundry work, especially for women with children. They could intermingle washing with the fulfillment of other responsibilities and incorporate help from other family members. "I could clean my hearth good and nice and set my irons in front of the fire and iron all day [with]out stopping . . . I cooked and ironed at the same time," stated Sarah Hill.[44] Male relatives sometimes picked up dirty clothes in wheelbarrows or wagons. Children could also help with pickup and deliveries, as Dorothy Bolden and her brother did, assist with maintaining the fire, or beat the clothes with sticks.[45]

THE RANGE of job options for black women was severely limited to working for white families. But within these strictures, laundry work was the optimal choice for a black woman who wanted to create a life of her own. The washerwoman was the archetypal domestic laborer in Atlanta. By 1880, laundry work engaged more black women than any other single category of domestic work, and washerwomen outnumbered male common laborers.[46] A significant shift had occurred in the proportion of laundresses among household workers between 1870 and 1880; general domestics and cooks combined increased by only 15 percent, while laundresses increased more than 150 percent.[47]

The intense struggles between workers and employers over the character of wage work following emancipation influenced black women's decisions to establish themselves in jobs that permitted some of the advantages of a home business. Their constant movement in and out of the labor market demonstrated their incessant effort to try to find better terms for their work. One important advantage of laundry work was that whites were not employers of laundresses as much as they were clients. This did not mean that washerwomen could unilaterally set prices or establish terms, however, as grievances prompting strikes in Southern cities would make clear. The sharp increase in the number of washerwomen can also be attributed to the depression of the 1870s, which affected employers' fortunes, compelling them to make decisions to send out their clothes to laundresses rather than hiring full-time domestics.[48] The influx of white migrants into the city who were wage-earners also increased the demand for laundresses, whose services many could afford. Atlanta, and the urban South more generally, had the highest concentration of domestic workers per capita in the nation. The large number of laundresses contributed disproportionately to this regional discrepancy.[49]

Domestic workers who spent most of their workday in white workplaces fought to gain concessions from employers to mitigate the impositions of wage labor. In constructing lives consistent with the freedom that emancipation had bestowed they established a number of goals and strategies for achieving them. The desire to distance themselves physically from erstwhile masters ranked high in their priorities. In a walking city like Atlanta, cooks, maids, and child-nurses could live in areas that were within easy reach by foot, yet were far enough to establish autonomous lives. Though the "marble-cake" pattern in antebellum cities intermixed servants' houses in white neighborhoods to keep them in check, ex-slave women's insistence on living in their own homes contributed to the growing pattern of de facto residential segregation by race.[50] A minority of household workers continued to live either in the homes or in the backyards of employers after emancipation, but most were interspersed among the wider black community.

This pattern was unlike the situation in the northeast, where most domestic workers, who were native-born white and European women, lived in the homes of employers.[51] Black women in the urban South perceived few advantages from living-in, as "free" accommodations and food were usually meager, especially in comparison to the personal sacrifices required of them.

White employers responded ambivalently to this trend. Some resented the loss of control the arrangement exacted. "Very few of them, cooks or servants, will consent to sleep on the premises where they work as servants. They seem to think that it is something against their freedom if they sleep where they are employed," an employer unwittingly revealed. "Married or unmarried. They will rent a little house, perhaps a mile off, and pay $10 a month for it, and go there to sleep, when perhaps you would be willing to pay them just as much and give them a comfortable bed or cottage on your own place," he continued.[52] But others had mixed emotions about living in close contact with blacks. As the early growth of upper-class suburbs such as the West End suggested, whites were increasingly creating exclusive retreats to escape from the inner city, though they wished to do so without relinquishing the convenience of having black servants nearby.

In the spirit of securing their independence and making decisions about wage work that were commensurate with the needs of their families and communities, black women continued to rely on the tactic of resistance they had employed with great determination during the postwar period—they quit. Their movement in and out of the labor market continued to evoke conflict and dominated the private conversations and public deliberations among whites about their perennial "servant problem." "One great need of Atlanta is cooks who won't leave families without notice, and breakfast and housegirls who will remain a month," stated a familiar news report, which broached an alternative. "Isn't Atlanta getting large enough to have a few white servants?"[53] The idea of hiring white servants would be bandied about in discussions about the "servant problem," but very few employers ever took any concrete steps to make it real.

One employer described the inconvenience caused by black women's audacious self-assertion: "It is actually dangerous to invite company three days ahead. I have known them to leave when they knew that invitations were out for a dining in the house; they would just leave without any particular reason at all, but simply from some foolish desire for change."[54] Rather than expressing "foolish desire," the workers wielded "incipient strikes" to deliberately sabotage a social event in order to cause embarrassment and shame to employers forced to entertain their guests without servants.[55]

Rather than abide by the strictures of unending hours of year-round toil, household workers also quit temporarily to labor in their own homes to take care of sick family or to participate in social activities. When church groups or secret societies sponsored train excursions as fund-raising and social events, employers were guaranteed sudden departures of their household help. "No matter how important the occasion may be, or how urgent the need for their services, whether you have a wedding in the house, or sickness, or whatever you may have, they will just leave the cooking-stove and the housework and everything else and go off on these 'scursions,'" one employer complained.[56] From the point of view of workers, however, time out of the labor market and unpaid work were as vital to the lives of working-class people as cash wages and more important to their personal enrichment.[57]

Quitting was a thriving strategy for resisting domination precisely because it could not be prohibited in a free labor system. Though some workers may have openly confronted their employers before departing, quitting did not require open or direct antagonism. Workers who had the advantage of living in their own homes could easily make up excuses for leaving, or leave without any notice at all. These small and fleeting victories of individuals accumulated into bigger results as workers throughout the city repeatedly executed this tactic, frustrating the nerves of employers.

In the process of everyday life, African-American household workers found other ways of seeking justice besides quitting. One such strategy was reappropriating the material assets of their employers for their own use. The "pan-toting" custom of taking away table scraps or dry goods presents a microcosm of the competing expectations of workers and employers and the encroachment of the wage system. This customary practice evolved during the transition from slave to free labor as an expression of a dissenting "moral economy." It is consistent with the "vails" and perquisites claimed by servants across cultures and dating back centuries, however.[58] African-American women claimed rights and privileges as waged workers in part on the basis of their former status as slaves who had produced the wealth of their masters without compensation. Household laborers expected employers to acknowledge their obligation to ensure basic subsistence openly, by supplementing wages with leftover foodstuffs, or else they literally reclaimed the fruits of their labor without the employers' consent.

Pan-toting helped to alleviate some of the onerous consequences of low-wage labor for black women. Some employers acceded to the practice, openly admitting that they paid low wages with table scraps in mind. Domestic workers who had no legal remedies to redress grievances sometimes used pan-toting to counter employers' tactics of dishonesty involving wages. Some employers interpreted "free" labor literally to mean expropriating labor without compensation. Outright refusals to pay wages, the use of coercion to pawn off extraneous articles in lieu of cash, depriving workers of wages for trivial "offenses," and assessing "insurance fees" were common occurrences.[59] Despite this, some employers attacked pan-toting as theft, as one employer celebrating the departure of a cook exclaimed: "This is our Emancipation day! We are free from *Susan Bell* . . . She has been robbing our table for months to support her mother."[60] The issue of perquisites would not be resolved to anyone's satisfaction and would become even more contested in the twentieth century.

Stealing breaks, feigning illness, and sloughing off at work were other strategies used by discontented workers. Child-nurses would sometimes schedule walks or outings with their charges in order to pass conveniently through their own neighborhoods to conduct business they would otherwise neglect. Feigning illness was a popular tactic, especially for live-in workers, who had less control over their time during or after work. On the spur of the moment, a dispute resolved without satisfaction to a cook or general maid could lead her to take action immediately by performing her job poorly. Even servants who were considered "well-raised" and "properly" trained by their employers would show "indifference" to their work if they felt unduly provoked. As one employer explained, "Tell them to wipe up the floor, and they will splash away from one end of the room to the other; and if you tell them that is not the way to do it, they will either be insolent or perhaps give you a vacant stare as if they were very much astonished that you thought that was not the way to do it, and they will keep right on."[61]

These tactics no doubt brought moments of relief and satisfaction to domestic workers, but gestures that outwitted employers or wore on their nerves were never sufficient to meet the needs of black women's subsistence. African-American women relied on their abilities to piece together a livelihood not only with the work they did for white families, but also with their non-remunerative labor for their own families.

The significance of laundry work to black families and communities is thrown into greatest relief within this context. The high visibility of laundry workers in black communities is illustrated by the prominent location of the wash tub in the center of the Shermantown village, or by the fact that one small Georgia town took its name—Shakerag—from the characteristic billowing clotheslines that enveloped the black settlement.[62] Laundry work was critical to the process of community-building because it encouraged women to work together in communal spaces within their neighborhoods, fostering informal networks of reciprocity that sustained them through health and sickness, love and heartaches, birth and death.

The practical value of communal labor was realized in sharing that broadened the meaning of kinship to create interdependence among women.[63] One widow washerwoman was given the assistance she needed from a neighbor who had saved the table scraps from her employer's table. Dinah Campbell explained other circumstances that could give rise to women pitching in for one another. "When my sister, what stayed home with Mandy and washed and ironed, took sick and died I had to take her place at the washboard," she stated. Sister Mandy picked up the story to explain how the circle of support continued: "Since Sister Jane done got no' count for work, Sister Ann come along here and axed us to take her in. We done it, and when she ain't workin' out she helps us with the washin' and ironin'." "Sister Ann," she noted when questioned about their relationship, "ain't no kin to us."[64]

This support system also facilitated the management of child care; washerwomen would watch the children of neighbors left at home or in the streets to fend for themselves while their parents worked away. And for washerwomen's own children, especially girls old enough to assist, laundry work nourished mother-daughter relationships. Girls learned the skills of their mothers' trades and were schooled in the lessons of adulthood within the camaraderie of women's work. Anna

Parks recalled her mother's words as she passed her knowledge and skills to her daughter: "Some day I'll be gone fum dis world, and you won't know nuffin' 'bout takin' keer of yo'self, less you learn right now." Parks remembered taking those lessons seriously and feeling proud after washing her first load of clothes and collecting her earnings. She saw this accomplishment as a rite of passage: "I felt like I wuz a grown [w]oman den," she stated.[65]

The intimacy of laundry work inspired unity, but it could also produce friction between women. Gossip cut both ways; individuals used it to pass on vital—literally life-saving—information. But as rumor and innuendo, it could also evoke jealousy or rouse ill will. A roaming reporter described the "true Lycurgus style" of a community laundry spot as a place "where all wash clothes harmoniously together until some sister gets in a bad humor."[66] Sharing did not occur indiscriminately, for past experiences determined one's reputation for adherence to social expectations. Nor did women redistribute scarce resources simply on the basis of abstract or sentimental principles. In the phrasing of the vernacular, working-class women gave with the understanding that what goes around comes around—they anticipated reciprocity. "Bad humor" could result from disagreements over the conduct or violation of this social rule. Public brawls and street fights were used as a method of airing grievances, seeking support, and obtaining resolution, with the sanction of the wider community. The passion with which women took their quarrels to the streets alarmed city authorities, who often dispatched the police. Though different assumptions may have informed this intervention, the arrests of working-class women for "disorderly conduct" frequently involved conflicts between individuals and groups within the community.[67]

Working in a communal setting also made it possible for women to use time during the day to salvage resources within their own immediate environment. Early in the morning before the business day commenced in Atlanta, women and children could be seen rummaging through the garbage pails of groceries, restaurants, fruit stands, and other merchants. They collected discarded cinders to generate fuel for cooking or for the laundry. Other goods from the public domain were recycled for use, trade, or resale in the neighborhood or in local pawn shops in exchange for cash. Sometimes children were sent out on their own to collect items for their mothers. "Troops of little black boys, bare-footed, bare-headed, and ragged 'to a degree'" were noticed picking up rags.[68] Some whites objected to poor blacks' scavenging the streets and blamed the women for spreading disease and contamination. Since "only the extreme processes of decay cause them to reject what may be discarded," these critics urged the city health officer to remove garbage dumps, or at least to force merchants to sort out the spoiled throwaways from the merely unattractive but recyclable items.[69]

Shopping for fresh foods and dry goods was a luxury that not all working-class women could afford. The chickens and pig spotted in Summer Hill provide evidence that rural migrants continued to produce some of their own food once they arrived in the city. Into the 1880s, a few African-American men farmed on small plots on the edge of town, returning to the city on the weekends to spend time with their families. The backyard gardens and livestock seen in Atlanta were characteristic of urban scenes in working-class communities—in the North as well as the South. Fertile plots not only supplied food to their owners but also enabled sharing and fostered sociability among family, friends, and neighbors.[70] When black women were able to purchase foods, they bought what they needed in small quantities from black or Jewish street vendors, peddlers, and grocery stores near their homes. This meant, of course, that they could not obtain volume discounts, which raised their food costs. Hardly a disregard for economy, as some of their contemporaries claimed, this minimal shopping prevented food spoilage and permitted budgeting of small cash outlays, especially when wages were paid irregularly.[71]

A select few black women were able to stretch their earnings, save money, and buy property. Elizabeth Pope, a washerwoman and cook, moved to Shermantown from Augusta with her husband Alfred and their five children during Reconstruction. The couple opened a store in Summer Hill and accumulated over $1,000 in property in Elizabeth's name by the time she was forty-two in 1873.[72] Annie Johnson was among the small number of black seamstresses in Atlanta in 1880 and held over $1,000 in property at the age of thirty. Unlike Pope, however, Johnson did not have the benefit of a husband. She raised three sons and cared for an eleven-year-old girl with the help of her mother, a washerwoman, in Jenningstown.[73] Pope and Johnson were exceptional black women able to accumulate relatively substantial property through domestic work. Most domestic workers did not accumulate property, however, beyond the pots and pans and modest furnishings in their homes. Those black women who did acquire property had to work overtime and combine their savings with resources of other relatives to buy even cheap houses.[74]

Despite the constraints of the Southern occupational structure, in which black women had only limited access to jobs outside private white homes, a few black women applied their skills to jobs elsewhere. Black women were hired in boardinghouses, brothels, and, increasingly in the 1880s, in hotels.[75] Working in commercial establishments sometimes paid higher wages than jobs in private homes and lessened direct paternalistic supervision. Immediately after emancipation, a woman identified only as Rachel moved to Atlanta with the idea of starting a laundry business. She hired several helpers before she arrived, including her daughter Frances. In a peculiar twist of customary Southern labor relationships, Frances returned to visit her ex-owner in the country to see if she would take care of her children while Frances helped her mother with the business. The ex-owner, appalled by the suggestion, later delighted in the apparent failure of the venture.[76]

Some black women established à la carte meal services or lunch carts. Dozens of these six-by-nine-foot establishments erected on busy streets were renowned for their fried fish, boiled ham, and bread. Some served as a catering service for white families as well. Many of these establishments became common gathering places for African Americans to meet and socialize. Some white residents found their presence objectionable, especially because they attracted large and boisterous crowds on Sundays and were rumored to serve alcohol in violation of the city's blue laws.[77]

WHATEVER their particular occupations, subsistence did not direct all the activities in working-class women's neighborhoods—though recreation and personal gratification could also serve economic ends. Lunch carts no doubt generated income and at the same time created outlets for leisure. Other places for leisure were the railroad depot, alleys, side streets, front porches, churches, and fraternal halls in African-American neighborhoods. In the conventional tone of a bemused outsider, a white Northern journalist traveling through the city just after Reconstruction described what must have been a typical scene near the railroad depot: "I find five laborers, each black as the deuce of spades, sitting upon a circle of battered stools and soap boxes, and forming a 'string band' despite the inconsistency of a cornet." Medicine shows that included displays of patent pharmaceuticals and minstrel performers to draw attention would be set up in a vacant lot downtown near the railroad depot. Blackface black entertainers dressed in burlesque fashion could be found "dancing jigs, reciting conundrums, and banging banjo, bones, and tambourine" as two to three hundred spectators watched, sang, and danced along with them.[78]

The sighting of African-American performers painted in blackface in the 1870s was consistent with broader national trends. Minstrelsy was the first form of popular culture, though it was originally performed by and for white men exclusively. But by the mid-nineteenth century, authentic slaves and ex-slaves challenged the monopoly once enjoyed by Caucasian actors mimicking Negroes. Within a few decades, black minstrel touring companies such as Silas Green's show from New Orleans and Pat Chappelle's Rabbit's Foot Minstrels from Port Gibson, Mississippi, traveled throughout the South; they featured musicians, singers, dancers, comics, and novelty acts under large canvas tents, performing material written and composed by other blacks.[79]

By 1880, outlets of commercial leisure in Atlanta were concentrated mainly on Ivy, Harris, Peters, and Decatur Streets, all located near the CBD and Shermantown, with the exception of Peters Street in the southwest, just above Mechanicsville and Pittsburg.[80] Blacks could frequent barber shops, billiard rooms, lunch rooms, restaurants, and beer saloons where they could play cards, gamble, smoke, eat, drink, and dance. At the corner of Decatur and Ivy Street stood the Willingham building, notorious for its association with worldly indulgences that landed people in jail. The building served as a boardinghouse and office space for a shoe shop, restaurant, billiard room, and beer saloon. As one investigative reporter described it: "Here by the light of a few smoky oil lamps, and to the soul-harrowing music of a string band, the colored beaux and dusky damsels, who rarely speak to a white person, trip the light fantastic toe, not forgetting to refresh themselves at the saloon counter when each dance is ended."[81]

Fun and reprieve from hard work awaited working-class women on the streets, but not without a price. If light-hearted fraternizing turned into open conflicts, or when the police launched gratuitous raids, black women and men were carted off to jail, subjected to severe penalties for alleged petty crimes. African Americans began publicly criticizing police brutality and calling for the city to hire black officers in the 1860s. They condemned the over-zealous record of arrests that were often inspired by ambitions for higher salaries and promotions. Denied changes in public policy to reflect these concerns, blacks united to reduce apprehensions by providing asylum to individuals chased by patrolmen.[82] Nearly 60 percent of the individuals arrested in Atlanta in the 1880s were black, although blacks made up only 44 percent of the city's population. Most of the alleged criminals were men, but black women were far more likely to get arrested than white. Blacks represented 80 percent of the women apprehended, and over 90 percent of those actually sent to jail. Yet black women constituted less than half of the female population.[83] Black women arrested for minor crimes were often sentenced to work on the chain gangs at the city stockade or leased to private firms that contracted convict labor. Beatings, rapes, and sexual harassment by male convicts and officials were common experiences. Some employers capitalized on this captive labor force by buying out prisoners' terms in exchange for release in supervised custody.[84]

Violence and crime were among the many challenges of urban life that required inventiveness for survival, in the absence of protection or support from governing authorities. Working-class women pieced together their livelihoods beyond the labor that they performed in exchange for wages, using the various consumption strategies described earlier that were critical both materially and socially. Scavenging, borrowing, and pan-toting helped to increase the provisions for subsistence of those with little cash. Domestic workers transformed raw products into consumable goods for their own families, the same labor that they performed in the homes of their employers, albeit with much more austerity.[85] They conducted this activity at the level of neighborhoods, creating informal social networks in communal laundry spots, on the streets, in lunch carts, and in dance halls. The casual mechanisms of mutual aid, in turn, facilitated the development of more formal institutions such as churches and secret societies which provided other outlets for social, spiritual, and political expression, as well as economic cooperation. Churches and secret societies then tended to reinforce the ties that bound people together as family, friends, and neighbors.

❧ CHURCHES played a critical role in the development of black community life immediately after emancipation. They had humble beginnings, often arising out of makeshift tabernacles such as abandoned railroad cars. Eight black churches were organized by 1870 and fourteen more by 1880, all within the four largest settlements.[86] They served as magnets for newcomers and facilitated the expansion of neighborhoods. Members of established churches created links across the city among parishioners by helping to start new churches in different settlements. Wheat Street Baptist Church was founded by members of Friendship Church who lived in Shermantown and wanted to build a sanctuary closer to their homes on the east side. Thus churches tended to beget more churches, and the relationship between different black institutions was reciprocal. Bethel AME Church was the first home of Storrs School and the midwife of Storrs Chapel, which became known as the First Congregational Church.[87]

African-American churches served a multitude of spiritual, social, and political functions. Sunday, of course, was dedicated to religious activities, as individuals attended Sunday school and worship service, sometimes crisscrossing between programs at several institutions on the same day. During the week, converts attended prayer gatherings and meetings of various organizations. Periodic revivals, most frequent during the summer, played especially important functions in spiritual rejuvenation, adding new members, reinvigorating the commitments of the long-lasting, and unifying different congregations. The seriousness of African Americans' commitment to these religious activities was demonstrated by their willingness to sacrifice time from remunerative labor, if necessary, to participate. Household workers provoked the ire of employers by abandoning secular toil for what some scorned as "fetish follies."

In the summer of 1878, a two-week-long revival held at Wheat Street Baptist Church occupied the days and nights of many African Americans, including domestic workers. One employer complained that a cook spent four days at the revival, forcing her to hire a replacement. Another noted a washerwoman who had "gone crazy with the prospect of getting religion," making it impossible to rely on her to wash clothes during the entire duration of the sacred jubilee. These grievances led the newspaper to editorialize: "Revivals may be a very good thing in their way, but when our cooks and washerwomen throw down their work and hurry off to the church to spend the week, they get to be a nuisance."[88]

Churches provided outlets of collective self-help, fostered leadership development, sanctioned group morals, and promoted public and private education. On special occasions, fairs were organized both as festive public events and as opportunities to raise money. The churches were sanctuaries for important secular and associational meetings, and they also provided settings for organizing ward clubs and political rallies, plotting electoral strategies, and coalescing votes.[89]

Religious institutions enhanced their power and position within the community not only by their individual acts but also by uniting in Sunday school and church associations that linked members of the same denomination within a city-wide and state network. These groups operated as umbrella organizations that carried out the same spiritual and social functions on a larger scale: they were involved in social reform movements like temperance, raised funds for black educational institutions, and allotted missionary funds. Their conventions promoted leadership development, skills in governance, and religious education, and also provided an arena for applauding the most dedicated religious converts. Those persons selected to represent their home churches as delegates, for example, were honored simply by their selection and obtained opportunities to partake in the widening of social networks.[90]

Although women composed the large majority of church members, their status and power were disproportionately small. Their leadership was significant and vital but usually subordinated to the most prestigious positions held by men, especially pastors. Toward the end of the century, some religious organizations devised rules for church governance that explicitly forbade women from voting and participating in official debates. A controversy over women's proper roles came to a head in the Missionary Baptist Convention of Georgia in 1893. Those who favored a stronger role for women split from the old order to form the General State Baptist Convention of Georgia. The dispute at the local level mirrored similar controversies at the national level, as Baptist women's outspoken advocacy of missionary roles and spiritual leadership was rebuked by male ministers.[91] The church could be stifling in other ways. Its commitment to governing the totality of people's lives addressed many of the needs of poor people beyond their spirituality, but it could also bring down the wrath of fire and brimstone against those who violated church rules or religious covenants, excommunicating or harshly punishing those who were judged as miscreants.[92]

Mutual aid and benevolent associations, also called secret societies, with antebellum roots in many Southern cities, rivaled churches in their popularity. They provided benefits for widows, orphans, and ill or unemployed members, as well as outlets for education, trade association, and political and social expression. Yet these were not always mutually exclusive institutions; some of these benevolent associations were organized through churches. Regardless of their origins, many exhibited religious influences. Names such as the Daughters of Samaria, Daughters of Bethel, Sisters of Friendship, and Sisters of Love demonstrated reverence for biblical figures and principles that meshed with their organizational purposes. It was not by accident that one group identified itself as the Daughters of Zion—the place of refuge, especially for the poor.[93] Church-affiliated organizations tended to emphasize raising funds for the church and aiding people outside of their organizations. The Daughters of Samaria, for example, started out as a small group in 1875 and grew to a membership of 500 by 1880. As in Jesus' parable of the good Samaritan who helped the traveler when he needed it most, the Daughters of Samaria identified themselves as latter-day missionaries to their people. When a yellow fever epidemic broke out in Savannah and Memphis in the 1870s, the Order sent charitable objects. Likewise, they aided the poor, sick, disabled, and survivors of the dead within their own city. By pooling their resources, they became the first black secret order in Atlanta to purchase property. Most secret societies did not achieve the material prosperity of the Samaritans, but dozens formed tributaries throughout the city that operated on a far more modest scale.[94]

The religious, secular, social, and political purposes of these organizations sometimes overlapped. For example, in its twelfth annual anniversary celebration in 1888, the Morning Star Lodge of the Good Samaritans and Daughters of Samaria staged a parade from their hall on Peachtree Street toward Bethel AME Church in preparation for a special sermon delivered in their honor. On the next night the group sponsored a social event at the Odd Fellows Hall that it billed as "*the entertainment of the season.*"[95]

At least a few of these associations were organized as labor unions or political leagues (and sometimes a combination of both). William Finch founded the Mechanics and Laborers' Union in 1868, which bridged labor issues and Republican Party concerns. Laundry workers formed Washing Societies in the 1870s and 1880s.[96] Another group known as the Union Benevolent Society may also have focused on work-related concerns. Disfranchised women exercised their influence in electoral politics through organizations like the Rising Daughters of Liberty Society—counterpart to the Sons by the same name usually affiliated with the Republican Party. The Rising Daughters of Liberty promoted political education among members and the wider community, raised funds, and stimulated enthusiasm for the campaigns of candidates or issues of their choices.[97]

Some associations were made up entirely of one sex or combined both women and men. But occasionally one finds the presence of a male officer, usually the secretary, in organizations where working-class women predominated and illiteracy prevailed. Though some female groups acted as subordinates to male groups, a striking feature of the Gospel Aid Society is the seemingly conscious effort to balance the power and positions of men and women. The president and secretary were men, the vice-president and treasurer were women, and an equal number of each sex served on the finance committee. Similarly, the Order of Good Samaritans and Daughters of Samaria, which operated separately as well as in a unified group, elected nearly equal numbers of men and women upon its founding.[98]

Whatever the makeup of their organizations, working-class women were active and visible members and leaders in these societies in Atlanta. Household laborers such as Amanda Bradbury, Rachel Oliver, Nancy Wilson, and Lizzie Ford helped to found the Daughters of Samaria. Rebecca Thomas not only served as president of the Rising Daughters of Liberty Society, but at various points she also headed the Daughters of Bethlehem and served on the bank committee of the Star of Bethlehem. Elizabeth Russell and Mildred Fane, president and vice-president of the Daughters of Bethlehem, were both washerwomen. The True Sisters of Honor elected Harriet Tolliver, a washerwoman, as vice-president, and her daughter Keziah Wood as a member of the finance committee.[99]

It is not just a coincidence that working-class women were involved in mutual aid and benevolent associations. The groups proved indispensable within the panoply of institutions designed for the purposes of urban survival, race advancement, and personal enrichment. Paying in small, regularly assessed fees, individuals pooled their resources and reserved them for emergencies. Blacks in Georgia paid $16.5 million to the lodges between 1870 and 1920, confirming that these fraternal orders were the most popular insuring agents in the state.[100] By their willingness to share their resources with others, they provided insurance for themselves. Secret societies in New Orleans, for example, contributed the largest share of health care services to African Americans in the late nineteenth and early twentieth centuries.[101] Societies contracted for physicians or pharmacists upon whom members could rely for treatment or medicines. Perhaps most important, laypersons from the order visited the sick, and in cases of serious illnesses they would move in with the patient to help with general household cares. The fervent spirit with which associations undertook these responsibilities is shown by the commitment to fine members who failed to carry out their duties diligently.[102]

Death benefits were critical to the very existence of these associations. The desire to ensure financial relief for surviving family members and to secure a respectable burial were among the most important reasons for joining. Secret societies facilitated the incorporation of community into the funeral as a public event. Mourners gathered special fees, collected food for wakes, dressed themselves and the deceased in the appropriate reverent apparel, and planned associational services in conjunction with the religious ceremony. They led elaborate processions and laid the physical body to rest, stressing a spirit of life embarking on a new stage in the world beyond, rather than the finality of death.[103]

Other rituals added to the secret societies' appeal for personal and group enhancement. Initiation, oath-taking, and self-improvement ceremonies with all manner of regalia, titles, and parades inspired a sense of collective objectives, and brought prestige and status to those who belonged. Elaborate rites taught members the secrets of symbols and instructed them to aid their fellow sisters and brothers and to live uprightly, according to principles such as love, charity, purity, and justice. Through the complex body of procedures and rules that regulated the conduct of meetings, rituals, and standards of membership, these groups promoted self-governance and discipline of a high order.[104]

The scant existing records do not permit a precise calculation of the number of societies in Atlanta during the late nineteenth century, but the general consensus among contemporary observers was that they were numerous throughout the South. In Richmond, there were four hundred secret societies organized by the early 1870s.[105] The well-established antebellum slave and free black community in Richmond, of course, gave that city a head start. But the promptness of these groups' appearance at the commencement of emancipation in a relatively new city such as Atlanta, enabling a major infrastructure for weaving together individuals and extended families, is testimony to the fact that they embodied and drew on preexisting values that stretched back over many generations, across time and space.

Critics were fond of disparaging the "natural proclivities" of African-American people toward congregating and socializing, but it was hard work rather than nature that cemented the ties in mutual aid societies, churches, and neighborhoods, all of which were crucial to meeting the challenges of urban life. Employers disdained this rich associational life that they perceived as upstart imitations of whites. Mutual aid societies were mocked as organizations with "funny names." "They have the society of the 'Immaculate Doves,' and the society of the 'Sisteren,' and the society of the 'Beloved Disciples,'" one employer remarked. Though the depth of meaning of African Americans' mutual aid groups may have escaped some employers, they undoubtedly understood the subversive implications of the collective culture that sustained domestic workers. The existence of secret societies, one employer admitted, "makes them perfectly independent and relieves them from all fear of being discharged, because when they are discharged they go right straight to some of these 'sisters.'"[106]

African-American women did indeed look to their sisters and brothers for mutual support. They responded to the growing pressures of exploitation in everyday life by pooling their resources through informal organizing in their neighborhoods and, increasingly, formed institutions that extended the boundaries of community across the growing metropolis. They pursued the line of least resistance when feasible, but took aggressive collective actions when necessary to secure their rights as workers and human beings.

"Washing Amazons" and Organized Protests

$\mathcal{S}$outhern black women's labor stood on the periphery of the burgeoning economy in the New South, but their work was essential to its effective functioning. Few events in history would demonstrate this more profoundly than the washerwomen's strikes. Domestic workers began to organize mass labor protests in the immediate postwar years. Strikes in Jackson, Mississippi, in 1866 and Galveston, Texas, in 1877 offer compelling examples of uprisings in this era. They reflect much of the impetus, substance, and structure of resistance that would emerge in Atlanta shortly thereafter. The women in Galveston were especially effective in launching their protests on the tail end of a national wave of protests led by railroad workers. But the Atlanta boycott, undertaken in the very heart of the New South, and its timing at a critical moment in the vanguard city's history, dramatized dissension most powerfully of all. The washerwomen mobilized in the summer of 1881 during preparations for the International Cotton Exposition, the first world's fair in the South. In a fitting gesture, they threatened a second boycott by all household workers at the fall opening of the gala.

Black women had reached the decision to undertake a direct, large-scale political action after years of trying other strategies to secure their rights which proved insufficient. Quotidian subsistence tactics and covert resistance were vital to sustaining working-class women and their families, but they were not enough to procure fair working and living conditions in a city that increasingly proved to be hostile to their interests. Black women drew on the leadership and political skills from their experiences during the 1860s and 1870s in the Republican Party, labor unions, churches, secret societies, and informal neighborhood networks. By the opening of the next decade, African Americans had won several pivotal victories in the electoral arena that engendered momentary bursts of hope and optimism. This reservoir of collective strength, knowledge, and experience would become decisive in the washerwomen's battle to secure autonomy in their trade and to subvert passive obedience to the whims of the free market. Black women in Jackson, Galveston, and Atlanta would strike a blow at the platitudes of progress broadcast by urban boosters to the nation and to the world.

LAUNDRY workers in Jackson, barely out of slavery, displayed conscientious leadership as well as a tightly articulated ideology of self-regulation. On June 18, 1866, they called a city-wide meeting. They then submitted an open letter and formal petition to the mayor, which outlined grievances over the conditions of their labor together with a proposal for ameliorating the situation. "The present high prices of all the necessaries of life," the petition read, "and the attendant high rates of rent, while our wages remain very much reduced," made it "impossible to live uprightly and honestly." Therefore, they resolved to "join in charging a uniform rate for our labor," warning that "any one belonging to the class of washerwomen, violating this, shall be liable to a fine regulated by the class." In establishing the justice of their position, they explained that "we do not wish in the least to charge exorbitant prices, but desire to be able to live comfortably if possible from the fruits of our labor." The women sought the mayor's support should he "deem it just and right" even as they forthrightly presented their demands: "We present the matter to your Honor, and hope you will not reject it as the condition of prices call on us to raise our wages."[1]

As the washerwomen in Jackson organized a collective action to voice their grievances and submitted their petition to the mayor, male laborers in the city also began organizing. The majority of the whites in the city probably agreed with the sentiment toward both strikes expressed by one reporter: "We regard this agitation so ill-timed, unfortunate and calculated to injure instead of better[ing] their condition." This was the alternative, oft-repeated explanation for the deleterious working conditions experienced by black workers: "Idleness and a disposition to change from one place to another without sufficient reason, are injuring the prospects of the freedmen more than low rates of wages."[2]

Critics disparaged black women's intelligence, political acumen, and organizational skills by attributing the strike's leadership to white male carpetbaggers. The newspaper acknowledged, however, that the washerwomen's strike could adversely affect employers who were already troubled by an insufficient supply of obedient workers. But in the end, it was predicted, employers would win and black women would lose their jobs.[3]

Details of how the strikes proceeded or the final outcomes have not survived, but the achievements are more significant than any evaluation of "success" or "failure" would indicate. The Jackson women formulated a structure with elements of both trade unionism and business organization. They set prices to ward off the potential of antagonistic competition and to maintain the advantages of independent labor. Yet they fixed fees according to a standard of fairness, rather than playing the market for all it would bear. Communal labor provided the basis for unifying women, as well as for censuring individuals who erred in undermining consensus. They solicited public recognition of the legitimacy of their claims, yet refused to leave the fulfillment of their human rights to the capricious free market. The constituent elements of their protest would surface in strikes elsewhere in subsequent years.

Domestic workers' protests were a part of a flourishing urban resistance campaign among African-American workers in the Reconstruction South. Municipal workers in Nashville, lumberyard workers in Washington, D.C., and coopers, brickmakers, common laborers, and tobacco workers in Richmond all organized strikes. Levee workers in Memphis and Mobile led strikes that threatened to break out into a full-scale riot, in the first instance, and turned into a mass uproar that spread to other industries, in the second. Longshoremen were particularly conspicuous in demanding higher wages or revolting against taxes on their trade—sometimes in solidarity with white compatriots—in Savannah, Richmond, Charleston, and New Orleans.[4] But more important, black workers signaled to postwar industrialists, who repeatedly denied dissension in the ranks of labor, that they would not assent passively to oppression. The strikes were important also for the organizations they generated. Barred in all but a few cases from participation in labor organizations with white members, black workers established separate unions, and in 1869 local unions coalesced under the banner of the Colored National Labor Union.

Severe economic depression in the 1870s, which left millions of workers unemployed across the nation, led to cuts in wages, and produced mounting dissatisfaction with generally intolerable conditions, stimulated one of the most epochal labor upheavals in American history. Railroad workers in Martinsburg, West Virginia, went out on strike to prevent the reduction of their wages in the summer of 1877. As workers mobilized, the national government imposed its most repressive measures to date against strikers, calling forth federal troops recently removed from the South who had been protecting freedpeople. The wildcat strike spread rapidly to Pennsylvania, Ohio, and the far West. Not only did the strike halt the nation's railroad system, it prompted the insurgency of workers in other industries en route.[5]

Just as the momentum of this national wave climaxed, black male common laborers, and a few whites in Galveston, caught the contagion of rebellion. On July 31, 1877, the men began a procession down the streets of the island city to protest against low wages and to refuse further cuts. Several hundred laborers from the wharfs, mills, construction trades, and railroads joined the march and convened at a central location, where they delivered speeches and passed resolutions stating their grievances.[6] Despite the city's efforts to break the strike with the use of force and intimidation, the strikers saw some positive results as some employers began to accede to their demands.[7]

Meanwhile, the working men's wives, mothers, daughters, and sisters who worked in private households or as independent laundresses initiated a movement of their own. Male strikers were sensitive to the unfair wages of domestic workers and discussed how to include the labor of women and children in their demands. A. Perryman, for example, stated that if "men of his color could not live on the pitiful sum of one dollar or a dollar and a half . . . neither could their wives on the fifty cents or a dollar they got, that their children could not be sustained by such pay." He pledged to fight for their rights.[8]

The women, however, were quite capable of speaking and acting in their own manner and voice. The paper pointedly derided the "colored women, emboldened by the liberties allowed their fathers, husbands and brothers . . . and being of a jealous nature, determined to have a public hurrah . . . of their own."[9] But jealousy had nothing to do with it. As the women later explained in an open letter addressed to "dear friend citisans," they demanded $1.50 per day or $9.00 per week, "because one dollar wood not feed our little children and pay our rent."[10] Low pay was only one of their grievances, however. If black women's confinement to household labor was to prevail, they would fight to maintain the autonomy of laundry work. The strikers along with male supporters made their first public appearance and recruitment campaign at the door of a steam laundry operated by J. N. Harding. As white women approached to enter their workplace, the strikers ordered them not to cross the symbolic picket line. "When met and told that they should not work for less than $1.50 per day, four turned back; but one, a Miss Murphy, went into the house and began working." Efforts to coerce Murphy to leave failed, and the strikers "caught her and carried her into the street, and by threats forced her to leave." When Alice, a black woman, approached the establishment to pick up her pay for previous work, "the cry was raised that Alice had gone back on them." The strikers allegedly assaulted the woman and a fight broke out, with Alice returning a "well-directed blow" which landed one of the assailants on the ground. "But they were too many for Alice, who was literally covered with women, clawing and pulling, until Alice's clothes were torn from her body and they could get no hold, then the poor woman was let up and driven off." With the most recalcitrant potential strikebreaker subdued, the mission appeared successful, but not complete: "The cry was raised, 'Let's lock them out for good; here's nails I brought especially.'" With the ready materials of an axe and nails, the determined strikers boarded up the windows and doors of the shop.[11]

The women warned Harding, the owner, that they would return later in the day for a repeat performance, and then directed their movement against another set of rivals—the Chinese laundries. "The women talked at once," stated the newspaper, "telling Sam Lee, Slam Sling, Wu Loong and the rest that they must close up and leave this city within fifteen days, or they would be driven away." According to this same account, the Asian immigrants agreed to this demand. "Chinese got no business coming here taking our work from us," at least one woman in the crowd was heard to say.[12]

Such xenophobia had driven Chinese men to seek refuge in self-employment in the first place. Many Chinese men who came to the United

States in mid-century to work on the railroads or in the mines during the California Gold Rush became launderers to fill in for the shortage of women. After the completion of the continental railroad and intensified racial strife, many Chinese men moved east to escape the hostility directed at them.[13]

Ethnic provincialism was also evident among some of the leaders of the men's strike, though their message was more contradictory than the women's. Martin Burns, an Irish American, stated that "this country belonged to the citizens, and that the citizens of the country came from every habitable part of the globe." But he went on to say that "there were no native Americans in this city; that that race were scalp-takers and lived by what they could steal and kill." Burns preferred to give the credit for nation-building to "the Irishman, the negro and the mule," who were thus entitled to expect jobs free of competition from "foreigners" such as the Chinese. Perryman, by contrast, indicated the importance of racial and ethnic unity among all workers without equivocating, and saved his censure for the wealthy who could afford luxury summer vacations at Hot Springs. Perryman "wanted more money—money that such as he, a colored man, and other laborers, Irish, Dutch, Chinese, and all earned for rich men."[14]

Black women's bold actions against Chinese commercial laundries put washerwomen in the spotlight, but cooks and maids were also active in the strike. Mary Pearson, Mary Granderson, J. Eastwood, and Rosetta Green, among others, met to unite all domestic workers as the Ladies of Labor. The first meeting was chaired by Granderson, who hosted the group in her home, and the group elected Green, who had initiated the meeting, as the president. Green noted the broad charge of their gathering: "Now we the ladies of labor, wives and mothers, have assembled ourselves to day to look into our best interest." Mrs. McLevain suggested that the organization was a manifestation of long suffering: "It afforded her great pleasure to participate in such a meeting, it being something that she had long looked for to see the leaders take steps to protect themselves." The reference to self-protection also reflected a critique of black male political leadership that echoed within the group. As Green put it: "We have intrusted our husbands, our sons and our brothers to provide us leaders, and up to this day and date they have provided as such as Mr. R. Cuney." She added, "and we disrecognize any such leader."[15]

The man in question was Norris Wright Cuney, the son of a slave and her white owner, and a rising leader in the Republican Party. In the 1870s and 1880s, Cuney served as inspector of customs at Galveston, alderman in a predominantly white ward, and, most notably, chairman and national committeeman of the Republican Party. Cuney had also founded the Longshoremen's Benevolent Association in 1869 for black workers excluded from white unions. Though he actively worked to open up waterfront jobs to black men, his relationship to the labor movement, and especially to radicalism among workers, was equivocal.[16]

During the 1877 strike, Cuney denounced black male workers at the public rally for "creating all sorts of discord and stirring up all sorts of bad blood." He entreated them to give up the struggle and go home to protect their wives and children, as they were "guilty in a vain attempt to revolutionize the industrial interests of the city."[17] Cuney's conciliatory appeals in the name of peace, order, and obedience to the free enterprise system would forever endear him to the white establishment. His standing among black and white workers, however, plummeted during the strike.[18]

Cuney's speech enraged many of the men: "he was treated with contempt by the rabid action in the crowd."[19] But his opposition to the strike elicited the most outspoken rebuttals from the Ladies of Labor. They chastised their brother workers for providing Cuney a platform to air his views, but highlighted Cuney in their critique. "I emphatically say that by such leaders for the last twelve years we have been bought out and sold out, and we declare to no longer keep in silence on the question," Mary Granderson stated. Granderson insinuated that Cuney's racially mixed ancestry compromised his loyalties, and she accused him of stealing workers' rights. The women set up a committee to invite—or dare—Cuney to deliver to them the same speech he had given to the men.[20]

The women did not confine their defiant tone to the deliberations in their meetings. Their open letter "to dear friend citisans," which outlined their concerns, also included a warning: "Mr. Stone our mayor you promise our husband you was going to do justice by our husband. Mr. Wright Cuney we dont thank you for none of your speech. Now Mr. Slam Sling Chinamen you better sling your shirt short cause we mean what we say, cause your time is growing old." The militant tone continued with barely disguised threats. "We are coming with our jockets fasten tite and our shoes fasten tite cause we mene what we say cause we expect to sail through bloody seas and we will die for our company. Miss Brooks is ready to sholder her rifle, Miss Sillese sharp shooter."[21]

As in the case of Jackson, the results of this strike in Galveston are difficult to interpret, since the newspaper provides few clues about its resolution. There was surprisingly little retaliation reported, despite the open confrontations and provocative oratory of the women. Responses apparently emanated from at least two sources. First, in an act of counter-resistance, white women employers pledged self-sacrifice. Rather than give in to the strikers' demands or burden their husbands' salaries, "some of the first ladies of this city have announced themselves as ready to carry their accomplishments into the kitchen rather than yield to the unjust demands of those who are clamoring for increased wages."[22] And second, a lithograph appeared from an anonymous source caricaturing the washerwomen's raid on the Chinese laundries—a depiction that belittled the store owners more than the strikers. In the usual pejorative manner, the media mocked a proprietor's response: "he was about as mad as Celestials usually get to be."[23] The strike eventually petered out, though it is unclear how many women received the wages they demanded.

Black women had objected to oppressive labor and to the competition of "foreign" immigrants during a combination of strikes that arose as a biracial battle of "laboring classes." Women acknowledged the significance of their contributions to their communities not just as wage workers, but also as participants in a grass-roots political culture. They criticized the external obstacles to justice and rebuked the presence of internal impediments, such as the leadership of Norris Wright Cuney. The women's insistence on "disrecognizing" Cuney for "stealing" their rights demonstrated their belief that autonomous voices in the political arena were as integral to improving their livelihoods as better wages. However much women's own voices were circumscribed by the dominant political system, they refused to be passive in withstanding attacks on their communities. Moving beyond the normal confines of "private" domestic labor in the homes of white employers or in their own neighborhoods, they paraded through the main streets in the commercial district, usurping public space for their rowdy protests. Their rough sport and assaults on private property dramatized their eagerness to halt business as usual in the city to call attention to their demands.[24] Undaunted by conservative whites or blacks, domestic workers in Galveston willfully acted to change the status quo. Their sisters in Atlanta would follow in their footsteps to that end.

THE International Cotton Exposition of 1881 was a masterful public relations campaign for the New South movement. An eager cohort of businessmen, politicians, and newspaper editors committed to remodeling the South in the image of Northern industrial capitalism were the leaders of the first world's fair in the South. They ardently championed laissez-faire as a panacea for regional development and touted Atlanta as the consummate example of an ambitious city prepared to lead the way.[25]

The idea for the exposition began in 1880 with Edward Atkinson, a Boston financier and friend of Hannibal I. Kimball, a railroad owner originally from Maine. Atkinson proposed a demonstration of advanced techniques of cotton cultivation, ginning, and baling to eliminate waste and refine the raw product that arrived in northeastern mills. He initially considered New York City for the exhibit, but Evan P. Howell, owner of the *Atlanta Constitution*, and Henry Grady, the editor, seized the opportunity to promote their hometown as the site for the fair. Despite the competition from New Orleans, Memphis, and Louisville, the "Atlanta Spirit" won out. The nascent industrialists transformed Atkinson's initial emphasis on the preparation of raw cotton to reflect their own interests in manufacturing textiles and attracting capital and immigrants to the region.

The planning of the exposition from its first conception embodied the values of the New South and furnished concrete proof that the urban upstart could compete among more established cities in the nation. A joint stock company headed by Kimball, the director-general, was formalized in April 1881 to generate assets. The *Constitution*, the unofficial organ of the campaign, solicited local funds and moral support by inundating its readers with news and promises of the harvests that the city would reap. Kimball embarked on a trip to New York City, Boston, Philadelphia, and Cincinnati to sell stock in the company and publicize the event. In a highly symbolic gesture, General William T. Sherman, whose troops had burned the city a decade and a half before, agreed to supervise a subscription drive in the northeast, bought shares for himself, and even agreed to make a special appearance at the exposition. Raising finances constituted only part of the planning. A hotel for visitors and twenty-one buildings were erected with startling speed to house more than a thousand exhibits, with many more overflowing into makeshift annexes. Guests numbering nearly ten times the city's population, representing every state in the union and seven foreign countries, would visit over the course of two months.

The long-awaited inaugural day on October 5, 1881, lived up to every bit of the promised festivity and pageantry; everything was accompanied by ideological preachings that defined the goals, values, and objectives of the New South. Visitors viewed the displays—machinery and appliances used in cotton cultivation and textile production were featured most prominently, followed by mineral, metallurgical, and agricultural products. Various manufactured items and handicrafts such as pianos, wagons, canned goods, furniture, and sewing machines were also on display. And guests participated in the self-congratulatory spectacles of speeches, parades, and dedications. During the evenings dignitaries were entertained in ostentatious private mansions that flaunted materialism. Governors Alfred H. Colquitt of Georgia and H. B. Bigelow of Connecticut appeared at one of these occasions attired in suits made from cotton that had been picked, ginned, woven into cloth, and sewn that same day.[26]

An ominous painting, "The New South Welcoming the Nations of the Earth," by James H. Moser, the illustrator for native son Joel Chandler Harris's Uncle Remus tales, was unveiled on the first day of the gala.[27] Moser portrayed a brunette woman draped in the American flag welcoming visitors as the personification of a region that had finally earned the approval of Uncle Sam and Columbia, both of whom looked on. Factories and buildings in the background suggested urbanization and prosperity. Yet older symbols could be seen as well. Another avuncular figure, Remus, and Old Si peeped out from behind bales of cotton while other blacks picked cotton in the fields. Against the backdrop of a booming city that professed to be openly apologetic about its tainted Confederate past stood the emblems of segregation and plantation slavery. The message was unmistakable. African Americans in the New South would be closely defined by the Old—in cotton fields or in servile labor in private homes, rather than in factory, managerial, or professional positions. Black workers would serve a visible and integral, yet subservient, role in the modern economy. These and other symbolic gestures imbued the fair with a characterization of the New South that idealized white supremacy as racial and economic progress.[28]

Despite the immense doses of propaganda invested in the exposition, not every one enthusiastically joined the commemoration. Spokespersons in other Southern cities such as Mobile mocked "the elaborate puffery" of the fair.[29] The Georgia legislature refused to allocate funds, despite the power of New South politicians who ruled it. This was, perhaps, unwitting justice since many of the same interests behind the venture also supported the retrenchment of the state's budget and favored subsidizing railroad, utility, and insurance companies over schools, roads, and other services that would benefit far more people. Even as New South politicos preached prosperity and optimism, their policies and investments defeated the undertakings that would have improved the quality of life for average people.[30] Urban workers and farmers, alert to this hypocrisy, were noticeably absent among the celebrants at the fair. Jobs were promised to laborers, but the few that were delivered required long hours and paid low wages. Consumers criticized the unfairness of skyrocketing prices for housing and food, as merchants and landlords began extorting profits in anticipation of shortages and high demand. For all these reasons, some observers suggested a more appropriate moniker for the fair—"the Cotton *Imposition*."[31]

New South proponents heralded Southern workers as "teachable, tractable, thankful for employment and utterly unacquainted with the strike," to appeal to Northern investors.[32] Meanwhile, workers in Atlanta belied these and other pledges of obsequious behavior. Though workers in the South were less prone to strike and demonstrate openly against repressive authority than in other regions, they were less docile and more attuned to injustices than industrialists would admit. In 1879 and 1880, white women's workplace strife at Kimball's Atlanta Cotton Factory helped push the mill into bankruptcy less than a year after the exposition.[33] White men at the Georgia Iron Works also walked out months before the brouhaha; black men previously discriminated against were hired to take their places.[34] The dialectic of these two phenomena—the image of the "Atlanta Spirit" and the reality of dissent—provides the context for understanding the laundry workers' strike during the summer of 1881.

WOMEN in Atlanta had begun organizing years before the idea for the Cotton Exposition germinated. Though the exposition was the most visible and poignant backdrop for the laundresses' uprising, other events percolating in the black community had spurred the women to action. The washerwomen had adopted a standard rate of pay just a few months before the Great Strike of 1877. The social space created by African-American women became a domain where they could wield power in their own right. Just as the women in Jackson and Galveston had promoted solidarity and enforced social sanctions against dissidents, women in Atlanta organized in a similar vein.[35] Laundry workers undercutting the fixed rates, one source reported, "[did] so at the peril of hair and eyes."[36] In 1879 and 1880 the women coalesced into a protective association.[37] The organization in 1880 "went to pieces," according to a police source.[38] But perseverance led to a new organization and a large-scale mobilization the next year.

Years of hard work using a variety of tactics to achieve racial equality had left African Americans in Atlanta with disappointing results. Yet they were still optimistic that the small, perceptible effect they were having could gain momentum. In the 1860s and 1870s, they had petitioned local and federal officials to hire black police officers and teachers, to provide jobs on the state railroads, to build school buildings, to pave streets, and to deliver potable water and sewer connections. They protested against lynchings and organized mass meetings to hammer out collective stances on public policy or to nominate candidates for city office. Only two blacks were elected to city office in Atlanta in 1870, the only time Radical Republicans were in control. African Americans would continue to run for office until 1890, although no others would be elected until 1953.[39] The very small numbers of blacks elected to public office during or after Reconstruction camouflaged persistent black self-activity prior to disfranchisement at the century's end. As the political fortunes of African Americans in the city improved ever so slightly, grass-roots organizing reached new levels.

Between 1879 and 1881 there were fresh signs of growing black political strength in Atlanta. In city council elections in 1879, black

candidates came close to realizing their demand for direct repre-
sentation by capitalizing on divisions among white voters. The black
community nominated William Finch for alderman and Mitchell Cargile for councilman, refusing to endorse white candidates. To forestall
Cargile's imminent victory, white Atlantans successfully closed ranks in
the final minutes and consolidated support for one white contestant.
Cargile's defeat underscored the effectiveness of the at-large election
system reinstituted by Georgia Democrats in 1871 to ensure that blacks
could not get elected to public office in predominantly black wards.[40]

In the spring of 1880, African Americans led a coup d'état at the state
Republican Party convention against the white party establishment.
After years of frustrating unrewarded allegiance to the Republican
Party, William Pledger, editor of the Athens *Blade*, used the power of
his newspaper to plan a takeover of the party by blacks in the state. He
and other black Republicans began organizing actively in early 1880.
By taking advantage of the flight of whites from the party of Lincoln
and the constant friction among remaining members over the distribution of spoils, a majority black delegation elected Pledger as chairman
of the central committee, the party's highest office. Pledger's victory at
the state convention came largely as a result of a resurgence of black
activism in party ward clubs where women and men threshed out their
positions and strategies. In the process, blacks in Atlanta came to
dominate Fulton County party functions. Their success at the local and
state levels led to a backlash by White Republicans, who instigated a
"Lily White" campaign.[41]

Refusing to be satisfied with their unprecedented victory, African
Americans in Atlanta rode the crest of their ascendancy by boldly
speaking out against the lynching of a black man and woman in nearby
Jonesboro in the summer of 1880. Thousands of circulars were distributed on the streets of Atlanta urging blacks to attend a mass meeting at
Morgan's Hall in front of Wheat Street Baptist Church to discuss white
terrorism. The gathering passed a resolution to condemn the Jonesboro
act and also assailed the systematic killing of African Americans by
white vigilantes who repeatedly escaped punishment. The resolution
called for the governor and law enforcement officers to take action to
ensure justice for black victims of such crimes.[42]

A wide range of views was articulated in the discussion of the resolution. The most militant tone was expressed by Jackson McHenry,

drayman and former candidate for city and state offices. A speaker before him "said something about our firing blank cartridges. That is just what is the matter with the colored people," McHenry began. "We have been shooting blank cartridges too long. We should shoot some loaded ones. Colored men have been killed upon all hands, and no white men. Now we must kill some white men and get even." McHenry concluded by calling on fellow black citizens to stand up for their rights—by whatever means necessary.[43]

The Jonesboro jury failed to be moved by the rhetorical warnings sounded by African Americans and refused to convict the white vigilantes. Regardless of the outcome, McHenry's outspoken tone and the mass meeting are important not only because they highlight black political activism at a moment when the prospects of black empowerment seemed bleak in the aftermath of Reconstruction, but also because they provide a context for one of the most important community-wide rebellions that would follow in its wake. It was against this backdrop of mounting dissension that the washerwomen would assume the mantle of leadership, heeding McHenry's challenge to stand up for their rights.

It was not coincidental that the resurgence of black militancy took place simultaneously in an electoral system dominated by men, and in domestic labor, dominated by women. The laundresses' rebellion brings to the surface the connections between black women and electoral politics that might otherwise be overlooked. By the testimony of women like Hannah Flournoy, who sought sanctuary in Atlanta to escape persecution by the KKK because of her political deeds, black women were active Republicans "tooth and toe-nail." They were integral to political organizing and fought to secure the party's goals. According to the reports of bemused observers: "Negro women, if possible, were wilder than the men" in defending suffrage rights during postwar election upheavals.[44] The explicit political activity during the Galveston strike also illustrates how African-American women participated in the grass-roots political culture, despite their disfranchisement by the dominant society. In fact, their formal exclusion from the electoral system animated their passionate intervention to protect community interests. African-American political concerns, during and after Reconstruction, were grave matters too important to be left to the dictates of one group. Whether related to electing public officials or improving conditions at work, political actions were community affairs that involved the participation of women, men, and children. Women in Atlanta would take advantage of the growing momentum of collective action, using the measure of power they enjoyed in a labor market that confined them to domestic work, yet also gave them the leverage of a monopoly.[45]

IN EARLY July of 1881, twenty women and a few men met in a church in the Summer Hill neighborhood to form a trade organization. As New South boosters promised Northern capitalists that their investments would be safe in a region of subservient workers, African Americans in Atlanta were already defying this impression. After the meeting, the group instructed black ministers throughout the city to inform their congregations of a mass public meeting in another church. At that time they organized formally as the Washing Society, electing officers, appointing committees, designating subsidiary societies for each of the city's five wards, and establishing a uniform rate at a dollar per dozen pounds of wash.[46] There are no extant records of the Washing Society or its course of action after the strike ended. Likewise, it is impossible to determine how much continuity or turnover there was among members of each successive organization. It is highly likely that all of the domestic workers' associations in Atlanta, as well as in Jackson and Galveston, adopted the institutional framework of secret societies. The resilience and legacy of secret societies in generating labor-inspired protests, whether they were explicit trade associations or not, would live on long after the strike.

On July 19 the Washing Society members called a strike, in order to achieve higher fees at a uniform rate. The protest was the largest and most impressive among black Atlantans during the late nineteenth century.[47] Railroad workers' boycotts in 1871 and 1875, for example, quickly dissipated when employers fired the discontented.[48] Despite the expectations of the same kind of instantaneous break, the women endured: "The laundry ladies' efforts to control the prices for washing are still prevalent and no small amount of talk is occasioned . . . The women have a thoroughly organized association and additions to the membership are being made each day."[49]

The "Washing Amazons," as they were christened by opponents, established door-to-door canvassing as the mechanism to widen their ranks.[50] A visiting committee went to the homes of all non-affiliated washerwomen to urge them to join the organization or at least to honor the strike. The recruiters approached several women after they had already picked up their wash loads and begun the work. With little consideration for the inconvenience to their customers, they joined immediately and returned the clothes unwashed or wringing wet.

Not all would-be associates responded with such alacrity, which led to confrontations. The police also accused the visiting committee of threatening to harm or kill other women with fire, cowhides, and other weapons. Like the defiant women in Galveston, strikers in Atlanta showed little attachment to prevailing middle-class conventions of femininity. As they did on other occasions, working-class women used street fights to settle disputes that jeopardized their unity and engaged in militant resistance. These public hostilities took on a ritual purpose of their own for involving the community in airing disagreements, spreading curses about another's reputation, and commanding sympathy for one's point of view. African-American communities embodied the full range of human emotions, behaviors, and differences; they were not utopian or monolithic societies. Quarrels, as much as harmony, were signs of passionate interpersonal relationships.[51]

Ten days after the strike was called, the police arrested a "sixtette of ebony hued damsels" that included Matilda Crawford, Sallie Bell, Carrie Jones, Dora Jones, Orphelia Turner, and Sarah A. Collier and charged them with disorderly conduct and quarreling.[52] All the women were fined $5.00 each, except Collier who received a $20.00 assessment that she refused to pay. Her obstinacy caused the judge to sentence her to a chain gang for forty days. But the undaunted Collier joined Emma Palmer, Jane Webb, and two anonymous white women to enlist new members outside of the major black enclaves. On this round they approached "an old white woman who lives over her wash tub" who had refused to abet the strike. "The infernal scoundrels," stated the police chief, William Starnes, "threatened to burn the place down and to kill her if she took another rag."[53] The involvement of white women, who constituted a mere 1 to 2 percent of the laundresses in the city, was an unusual display of interracial solidarity, though little is known about these women since the paper declined to print their names in order to protect them from scorn. But if they were representative of the working-class whites who lived nearest African Americans, they were probably very poor, single or widowed, and Irish.[54]

In another incident, the police caught Dora Shorter, Annie King, and Sam Gardner allegedly threatening to kill another reluctant participant. Sam Gardner not only induced his wife, Sarah, to participate in the strike, but he joined the movement himself. He was caught helping to berate the woman who worked as a maid for Mrs. Richardson, his wife's client, and was hired to substitute as the laundress. Shorter, King, and Gardner did not stop at heckling the new washerwoman; they also taunted Mrs. Richardson. Starnes may have been describing Gardner when he stated that "the men are as bad as the women. When a woman refuses to join the Society, their men threaten to whip 'em, and the result is that the ranks are daily swelling."[55] If any men fit this description, the courts did not punish them as harshly. The court charged both women with disorderly conduct and quarreling and fined them $20 each, but Sam Gardner may have escaped chastisement.[56]

Biographical information can be pieced together about some of the strikers whose names appear in public records as a result of their arrests. Of those who could be identified, their residences were spread out in the city. Sarah and Sam Gardner lived on Walker Street, wedged between Jenningstown and Pittsburg. Annie King, at age twenty-nine, held the distinction of living alone, south of Shermantown near the Oakland cemetery. Orphelia Turner, one of the youngest members of the clan at twenty-two, lived in the Mechanicsville area with her husband Jack, a drayman, and his two young daughters from a previous marriage. Sarah A. Collier, at age forty-nine the oldest identified protester, was married to Thomas, a common laborer, who was disabled and unemployed the year before the strike. Collier herself suffered from asthma that apparently diminished her capacity for sustained work. The couple had two daughters aged four and ten and lived on Greensferry Street, southwest of Jenningstown. Jane Webb was also married to an unemployed laborer and had six children ranging in age from two to eleven. She lived on Greensferry Street next door to Sallie Bell, a twenty-one-year-old who boarded with Sandy and Charlotte Meyers, a laborer and washerwoman. And forty-five-year-old Matilda Crawford lived with her husband Zachariah, a day worker, on Fraser Street in Summer Hill. The profile of this group of mostly older married women with children, some with unemployed husbands, indicates the important role that their wage labor played in their families. Their willingness to jeopardize what was sometimes the sole family income shows their determination to fight for a just cause to improve their immediate circumstances and the long-range prospects of their lives.[57]

The effectiveness of the strikers, whatever their methods of convincing others to risk similar sacrifices, is borne out by the fact that their ranks swelled from twenty to three thousand strikers and sympathizers within three weeks.[58] The Washing Society maintained solidarity by meeting together almost nightly as one body or in decentralized ward divisions. Given the broad support and participation within the black community at large and the wide range of households outside that community that relied on manual laundry workers, the entire city was affected by this event. Communal laundry work, again, proved critical to facilitating this mobilization.

Whites acknowledged the magnitude of the matter and appeared to take the strike seriously: "I tell you, this strike is a big thing," stated Starnes. But they also tended to take the short-sighted—and familiar— view that forces outside the community were responsible for the expressions of discontent. Echoing charges made earlier in Jackson, Starnes claimed that a white man, unnamed, headed the organization.[59] As employers waited for an impending doom, others in the city busied themselves to find alternative methods to suppress the strike. Consistent with New South ambitions, leading capitalists raised funds for an industrial steam laundry and offered to employ "smart Yankee girls" who would operate the latest technological machinery. The planners requested a tax exemption from the city council to subsidize their costs and efficiently undercut the prime competition. If the washerwomen charged $1.00 per pound of laundry, the new enterprises would charge 20 to 30 cents for same-day service.[60] But the large ratio of laundry workers to employing families in Atlanta made it difficult for one laundry firm to eliminate the demand for manual workers.[61] Almost every white household in the city continued to hire black independent laundry workers. Steam laundries would not begin to rival the hand trade until the 1910s in Atlanta. They became serious contenders for a larger share of white family wash in the 1920s, as commercial laundries began to offer a variety of incremental services affordable to a broad spectrum of the population. But even then the commercial business would never compete for the entire family wash. It was the automatic washing machine, which became widely popular after 1940, that spelled the final decline of manual washerwomen, who would survive longer in the South than the rest of the nation.[62]

Municipal authorities undertook the most direct action against the strikers by arresting and fining members of the visiting committee, and they threatened to go even further. "Can't the city council take hold of this matter and govern their demands as they do the draymen?" some asked impatiently.[63] The city council had started regulating the predominantly black male transport occupation in 1875. Previously, the draymen had ranked among the most economically successful of the unskilled black workers. The twelve wealthiest blacks in the city in 1873, those owning over $2,000 in property, included three draymen. But the municipal license requirement caused the men to lose the leverage once achieved through domination of the trade.[64] By preempting the right of self-regulation, the city hired and fired workers at its discretion, which often meant replacing blacks with whites and setting lower wages. Black draymen tried to resist the new regulations by refusing to pay the license fees, but those who did were arrested and jailed.[65]

The City Council debated a resolution on August 1, 1881, to regulate the laundry workers in hopes of achieving comparable results. It would require each member of any washerwomen's organization to pay an annual business tax of $25.00. The council introduced the resolution on the same day when the tax exemption proposal of the commercial laundry investors was to be entertained. Predictably, the legislation gave wealthy entrepreneurs non-profit tax status while burdening the poorest laborers with heavy license fees. The newspaper misled the public by reporting two days later, on August 3, that the council had actually "passed" the ordinance to tax the workers. "This action of the council has fallen like a bombshell in the camps of the strikers, and has induced quite a number to withdraw from the organization." But the paper also admitted that "there are many however, who laugh at the resolution, and say emphatically that they will neither give in nor pay the license fee. *Of this latter class there is a majority."*[66]

Faced with this determination, businessmen expressed astonishment "at the colored people's stupidity in not seeing that they are working their own ruin."[67] They invoked welfare payments as a form of social control by threatening to deny winter aid to those who refused to accept "fair" pay; in reality, no such comprehensive charity originated from white businesses. Other employers found different means of retaliation. Mary, who worked as a laundress for her white landlord, informed her client of her new rates. "'All right,' said the gentleman, and the woman started off, happy in the thought that she had succeeded, but just as she reached the door with the clothing the gentleman said: 'Mary, I have decided to raise my rent. Hereafter, you must pay me $25 per month rent.'" Mary questioned the landlord about the hike and was told "'you have gone up on washing, I will go up on house rent,'" which forced her to change her mind. The *Constitution* used this example to warn of the dangers of not heeding the laws of supply and demand. If the strikers "persist in their exorbitant demands they will find house rent going up so rapidly that they will have to vacate."[68]

The washerwomen responded to these measures with outrage. Five hundred women of the Washing Society along with some men met on August 2 at Wheat Street Baptist Church in Shermantown to discuss the City Council's action. "Many of the speeches were of the most 'expressive' character," reported the newspaper. "They openly denounced the council for imposing the tax, and defied an attempt to collect the same. But this spirit of bravado, was not entertained or manifested by all." According to the newspaper, "quite a number" of women apparently wanted to resume their labor at whatever price they could obtain. This indication of division prompted the paper to predict confidently that "in a week at the furthest the washer-women will be bending over their tubs, singing songs as if they had succeeded."[69]

The persistent strikers drafted a letter to Mayor Jim English at the same meeting that promised a different song. "We, the members of our society, are determined to stand our pledge and make extra charges for washing, and we have agreed, and are willing to pay $25 or $50 for licenses as a protection so we can control the washing for the city." If city officials harbored any doubts, the women insisted that they could "afford to pay these licenses and will do it before we will be defeated." They continued, "and then we will have full control of the city's washing at our own prices, as the city has control of our husbands' work at their prices." They concluded in an outspoken tone: "Don't forget this. We hope to hear from your council on Tuesday morning. We mean business this week or no washing."[70]

The shrewdness of a group of uneducated and formerly enslaved black women submitting this letter must have stunned those who considered themselves better schooled in political economy. Rather than accept the license tax as a penalty, the laundry workers turned the resolution on its head and transformed it into a protective fee. If the council would seek to control their labor by imposing the unreasonable costs usually levied on businesses, the strikers desired to pay those fees with expectations of contracting the privileges of self-regulation as well. When the women boasted that they would be able to pay the high fees, they may have been counting on the $300 treasury of the Washing Society and contributions from their other affiliations with churches and fraternal orders, as well as personal savings. In reality, the tax would have cost each woman several months of wages, far more than any of them could afford. But regardless of their actual resources, it is clear that higher wages alone would not satisfy the laundry workers.

Just as the strikers in Jackson sought respectability in their own terms, the women in Galveston and Atlanta were attempting to prevent the control they exercised over their productive labor from slipping away. Their demand for self-regulation drew on the strength of the communities that they had been building successfully since Reconstruction. They tested the resilience of these community bonds by reprimanding internal dissension. Household workers' strikes also revealed an astute political consciousness by making women's work carried out in private households a public issue—exploding the myth of the separation between private (family and household) and public (business and economics) spheres. The Galvestonians and Atlantans went further by making explicit political connections to male workers. While the Texas men tried to offer protection to their wives and daughters, their women criticized elements that impeded their own autonomy as well as men's. And the message in Georgia contained an element of retribution. Atlanta officials may have controlled black men's labor, but the washerwomen seemed determined to divest them of authority over all black workers by using the threat of regulation to their own advantage.

The creation of a competing industrialized laundry facility, police arrests, court fines, and proposed city taxes had all failed to defeat the washerwomen and the growing contention within the larger black community. Beginning early in the strike, rumors surfaced indicating that other black household workers were organizing.[71] The laundry workers' actions had inspired cooks, maids, and nurses to demand higher wages. The seriousness of this matter would be borne out later. Meanwhile, black waiters at the National Hotel refused to enter the dining room until their employers agreed to increase their monthly wages. In similar efforts in the past, hotel managers had dismissed the complaints, fired the waiters, and hired new ones.[72] But this time the employers may have been aware of the magnitude of black labor unrest and less confident that they could find replacements given the atmosphere of discontent. As the clamor of the laundry workers' protest reverberated, the management acceded to the waiters' demand.

The impassioned advocates of the New South had stirred up the opposition to the laundry strike, yet they were conveniently silent after the premature August 3 report on the ordinance. Had the bombshell fallen in the laps of the opponents and not the strikers when the City Council decided to reject the license fee on August 15?[73] The newspaper reported the failure the next day, but without comment on the resolution or the outcome of the strike. The washerwomen had succeeded in frustrating the retaliation against them by threatening to use municipal regulation as a tool of self-protection. New South capitalists revealed their own ambivalence toward laissez-faire by yielding to counter-attacks, ultimately balking at legislating labor control. Employers were perhaps torn between their prerogatives as managers of labor and the intervention of public authorities, literally, on their home turfs. African-American women's opposition may have thwarted employers' efforts to subdue them, but other factors may also have hindered the realization of the optimal balance between compulsion and free labor. In an economy moving toward modernization, even in the constrained version of capitalism in the South, the relationship between state power and individual employers' authority would never be consistently resolved. In any case, the outcome of the strike favored the workers, if not by raising the wages of some workers, then at least in heightening the city's awareness of laundry workers' role in the New South economy.[74]

On September 6, local reports cautioned vigilance among white housewives as the specter of the laundry strike reappeared in an even more menacing form. Household workers threatened to call a general strike upon the opening of the International Cotton Exposition in October. "The same persons that engineered the washerwomen's strike are said to have the new management in hand," the *Constitution* reported. "Prepare for the attack before it is made."[75]

Employers apparently heeded the warnings and prevented another massive walkout of household workers at a time of unparalleled need. There is no evidence that the second strike came to fruition or how it was stopped. But the shrewd strategizing that undergirded the mere threat of a "general strike" at this critical historical moment was highly symbolic. The exposition represented "the most important and encouraging sign of the dawn of a regenerative era for the South," the *New York Times* reported.[76] Hannibal I. Kimball summed up the spirit of reconciliation in his address at the event's conclusion: "I have lived to see sectionalism ended—the Exposition has driven out the last vestige. From thenceforth there will be no sectional controversies in our land; we are one people, rejoicing in a common heritage, hopeful of a glorious destiny."[77] Yet the cornerstone of this apology to Northern capital was the institutionalization of white supremacy through the segregation and subordination of black labor. African-American women threatened to expose the tyranny in the New South by disrupting this celebration of new-found harmony at an early stage of its public relations campaign.

From a practical standpoint, the exposition would attract thousands of visitors who would require living accommodations. Early in the year there were indications that even with a new hotel all housing needs could not be met, and the planners encouraged white families to board incoming visitors, which accounted for the nearly 50 percent increase in boarding establishments advertised in 1881. Indeed, the budding hospitality industry relied on private boardinghouses to cater to business and leisure travelers, because the construction boom in hotels was just getting off the ground. These boardinghouses also depended on black women's labor—their cooks in particular were their marks of distinction. Visitors to the city had to rely on these establishments to get their meals because there were few full-service restaurants.[78] As one Georgia newspaper put it, the exposition "will be a great advantage to the South, in inducing respectable northern people to come here and see us as we are."[79] But ironically, it was precisely the prospect of visitors seeing them as they were that made the threat of a strike troubling. Striking household workers would not only expose the underside of the New South image, but also would renege on the city's pledges of hospitality and service to the exposition's guests.

The washerwomen had exercised remarkable leverage in the face of class, gender, and racial hostility. Through the use of formal and informal community networks in which they shared work routines, work sites, living space, and social activity, the strikers organized thousands of women and men. The importance of these everyday networks and sequestered social spaces was thrown into relief by the strike: they not only promoted quotidian survival, but also built a base for political action. The areas of everyday survival, on the one hand, and resistance and large-scale political protests, on the other, were mutually reinforcing; both were necessary parts of a collective cultural whole of working-class self-activity.[80]

The strike is also suggestive of the character of domination in the emergent New South. White employers certainly had the power to confine black women to domestic work, but not the unilateral power to determine how and under what conditions that labor would be organized and performed. African-American women's pragmatic adaptations to the former did not constitute consent to their own oppression. They openly and clandestinely contested the conditions of domestic labor in multiple ways. In the summer of 1881, their contestation took the form of a strike, not only because by then the prerequisite community institutions were in place, but also because of the broader political struggles and period of relative optimism that characterized the black community. The surge in Republican ward activism, the takeover of the state and county parties, the public debate and protests against the Jonesboro lynching all combined to create an atmosphere which made organizing a successful strike seem promising. The women used the practical skills they had learned in grass-roots politics. Their spirited rallies with prayers, speeches, and singing in black churches closely resembled the form of other political meetings. Their letter to the mayor likewise drew on prior experience in writing petitions and resolutions. The period from 1879 to 1881 was a brief time of opportunity, and African Americans pressed it as far as they could before the full force of New South political and economic development made itself felt.

The protests did not end here, however. The articulation of discontent would be channeled through other tactics in response to the changing character of domination as de jure segregation evolved and hardened. In turn, the forces of power searched for the most effective techniques for keeping blacks in check in the era of Jim Crow.[81]

CHAPTER FIVE

The "Color Line" Gives Way to the "Color Wall"

By the end of the century, African Americans had deployed a multitude of strategies in the workplace, in their neighborhoods, and in the political arena to protect their personal dignity and the integrity of their families and communities. But despite effective community mobilizations on many fronts—indeed, because of their effect—blacks were increasingly met with systematic encroachments on their civil and human rights. After the washerwomen's strike, black women continued their direct protests. In response to official indifference toward police brutality, they retaliated in the streets. Initially, their physical resistance exasperated authorities unable to control their spontaneously organized eruptions. But the consequences of impudence became more hazardous. Political disfranchisement, vigilante violence, and de jure segregation intensified in the 1890s and began to tip the scales of justice decidedly in favor of whites.

The epic moment in the ascendancy of white rule was the infamous race riot of 1906. This violent rampage against black residents signaled that whites in the city would stop at nothing to stamp out all but the most deferential black presence in the urban landscape. Fear, resentment, and anxiety fueled the increasing demands for inscribing segregation in the law. With each passing decade Jim Crow became more firmly established in urban life, most visibly in public accommodations, residential patterns, and employment.

MODERNIZATION and Jim Crow grew to maturity together in the New South. African-American women's lives and labor were se-

verely circumscribed by the harsh consequences of this pairing, as Jim
Crow moved from its embryonic de facto stage to its more stringent de
jure form. With each adoption of advanced technology or each articulation of platitudes of progress, Atlanta also strengthened its commitment to keeping blacks subordinate and unequal.

By the end of the century, the streetcar replaced the railroad as the
most visible icon of the aspiring metropolis and became one of the first
institutions tainted by official Jim Crow regulations. In 1891, the Georgia legislature passed one among a forthcoming onslaught of laws
regarding segregation, permitting cities to demarcate the color line in
public conveyances "as much as practicable."[1] Blacks were relegated to
the rear of electric trolleys and forced to stand even if seats designated
for whites in the front were vacant. Streetcar conductors and white
passengers policed and adjusted the fluid boundary to reduce inconveniences to themselves. African Americans resented these proscriptions
because they were humiliating and unjust; they deprived them of their
personal dignity and their rights as consumers.

When streetcar lines attempted to implement the state law, black
residents in Atlanta responded by refusing to sit in the rear, at the risk
of being arrested for disorderly conduct. They also boycotted the
companies several times from 1892 to 1906. In 1896, an unidentified
group of women led a boycott when a streetcar company arrested and
imprisoned a black man for refusing to sit in seats designated for his
race. "These ladies have declared that they will not patronize that
streetcar company, and admonishes all race lovers who cherish their
manhood and womanhood to do likewise," a neighboring black newspaper reported. "The time has come when such actions are necessary
to secure our rights."[2] Black passengers arranged for other forms of
transportation—they walked, rode bicycles, or used the services of
black hackmen. The streetcar companies, not eager to lose valuable
customers, no matter what race, yielded to black protests in the early
1890s. But by 1900, increasing sentiment for racial separation by white
residents led the city to pass its own legislation, which denied discretion
to individual companies previously left alone in interpreting the 1891
state law.[3]

White racial attitudes that inspired de jure segregation on streetcars
were also operative in de facto patterns of residential development. Jim
Crow became more pronounced as African Americans occupied larger

clusters in the city. The overall population of Atlanta quadrupled between 1880 and 1910 and the black population tripled, which pushed the boundaries of the city limits outward to accommodate the growth and increased the competition for residences within the city's core. By the turn of the century, a clear pattern of black expulsion out of the inner core and greater concentrations on the east, west, and south sides of the city was starkly evident.

The rising tide of Jim Crow profoundly affected the geography of the city by restricting where blacks could live. But African Americans used segregated spaces to bolster their autonomy and collective power and to escape exploitation by whites.[4] Black neighborhoods were products of the twin forces of exclusion and seclusion—the former forced, the latter embraced to deal with a hostile climate. As old neighborhoods expanded to adapt to new migrants searching for havens near family, friends, and amiable strangers, new ones were juxtaposed nearby. Black institutions continued to attract residency in certain areas. Southeast of Summer Hill, Brownsville (also called South Atlanta) was established with the building of the original Clark University in 1883. The construction of Gammon Theological Seminary in 1889 furthered community growth.[5]

A diversity of largely black neighborhoods began to sprout in and around Shermantown on the east. Annie and Albert Ford, a teacher and a painter, were among the first settlers in an area later known as Bedford Pine, due north of Shermantown. The couple built a recreation facility known as Ford Springs for fellow African Americans in the 1880s, which provided space for traveling tent shows, swimming, dancing, picnics, and food concessions. Bedford Pine's tree-lined streets and grand rolling terrain made it attractive to well-to-do whites, who bought homes on the highest elevations along Boulevard Drive. This area was among the few places in the city on high ground available to blacks. Most blacks, however, tended to live in the alleys and on lower elevations of crowded neighborhoods such as Buttermilk Bottom and Dark Town. Bedford Pine followed the pattern characteristic of residential development throughout the city. When the Fords first moved there in the 1870s, blacks and whites settled in a checkerboard pattern along street blocks, but after the turn of the century residents were increasingly living in either all-black or all-white expanses.[6]

In the heart of Shermantown, one of the most significant residential and commercial developments of early twentieth century Atlanta took place on Auburn Avenue. Auburn was originally dominated by white professionals. In the 1880s and 1890s, black domestic and unskilled workers began to settle there in large numbers. The modest Victorian bungalows on Auburn and contiguous streets stood in marked contrast to the ramshackle shanties available to wage-earners elsewhere in the city.[7] Black businesses including grocers, a jeweler, tailors, drugstores, restaurants, and a hotel also made it appealing to live there.

Black entrepreneurs made a conscious effort to develop Auburn Avenue as an alternative business district, especially after the race riot of 1906 heightened white hostility toward blacks. The Odd Fellows erected a flagship edifice in 1904, which provided rental office space, a sizable auditorium, and a roof garden dance floor. Black-owned financial institutions such as a bank, real estate brokerage, and insurance companies also built headquarters there by the early 1910s. But "Sweet Auburn" is perhaps best known as the birth home of Martin Luther King, Jr., and the home of Ebenezer Baptist Church, where he was pastor.[8]

While the commercial development of Auburn Avenue anchored black community life on the east, educational institutions were the focal point on the west. All the black colleges would eventually converge by mid-century in the vicinity of Atlanta University. Other institutions such as the Neighborhood Union, a social settlement organization, and the Leonard Street Orphans Home were also located in the area. Though working-class and middle-class blacks were interspersed throughout the neighborhood, there were distinct class enclaves as well. Beaver Slide, Fair Street, Whites Alley, and Peters Street were noted for crime, gangs, prostitution, beer saloons, "blind tigers" (bootleg liquor outlets), overcrowding, and poor sanitary conditions. Black faculty and business elites lived on more spacious and better maintained streets close to the college campuses.[9]

As African Americans moved east and west, wealthier whites moved south and, especially, north. The toniest white neighborhoods continued to evolve in the northern section of the city along Peachtree Street and to the east. White upper-class mansions sprang up in the northeast around Piedmont Park, built in 1910 as Atlanta's answer to New York's Central Park. Inman Park, Druid Hills, and Ansley Park were the first planned landscaped suburbs in the city, accessible to town by streetcar and later benefited by the automobile.[10]

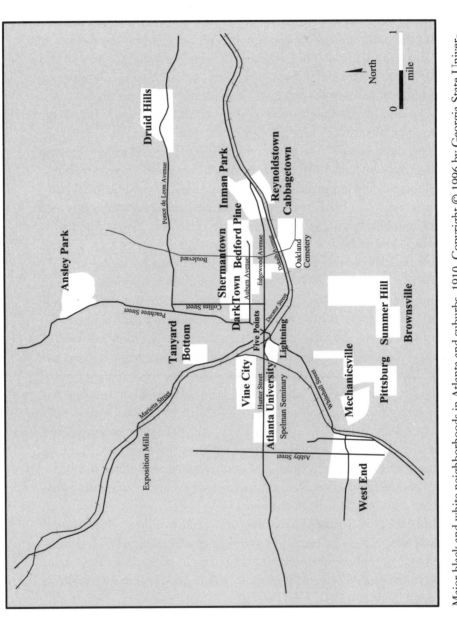

Major black and white neighborhoods in Atlanta and suburbs, 1910. Copyright © 1996 by Georgia State University, Department of Geography, Cartography Research Laboratory.

A by-product of the growth of white upper-class suburbs became apparent by the 1910s. As whites moved further away from blacks they continued to demand the services of cooks, maids, yardmen, and chauffeurs. To satisfy this demand, blacks began to establish small satellite communities within easy reach of their workplaces. Tanyard Bottom, located northwest of Peachtree Street near old tanneries, and Johnsontown, located in the far northeast, are examples of this phenomenon. Johnsontown developed in 1912 when two wage-earners, Callie and Columbus Johnson, purchased a house in a heavily wooded area near the Southern Railway line, an abandoned white subdivision. The neighborhood was literally built by the labor of black stonemasons and carpenters, who constructed wood-framed "shotgun houses" (generally one room wide and three rooms long) for their families and friends. A few houses, Zion Hill Baptist Church, and Henry Walker's Restaurant and Grocery Store were the seedbed for this community's unfolding.[11]

There were a few small, adjacent, in-town black and white working-class communities. Though white wage-earners were dispersed throughout the city, the largest concentrations were most prominent along a northwest by southwest projection. Reynoldstown, a community of black railroad men and their families, was sandwiched between Inman Park and Cabbagetown (formerly Factory Town), the home of Atlanta Fulton Bag and Cotton Mill. Lightning, a small black community south of the CBD, was next to manufacturing plants and boardinghouses that attracted numerous white women by the end of the nineteenth century.[12]

Despite the growth of new communities, the extension of the city limits, and the rhetoric of boosters promoting Atlanta as a modern metropolis, there were areas within the city limits still described as "country" into the 1920s. Uneven development of the basic city infrastructure and class-biased delivery of municipal services continued to plague the city. Black and working-class leaders criticized the persisting inequities. "Atlanta streets, in which whites and the rich live, are cleaned daily and the pavement is taken up and re-laid every half dozen years, while the negroes and poor whites in many instances live in communities seldom cleaned and never paved," it was stated in the *Independent.* "There are thousands of negroes in Atlanta living in alleys more unsanitary and filthy than a Peachtree street horse stable. The color line is too often drawn in the distribution of public services."

Similarly, white trade unionists christened Peachtree Street "Tax Dodgers Row."[13]

The problems of municipal delivery of sanitary services were closely tied to the problem of housing. Most African Americans lived on crudely constructed roads and in the dark hollows of alleys, and the houses they inhabited were poorly constructed of cheap materials atop shaky brick piles that invited disasters like floods. Most of the houses occupied by blacks were wood frame dwellings containing three rooms or fewer. Many families shared outhouses in backyards and public hydrants with their neighbors. The furnishings inside were spare—bed, table, bureau, wardrobe, pots, pans, and wash tubs.[14]

Most African Americans paid relatively high prices to lease substandard property.[15] Lugenia Burns Hope, founder of the Neighborhood Union, castigated landlords who exploited their tenants: "Poor people pay vastly more for the rent of their shanties than do the better class for better homes, yet the greed of the landlords and their desire for larger profits on their investments makes them slow to repair." The landlords shuffled in family after family without proper maintenance. "These men receive their 'blood money' and care nothing for the people or the community," Hope concluded.[16]

Poor people in general were disadvantaged by the politics of city governance that favored the interests of the white elites. But Jim Crow deprived all African Americans, regardless of economic status, of basic liberties. By the time the law dictated residential segregation, restrictive covenants and de facto practices of exclusion had long been practiced. Although Atlanta was already more segregated than any other city in Georgia, in 1913 it passed the first residential segregation ordinance in the state, mainly to prevent affluent blacks from encroaching upon upscale white suburbs like Ansley Park and Druid Hills. The state Supreme Court struck down the law two years later, but extralegal pressures and vigilante violence substituted for legal mandates.[17] The emphasis on keeping black middle-class and upper-class home owners from living near whites was not so much a concern about minimizing interracial contact as it was a desire to restrict the terms of interracial interactions in order to keep blacks subordinate.

This thinking was betrayed in contradictory white attitudes toward domestic workers and middle-class blacks regarding Jim Crow residential patterns. Most household workers continued to insist on living in their own homes. The small percentage of live-in domestics declined even further between 1880 and 1910. While the highest concentrations of live-in servants were always located in the most affluent white neighborhoods, this trend became especially marked by 1910 as a third to nearly one-half of live-in domestics were located on the north side alone—near Ansley Park and Druid Hills.[18] As Jim Crow intensified the physical and social distance between most blacks and whites in the city, the wealthiest whites had the most sustained contact with blacks who worked or lived in as servants. Clearly, the advocates of the 1913 ordinance did not have the exclusion of this group from white suburbs in mind. As long as blacks were living in close contact as servants or subordinates, physical proximity was not only acceptable but desirable. It was usually when blacks moved into white neighborhoods on equal footing that physical proximity became an aberration.

Jim Crow and domestic labor thus represented contradictory desires among urban whites striving to distance themselves from an "inferior race," but dependent on the very same people they despised to perform the most intimate labor in their homes. White urbanites revolted from situations where they might literally brush shoulders with black urbanites on city streets, as if to do so would expose them to contagious germs. African Americans challenged the logic of the pernicious contagion theory that undergirded the rationale for segregation. "It is no more contaminating or humiliating for colored persons to ride in the same car with white persons than for them to cook for them and do other domestic duties," one person stated.[19] The ambivalence of whites' feelings toward black women was a compelling paradox in the age of Jim Crow that would be expressed in a variety of ways.

Convenience took precedence over concerns about racial separation as decisions were made to hire household help; many whites preferred to hire live-ins. Convenience also accounted for the minority of black women who acquiesced. As wealthy whites moved to the northern limits of the city, it became harder for African Americans employed by them to reach work by foot. In the 1890s and early 1900s, the largest proportion of live-in domestics were cooks.[20] This is not surprising given that the cook's workday began earlier than that of other household workers, in order to serve morning meals.

Although a relatively small number of African-American women willingly made commitments to live on the premises of employers, most considered this a last resort. "I see my own children only when they happen to see me on the streets when I am out with the [employer's] children or when my children come to the 'yard' to see me," a veteran of the system reported. But even these slight glimpses of loved ones were infrequent, she explained, "because my white folks don't like to see their servants' children hanging around the premises." The demands of perpetual labor restricted her family life, friendships, and participation in social events. "You might as well say that I'm on duty all the time—from sunrise to sunrise, every day in the week." She expressed the familiar feeling of confinement that most black women had historically tried to escape: "I am the slave, body and soul, of this family."[21]

The fear of sexual exploitation also discouraged women from choosing to live in. A black woman's body, in slavery and freedom, was treated as though it were not her own, nor even the conventional prerogative of her father or spouse. White employers' displays of disgust toward interracial contact in public in the age of segregation did not match their behavior in private. Black women were the victims of sexual abuse in their workplaces, yet they were accused of being the aggressors. The same woman who spoke out about the disadvantages of living in described how she lost a position after rebuking the seductions of her employer. Her own mate confronted the assailant and was arrested and fined $25 for disputing the word of a white man. The victim of the assault summarized the lesson she learned: "I was young then, and newly married, and didn't know then what has been a burden to my mind and heart ever since: that a colored woman's virtue in this part of the country has no protection."[22]

Black women could not protect their bodies, and they had no more control over claiming the just fruits of their labor whether they lived in or not. It was common for employers to rob workers of their rightful cash wages. Some used a bait-and-switch tactic to lure workers with high wages and then gradually reduced the rates once employed.[23] Willie Mae Cartwright described a ritual she regularly endured of being coerced to accept deductions in her wages in exchange for items of dubious value. "One woman I worked for, I'd work all week and then she'd say: 'Here's a nice dress I'd like to sell for fifty cents.' It be so big I could have flung a fit inside it and never popped a seam." Cartwright suffered the loss of half her wages rather than risk losing her position, even if it meant buying a Rhode Island rooster, as she did on one occasion. "Regular, every week, she'd palm off things on me that way," she stated.[24]

Paying low wages and withholding payment were not deviations from a system otherwise designed to permit black women to earn a fair living. And the stipulation of paltry wages was not a function of mean or spiteful employers. Paying low wages was the standard even among employers who were otherwise liked and respected by domestic workers. Alice Adams described her relationship with her boss: "We got along lovely, just lovely. She was one of the loveliest people you could be around. The only objection was the long hours and little pay. But it was lovely peoples." Adams continued, "She was willing to do anything to help me but the money—no money." Adams stated that if she fell short of money needed to pay rent or to buy necessities, her employer would sometimes pay her rent or buy what she needed, but would not give her the money directly in wages. She reiterated, "the onliest trouble we had, the onliest difference was the long hours and no pay."[25]

African-American women workers refused to accept the illogic of low wages for long and arduous work. As Daisy Johnson stated with irony: "There is one thing that I don't think white people have ever given enough thought to, and that is the smallness of wages paid cooks, maids, butlers, and in fact, all servants." Johnson spoke for many of her fellow workers in criticizing wages too low to satisfy the most basic human needs. "What self-respecting white people would be willing to have us working in their kitchens and all through their homes if we were filthy, ragged, and barefooted? But how many of them are willing to pay enough to provide the things they expect of us?" she asked.[26] Another domestic worker pointed out the incongruence between employers' high expectations and their aversion to fair pay: "When I think of the low rate of wages we poor colored people receive, and when I hear so much said about our unreliability, our untrustworthiness, and even our vices, I recall the story of the private soldier in a certain army who . . . being upbraided by the commanding officer because the heels of his shoes were not polished, is said to have replied: 'Captain, do you expect all the virtues for $13 per month?'"[27]

The captains of white Southern households would answer yes and more. They justified the low wages by arguing that black women were paid what they were worth, given their poor skills and abhorrent personal traits. Employers complained of the troubles they had to endure, the resources wasted by inefficiency, the time lost by laziness or the agonizing repetition of workers quitting.[28] Other employers openly rationalized low wages as a necessary strategy for lengthening the workday. They justified coercion by saying that when black workers were paid good wages they worked less, not more.[29] "The poorer class of Negroes, naturally indolent and happy-go-lucky, found that they could make as much money in two or three days as they had formerly earned in a whole week," a Northern journalist explained. "Why, then, work more than two days a week? It was the logic of a child, but it was the logic used."[30] African Americans who valued subsistence and consumption over the illusory goals of accumulation were penalized by white employers who put the highest value on keeping blacks subservient in a restricted labor market.

Low wages made domestic workers accessible to virtually the entire white population. The large concentration of domestic workers in Atlanta, one of the highest per capita in the nation, and the propensity for domestics to work by the day also increased access. Poor white women no doubt did the overwhelming bulk of their own housework, but some hired help. In rare cases, live-in maids were employed and slept in cramped quarters with the children. Day laborers were sometimes hired to cook, clean, or to take care of the children. In the urban North, some white women living in tenements and lacking access to water and supplies might send their wash to commercial laundries. In the urban South, where the adoption of technology lagged and manual laborers were not only readily available but preferred, many white wage-earners hired black women to do some or all of their wash.[31]

Emily J. W. Bealer exemplifies the humble circumstances of some white employers of domestic labor. Bealer moved her dying husband and four children to Atlanta from Savannah in the 1880s. Though she struggled financially before and after her husband's death, she still considered hiring maids, cooks, and washerwomen a necessity. Bealer's only apparent income, except for help from her children, came from rental property that did not produce a stable profit. And despite her ownership of real estate, she rented her family's home. The following typifies Bealer's plight: "I am so depressed not sinfully I hope. But my houses are not rented. My children and myself need clothing. I owe for milk, groceries and a few other accounts, and under the present circumstances, dont know how to pay for them. Oh my poor me!" Once she revealed: "I have not been able to buy a decent dress, since June [in three months], or anything else, even my shoes are worn to the ground. I cannot make a genteel appearance in the street. And George and Pierre are too shaby to go to Church. Several of my bills are unpaid and God knows how I deplore the condition I have been in."[32] But despite her hardships Bealer continued to hire domestic workers. In one week she complained about a cook leaving and noted that dire straits forced Bealer to borrow $10 for her rent. Given her frequent references to workers leaving and new ones entering her employ, Bealer's financial instability no doubt impeded the retention of servants.[33]

Bealer's seemingly contradictory position as an employer of domestic labor on an income that fell short of enabling the middle-class existence she aspired to was not unique. "No white family ever did its own washing," Polly Stone Buck explained. Buck came from a genteel but poor background. Her father was a college professor who died and left her mother and siblings with few means of support. Buck's widowed mother made a living renting rooms to students at Emory College and occasionally worked as a seamstress. "Even at the time when we were poorest, the soiled clothes were regularly 'counted out,'" Buck remembered.[34]

Glenn Rainey had a similar story to tell about growing up working-class in Atlanta. "My father had left home early, and had come from Virginia to Georgia. And he lived pretty much the hard way," Rainey remembered. "We lived pretty modestly. We had five children," he noted. "But we always had a servant, you know, or nearly always had a servant . . . It would be some black woman who'd come in and work for a dollar and a half a week—I don't know what—fifty cents a day, maybe, at the most."[35]

A Northern journalist traveling in the South found this a curious phenomenon. "One day I visited the mill neighborhood of Atlanta to see how the poorer classes of white people lived," he wrote. "I found one very comfortable home occupied by a family of mill employees. They hired a Negro woman to cook for them, and while they sent their children to the mill to work, the cook sent her children to school!"[36] The irony, of course, was that most white workers in factories, retail shops, and clerical positions in the South were paid relatively lower wages than their counterparts elsewhere in the nation. The wages in cotton textile mills were especially low, usually requiring the labor of every able-bodied person in a family—women, men, and children alike—to achieve a satisfactory standard of living. But comparatively, the wages of black women were worse.[37]

African Americans often resented working for poor whites whose life-styles were similar to their own. As an Athens woman stated, "I worked for the rich white folks, myself, and when I'se able to work I still works for them kind of folks." She explained, "You ain't catching me fooling along with pore white trash. If you does they work, they can't pay you nothing, and ain't got nothing to give you besides."[38] Yet working for rich people did not always yield better pay or working situations. Quite often employers with higher incomes, larger houses, and greater material possessions demanded harder and longer hours of work.[39]

The cheapness and abundance of domestic laborers not only put them in reach of working-class whites but also enabled, to a lesser degree, some African Americans to hire them as well. Sometimes, single black men may have relied on hiring women to cook, clean, or wash their laundry. Usually, wealth and prestige determined when blacks hired help. Atlanta had a cadre of blacks who were educated professionals (professors, ministers, and physicians) and well-to-do business entrepreneurs in insurance and real estate. Families such as the Du Boises, Ruckers, Herndons, and Hopes were part of the employing class. W. E. B. Du Bois himself commented on this phenomenon, noting that for black employers domestic work did not represent the same denigration it did for whites: "The employers in this case in no respect despise common labor or menial duties, because they themselves have performed such work all their lives," Du Bois argued. The relationship resembled an antebellum form of hired help found in New England, where a neighbor's girl lived in "like one of the family." But Du Bois also recognized that class biases influenced the attitudes of some black employers who spoke as condescendingly about "the servant problem" as their white counterparts.[40]

African-American employers were held in contempt by whites who resented the social status that hiring help conferred. Some whites ridiculed elite black housewives as sloppy and irresponsible for delegating their work to others as they abstained from gainful labor and spent time socializing and hosting afternoon tea parties. "It is such ones as these who are guilty of the grossest impudence to white women who come into the community to employ servants," wrote an investigator. "One [white] woman upon inquiring as to where she might find some one to cook, was told [by a black woman] to 'go home and look in the mirro[r].'"[41]

In the urban South domestic labor was made a commodity, valued at the bottom of the wage scale, and placed within the means of at least a portion of the white working class whose own labor power was valued among the lowest in the nation. Deliberately low wages paid to black women helped to subsidize in some small way a portion of the costs of sustaining white workers. White Southern domesticity at nearly every level of society was built on the backs of black women.

THE DISADVANTAGES of household labor were especially troubling to black women because they had so few other options for wage work. More than 90 percent of black female wage-earners were still confined to domestic work at the turn of the century. As of 1890, there were some black women who had escaped private households, but had not left domestic labor entirely. They worked as maids and cooks in hotels, boardinghouses, transportation, and commercial industries. A few became caterers or cake bakers, such as Myra Miller, highly regarded for her edible works of art.[42]

The first sign of any measurable change in black women's occupational choices occurred between 1900 and 1910, when the proportion of black women in domestic work dropped from 92 to 84 percent. The number of seamstresses, dressmakers, tailoresses, and milliners increased during this period.[43] The rising popularity of the fashion industry, mail order catalogs, and department stores whetted the appetites of middle-class consumers to buy more clothing, which stimulated the demand for seamstresses. The black middle and upper classes in Atlanta sought the most talented dressmakers for christening garments, wedding dresses, and ball gowns. Some black women also did piece work at home for some of the thriving clothing manufacturers, though these jobs were mostly reserved for white women and girls. Most black dressmakers were independent artisans or helpers working at home or in shops that they owned.[44] Sewing gave black women many of the advantages that laundresses enjoyed in terms of autonomy, only it was more lucrative, creative, and enjoyable for the highest-skilled.

Ida L. Wimbish, who received training at a dressmaking school in Boston, advertised her skills as a "fashionable dressmaker" specializing in fancy suits, wedding trousseaux, and walking skirts. She owned a shop at Houston and Piedmont Streets, hired other seamstresses to assist her, and taught day and evening sewing classes as well. Fannie Pepper used her fifteen years of experience as a dressmaker and opened a formal school to teach other women and girls how to make dresses and corsets. Pepper promised that graduates of her program "can be made thorough in a reasonable time to cut, fit, make and finish work to compare with the best establishment of the country."[45] If the aspirations of black girls in Atlanta were any indication, dressmakers were held in high esteem; more girls wanted to become dressmakers than any other occupation, followed by teachers and musicians.[46]

Very few black women worked in the professions. Teachers were the largest group, followed by a few nurses and midwives. Black women also made small gains in white-collar clerical and sales jobs in black-owned insurance and retail shops. Several black women ran businesses of their own, or with other women or spouses, including boarding-houses, lunch rooms, restaurants, groceries, secondhand clothing stores, hairdressing shops, dry goods stores, and ice cream and cold drink parlors; some peddled their wares on the streets. Laura Ryals had the unusual distinction of running a man's business: she owned a valu-able line of hacks that transported goods and people across town. Though black women were excluded from most factory jobs, except for a few hired as cleaners, between 1900 and 1910 several hundred black women entered the commercial laundries, whereas a decade before there were none recorded.[47]

A nascent underground economy supplied black women with alter-native sources of income and employment as gamblers, "blind tigers" or bootleggers, and prostitutes. Some women found they could maxi-mize their options and evade detection by the police if they maintained a semblance of legal employment in domestic labor. Games of chance offered fun and recreation as well as the potential to earn extra cash. Similarly, bootlegging granted women a way to evade laws prohibiting their entry into Atlanta saloons and gave them access to profits that accrued from peddling liquor in alleys and side streets.[48]

Prostitution was a thriving business beginning in the 1880s and 1890s as the commercial fortunes of the city rose and attracted traveling businessmen, railroad men, and visitors to fairs. White women entrepreneurs consolidated their control over the trade headquartered in brothels, small hotels, and boardinghouses at the sufferance of real estate companies, landlords, police officers, and politicians—individuals who did not simply look the other way but took a cut of the profits. Most of the city's prostitutes were whites working individually or in houses on Collins Street that catered to white men. In 1900 there were ten identifiable brothels on Collins Street; eight of them were occupied by white prostitutes, two by blacks. Black women were more likely to be found streetwalking or working in brothels on Decatur Street, where black men were permitted to buy sex.[49]

African-American women were often hired as live-in servants or day workers, not prostitutes, in the prosperous brothels operated by white women. Ruby Owens worked for fourteen years at the beginning of the century at the San Souci Hotel, a brothel, boardinghouse, and gambling spot. The San Souci catered to business and leisure travelers waiting for trains, professional entertainers and soldiers visiting the city, and local rich men. Owens and another black woman alternated between roles as cook and maid: "When I be cooking the maid be tending to white folks business. And when I be tending to they business she be cooking."[50]

But aside from cooking and cleaning, Owens sometimes ran the house in the madam's absence. In addition, Owens' and the other maid's names were used by the owner to purchase illegal alcohol, after Atlanta passed a prohibition law in 1908 that forced persistent consumers to buy liquor from out of town. Serving liquor was one way to entice men looking for multiple pleasures into the brothels. The madam, however, neither obtained Owens' consent nor shared the loot. "She wouldn't give us none," Owens stated. "Wouldn't pay us for using our name. She order it for herself to make her money on."[51] Owens and the other servant were responsible for selling beer to customers and were instructed in techniques for cheating customers to maximize profits. They became adroit at taking occasional sips for themselves without the owner detecting them.

Owens' multiple roles as maid, cook, manager, and confidante, and the fondness she inspired in the prostitutes and customers, led them to think of her as the madam of the house. At a time when most domestics still earned on average $1.00 to $2.00 a week, Owens earned $4.00 plus carfare and tips that usually added up to $10.00 or $11.00 by the end of the week. Though she worked long hours during the day and at night, she was able to earn and save enough money to buy a house for her family and other real estate. Years later, she expressed some regrets about the sordid events she was exposed to in the brothel and resisted talking about "white folks business" and "a whole lot of old nasty stuff" that "wasn't fit to tell." Owens reconciled her regrets, however, by emphasizing that she had simply been doing what she needed to survive: "I wasn't working for nothing but for a living."[52]

WOMEN like Ruby Owens were caught between the proverbial rock and a hard place. In the urban South black women and domestic labor were virtually synonymous, and they were locked out of relatively better paying jobs reserved for white women exclusively. The difficulty black women faced in breaking out of segregated domestic labor was demonstrated most dramatically by a strike by white women in a local textile mill in 1897.

On August 4, twenty black women were hired to fold bags at the Fulton Bag and Cotton Mill. In response, two hundred white women who worked in the folding department refused to go to work. Twelve hundred women, men, and children, except three who stayed behind to train the new recruits, followed the strikers by the next day. The mill women used their social networks, as the black washerwomen had done, to garner support for the strike in the village near the mill and other areas inhabited by workers. But the male-dominated Textile Workers Protective Union took over the leadership of the strike. One male strike supporter conceded that the movement was "started by the ladies and was being directed by the ladies," but men in the union assumed the mantle of public leadership of the strike, making most of the speeches at rallies and meetings, serving on committees, and representing the grievances of the workers before the owners of the mill.[53]

The workers complained about low wages, long hours, and the lack of extra pay for evening work. They accused the management of preparing for their wholesale replacement by blacks, as it had been undermining their position by hiring blacks one at a time over the past year while turning away white female applicants. Before the hiring of the new women, according to one estimate, there were already fifty blacks working in the mills; in all likelihood these were mostly men hired to do the dirtiest jobs as sweepers, scrubbers, yard hands, and roustabouts. The few black women in any mills in the city were scrubwomen or cleaners. Production jobs were reserved exclusively for whites, except on occasion when they left their machines idle during breaks or under other special circumstances.[54]

The owners argued that white workers were treated well at the mills and paid good wages, which should have given them no justifiable cause for complaint. The company had fallen behind on its production schedule and had explicitly advertised vacancies for white women, only to be rebuffed by prospective applicants who objected to working in the heat and for the hours requested. The owners ended up hiring black women out of necessity, not by choice. Labor shortages were chronic problems for cotton textile owners, who were often unable to find sufficient numbers of women and children to meet their needs or too dependent on transient workers moving in and out of the mills. Textile mills were also competing for white women workers within a burgeoning field of manufacturers in Atlanta.[55]

The strikers spurred on their troops by holding rallies in their neighborhoods and delivering passionate speeches. One orator "won eternal fame" at a rally as he exclaimed: "it was a shame and an outrage for 'our wives to be forced to work along side nasty, black, stinkin' nigger wimmin.'" The strikers won a lot of sympathy for fighting to preserve racial purity, especially from fellow trade unionists who believed the strikers were fighting on behalf of a "greater principle than any ever presented to the laboring people."[56] A resolution by the Painter's Union helped to goad the owners into a defensive posture as it demonstrated that other whites in the city would not stand by silently in the face of a threat to the color line in the industry reserved for whites only. The painters condemned the textile owners' actions as "one of the most dastardly and disreputable acts ever perpetrated on the white working women of the south." They ended their resolution with a stinging insult to discredit the mill owner's loyalty to the race: Jacob Elsas "should be required to do himself what he has endeavored to force white women to do—make social equals of negro women."[57]

Elsas tried to minimize the importance of the strike by attributing it to a misunderstanding and by underscoring his intention to segregate the races. He had never planned for there to be direct contact between black and white women in his factory. "I have no desire to oppress any of the people, nor am I forced to take the advice of the Painters' Union," Elsas stated defensively. "I do not mind having my dinner served by a colored cook, but I don't say that they should sit down to my table."[58] Elsas expressed solidarity with the fundamental premise of the strike—that black women's proper place in the Southern political economy was as servants to whites, not as "social equals." In this instance, however, Elsas's needs as a businessman, in search of labor that was in short supply, conflicted with his views that were otherwise consistent with keeping black women in their "natural" place.

After the first day of the strike, union representatives were sent to meet with Elsas to present their demands and negotiate a settlement. Though the committee had been instructed to demand that the owner fire the newly hired black women and to exact a promise from the boss not to retaliate against strikers returning to work, the spokesmen audaciously asked for the discharge of all blacks except for janitors, scrubwomen, and yard hands assisting white firemen. In return, Elsas asked the workers to work extra hours in order to compensate for the loss of the black workers, which they agreed to do.

Though workers rejoiced in the streets at the news that an agreement had been reached, their victory celebrations proved to be premature. The next day conflict erupted again as the workers accused Elsas of reneging on his promises and refusing to sign a written contract. Elsas claimed that he had agreed to fire only the newly hired black women, not all black workers. White workers had not complained about any other blacks in the mill before the strike, and he saw no reason to unnecessarily punish good, industrious workers, some of whom had worked there faithfully for twenty years. "I have no right to tell them to get out," Elsas argued. The strike had opened the floodgates of the race issue and exposed the unstable quality of the color line in Southern industry, which fluctuated depending on the needs of management and the reaction of white workers. White workers seized the opportunity to secure their total domination in cotton mills except in stereotypical "black" jobs. "We want all them niggers out of there, and that's what we are going to have," one woman cried out at a meeting of the strikers. Another woman criticized a black man she called "a nigger second boss" who, it seems, held a rare position on the shop floor. "We want that nigger boss to git out of there," she demanded, "he orders us about just like he owned us."[59]

In the end, a compromise was reached. Elsas did not sign the agreement but made a verbal promise to transfer all blacks from departments where they had any contact with white workers and agreed to take no retribution against strikers returning to work. Both sides seemed happy with the settlement, and both were praised by observers for doing "the right thing." The union took pleasure in having forced some concessions from the owner, which increased their membership rolls by the hundreds. Workers at the Exposition Mill in the northwest section of the city amassed enough new members to form a separate branch of the textile union. The women who had initiated the walkout enhanced their prestige in the labor movement and were honored in the Labor Day parade. The workers had displayed more unity in the strike against black women workers than they would ever show in the entire seventy-five-year history of the mill. Their success reverberated in an unprecedented invigoration of white organized labor in the city and contributed to the rapid growth of the National Union of Textile Workers in the region. In the first two decades of the twentieth century Atlanta had a percentage of workers in trade unions that was higher than the national average. White workers' power would be felt at the ballot box as they put James G. Woodward, a union printer, in the mayor's seat four times between 1900 and 1916.[60]

Within a few months, however, the compromise broke down again. By the end of the calendar year the textile workers had called another strike against the Fulton Bag and Cotton Mill. The strikers protested against discharges of workers associated with the August strike and criticized the owners for refusing to treat their grievance committee with the proper respect. The Atlanta Federation of Trades called for a general strike by all unions affiliated with mills owned by Elsas. Elsas returned the favor by attributing the walkout to union members' misinforming workers that management had authorized them to leave the factory early and to lazy workers eager for any excuse to quit. He scorned the union as an "outside organization," refused to meet with representatives of the mill workers, and defended the firing of certain workers since the August strike. Elsas also tried to correct the public perception that the race question was still unsettled at the mill and accused the workers of unfairly using race to elicit public sympathy. In the minds of the workers, however, race was still an issue in the absence of blacks from the mills; it served to rally supporters from within and outside the city.[61]

The American Federation of Labor was holding a meeting in Nashville at the time of the strike and pledged to support its brothers and sisters in Atlanta. The local union of the National Paper Hangers' Protective and Beneficial Association of America, the streetcar conductors, and other unions passed resolutions supporting the mill workers. A mass meeting of whites "representing all classes of citizens" was held in support of the strikers and passed a resolution criticizing "the encroachment of organized greed upon the rights and liberties of labor." The group called for a boycott of all goods produced by the Fulton Bag and Cotton Mill because "the issue at stake means either the reduction of white labor to a level of social equality with negro labor, or the supplanting entirely of white labor by negro labor." It pledged moral and financial support of the strikers' cause "to the end that white supremacy may prevail and that the combination to crush out the Caucasian laborer may prove a total failure."[62]

Both the American Federation of Labor and the National Textile Workers Union sent representatives to Atlanta to meet with the mill management, but no agreement was reached. The workers were fighting a battle they would not win. Unlike the strike during the previous summer, the second walkout had lasted longer but the workers were less unified than previously when the stakes had seemed, literally, more black and white. As workers trickled back to work and replacements were hired to take the places of those who did not, the union was unable to hold out any longer.

"Hate strikes" against black workers were not unique to Atlanta. In this same period, white textile workers in Rome, Barnesville, and Savannah staged walkouts to keep black workers out of the mills. Similarly, white workers in other industries protested the presence of black men at the Atlanta Machine Works and the Georgia Railroad Company.[63] Black and white workers in Atlanta had formed brief political and trade union alliances during the period of the Knights of Labor in the mid-1880s, but by the end of the century those alliances had splintered as white workers sided with the middle and upper classes on racial segregation. In the 1870s and 1880s, compared with the 1890s and beyond, the social geography of the city had been more conducive to casual interactions on the streets as working-class people engaged in scavenging, shopping for groceries, peddling, or using wells and privies. African Americans were pushed out of the CBD, where a thriving living and working district was dominated by working-class whites, just as they were kept out of middle- and upper-class white neighborhoods.[64] Segregation was not a system imposed entirely from above; it also helped to advance the interests of white workers, who were able to gain status from their position in the social hierarchy above all blacks. Decatur Street, the premier red light district, within easy reach of both black and white working-class enclaves, would remain the last refuge for interracial intermingling.

The segregation of working-class neighborhoods may have had more severe ramifications for the relationship between women across races than for men. If black and white women did not encounter one another in residential areas, there were few other places considered respectable where they could meet since women's work was the most segregated work of all. Black men were concentrated in unskilled manual labor and were employed in a diversity of industrial, commercial, and public jobs where they inevitably came into contact with white men. Compared with men, there were few jobs that black and white women shared, and even fewer that involved the same work sites. The one exception was the commercial laundry. Though laundry work had historically been considered "black women's work" in the South, its standing rose in the estimation of white women when it began to move out of private homes, where wage labor was associated with servility, into commercial settings. However undesirable it might have been for white women to do black women's work, whites had the prerogative of crossing over into racially stigmatized occupations. No such opportunity existed for black women.

White women at the Fulton Bag and Cotton Mill had walked out at a propitious moment in the evolution of the local political economy. Their strike reinforced the pervasive association among black women, degradation, and domestic work just when more employers were in search of women workers. Wages for women remained low or declined during the depression of the 1890s, but Atlanta was becoming a city of working women because of the expansion of cotton textiles, clothing manufacturers, cracker makers, candy factories, patent medicines, paper box factories, mattress makers, wholesale distributors, and printing establishments. Telegraph and telephone companies, bookstores, dry goods shops, and department stores also hired more women in clerical and sales positions. Yet nearly all of the women employed in these jobs were white. In 1900, white women made up 28 percent of the wage-earning women in the city although they represented 56 percent of the women in the population. By 1920, however, 48 percent of the women gainfully employed were white, though by then they constituted 67 percent of the women in the population. Atlanta had more women in the work force than most cities in the nation, except Washington, D.C., and a few textile cities in Massachusetts. Forty-two percent of all Atlanta women aged sixteen and over in 1920 were gainfully employed.[65]

One strike cannot be held responsible for keeping black women locked out of cotton textile mills and other manufacturing jobs. But the strike and the widespread sympathy it elicited symbolized the powerful forces that diminished economic opportunities for black women and maintained their confinement to domestic work. White women mill workers were not simply repulsed by working next to "stinkin' nigger wimmin" whom they perceived as agents of moral and social contagion; they may also have objected to working next to women whom they felt entitled to hire as their personal servants.

The mill workers' strike demonstrated just how far white workers would go to protect their position in the social hierarchy. The increased antipathy among white workers toward blacks' pursuit of economic justice in the marketplace reflected the hostility of middle-class whites who insisted on legalizing racial segregation to prevent the incursion of black elites into their neighborhoods. Most white workers and middle-class professionals alike agreed that social equality, whether in the labor market or in residential neighborhoods, could not be tolerated. Their actions and their attitudes about labor and residency were symbolic of broader frustrations that were exploding in the city to make Jim Crow an inescapable part of urban life.

RACIAL tensions in the workplace mirrored conflicts on the streets, especially conflicts between black citizens and white police officers. Police brutality was a chronic problem in Southern cities. Atlanta had one of the highest per capita arrest records in the country, and most of the people apprehended were blacks subjected to indiscriminate raids on their persons and property on spurious grounds of suspicion. Individuals walking down the street, minding their own business, were stopped for carrying items for which they could not document ownership on the spot. Once arrested, blacks were not presumed to be innocent, nor were they assured the conventional protections of due process.

African Americans had begun complaining to public officials in Atlanta in the 1860s and urging them to correct this problem by hiring black policemen. The city refused to make any amends, and the tensions grew worse over the years. Blacks summarized their mounting frustrations in 1881: "We have lived in Atlanta twenty-seven years, and we have heard the lash sounding from the cabins of the slaves, poured on by their masters. But we have never seen a meaner set of low down cut throats, scrapes and murderers than the city of Atlanta has to protect the peace."[66]

As a last resort, African Americans began to fight back against police brutality by attempting to forestall arrests. Incidents of collective self-defense were most conspicuous in the 1880s and 1890s.[67] A typical example occurred two months following the washerwomen's strike. A policeman grabbed a young black man, John Burke, for allegedly pushing a white woman off the sidewalk as he tried to gain access to the stairway of the Opera House. Burke resisted the arrest by trying to jerk away as the officer dragged him down the steps. Once at street level, Burke tried to escape and this time hit the arresting officer and his colleagues who joined in to make the arrest. As the policemen began to overcome their charge by banging him over the head with their sticks, a sympathetic circle of black bystanders formed to try to prevent the arrest. According to a news report: "There are at least five hundred colored people about the opera house, and as there was only a half dozen police, they felt sure of success."[68] The crowd was pushed back, however, as the officers pressed on with the initial arrest. A fierce battle ensued as more officers joined the fracas and the insurgents grew more determined in their yelling, cursing, and assaults. People in the crowd noticed guns belonging to the Fifth Artillery stockpiled near the Opera House and tried to retrieve them. The police kept everyone away from the rifles, except for John's mother, Gertrude Burke.[69]

Gertrude Burke picked up one of the guns, aimed it at the face of police officer Dennard, and pulled the trigger. An empty barrel spared Dennard from a point-blank blast that could have cost him his life. "For a few seconds the air was wild with the shouts and oaths of the infuriated mob, as they advanced upon the police." The police again prevailed in making more arrests, but an undaunted crowd of more than two hundred people followed behind them en route to the station house. The marchers toasted the officers with a variety of boisterous epithets including calls to "cut their d——n throats."[70]

It is not coincidental that the incident precipitating the arrest of John Burke was a conflict over access to public space. Burke may have been guilty of pushing a fellow pedestrian off the sidewalk—deliberately or not. It is also possible that his mere physical proximity to a white woman on a public street was perceived by her or others as an invasion of her personal space. Conflicts over the propriety of casual, public, interracial mingling were increasingly causing friction among urban Southerners. Though young, vibrant, and ostensibly progressive cities like Atlanta offered the best hope for fulfilling black expectations for freedom, they were often repressive. The so-called modern cities were the first to rationalize segregation as the solution to the race problem. An all-white police force was the most visible symbol of the enforcement of Jim Crow codes and of the unwritten rules of racial etiquette.

African Americans continued to demand fairness from the criminal justice system and sometimes pressed charges against the police. Though a few cases of gross civil rights violations were ruled in their favor, resulting in the punishment of policemen, this did not occur often, despite the fact that the overwhelming number of grievances were never reported.[71] After blacks in the city attempted unsuccessfully to get a police officer dismissed for assaulting the black suspect of an alleged petty crime, blacks openly articulated the dilemma this presented: "Are we going to be murdered like dogs right here in this community and not open our mouths?" The more compelling alternative was that "something must be done and that soon."[72]

In the absence of justice from the city, blacks continued to pursue self-defense. Isabella Ridley, a healer, sought vengeance by calling on God the Almighty to strike down a policeman—a prayer for which she was arrested.[73] But many other African Americans applied the methods used by Gertrude Burke. By the 1880s, each time policemen entered the black community to make an arrest, they faced the possibility of being tormented. Sometimes the civilians recaptured the person being taken away, but sometimes not. At a minimum, insurgent crowds subjected the despised law enforcement officers to verbal taunts, fisticuffs, or chases in parade fashion down the streets. In other cases, they wielded guns and other weapons, sometimes with injurious results for either or both parties.

Whites in the city became alarmed by this pattern of retaliation. They were especially disturbed by the collective quality of protests. "The moment that a negro steals, or robs, or commits some other crime, his person seems to become sacred in the eyes of his race, and he is harbored, protected, defended and deified," one source complained. "The leading negroes drum up a mass meeting and proceed to pass a string of senseless but sympathetic resolutions, after a series of harangues that would be a discredit to the Zulus," it continued.

Black women added insult to injury as they boldly taunted and beat up grown men. "If an officer refrains from using his pistol, he is followed by a mob of howling women who throw stones at him and attempt to rescue the criminal," stated a typical news report.[74] Mothers like Gertrude Burke intervened to protect their children from police abuse. At other times women acted to protect themselves, each other, and adult men—who in turn fought to defend women in distress. Forbearance by the police, some whites argued, was threatening pandemonium. Policemen were implored to use all necessary physical force against unruly black women and men alike.[75]

The escalation of retaliations by African Americans in the 1880s and 1890s distressed whites, who feared that a major race riot would erupt—a self-fulfilling prophecy. Ironically, the decade-by-decade increase of Jim Crow hastened black self-defense efforts in racially sequestered neighborhoods. Though white police officers had the advantage in areas where whites predominated, they were often disadvantaged when isolated in black neighborhoods. By the 1890s, matters had become so serious that some officers refused to go alone into certain places, such as one "Elbow Bend," notorious as "the resort of the lowest criminals" and of prostitutes known to attack policemen.[76] When prospective officers were interviewed for positions on the force, a police commissioner asked them a hypothetical question: "What would you do in case you tried to arrest a couple of niggers on Decatur Street and they started to fight you?" The applicant responded: "What wud you do and what wud any sensible man do? Blow your gong and run like the virry devil!"[77]

African Americans' self-assertions against the police were pronounced because they were part of a broader political agenda. Beneath the surface of major political defeats since the decline of the Republican Party during Reconstruction, black political agency in the city had persisted into the 1880s before it was finally crushed with disfranchisement in 1891. As whites expressed fears about the security of the city, they were also caught off guard by the efficacy of black political action. African-American voters shrewdly took advantage of splits in the white electorate to win concessions from white candidates. But as they gained leverage and began demanding support for their own candidates, white politicians balked. Whites began to unify to eradicate blacks from the electorate and from civic life once and for all.[78]

THE IMPACT of increased black political leverage, the retaliatory campaign against police brutality, the acquisition of property by blacks, and the development of thriving African-American social and educational institutions unleashed more white violence. By 1906, the tensions generated by black social and economic mobility reached a boiling point that would spill over into one of the worst race riots in the South.

The event most responsible for fanning the fires of racial hatred was the 1905–1906 gubernatorial election campaign. Hoke Smith, the Democratic candidate, former Secretary of the Interior under President Grover Cleveland, was running against Clark Howell, the editor of the *Constitution*. Both candidates repudiated their former record of racial moderation and tried to surpass each other in their promises to defend white supremacy by any means necessary. Both made the elimination of the threat of "Negro domination" the cornerstone of every conceivable reform plank offered to the white electorate. Both preyed on the fears of white workers at a time when their migration into the city was increasing, as was their anxiety about competing with blacks for jobs. Smith rode to victory with speeches that lifted applauding well-wishers out of their seats as he deliberately summoned the memories of the Wilmington Race Riot of 1898 as a model to be imitated. The call to arms for a racial massacre implicit in Smith's messages was not lost on his audience.[79]

The gubernatorial campaign revealed an insidious proclivity of some white Southerners to identify themselves as progressive reformers in order to explicitly link social reform and racial repression. Under the guise of Progressivism, Jim Crow was justified as a civic reform that would alleviate racial conflict and improve race relations. Segregated parks and playgrounds were defended as essential places of recreation that would siphon off friction that might otherwise be vented on the streets. Most important, disfranchisement was justified as purifying the electoral system and purging it of corruption caused by black political clout. African Americans had already been effectively disfranchised in 1891 by the establishment of the white-only Democratic primary. Neither Smith nor Howell was satisfied with this restriction, and they fought over better methods to ensure that blacks could not organize a counter "black primary" nor ever again be able to muster an iota of political will.

The gubernatorial campaign coincided with growing white sentiment linking black disfranchisement not only with purifying the body politic, but also with purging black autonomy in economic and social life. Disfranchisement ensured that whites could increase legal restrictions against blacks uninhibited by the need to show moderation toward people with no power to vote. The grip of Jim Crow was tightened most severely in Atlanta during the summer and fall of 1906 during anti-vagrancy and anti-vice crusades.

African Americans were increasingly harassed by the police for violating "vagrancy" laws. Blacks walking the streets or found in pool halls, saloons, dance halls, and restaurants were subjected to raids under the pretext that they were committing "fraud" and "criminal evasion" against white employers by depriving them of laborers. Even persons caught in their private homes during the day were arrested for tarrying in "Negro dives."[80]

The crackdown on "vagrants" also enabled reformers to attack "vice." The consumption of alcoholic beverages by blacks had long been held responsible for debauchery that spilled over into the political system by making blacks vulnerable to selling their votes. During the gubernatorial campaign and after, however, the link between alcohol, suffrage, and "vice" was taken to a new level as supporters of prohibition seized the explosive racial hysteria to advance their cause. Members of the Woman's Christian Temperance Union, the Atlanta Anti-Saloon League, the Businessmen's Gospel Union, and other white organizations and individuals joined forces to preach against the evils that transpired when blacks entered the saloons and reveled in drink.[81]

The gravest concern for reformers opposed to alcoholic consumption by blacks was not the danger they posed to the political system, but the danger they posed to white women. This concern was exacerbated by the social context in which much of the drinking occurred—on Decatur Street, the last preserve of interracial socializing and also the headquarters of "vice." Decatur Street became the focal point for cleaning up the city and ridding it of the evil influence of the "demon rum." The presumption of social equality between black and white men in barrooms was sufficient cause for concern, but the most objectionable aspect of the saloons was the threat that black men posed to white women. Black men, it was presumed, were enticed to lust after white women in these bars, titillated by illustrations of nude women on bottles of gin and by their natural "animal insanity." Both the broader white populace and the popular press reinforced these fears with stories about an "epidemic" of a "new negro crime" against white women. Between August and September newspapers inundated the city with salacious stories of black men raping white women with impunity. In one case of alleged assault, a ninety-year-old white woman had screamed at the sight of what she imagined to be a black man walking down the street as she drew the window shades in her bedroom. In another case, two men inadvertently knocked over a white woman on the street—a situation reminiscent of the John Burke incident which had provoked less harsh retribution, in retrospect, a decade and a half before.[82]

On Saturday, September 22, 1906, these stories reached a fever pitch when the newspapers issued several extras during the day to update its readers about new assaults. An angry white mob, not coincidentally standing on Decatur Street, began to attack every Negro in sight. Hundreds and eventually thousands of other men had joined in within two hours of the riot's commencement, targeting black businesses, but showing little other discrimination; they assaulted men, women, and children, beating, torturing, and killing their victims in a rampage that lasted for four days. With the sanction and participation of the police and prominent whites, the urban mob, consisting mostly of working-class whites, went on unimpeded. The rioters were described as "patriotic citizens" seeking "swift justice," forming a "people's court and jury" against "savage" blacks who "met just fate."[83]

The brutality against blacks was favorably regarded by most whites in the city in the name of protecting innocent white womanhood. By sounding the clarion for black male castration and female sterilization in its stories leading up to the riot, the newspaper had induced the mob to link racial and sexual hysteria. The attitude of Rebecca Felton, suffragist, prohibitionist, and later the first woman U.S. senator, exemplified the white consensus that endorsed violence to punish alleged black rapists: if a rapist "was torn to pieces limb by limb and burnt with slow fire, or hung by the thumbs until the buzzards swarmed around him, he would still be saved some of the revolting torture already inflicted upon a harmless victim."[84] Despite the fact that the reported cases of rape were later to be proved groundless, the riot would go down in infamy as a quest for the preservation of white female virtue.

Despite Atlanta's proud reputation as a progressive "gate city" and model for the New South, the riot had raised questions about the real meaning behind these platitudes. J. Max Barber, the editor of *The Voice of the Negro* who was forced to flee the city because of his outspoken views, criticized the hypocrisy of racism. According to Max, Atlanta was "a city that struts before the world as a liberal gateway of a great section but which is really the same old Atlanta steeped in the foul odours of the antebellum traditions and held firmly in the remorseless clutch of a vile and unreasonable race prejudice."[85] In one of the most symbolic and sadistic acts during the riot, the marauders presented the corpses of disfigured black bodies as a tribute to the statue of Henry Grady, the father of the New South movement. In the 1880s, Grady had presented segregation as the last hope of salvation for the white South, providing an eerie preview of the famous speech that Booker T. Washington would make nearly two decades later at the Atlanta Cotton States and International Exposition. "What God hath separated let not man join together . . . Let not man tinker with the work of the Almighty," Grady had preached.[86] Mob violence followed from such preachments on the eminence of white rule, exposing the contradictory nature of segregation—a modern, but retrograde, political tool initiated in the self-styled progressive cities of the South.

The Atlanta riot was not an isolated incident. Some forty other similar episodes erupted in the South between 1898 and 1908, all of them aided by the indifference toward Jim Crow prevalent in the rest of the nation. General Sherman's return to Atlanta as a civilian during the 1881 Cotton Exposition to submit his blessings to the architects of the New South had been a sign of the truce already in place between the nation and its erstwhile wayward child. A national consensus on Anglo-Saxon superiority, defended at home and abroad in foreign policies that justified the expansion of the American empire into the Pacific and Caribbean at the expense of the subjugation of people of color, had been reached. The 1896 *Plessy v. Ferguson* Supreme Court ruling validating the "separate but equal" principle was further evidence of the nation's repudiation of justice and equality.[87]

The riot marked the turning point of the institutionalization of Jim Crow in Atlanta. From that time forward, race relations in the city would never be the same. Many blacks left the city in the wake of the riot, and some never returned. Those who stayed were haunted by the indelible images of raging vigilantes. African Americans who were caught downtown at the time of the riot had been in the worst position for self-defense, since they were isolated from their communities and outnumbered by angry howling men, boys, and jeering women on the sidelines. Other African Americans organized bands of armed men for protection and retaliation in predominantly black neighborhoods. White streetcar conductors refused to travel in these sequestered areas out of fear. Residents in Darktown shot out the street lights to discourage encroaching rioters and shot at any whites who dared to enter. When a crowd of white county police officers and civilians entered Brownsville to arrest blacks possessing weapons, they were surprised by an ambush. Brownsville residents killed one police officer, and several other people on both sides were injured. The next day three hundred blacks from Brownsville were arrested and marched through the streets escorted by police—a reversal of the parades that had regularly formed in the 1880s when police were followed by hundreds of blacks protesting arrests. Although retaliations against the police would continue into the next decade and blacks would continue to fight back against other injustices, the brute power of the riot had shifted the momentum in favor of whites.[88]

African Americans had traveled a long way from the apogee of hope, in the era of the washerwomen's strike, to the nadir of despair, by the time of the riot in 1906. When the entertainer Ethel Waters entered the city after the riot had settled down, she was stunned by the palpable, virulent racism in the city. "I'd encountered Jim Crow all over the South and in many Northern towns as well," she stated, "but it was in

Atlanta that I learned how racial discrimination can hedge in a colored person and make him feel boxed up."[89] It was here that segregation matured amid the contradictory but complementary forces of modernity and antiquity, coerced labor and a thriving free labor market, racial distance and racial propinquity. The leadership that Atlanta exercised in implementing de jure segregation was as sure and as determined as its commitment to building railroads, textile mills, and large corporate enterprises like the Coca-Cola Company. The rules of segregation became increasingly petty and rigid after the turn of the century. Blacks and whites could not touch the same Bibles in courtrooms, could not sit next to one another on streetcars even as prisoners riding to the stockade, could not patronize the same restaurants, parks, libraries, and zoo. Ethel Waters was perceptive in seeing that what underlay this aversion was white fear. "What could be more pitiful than to live in such nightmarish terror of another race that you have to lynch them, push them off sidewalks, and never be able to relax your venomous hatred for one moment?" she pondered.[90] African Americans bore the burden of this bad dream every day.

CHAPTER SIX

Survival and Social Welfare
in the Age of Jim Crow

The hardening of segregation in the South led black women to redouble their coping efforts. In the wake of the riot, the development of private institutions became especially important to substitute for the public services that were denied to blacks by the white establishment. This institution building coincided not only with the development of segregation, but also with the Progressive reform movement that was sweeping the nation.

Progressive reformers tried to remedy the social imbalances produced by industrial capitalism, especially in urban America. The reformers represented a diverse group with wide-ranging political views and varying, often contradictory, ideas about how to accomplish their goals. The regulation of big business, consumer and worker protections, electoral reform, and moral improvement were leading issues on their agendas. Progressive reformers were typically middle-class professionals and their objects of reform were generally working-class women and men—regarded as menaces to society to be studied, controlled, and transformed. Working-class people were not passive beneficiaries of altruism, however. Many were reform leaders in their own right.[1] Whether in cross-class organizations like the Neighborhood Union or in other groups, black women diligently built clinics, kindergartens, orphanages, and reformatories to meet the exigencies of living in a separate and unequal society.

Renewed institution building did not preclude the need for black women to continue drawing on the survival strategies that had served them well for decades. Their neighborhoods persisted as the launching pads for informal and formal collective action and mutual support, to meet the goals of mobilizing resources for daily sustenance and fighting against oppressive working and living conditions. Refusing to leave their fates entirely to the capricious market economy or to Jim Crow, black working-class women in Atlanta attacked persistent social and economic problems from every angle.

Low wages continued to plague black women engaged in domestic work, which kept them constantly searching for alternative ways of increasing provisions for their families and augmenting their incomes. The memory of the 1881 washerwomen's strike had not faded ten years later. Laundresses still dissatisfied with their pay struck again in 1891. "I have never had such trouble as this before," one victim of the strike exclaimed. "My regular washwoman came around and got the regular week's wash Monday, and on Wednesday she came back and said that she could not do it for the regular price I had been paying her." The washerwoman's request was refused and the patron made another attempt to have her laundry taken by a different worker, but encountered the same demand for higher pay. "The strike is on, and the consequence is soiled linen and perplexed housewifes," the newspaper stated. No further reports were made about the progress or the result of this strike.[2]

Not all of the efforts to improve working conditions or resolve conflicts were antagonistic, however. A group of women organized the Cooks' Union, a mutual aid organization designed to care for members during illness and other urgent times. The organization's fraternal purpose was intended to be in harmony with the interests of the employing class, according to one source. "Its object is not to create strikes and close up kitchens and demand higher wages. The object here is a noble one; to do good, keep well, and if sick to aid each other to speedy health and a quick return to work again."[3] Other African-American women from diverse class backgrounds formed an organization called the Colored Working Women and Laundry Women "for the purpose of uplifting their class and color, to make better their conditions in social lines." They defined "working women" broadly to include women who were laundresses, cooks, and maids as well as many teachers and housewives of elite men in business, politics, and the professions. The group endeavored to improve the lives of wage-earning women by promoting better conditions of work, cultivating good relationships between workers and employers, and uplifting the race.[4]

Organizations like the Cooks' Union and the working women's group were important resources for enhancing the survival of wage-earning women. Black working women developed other routine strategies to make ends meet. They continued to assert the right to customary appropriations of products of their labor. Cooks relied on the nonmonetary compensation of cooked leftovers, unused scraps produced during meal preparations, and a cut of pantry staples. Pan-toting proved to be an essential supplement to the diet of domestic workers' families and communities. "Others may denounce the service pan, and say that it is used only to support idle negroes," one worker stated. "But many a time, when I was a cook, and had the responsibility of rearing my three children upon my lone shoulders, many a time I have had occasion to bless the Lord for the service pan." She emphatically rejected the idea that the practice was stealing: "I indignantly deny that we are thieves," she declared. "We don't steal; we just 'take' things— they are a part of the oral contract, exprest or implied. We understand it, and most of the white folks understand it."[5]

Some employers concurred that pan-toting was part of the worker's remuneration and used it to justify low wages. "We know that most of this so-called 'food' is left-overs, cold scraps and the like which we would not use on our tables again," a self-proclaimed "Old Time Southerner" admitted. "We know that our servants are paid a small wage."[6] Another employer similarly conceded: "'Totin' was a well-established custom, and should be remembered if the wages paid seem horrifyingly small." Others portrayed the custom as charity, disavowing any culpability in paying substandard wages that engendered the need for the "gift." "There are hungry children in the cabin awaiting their mother's return," one employer explained. "When I give out my meals I bear these little blackberry pickaninnies in mind, and I never wound the feelings of any cook by asking her 'what that is she has under her apron.'" She added, "I *know* what it is—every biscuit, scrap of meat, or bit of cake she can save during the day, and if possible a little sugar filched from the pantry."[7]

Most of the women who engaged in pan-toting were maids and

cooks. Laundry workers sometimes asserted their own customary rights by borrowing garments before returning them. One white woman recalled memories from her childhood about washerwomen who rarely mixed up items although they were entrusted with the laundry of many families. But she also believed that "occasionally a few items were not delivered until the following Monday [a week later] at pick up time." She explained the rationale for the time lag this way: "If my best white dress, for instance, failed to appear on Saturday, there was sure to be a special children's service at the black church on Sunday, and my dress would be needed by the washwoman's daughter, who was my age." The washerwoman in turn might use the excuse of rainy weather to explain the delay. Another laundry worker, Cleo, explained the missing shirt-waists and skirts from Emmie Stewart's bundles with the simple statement: "You see, me and Miss Emmie is hipted and busted jes' the same." Employers were exasperated, but acquiesced: "There was not a thing we could do about it."[8]

Tolerance did not mark the responses of all employers; some perceived a thin line between the practice of clandestine borrowing and theft. At the turn of the century, a police officer argued that "stealing clothing by washerwomen had become almost epidemic" as judged by the large number of reports of theft filed by customers complaining of missing linen and clothing.[9] Many black women were arrested and convicted of petty theft of laundry as well as missing household goods, usually on the basis of the employer's word alone and without due process. One washerwoman described an incident of false accusation, stating that "white folks tends to lose what they ain't never had." The police searched her home for missing items, indiscriminately rummaging through her belongings, even cutting open the bed tick. Although this investigation failed to uncover the alleged stolen goods, the police forced the laundry worker to compensate the employer by performing a month of labor without pay. But when the complainant later discovered that some of her own visiting relatives had taken the items, she refused to reimburse the laundress for the punitive labor.[10]

Some washerwomen did in fact deliberately withhold their patrons' laundry or steal from employers, motivated by retribution against employers' nonpayment or late payment of wages, when no other avenues existed for redress. Employers usually denied the economic and political import of these acts and the underlying protests they symbolized.

Instead they criticized pilfering as a moral failing of an inherently inferior race and exacted disproportionate punishments.[11] In other cases, devious women and men who were not all associated with laundresses tricked unsuspecting customers into turning over bundles of laundry with no intention of ever returning them.[12]

In addition to nonmonetary supplements and borrowing from employers' resources, African-American women devised other strategies to stretch their meager earnings. They salvaged goods from the public domain for use, trade, or resale in the neighborhood, or sometimes exchanged them for cash in local pawn shops. Children might be enlisted to help their mothers scour the streets or the trash of merchants, though they were treated with suspicion by police who suspected them of theft or by fellow citizens who accused them of avoiding "useful labor."[13]

Working-class women also increased their incomes and decreased their living expenses by renting rooms to boarders. Bed and meal services in private households, like boardinghouses, provided significant aid to poor newcomers, transients, and single men not in the habit of doing their own routine household chores. Young single women who migrated to the city benefited from these arrangements and offered babysitting or assistance in household work in exchange for their stay. Some of the boardinghouses offered informal and makeshift accommodations for guests, giving them no more than a place on the floor or a rotation in a bed for a nominal fee.

Renting rooms or space on the floor could bring in extra cash, but sometimes families had no room to spare. Working-class women short of cash were vulnerable to merchants and moneylenders who offered loans at high interest rates. Poor women often borrowed money in meager amounts, less than one dollar at a time, amassed running accounts for several months or years, and repaid ever-accumulating interest in small installments.[14] Many moneylenders were usurious. It was common for borrowers to pay 250 to 3500 percent interest on small sums, which exacerbated poverty with interminable debt. Fannie Holman, a washerwoman, borrowed between $60 and $90 over a two- or three-year period. Though she would repay over $1,000, the creditor applied it to defray the interest but not the principal of the loan.[15]

These unscrupulous practices undoubtedly affected household workers living on shoestring budgets very severely. The frequency with which their names appeared under chattel mortgages in the county's court reports is further testimony to their situation. Not only did these workers pay high interest rates and penalties, but when their money was completely exhausted they were forced to relinquish personal property that was essential to their wage labor or that added to the comfort of their modest homes, such as pots, pans, curtains, carpets, pictures, and other furnishings.[16]

The Working Women's Society, a mutual aid and trade organization, instituted an alternative to the moneylenders by lending funds to its members without interest; this service was paid for by weekly membership dues. Disturbed by the pattern of abuse that black women regularly endured, the organization prohibited its members from borrowing money from loan sharks and from mortgaging personal property to get cash.[17] Similarly, a washerwomen's organization petitioned the Macon, Georgia, City Council to protect its members from the abuse and harassment of loan sharks and furniture store dealers. The women placed the onus of debt on employers who paid insufficient and irregular wages and solicited the forbearance of their creditors from exacting usurious fees.[18]

African Americans were not the only borrowers to suffer, however. The system was corrupted by the collusion between justices of the peace, bailiffs (some of whom ran moneylending operations), and loan sharks. Blacks accounted for 60 percent of the borrowers, but the sum total of their loans was less than that of whites. Blacks were likely to suffer disproportionately, however, when facing a justice system decidedly stacked against them. This led some African Americans to resort to self-defense, as they had done to protect themselves against police brutality. Hundreds of residents were known to arm themselves with sticks, axes, bricks, and rocks to intimidate bailiffs coming into their neighborhoods to seize household goods on behalf of moneylenders.[19]

Everyday strategies like pan-toting, moneylending, borrowing clothing, scavenging, and boarding helped working-class women stretch their slim material resources and made the difference between starvation and subsistence. Mutual aid and trade organizations like the Working Women's Society, the Cooks' Union, and the Colored Working Women and Laundry Women were viable methods of pooling meager fortunes in the tradition of longstanding cultural practices. In more rare instances, black women could turn to the strike as a weapon to seek redress from employers. Times were changing, however; the racial atmosphere in the city in the wake of the riot did not bode well for African Americans hoping to achieve economic and social justice. Black women began to search for systematic solutions to improve the well-being and protection of their community.

THE RACE RIOT marked the nadir of race relations in the city, but it also accelerated black institutional development. Lugenia Burns Hope was among those whose sense of civic activism was heightened by the tragic violence and deaths. Less than a decade before, Hope had arrived in the city with her husband John, who moved there to teach at Atlanta Baptist College and shortly thereafter became the president of its successor, Morehouse College. Lugenia Burns Hope, a teacher and social worker, brought an enthusiasm for continuing the settlement work she had begun in Chicago, which included an affiliation with Jane Addams's Hull House.[20]

When Hope came to Atlanta, she entered an established voluntary reform world. African Americans had diligently built a network of mutual aid and fraternal organizations, churches, and Sunday school associations that had aided the sick, built schools, and housed orphans and the elderly. In 1899, Hope attended a conference at Atlanta University on "the Welfare of the Negro Child" that propelled her onto the Atlanta social reform scene. The conference concluded that wage-earning mothers who worked long hours for low wages needed help with child care during the day and information on child development. When the conference was over, several women began to work immediately on these goals. Alice Dugged Carey, a Morris Brown College teacher, organized mothers' meetings and a kindergarten in the basement of Fort Street Methodist Episcopal Church in 1900.[21] Hope and several other women started the Gate City Free Kindergarten Association five years later, to which Hope was elected president. They opened their first kindergarten on Cain Street, and by 1908 they had four additional kindergartens in operation serving a total of one hundred and fifty children. By 1917, three thousand children were cared for in structured learning and recreational programs in day nurseries located in poor neighborhoods.[22]

Hope drew on the strength of the women in the Gate City Free

Kindergarten Association in 1908 when she started the Neighborhood Union (NU) to dispense social welfare services among African Americans; the NU complemented the work of existing institutions but extended beyond the reach of any other organization by taking the entire city as its jurisdiction. Hope had been inspired not only by the horror of the riot, but also by the conditions of everyday life she witnessed in the poor neighborhoods in the vicinity of her west side home. The direct impetus for establishing the NU was an incident in which a woman had endured an illness, unbeknown to neighbors until it was too late, just before her death. Hope considered this a tragic incident that could have been avoided, had the woman known her neighbors. Hope vowed that such an episode would never happen again, adopting a motto from the Bible that would exemplify the NU's central purpose— "thy neighbor as thyself."[23]

The Neighborhood Union provided many services associated with settlement houses of the period.[24] One of its first priorities was to educate reformers and the broader community on the prevention and care of infectious diseases like tuberculosis. The NU provided the core leadership for an anti-tuberculosis campaign and the development of community clinics. Given the neglect of black health care by city officials and the slow response from white public health reformers, the NU provided essential services. It opened the doors of its first clinic, on West Fair and Mildred Streets, shortly after its founding.

Recalling its roots in the kindergarten movement, the NU regarded the well-being of youth as central to its mission. There were no playgrounds for black children to play in safety and freedom, and the NU began advocating for the city to make amends. The NU adapted a portion of the grounds of Morehouse College as a playground in the absence of city support. Though Hope showed a concern for all youth, she was especially touched by the plight of young women. As one associate recalled years later, Hope felt that "the girls on the street, or the girls around here had no place to go unless they were going to a public dance."[25] In Hope's opinion, and that of many other middle-class blacks, the dance halls were not places of virtue that would uplift women, or men, of the race. Hope designed the NU as an alternative to the dance halls: "to encourage wholesome thought and action in the community by disseminating good literature among the young" and "to provide harmless and beneficial sports and games for the young."[26]

The Neighborhood House opened in 1913 and served as a laboratory of domesticity for neighbors eager to partake in the rich array of programs offered. There were clubs for boys and girls, and classes were offered in sewing, dramatics, basketry, embroidery, financial planning, domestic science, hygiene, and literature. Other activities sponsored by the NU were concerts, lectures, and better home and clean-up campaigns. The programs were designed for personal enrichment, the improvement of home and family life, vocational development, and the promotion of strong citizenship in a modern industrial world. The organization also offered direct relief, such as food and clothing, to destitute families during emergencies, economic depressions, and wars.

The nucleus of the NU program was self-help activity, but the women also worked for the expansion of municipal services despite the city's record of gross neglect. The NU organized extensive investigations of conditions in public schools, including salaries of black teachers, lighting and ventilation of school houses, and conditions of overcrowding. They lobbied the mayor and city council, as well as other influential whites who would listen to their concerns, and they met with some success, including some raises for black teachers and eventually the construction of the first black public high school in 1924.[27] They also lobbied city hall for the improvement of unpaved, neglected streets, the repair of open sewers, and the removal of foul privies. The group criticized irresponsible landlords for charging exorbitant rents for ramshackle housing and urged the city to pass stricter regulations. They chastised unscrupulous merchants for unsanitary stores and exposed fraudulent business practices, such as grocers conducting special "sales" to entice black customers; the prices would be lowered on goods such as sugar and flour, but the sacks would contain rocks and debris to inflate their weight.[28]

Women in the NU did not shrink from criticizing errant members of their own communities. They took especially seriously their roles as advocates for children and families, and intervened when necessary to protect children and women from abuse. They attempted to pass a law against incestuous rape after an incident in which a father escaped punishment for abusing his daughter, sought indictments against men who beat their wives and children, and made referrals to charities on behalf of families deserted by breadwinners.[29]

But family and neighborhood investigations proved to be a double-edged sword. The reformers portrayed themselves as moral crusaders who would "clean up" black neighborhoods—physically and socially. The NU's charter defined as part of its purpose "to unite our efforts in breaking up dens of immorality and crime" and "to aid in the law of the land in suppressing vice and crimes therein."[30] The organization formed an investigation committee to report "everything that seems to be a menace to our neighborhood." It censored individuals "breaking the Sabbath," gamblers, drinkers, prostitutes, late night dancers, and "holy rollers" and reported the "undesirables" to the police. Several families and individuals identified as engaging in "immoral" activity or being of "questionable" character were evicted from the neighborhoods after petitions were circulated among other residents. In 1911 a secret backyard committee was formed, apparently to carry out vigilance more surreptitiously.[31]

The Neighborhood Union exhibited some class presuppositions typical of other contemporary reform organizations.[32] But NU reformers were mostly socially responsible individuals who were neither materially nor emotionally detached from the masses. Unlike most white settlement houses in which middle-class whites left the comforts of their sheltered environs to live and work among the poor in the slums, the homes of social workers in the NU were located among the poor or a stone's throw away. Jim Crow tied the fate of all African Americans together. Sometimes they were more entangled than the elites would have liked. Hope herself was known to lament the proximity of black colleges and the slums.[33]

Nonetheless, NU activists took on the formidable challenge of confronting an intransigent city government at a time when prospects for improvements were bleak. Their success with the city bureaucracy, however, was limited. City officials were not eager to remedy the injustices exposed by the group, but they did show themselves appreciative of the NU's moral scrutiny, missing few opportunities to arrest blacks identified as miscreants. In a telling example of the city's response, it delegated its settlement work related to African Americans to the NU, which acknowledged the importance of the women's leadership while at the same time giving municipal officials the opportunity to relieve themselves of important responsibilities for the welfare of black citizens.

The brilliance of the NU was that it built on the strength of Atlanta as a city of neighborhoods. Hope started her work in her own neigh-

borhood—the area sandwiched between Atlanta University on the
north, Spelman Seminary on the south, and Ashby and Walnut Streets
on the west and east. After organizing the people in this area, she
developed an elaborate structure to enable the NU to reach across
the city, as one by one, neighborhood groups joined the coalition.
The city was divided into zones, neighborhoods, and districts. At
every level there were checks and balances to ensure that leaders who
were elected by constituents or selected by fellow NU organizers
could monitor and respond to the needs of their communities.[34] These
women took grass-roots organizing seriously, undaunted by the sheer
physical energy required to visit and stay abreast of the people in
every home in their surrounding areas. The structure of the NU not
only facilitated communication with virtually every African American
in the city, it also spread the responsibilities of leadership broadly,
allowing for both autonomy and connectedness for a diverse group
of women and families.

This distinctive infrastructure enabled and required the participation of many working-class women.[35] Though middle-class, college-
educated women affiliated with black colleges and businesses, in their
own right or by marriage, have been credited with the leadership of
the NU, there were domestic workers and other wage-earning women
who were active in the leadership from its inception. In addition, some
professional women were married to artisans and manual workers.
Though middle-class women were often more prominent, the Neighborhood Union in its early years reflected a cross-section of class
backgrounds. An organization of this scope and nature could not function without the active involvement and leadership of the women the
NU was designed to reach. This situation changed somewhat after
1920, however.

Lugenia Burns Hope and the Neighborhood Union not only established an extensive voluntary social work infrastructure, but in the
process they were instrumental in professionalizing black social work.
They collaborated with sociologists conducting research and teaching
at Atlanta University and established the Social Service Institute, a
training program in social work held at Morehouse College, with a
faculty of black and white educators, reform leaders, and other professionals. In 1920, the Social Service Institute was transformed into the
School of Social Work, which later became a part of the Atlanta Uni-

versity system.[36] Hope taught in the school and allowed its students to receive practical experience by working in the Neighborhood Union. The graduates of the school received certificates that qualified them for a variety of positions in charitable and social welfare organizations in need of their expertise. The impact of the professionalization of social work on the NU was noticeable in the professionalization of the NU's own leadership. Although this change did not occur overnight, the NU appeared to take more of a top-down approach to forming its leadership after 1920. The names of ministers, physicians, businessmen, and other elites were more prominently displayed on boards, committees, and the public face of the organization.

In the years before 1920, however, working-class women were indispensable to the success of the NU. A few examples of working-class activists highlight their roles. Laura Bugg, a domestic worker, was one of the original nine members who attended the founding meeting in Hope's home in 1908. Bugg lived with her husband Jordan, a carpenter, and their three children. She often spoke as the group's spiritual leader, guiding the group in prayer in preludes to meetings. She also served on the board of directors and led committees, and in 1915 her peers elected her to the position of first vice-president.[37] Her husband lent a hand on the "gentlemen's committee," and donated his carpentry skills to fix the Neighborhood House. Bugg's devotion to the NU, however, did not consume all of her time for community work; she also joined Friendship Baptist Church and a secret society. Hattie Barnett worked variously as a domestic and a laundry worker, while her husband Samuel was a cook. She served on the board of directors of the NU and as second vice-president in 1913. When her peers chose representatives for a meeting at city hall, they selected Barnett along with Hope to discuss a joint mission school with the government. Outside the NU, Barnett was an active member of Warren Chapel. Mary Brawner worked as a cook and laundry worker and was married to James, a porter. The couple had three children, who also worked in domestic and manual occupations. Brawner served as a district manager of the NU in 1908. Ella M. Crawford, a domestic worker, and her husband Dock, a minister, were both community activists. She held positions in the NU as a district manager, a member of the board of directors, a committee chairperson, and assistant secretary. She also belonged to a secret society. And Maggie F. Williams, who served both on the board of directors and as secretary, was a laundry worker who lived with her widowed mother Missouri, a maid and cook.[38]

The participation of working-class women in the Neighborhood Union exemplified their participation in the full range of black institution-building in the city. They formed alliances with men, established cross-class institutions with other women, and organized among themselves. Some of the first sustained reform activities in the city had already been organized by working-class women before the establishment of the NU. Former slave Carrie Steele, a stewardess and cook at the train station, volunteered her time as a probation officer for children in trouble with the law. This experience and her childhood as an orphan inspired her to start an orphanage in 1890. She believed that many of the children she came in contact with had fallen on hard times because they had no families to take care of them. Steele raised money to purchase four acres of land and the orphans' first home by selling her own house, writing and selling her autobiography, and soliciting funds from generous individuals, black and white. By 1898 the Steele orphanage consisted of a brick building, hospital, and schoolhouse, and more than two hundred children had passed through its portals since its founding.[39]

A group of working-class women "with no aid save their own courage and simple faith" started a state network of women to build the Georgia Reformatory for Boys and Girls on forty acres of land in Fulton County in 1905. Fannie Slack, Cynthia Showers, and S. A. Moon, the president, vice-president, and treasurer, were all laundresses. Lillie Davis Turner, the president of the Fulton County chapter, was a teacher. These women shared aspirations similar to Steele's in addressing the problem of juvenile delinquents. While Steele focused on preventing youth crimes, Slack and her associates dealt with adolescents after they were convicted of misdeeds. Their goal was to provide an atmosphere for rehabilitating youth away from the negative influences of adult penitentiaries.[40]

Working-class and middle-class women formed alliances in many other social reform efforts. Women, men, and children of modest means were vital supporters of many charitable, community, and reform organizations. When the Gate City Free Kindergarten was organized, for example, it relied on the donation of small sums of money from many of the people that it ultimately served. Poor people contributed to the building of social reform institutions by giving in-kind labor, donating money, and participating in fund-raising events like bake sales, bazaars, athletic competitions, and baby contests—events that had the added benefit of deepening community bonds.[41]

Churches continued to build links between various segments of the black population. Many identified themselves as "institutional churches" with explicit goals similar to those of social settlement organizations in addressing the holistic needs of the urban poor. Bethel African Methodist Episcopal Church offered an employment bureau to match domestics and employers. Wheat Street Baptist Church opened a home for elderly women and a day and night school that attracted hundreds of laborers. Friendship Baptist Church built a house to care for the indigent and elderly. The Central Avenue Methodist Episcopal Church operated a kindergarten.[42]

The First Congregational Church, with Henry Hugh Proctor at its helm beginning in 1894, was the first "institutional church" in the South and the most distinguished in Atlanta. Like Lugenia Burns Hope, Proctor was inspired by the riot to infuse his church with a mission to transform the conditions of city life. Like Hope, Proctor designed wholesome programs for personal enrichment that he considered alternatives to unseemly Decatur Street entertainment. Proctor became profoundly aware that whereas the "dives" and dance halls on Decatur Street were attractive, wide open, and beckoning eager patrons, the doors of his own church were closed—literally and metaphorically. "God helping me," Proctor vowed, "I will open my church and make it as attractive as the dive."[43] By the 1910s, facilities at the church included a library, gymnasium, bath house, model kitchen, working girls' home, kindergarten, and employment bureau. It sponsored the Working Men's Club, Woman's Aid Society, Young Men's League, a chauffeur's association, a temperance society, and an annual musical festival. And the church organized several neighborhood missions on Cain, Irwin, and Decatur Streets as well as prison missions at the county jail and federal penitentiary.[44]

By the 1910s, African Americans had developed a web of social services and institutions stimulated by voluntarism, altruism, and the necessity of countering economic, social, and political deprivation. In the wake of the riot, blacks had worked harder to fortify the foundation that protected them from the insults and injustices of Jim Crow. But despite the best efforts of leaders like Hope and Proctor, working-class women would find relief not only in the settlement houses or institutional churches, but also in places that many considered taboo—the clubs, theaters, and dance halls on Decatur Street.

After the Civil War, recently freed slaves settled together in several clusters in Atlanta. This 1879 lithograph from *Harper's Weekly* depicts Shermantown, located east of downtown, as a collection of wooden shacks encircling a well. The clotheslines stretched between the buildings and the implements of the washerwoman's trade underneath the thatched roof in the center highlight the significance of black women's labor.

Washing clothes occupied much of black women's time and energy as they transformed their slave skills into paid labor. Laundry work was one of the most arduous chores of the era, but it also gave women more autonomy and flexibility than other domestic work. This scene from 1900 shows laundresses at work with the help of children, who performed tasks such as stirring the pot of boiling water. *Source*: Library of Congress.

Domestic workers pose in front of the home of their employer, Isabel Boyd. Many middle-class white families hired a number of domestic workers as maids, cooks, yardmen, and coachmen. The presence of the child pulling a wagon suggests that children were often groomed early for service occupations. *Source*: Atlanta History Center.

The term "child-nurse," the designation used for hired child-care providers, took on a double meaning as young black girls were hired to watch white infants. One of these girls was so small that her feet had to be propped up for the photographic sitting in 1903. The girls from Macon, Georgia, are unidentified, but the two infants in their arms are John and Allie Lamon. *Source*: Georgia Department of Archives and History.

Adult workers were also hired as child-nurses. Here, a woman named Autie poses with the children of the Inman-Grant family in the 1890s in a typical "family" genre shot of the era. *Source*: Atlanta History Center.

African-American women spent much of their time performing wage work for white households, but they also had family responsibilities of their own. This portrait of a mother and her own child at the turn of the century reminds us of the importance of family life to working-class women and is a departure from the typical photographs of black child-nurses with white children. *Source*: Atlanta History Center.

Around the turn of the century, new forms of leisure were enjoyed by African-American women and men in southern cities. The bicycle, a means of mobility and a symbol of modernity, was in vogue in the 1890s, especially for women. This studio shot of a young woman shows the growing popularity of biking as well as the novelty of taking pictures like this one for fun. *Source*: Atlanta History Center.

Working-class and middle-class black women built and sustained community institutions like the Neighborhood Union, founded in 1908. In this photograph, children from one of the areas surrounding Atlanta University are shown with women from the Neighborhood Union. *Source*: Clarke Atlanta University.

Lugenia Burns Hope, a social worker by training and the wife of the president of Morehouse College, combined her talents and skills to fulfill her responsibilities as citizen, reform leader, wife, and mother. Hope is shown here *(top, center)* with her son, John Jr., and the child's nurse in the 1910s. Hiring domestic help was a rarity among African-American families, except for elites like the Hopes. *Source*: Clarke Atlanta University.

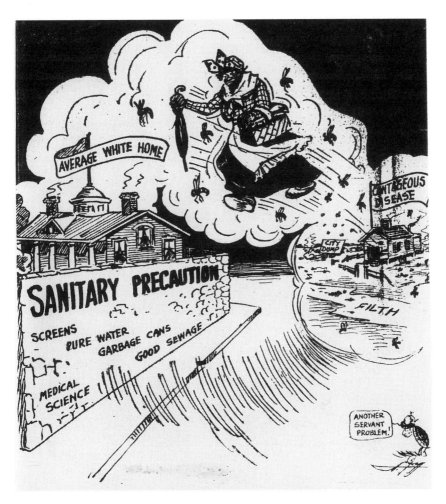

Although most middle-class and upper-class white families in the South considered black servants to be indispensable, they had ambivalent feelings about living in proximity to blacks in the era of segregation. Cartoons such as this one published in the *Atlanta Constitution* in 1914 warned the white public about the danger of germs and disease carried by laundresses and servants who entered their homes.

The original headline for this cartoon from the *Atlanta Constitution* in 1914 was "Can you wonder it spreads?" White readers were again reminded of the dangers of contagion from black servants. However, this caricature also offers a subtle critique of the city's culpability in exacerbating disease—the rejected application for hospital care on the floor.

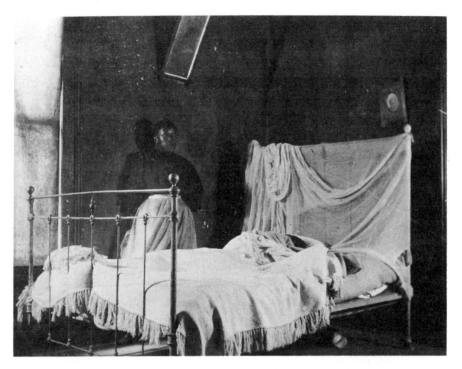

One of the photographs taken by white women of the Atlanta Anti-Tuberculosis Association to document poor living conditions in black neighborhoods shows Minnie Freeman sick in bed. Freeman, a twenty-year-old washerwoman and TB victim, achieved infamy because she lived close to a distinguished white neighborhood, which she allegedly contaminated. The woman standing behind the bed is probably her mother, also a washerwoman, who was accused of spreading germs because she nursed her sick daughter and continued to take in laundry. *Source*: Atlanta History Center.

Another photograph taken by the Atlanta Anti-Tuberculosis Association shows Maria Greer sitting near her house. She was considered a danger to whites not because of her own poor health, but because her son and husband were ill. *Source*: Atlanta History Center.

Pan-toting, taking home leftover foods or pantry goods, was considered a customary right by many cooks, maids, and employers after slavery ended. But the practice also had its critics, who considered pan-toting theft or who believed that it encouraged laziness. This 1916 caricature from the *Montgomery Advertiser* depicts a black cook as a crow delivering a basket of food scraps (with a white man inside) to her husband, who is lounging on the "family tree."

As the Great Migration of blacks to northern cities began to take an economic toll on the South's economy, some white moderate business and political leaders launched a public relations campaign to dissuade black workers from leaving. This cartoon from the *Montgomery Advertiser* in 1916 mocked would-be migrants, extolling the virtues of easy life in the South in contrast to the harsh winters, rigid time clocks, and lack of sympathy from northern employers unfamiliar with southern customs.

CHAPTER SEVEN

"Wholesome" and "Hurtful" Amusements

When Alice Adams, a domestic worker, moved to Atlanta in the early 1900s, her family members warned her about the perils of unseemly places that she should avoid. As she recalled years later, they said to "stay off Decatur Street, and I did just that." But as Adams admitted, despite the street's notorious reputation for "vice" and crime, she was drawn to experience its attractions for herself. "They had one restaurant on . . . Decatur Street and Central Avenue. We would go in that restaurant and go from there to Eighty One Theater." Mary Morton, also a domestic worker, had a similar story to tell. "Decatur Street was terrible, momma didn't allow us on Decatur Street," she reported of her youth. "One night my sister and me went over to spend the night with a girl that lived out in that section, and momma didn't allow us to go in no shows or nothing like that, but we went to a picture show and so—and this girl took us."[1]

Despite familial admonitions, working-class women like Adams and Morton found relief from their workaday lives in Atlanta's central amusement district. Though old forms of leisure persisted, African Americans increasingly turned to commercial outlets for pleasure amid the rigors of their daily labors. Lugenia Burns Hope had created the Neighborhood Union, in part, to provide "wholesome" alternatives to Decatur Street's "hurtful" amusements for young women like Adams and Morton. Henry Hugh Proctor expanded the community outreach programs in his church with a similar goal in mind. But thanks to rapid urbanization, advances in technology, and electricity, many new and controversial amusements had become accessible to a wider public by the turn of the century. The changing rules and expectations of public decorum and social conviviality as strangers encountered one another more casually and intimately on this new terrain heightened the tensions that accompanied modernization throughout urban America in the Victorian era. The imperatives of de jure segregation exacerbated anxieties in the South even further. Blacks in Atlanta vigorously created and defended a separate and unequal, but vibrant and distinctive, world of entertainment that was at once removed from and subjected to the limitations imposed by Jim Crow. Alice Adams and Mary Morton would encounter this rich, contradictory, and contested domain at its most typical on Decatur Street, the center of urban leisure.

During the post-riot era, Atlanta tried to rescue the tainted reputation of downtown by remaking it into a white consumers' fairyland. Electric lights, sidewalks, and wide streets connected stores, restaurants, and sanitary facilities into a shopping promenade where consumers could stroll and shop in a pleasant and secure environment. "The Great White Way" at Five Points, where the intersecting railroad lines met at the center of the city, followed the lead already established by cities in the northeast. Store owners targeted women shoppers in search of fancy clothing and accessories, or those who were simply enjoying the multitudes of goods in window displays.[2]

Complementing the new look of downtown as a respectable place for pleasure after business hours were the rural retreats within the city. Ponce de Leon Park was transformed from a spring and picnic ground into a thriving amusement park by the 1910s, offering manicured gardens, swimming, boating, band concerts, skating, and mechanical rides like a merry-go-round and a Ferris wheel. Piedmont Park, like New York's Central Park, offered landscaped gardens, lakes for swimming and boating, and amusement rides like chute-the-chute. Frederick Law Olmsted, the landscape architect for both parks, believed that municipal parks would encourage democratic ideals because they would bring "all classes largely represented, with a common purpose . . . poor and rich, young and old, Jew and Gentile." Commonalities would be emphasized, differences minimized.[3]

In the New South, however, democracy in the parks was reserved for whites only. Exceptions were made for black child-nurses carrying white children to the park, but even this custom was challenged. The operators of Ponce de Leon Park decided that leniency shown to servants should end because "there is a tendency on the part of some colored nurses in the care of children to try to be conspicuous." Park officials feared that black women's presence on the amusement rides "proved quite objectionable to ladies and young girls" and drove them away.[4]

Jim Crow was embodied in the design of white consumer fairylands from their initial inception. Names such as "the Great White Way" were not incidental to their expressed purposes of entertainment. These parks also provided ways of reaffirming whiteness through ritual play and reinforcing racial unity against a perceived black threat. During the era of the riot, promoters and advocates of parks made explicit the rationale of creating playgrounds exclusively for whites. Jim Crow parks were designed not simply to put white urbanites closer to nature, but also to give them moments of reprieve and distance from blacks in order to channel racial friction in "wholesome" directions.[5]

As opportunities expanded for working-class and middle-class whites to mingle in public, class proclivities were still detectable. The upper crust tended to prefer Ponce de Leon's pristine and sedate amusements, while white workers headed off more often to "White City," an amusement park with a more daring fare of mechanical rides and an atmosphere of raucous entertainment. Class tensions were evident as the city's elites tried to create idealized public spaces for whites and scoffed at the increasing array of recreation enjoyed by the burgeoning white wage-earning population. Cheap theaters, vaudeville shows, moving pictures, saloons, dance halls, and house parties all beckoned and reached eager white working-class patrons.[6]

Jim Crow laws and customs governing public amusements and work restricted the leisure opportunities for women like Alice Adams and Mary Morton. Unlike white working-class women whose work lives were increasingly regulated by industrial time clocks, which gave them set hours and time off for play, domestic workers had to struggle to make space for leisure. Adams noted that going out late in the evenings while working a seven-day work schedule did not satisfy her personal needs. "I wanted time off," she stated. "Time off to visit my friends and my friends to visit me, just like I was entertaining [my employer's] friends, I wanted to entertain my friends, and I wasn't satisfied until I did." Adams clearly recognized that it was her labor that made possible her employer's social life. Though her husband reminded her that she was fortunate to have nice employers who "are so good to you," Adams persisted. She explained to her husband: "I say, that's not the thing, I wants time off. And I got it."[7]

Adams's yearning for informal socializing reflected the general character of black women's leisure lives, which continued to be centered in church social events and fund-raisers, secret society celebrations, picnics, and gossip sessions at the wash stand or on front porches. A network of social clubs and private parties which met in homes or clubhouses enhanced the cultural life of black Atlantans. The precise chronology of when most of these clubs emerged and how long each existed is not available, but they were clearly prolific after the turn of the century. The Eureka Social Club, the Gate City Club, the Gate City Girls, the Belmont Social Club, the Imperial Social Club, the Fulton Social Club, the Ladies Savings Union, the Twilight Social Club, the Douglas Literary Club, the F. D. Literary Society, the Smart Set Social Club, the Ladies Pleasure Club, the Workingmen's Pleasure Club, the Young Ladies Criterion Club, the Ladies Needle-Work Club, and the South View Floral Club were just a few of the multitude of names.

The social status of these groups and their members is revealed in the location of stories about them in the local press. Clubs dominated by wage-earners were more likely to appear in white newspapers in the crime section. Lacking the means to conceal their activities from white scrutiny, members of these clubs were often the victims of police surveillance and arrests. Their quarters were often bare, makeshift, multi-purpose buildings shared with other institutions, such as saloons or possibly trade unions.

In contrast, clubs dominated by the more prosperous African Americans were often discussed in rich detail on the social pages of the black newspaper during the early 1900s. In this period, a small but significant number of affluent blacks were becoming increasingly visible. Doctors, lawyers, real estate owners, insurance executives, bankers, college professors, and well-to-do ministers constituted Atlanta's black upper class. A larger middle class of skilled artisans, nurses, tailors, barbers, blacksmiths, caterers, teachers, and small entrepreneurs also existed. The relatively greater financial means of the better-off African Americans improved their ability to socialize in privacy away from white official-dom's punitive reach. Middle-class blacks sponsored barbecues, whist parties, Russian teas, and even regular club meetings that were remark-able in their display of material achievement. "Palatial" and "artistic" homes decorated with an effusive array of American beauty roses, ferns, or other fresh floral arrangements were typical of the settings described in newspaper stories. The host or hostess's attire (the fabric, accesso-ries, and color scheme) would be delineated in detail, along with com-ments on their "charming" personalities. "Sumptuous" refreshments and delicacies such as oyster soup, Saratoga chips, broiled pompano fish, wreaths of California grapes, and peppers stuffed with calf's brain were served to club members.

Expressions of gentility and prestige were often clearly conspicuous, if not in the names of some clubs, then in the professional titles of the members, or in other telling signs. The members of the Independent Ten Social Club, for example, were privileged to have among them Robert Webb, who purchased an automobile "for the comfort of his friends and club members." Other avid car-lovers purchased property for the Negro Driving Club. The correlation between skin color, mixed-race heritage, and social status influenced club membership as well. Though a deeply rooted mulatto class was not as strong in Atlanta as in some other Southern cities, color caste was evident. Some clubs explicitly excluded dark-skinned blacks from membership. Others may have been more subtle in their self-selection. Women of the White Lily Club spent their summer vacation at Niagara Falls. And the Idle and Wild Club consisted of mostly fair-skinned young adults, judging by a photograph which showed them tamely and politely posed in their formal tuxedos and gowns at a formal ball with British and American flags draped across the ceiling of the hall.[8]

College, intramural, and semi-professional sporting events such as boxing, baseball, and football were enjoyed by both women and men. Ruby Owens, who worked as a maid in a brothel, enjoyed going to baseball games after work with her girl friends; they would make bets with each other on their favorite teams, using peanuts instead of money.[9] One of the most important athletic matches was a national prizefight between Jack Johnson, a black fighter, and Jim Jeffries, who was white, in 1910. Though boxing was usually a sport enjoyed by male spectators, this event sparked broader interest. Many blacks made bets on the match or sported buttons on their lapels and collars showing Johnson's likeness. Bishop Henry McNeal Turner installed an Associated Press wire service on the pulpit of his People's Tabernacle. When Johnson beat Jeffries, "the white hope," blacks in Atlanta and throughout the nation celebrated the victory as a symbolic gesture of racial retribution. City officials, however, took the usual steps to restrain jubilant crowds in the streets as angry and disappointed whites lashed out violently. Several cities in Georgia, as well as the state legislature, moved to prohibit films exhibiting prizefighting. The Atlanta Police Board sent a public warning to Johnson that he should not dare to even visit Atlanta or the rest of the South.[10]

The celebration of holidays marked important occasions for revelry. Following emancipation, African Americans redefined the Fourth of July, for example, as a tribute to emancipation, much to the consternation of many whites. One source complained, without any apparent awareness of the irony, "It is a curious fact that many negroes in the south appear to associate the Fourth of July with their deliverance from slavery. Freedom and American independence has become a mixed metaphor in their patriotism."[11] The celebration would begin with a welcoming committee of vendors peddling lemonade, watermelon, and other foods at the railroad depot as arriving guests from other cities disembarked from the locomotives. The day would continue with picnics, street parades, baseball games, and dancing at night clubs.

Each year the local press and municipal officials attacked these celebrations for one reason or another. Sometimes efforts were made to curtail public congregations, as occurred in 1904 when the chief of police and city clerk decided unilaterally to deny black hawkers the right to obtain street licenses near the railroad depot. "The booths have been eye-sores, for they were hastily built, rickety concerns constructed of old boxes and dirty cloth," and the odors of fried fish and tainted ham were offensive to white passersby, the newspaper rationalized.[12] At other times, whites complained that blacks unduly dominated the city on that day with their public festivities. Some whites were sufficiently disgusted that they refrained from planning an observance of their own.[13]

The steam engine excursions that brought visitors to town on special holidays also served as a conduit for the exchange of news, information, and cultural practices throughout the South. Train companies offered discount fares for travel between popular destinations that blacks took advantage of frequently. Friends, families, social clubs, church groups, and fraternal orders boarded the caravans to and from Atlanta to attend carnivals, cakewalk contests, religious revivals, and state and regional fairs. Visiting excursions enabled family and friends to maintain contact over long distances, as many blacks migrated throughout the South and further north. They encouraged the development of broad networks of community and helped to spread a common culture throughout the region and beyond. But these seemingly innocuous outings could turn sour when fights broke out. Many African Americans were quick to point out when criticized that most excursions were amicable affairs.[14]

The church continued to be a refuge for black recreation, even hosting popular cultural entertainment. Wheat Street Baptist Church sponsored events such as a lecture by "a colored humorist." For ten cents, patrons could watch "a series of characters, impersonations, dialect sketches and witty sayings." In a reversal of the traditional blackface minstrelsy, in which white performers mimicked black singing and dancing, black performers imitated various other ethnic groups, such as Irish, Dutch, Chinese, Italians, and Jews, "with striking fidelity to nature."[15]

WHILE many leisure activities were centered around special occasions or limited to small and private circles, African Americans increasingly sought pleasure in commercial places by the end of the nineteenth century. An occasional circus came to town with East Indian snake charmers and elephants in tents erected on Grant and Fair Streets. A skating rink provided fun in the afternoons for ladies and opened in the evenings for gentlemen. On occasion, blacks could patronize Piedmont Park to watch drills by militia companies, play baseball, watch horse, mule, or bicycle races, or listen to music and speeches. Blacks also hosted exhibitions at the park featuring Wild West shows, baby contests, and equestrians.[16] By the 1910s the array of commercial entertainments had widened considerably. African Americans enjoyed a flourishing leisure life in saloons, dance halls, billiard rooms, restaurants, gambling dens, and vaudeville and motion picture houses. Just as white workers frequented "White City," an obvious reference to the amusement park popularized by the World's Columbian Exposition in Chicago in 1893, blacks enjoyed "Luna Park," a modest storefront imitation of the heart of New York's Coney Island.[17]

Most of these outlets were located on the infamous Decatur Street, the center of the urban leisure district. Its resemblance to other seamy metropolitan districts sometimes evoked comparisons with Canal Street in New Orleans, the Bowery in New York City, the Champs Elysées in Paris, and Chinatown in San Francisco. Decatur Street was "a kaleidoscope of light, noise and bustle from dawn to dawn," especially on Saturdays. On the weekends, local residents and country transients flocked in large numbers to conduct business with street vendors or auctioneers waving their wares, as the smells of peanuts, tobacco, near-beer, hot dogs, fried fish, horse manure, and cheap perfume mingled in the air. Second-hand clothing stores along with a multitude of shoe and boot stores attracted scores of consumers looking for snazzy outfits at bargain prices. Others brought items to exchange for cash in the pawn shops—the places where victims of larceny headed hot on the heels of thieves in hopes of reclaiming stolen property. Dozens of bars, eateries, poolrooms, bordellos, barbershops, drugstores, delicatessens, grain merchants, seafood vendors, and dry goods stores lined the street awaiting customers. Meanwhile, one could have an instant tintype photograph taken by a street camera fakir, catch up with passing friends and trade news, or perhaps sneak a drink of moonshine from the Appalachian farmers who sequestered the contraband in between piles of fresh corn, peas, and greens brought to market.[18]

The conspicuous presence of Chinese laundrymen, Jewish and Greek shopowners, Yankee spielers, Italian chorus men, and moonshine mountaineers rubbing shoulders with one another reinforced the street's reputation as the "melting pot of Dixie." Ella Jackson and Nettie Penn, two black women who owned lunch rooms, were located in the same block with Fred Ketchum's jewelry store, Nathan Weitzman's barbershop, and Luna Park. Similarly, Lina Richardson, a black lodging house owner, ran her business a few doors away from Isaac Sinkovitz's pawnshop, Evan Williams's grocery store, and Lula Edwards's brothel. The reputation of Decatur Street as a "melting pot" meant more than the coexistence of a diversity of ethnic businesses, however. Decatur Street was also one of the few places where different racial and ethnic groups mingled relatively freely. Lunch rooms, mostly run by black women, were popular places for cross-race interaction.

The City Council tried to stop this practice in 1910 by passing an ordinance "to prohibit lunch or meals being served to whites and blacks in the same place."[19]

Despite this reputation for the intermingling of people from diverse nations and cultures, Decatur Street made its name as a "negro playground" on the basis of its prominent "African majority." Decatur Street attracted more peripatetic African Americans than any other local thoroughfare. Its only rival was Auburn Avenue, the black "Great White Way." The two fairways were perceived by some residents as representing opposite ends of the spectrum of respectability, character, and status. Benjamin Davis, the outspoken editor of the *Atlanta Independent*, promoted the notion of the "Auburn Avenue Negro" and the "Decatur Street Negro"; the first he defined as industrious and thrifty, the latter as shiftless and fun-loving.[20] Sweet Auburn in its heyday was the ideal of an unsullied, beautiful promenade that exemplified black uplift and capitalist enterprise. As Alice Adams fondly remembered: "Auburn Avenue was a place to go at night and dress up. Had to be well-dressed to go down there." She added: "it was what they called 'black folks' Peachtree.'" Decatur Street, by contrast, was rough, she stated. "That was no place for me. And I stayed on the safe side I'd go to Auburn Avenue, Sweet Auburn Avenue, that was my street." Kathleen Adams, a teacher who grew up in a middle-class family, reiterated these distinctions. She recalled the romance of Auburn Avenue on Sunday mornings as African American women were dressed up for church in taffeta, brocades, and bellback skirts. Men, like her father, might be seen with striped pants, two-button cutaway coats, Stetson hats, walking canes, and tan gloves.[21]

The perceived distinctions between Auburn Avenue and Decatur Street highlight the tensions over ideas of decency and indecency that swirled through discourses on public amusements. Nevertheless, the contrast between the two streets would soon be blurred, as houses of prostitution and boisterous street play began to appear on Auburn Avenue by the First World War era. Condemnations of the "Decatur Street Negro," typically by middle-class black and white spokespersons, were usually taken to refer to the ill-bred behavior of the working-class. Decatur Street was not just a popular place for the "African majority," but mostly for the black masses. Not all working-class people wanted to be identified with this reputation, however. Alice Adams, for example, was ambivalent about her excursions there in light of her family's warnings about the district. Despite this tension, Decatur Street was an alluring subterranean world, tempting to a broader cross-section of the populace than many would readily admit. Groups of "stylishly dressed" white "society men and women" who were "anxious for diversions" would cruise through Decatur Street in automobiles on Saturday night. This "slumming craze" allowed polite white society to participate in the pleasures of Negro play, by mimicking and ridiculing blacks congregating in the streets.[22]

By the 1910s, Decatur Street presented more opportunities for black women as consumers, small entrepreneurs, and entertainers. Women's presence in show business reflected a significant shift in dominant ideas about gender in a society highly influenced by Victorian values and standards. Entertainment that took place beyond the confines of private parlors and church sanctuaries had been tightly controlled to ensure that middle-class propriety prevailed in keeping individuals from socializing across class, racial, and gender lines. Intermingling of the sexes and social groups had been considered improper, except between prostitutes and men, which prevented women from freely enjoying most public entertainments as either performers or consumers. When exceptions were made, such as in opera houses or polite theaters, women were expected to be chaperoned or escorted by men, and a hierarchy of seating insulated the bourgeoisie from the despised "others" to prevent breaches in social decorum.[23]

Many women from immigrant, working-class, and African-American backgrounds helped to reconfigure gender conventions in public amusements. Their defiance of the Victorian standards of "true womanhood" that defined respectability as middle-class propriety provoked controversy.[24] Middle-class reformers, black and white, targeted women most passionately in their criticisms of public amusements, proposing regulations and police crackdowns. White wage-earning women were usually described as vulnerable, innocent victims exploited by entertainment companies, saloon keepers, and unscrupulous men.[25] Black women of the same class, however, were usually described as agents of moral decline and decay.

The criticisms may have delayed women's entry into show business, but women persisted in showcasing their talents on stage. Their prominence in minstrelsy and vaudeville shows increased as urbanization, migration, and an expanding market for their labor enhanced social mobility. Women actors became stars in their own right, as well as parts of ensembles and duos with men. Husband and wife pairs such as Jody (Butterbeans) and Susie Edwards, or Leola B. (Coot Grant) and Wesley (Kid Sock) Wilson, were celebrated teams who parodied marital feuds.[26]

Black audiences in Atlanta were treated to performances by entertainers like Anna Madah and Emma Louise Hyer, known as the Hyer Sisters, who penetrated the all-male minstrelsy field. They were featured in plays such as *The Underground Railroad* and *Out of Bondage.* Women minstrels continued to make strides in Sam T. Jack's production, *The Creole Show* (1890), which included a cast with sixteen women, a woman interlocutor, and the first black female chorus line. Black Patti's Troubadours, led by the opera singer Sissiretta Jones, became the first black road show to tour the East and South in 1897 and made frequent appearances in Atlanta.[27]

Though minstrel shows continued to appeal to Southerners, they had begun to decline in popularity among audiences elsewhere by the turn of the century. But the gates of the entertainment world had been opened irrevocably for black performers, who funneled their talents into vaudeville—the new vogue.[28] Black audiences in Atlanta enjoyed going to see vaudevillians such as Fanny Wise, Billy King, Tom Fletcher, Ernest Hogan, the Whitman Sisters, and Ethel Waters (Sweet Mama Stringbean). In 1909, the Theater Owner's Booking Association (TOBA) began formalizing the booking of such acts and organizing a chain of theaters in the South that featured these performers. By 1921, this institution had created a network across the country that opened doors for blacks in show business and facilitated broader access to audiences. TOBA, a white-owned company, did not always treat its clients fairly, however, and acquired a tongue-in-cheek moniker—*Tough On Black Asses.*[29] Most of the venues for TOBA and other black vaudevillians were white-owned and white-operated theaters until the 1910s. In 1903, there were only a few black facilities in Southern cities that performers could count on regularly, including the Blue Room in Louisville, Tom Baxter's in Jacksonville, the Hottentot in Pensacola, and Tom Golden's in Savannah. But the number of black theaters skyrocketed, ensuring theatergoers a steady menu of shows and entertainers and managers regular profits. The South became the best testing ground for black talent in the 1910s.[30]

Atlanta was pivotal to the growth of this burgeoning field. Entrepreneurs established theater houses that featured the famous performers and supported young artists, making Atlanta a pacesetter in popular culture. African-American businessmen were involved in these ventures, such as James T. Lynch, who opened the Central Theatre and hired Billy King, a former black actor, to manage it. The club thrived under King's leadership, and he started a house stock company and produced shows that created steady jobs for local artists to practice in a variety of genres.[31] The Southern Amusement Company's Auditorium Theatre was renowned as the finest black-owned playhouse in the South and a favorite on the vaudeville and road show circuits. Occupying an entire city block of Auburn Avenue, the Auditorium had over seven hundred seats on the main floor and more than five hundred in the gallery.[32] The most influential nightspot in Atlanta was the Eighty One Theatre, owned by the white businessman Charles Bailey and located on Decatur Street. An endless roster of celebrities, such as Ma Rainey, String Beans, Skunton Bowser, and Buzzin' Burton, would perform there, especially in the 1920s and 1930s. This vaudeville house was most influential as the launching pad for stars on the rise.[33]

Bessie Smith, the "Empress of the Blues," regularly hung out at the Eighty One as a teenager in 1913. Unlike most young women of her age aspiring to find alternatives to domestic work, Smith was able to capitalize on her talents to avoid being wedded to pots, pans, mops, and brooms. Show business offered black women a rare opportunity to merge avocation with vocation and earn good pay. Singing live in theaters accompanied by piano players and other musicians was pleasurable, rewarding, and hard work. The young Smith practiced her craft in the backyard of the Eighty One during the day, trained chorus girls using the expertise she had acquired in the road shows where she performed before moving to Atlanta, and sang on stage at night. The audiences loved Smith, especially when she sang their favorite, "Weary Blues," and would throw tips on the stage to show their appreciation—adding a few extra dollars to her typical $10.00 weekly salary. When she began touring on the TOBA circuit a few years later, the Eighty One Theatre served as her home base.[34]

Atlanta theaters nurtured other local talents. The Whitman Sisters, consisting of Mabel, Essie, Alberta, and Baby Alice, were the highest paid performers on the black vaudeville circuit in the 1910s. Mabel, the oldest sister, was born in Lawrence, Kansas, but the girls grew up in Atlanta where their father, Albany, was a minister at Big Bethel African Methodist Episcopal Church and a dean at Morris Brown College. They received their informal training in church music, local socials, and jubilee concerts and their formal training at the New England Conservatory of Music and Morris Brown College. The sisters made their professional debut in the 1890s as a filler act at the Orpheum Theatre in Kansas while accompanying their father on an evangelical tour. They sang and danced in New York as the Daznetta Sisters before touring with the Kohl, Castle, and Orpheum circuits at the end of the decade, and later they joined TOBA. In their early years in show business, they were obliged to perform minstrel acts in blackface makeup and wigs that covered their own fair skin and naturally blonde hair, only to expose the farce of their disguise by unveiling their true identities in the finale. Passing and cross-dressing recurred in their career in another manner as well. Alberta, who assumed the stage name Bert, cut her hair short, donned masculine apparel, and became one of the best-known male impersonators. Bert's manly stage presence was not unique, but was still uncommon. Other black women entertainers such as Gladys Bentley and Josephine Baker would impersonate men in the 1920s and 1930s. Cross-dressing was usually the prerogative of men, however. Double cross-dressing (the inversion of race and gender) was mostly performed by white men, dating back to early nineteenth century minstrelsy.[35]

The Whitman Sisters Novelty Company—consisting of twenty to thirty artists, including actors, singers, dancers, a brass band, an orchestra, and comedians—returned to Atlanta frequently to perform at Turner's Tabernacle, other theaters, or under a canvas tent at the Jackson Street baseball field.[36] The sisters could always depend on their hometown fans' loyalty, and they repaid this reverence and esteem by maintaining ties to the community, incorporating local talent into their shows, and donating portions of their proceeds to churches and secret societies.

Not all Atlantans greeted them with enthusiasm, however, as a crowd of fans learned while waiting in line for tickets at the white-owned Lyceum Theatre on Edgewood Avenue one hot summer day in July in 1900. New management at the Lyceum had canceled the Whitman Sisters for failing to meet its standards as a "higher class of attractions."[37] Even some within their own race looked askance at the women's secular theatrical enterprise, accusing them of disrespect toward their father's ministry.[38]

Fans who appreciated the Whitman Sisters' talents were especially fascinated by their dancing. The sisters and other members of their company were some of the best dancers in the country over the course of their careers from the 1890s to the 1940s. Alice, "the Queen of Taps," was especially talented in this regard and had acquired her flair very early in life. "As a kid I'd be 'Georgia Hunchin' up and down Auburn Avenue in Atlanta, just a little shuffle with taps, but you could move along," she later recalled. "I even used to do it after Sunday School in front of the church, and the people would shake their heads disapprovingly and say, 'Oh, look at Alice.'"[39]

Unwittingly, and perhaps to his own chagrin, Albany Whitman had nurtured his daughters' dancing by teaching them the "double shuffle"—though he insisted that it was "just for exercise." The Whitmans took these lessons further than their aerobic intention, however, and became innovators in dance; they were credited with starting a cakewalk craze in Atlanta after winning a contest in the early 1900s.[40] Dancing in the Whitmans' repertoire was showcased for its own aesthetic value rather than used simply as incidental comic relief, as was often the case in vaudeville. The sisters contributed to the exchange between vernacular and theatrical dance as they adopted dance steps they learned from audiences and featured new dance steps in their shows that their fans in turn adopted. Black dancers who got their first break with the Whitmans would continue to draw on this legacy in Broadway shows once vaudeville subsided.[41]

Black Atlantans would have many opportunities to enjoy the performances of home-grown national talents who were women, but they were also treated to the rising stardom of young men. Several talented men, sons of domestic workers and laborers, began their performing careers in the city's clubs and theaters. Thomas Dorsey, though later known as "the father of gospel music," began his career as an adolescent in the secular world of the Eighty One Theatre. Dorsey used his job as a "butch boy," selling soft drinks and popcorn during intermission, to learn from veteran piano players in the early 1900s. Dorsey's mother Etta, a washerwoman and organ player for his father's church, inspired his initial interest in music. Dorsey took a detour from his religious roots, however. By the time he was sixteen he was already a sought-after musician, playing at the Eighty One, the Ninety One Royal Theater, other vaudeville clubs, movie theaters, social halls, house parties, and dance halls.[42]

Like Smith and Dorsey, Perry Bradford started his career as a young-ster, performing at local clubs and theaters in the city. His family lived in a four-room shack next door to the Fraser Street jail in Summer Hill. His father, Adam, was a common laborer, and his mother, Bella, worked as a washerwoman and conducted a small catering business, serving coffee, biscuits, cornbread, molasses, peas, and rice to prison inmates. Like Etta Dorsey, Bella Bradford stimulated and encouraged her son's musical interests. She had lulled her child to sleep with lullabies, nourishing him with indelible lyrical memories inspired by the blues and ragtime melodies that careened between the iron bars of the prison. Bradford learned the piano, sang, and danced on the min-strel circuit with Jeanette Taylor Bradford, his partner and his first wife. He became a leading composer of his generation, best known for translating traditional blues into commercially successful hits.[43]

Performers like Bradford, Dorsey, Smith, and the Whitmans were popular among Atlanta audiences because they combined the tradi-tional and familiar with new and transformed idioms. In addition to homegrown talents, Atlanta audiences were treated to an array of per-forming artists throughout the 1910s: Ulysses the Magician, W. C. Handy's orchestra, Billy Kersands Minstrels, Rabbitt's Foot Comedy Company, Wells and Wells Acrobat team, and the Black Patti Musical Comedy Company. Cheap theaters competed for patronage by staging these acts as well as local contests (such as fancy dress cakewalks and bowling), roller skating, and merry-go-rounds. The Majestic Theatre, Famous Theatre, Gayoso Amusement Company, Afro-American Elec-tric Theatre and others all aimed to please those who were looking for a pleasant place to spend an evening enjoying "wholesome" entertain-ment in a safe setting.[44] An advertisement for the Afro-American Elec-tric Theatre, for example, emphasized "first-class, clean, and instructive entertainment." And it noted: "any lady or child can attend . . . with the satisfaction of knowing that nothing unclean will be seen or heard" in a facility on a par with the best white theaters.[45] Claiming to have the endorsements of "leading colored men" or "pulpit and press," theater owners tried to bolster the reputation of their venues. The language of the advertisements emphasizing middle-class respectability helped to create the sensation of upward mobility for family audiences that were in reality largely working-class. Playing on the fluctuating line between "us" and "them" in the debate about "wholesome" and "hurtful" amusements, these ads promised "first-class" entertainment on a wage-earner's budget. These popular amusements provided escapes from the everyday social order; normal rules were suspended, and fantasies could be realized for brief moments without the stigma of being sordid.[46]

Cheap theaters faced their strongest competition from the rising popularity of motion picture shows after 1905. Many theaters, however, were flexible and adapted to new consumer demands. At the Gayoso Theatre one could find a variety of live theater acts as well as movies like *James Boys in Missouri*, *The Cat Came Back*, and *Sherlock Holmes as a Woman Spy*, which changed every twenty minutes; these were all white-produced films until "race" cinema took off in the 1920s. Some theaters showed silent film exclusively. These included the Washington Theatre, which advertised new movies and a live orchestra accompanying them, and the Princess Theater, which premiered shows not seen in other black venues.[47] The demand for movies was sufficient to gross one thousand dollars in receipts per theater per week; at the rate of five to ten cents per show, every African American in the city could have attended at least once in a two-week period. Movies attracted a broad audience because they were suitable for all ages and were relatively short in duration.[48]

The appeal to black spectators, however, was not just the films themselves, but the simultaneous blending of many cultural idioms. "Silent" movies were often accompanied by live music, usually a piano. Musicians cued their own compositions to the images and narrative of the films. Though movies were intended to be the main attraction, musicians often improvised beyond the dictates of the story line to foreground their instruments. The mimetic power of black music was reinforced as the performer, audience, music, and visual art meshed. Audiences were often transformed from passive consumers to active performers as the rhythms of ragtime and blues music evoked visceral responses to the visual images and dramatic enactments zooming across the big screen.[49]

Many black Southerners had left the countryside and migrated to urban areas like Atlanta, in part, to find new opportunities for social diversions as well as work. African Americans wanted to have the option of attending and participating in public entertainments that were not offered in black theaters. But theaters designed for whites either excluded blacks altogether or offered second-class seating for first-class prices. Jim Crow theater practices forced blacks to enter through dark alleyways and back doors and to settle for seating variously derided as the "buzzard roost," "peanut gallery," or "nigger heaven."

Some African Americans refused to patronize segregated theaters and chastised others who did not do likewise. E. B. Barco, a newspaper columnist, kept close tabs on individuals who attended Jim Crow theaters and threatened to expose them publicly. A "true" lady or gentleman would not tolerate such inequitable conditions, he argued. But he reserved his most unrelenting criticism for women: "If the Negro women will just stay in their places, it will be an easy matter to control the men, and soon or late we will have an opera house which you can go [to] and not be molested nor criticized."[50] Attending segregated theaters did not necessarily mean passive submission, however. African Americans who watched Thomas Dixon's racist dramatic production *The Clansmen* in 1905, which was later adapted as a film, the infamous *Birth of a Nation,* laughed in places unanticipated and unappreciated by the writer. They also hissed and taunted in opposition to racist responses from white theatergoers, and threw soda bottles down on whites seated below.[51]

Despite Jim Crow, the period before 1920 was perhaps rare in theater history in the opportunities available for all-black audiences to enjoy productions by black writers, artists, producers, and composers.[52] African-American audiences in Atlanta were not only beneficiaries of these enriching experiences, they helped to shape them. The genius of Bessie Smith, Thomas Dorsey, Perry Bradford, and the Whitman Sisters was not just their individual talent, but also their ability to capture and transform vernacular idioms, using minstrelsy and then vaudeville as vehicles for the cross-fertilization of old and new cultural forms. In turn, they learned from the responses of black audiences, which inspired them to greater bursts of creativity in new song and dance numbers.

WHEN blacks in Atlanta entered amusement establishments they sought, and to a large degree achieved, respite from the trials and tribulations of their workaday lives, yet they traversed a terrain as hotly contested as wage labor or electoral politics. The proximity of legal entertainment and the underground world of vice in the era of prohibition and social purity crusades exacerbated tensions over physical pleasures and indulgences. The red-light districts in Atlanta were the crossroads for the intersection of these two worlds, and it was here that a subterranean nightlife originated and fostered opposition to the demands and values of the dominant culture.

While white pimps such as George Jones, Pretty-boy Redmond, and Fashion-plate Charley held sway over the illicit trade on Courtland Street, black gangsters such as Joe Slocum, Lucky Sambo, and Handsome Harry controlled the sporting action and barrooms on Decatur Street. Rowdiness, violence, and gangsterism were common occurrences. As Perry Bradford recalled from his childhood: "It was a tame Saturday night in the notorious Decatur Street section if there were only six razor operations performed, or if only four persons were found in the morgue on Sunday morning."[53]

Decatur Street's reputation for colorful characters, violence, and illicit sex led moral reformers to confront the sinful and extend "the right hand of fellowship" to wayward souls. One group of women organized open-air religious meetings at the height of merrymaking on Saturday nights "to bring the frequenters of that thoroughfare to a higher moral plane."[54] But despite its notoriety, Decatur Street patrons were typically not the larger-than-life pimps or mobsters but ordinary women and men in search of social diversions and alternative financial prospects denied to them elsewhere in their lives.

The saloon, in its multiple guises, was one of the most common and most controversial sites where these expectations were met. The emergence of industrial capitalism in the late nineteenth century stimulated the popularity of the saloon as a distinctly class-based institution. Mechanized labor, tighter work discipline, shorter workdays, relatively higher wages, and intensified regulation of public recreation were all factors that led workers to drink in saloons.[55] Though saloons were dominated by men, women visited them as well. Some workers went to saloons and clubs after work in the evenings. Others who were unemployed because of the seasonal nature of many jobs patronized the bars during the day as well. Still others took time off from jobs that offered no vacations.

Drinking was not the only appeal of saloons in Atlanta, nor was it necessarily the main attraction. Prostitution and gambling also thrived in the tenderloin bars. The blues and ragtime melodies, played by pianists like Thomas Dorsey, brought in patrons to listen and dance. As Dorsey described the music and the atmosphere, it was a "lowdown type music, they put any kind of words to it they wanted . . . In these places, they'd shine out with anything, say 'Yeah!', you know, so I think that's why they called it barrelhouse, you'd go down to where they'd opened a keg, and you'd hear anything, did anything, you could get arrested."[56] It was precisely the "doing anything" that disturbed city officials, who decided that the music was as much of an "improper" stimulus as alcoholic drinks.[57]

Drinking was a pastime widely enjoyed and a habit difficult to break; as Spelman College students discovered in the 1890s in their proselytizing missions across the state, wage-earners were not easily persuaded to give up drinking or other "hurtful" amusements.[58] Though religious faith and biblical teachings had the strongest influence in deterring the use of alcohol, devout Christians did not necessarily think of drinking per se as evil. Still, not all working-class people chose to indulge, since drinking created or exacerbated family stress and diverted hard-earned wages away from family coffers toward fleeting gratification.[59] Temperance societies, sponsored by the American Missionary Association, were popular among black working-class people shortly after the Civil War in Atlanta. Under the banner of the "Lincoln Brigades," the "Bands of Hope," and the "Morning Stars," freedpeople dedicated themselves to abstaining from liquor, tobacco, and swearing. Woman's Christian Temperance Union branches, such as the Sojourners of Truth, were active in the early twentieth century and picked up where the early leagues left off. Some secret societies also enforced morality rules among their members that prohibited drinking and other vices. Bettie Dacus was expelled from the Household of Ruth, for example, after it was discovered and verified by official records that she had been arrested, fined, and jailed for "disorderly and immoral conduct."[60]

Middle-class reformers and city officials led the most intense campaign against alcohol and sounded the loudest alarm against the heterogeneity of drinking crowds. "White men and black men, white women and black women, and even children, are now seen at the bars of the beer saloons, drinking together," one source reported. The city tried to prevent this intermingling across color and gender lines by requiring "near beer" saloons to designate one race of customers exclusively and to prohibit women altogether.[61] Working-class blacks and whites defied the law in saloons and "dago bar joints," which led many whites, and some blacks, to fear the violence—or, what was more troubling, the affection—that could develop between these two groups. Rumors of an interracial crime ring operating on Decatur Street in the 1910s made these fears palpable.[62] But even when segregation was adhered to, many of the saloons designated as "colored only" were owned and managed by whites. At times, a semblance of "social equality" prevailed between the white owners and the black customers: "Some of the saloon men allow the negroes to curse them, applying the vilest epithets, while they in turn call the negroes 'mister' and speak of them as gentlemen," one source reported. On the other hand, some white saloon owners, in the spirit of Jim Crow, charged their black customers inflated prices for diluted drinks.[63]

The electorate in Atlanta debated the pros and cons of public drinking in highly visible political campaigns beginning in the 1880s. Voters flip-flopped from one election to the next, variously passing and rejecting prohibition, with blacks carrying critical swing votes. Prior to 1908, when prohibition against the manufacture and selling of alcohol was enacted throughout the state, the city made efforts to regulate the liquor trade through licensing saloonkeepers, restricting their hours of operation, and barring women and children. Alcohol was a substance that could not be easily regulated through the law, however.[64] After 1908, suppliers from Chattanooga, Tennessee, and Jacksonville, Florida, regularly delivered gallons of bootleg whiskey and beer to barrooms and residences. Saloonkeepers resorted to a quasi-legal selling of "near beer." In reality, critics argued, "near beer" was a clever euphemism for the real thing and was more widely available than undisguised alcoholic beverages prior to prohibition. "Near beer" could be bought at some soda-fountain stands, and since it was presumably a nonintoxicating substance, it was difficult for city officials to justify special regulations or taxes on it.[65]

Despite the interracial character of saloon customers, police officers disproportionately targeted African Americans in their raids and arrests. The Atlanta riot of 1906 was ample demonstration of the sinister power of racial paranoia that fantasized a biological disposition for inebriation based on race. The Georgia Anti-Saloon League alluded to memories of the riot in its campaign against "near beer" saloons.[66] These attitudes led to simultaneous raids throughout the city to empty black bars, poolrooms, and other such places of "idlers" and "vagrants."[67]

The victims of barroom raids were predominantly men, which reflected the fact that the saloons attracted a mostly male clientele drawn to other by-products of the saloon, such as gambling and prostitution. The coupling of sex and drinking was not merely coincidental to the disproportionate number of attacks on black men in particular. White fears of black male sexuality running rampant under the influence of alcohol and leading to attacks upon white women were exacerbated by the casual attitudes toward racial etiquette shown on Decatur Street.

Black women were also the target of complaints, however; they were criticized for violating both prohibitions against consuming intoxicating drinks and gender restrictions.[68] And though black women were arrested less frequently than black men, they were picked up, far more than white women, for drinking, gambling, using or selling cocaine, and running "blind tigers" of their own.[69]

The moral implications of women consuming intoxicating substances troubled many middle-class blacks and whites. Women not only evaded laws prohibiting them from entering saloons, they frequented bar room "annexes," they drank alcohol in alleys and streets, and they sold beer from their homes. Jackson McHenry, one of the leaders in the prohibition campaign during the 1880s, complained to city officials in 1904 about women evading anti-liquor edicts. Some restaurants were simply charades for "women bars" designed expressly to cater to women of all ages who were carousing all day and late at night "when they ought to be at work," he argued.[70] As McHenry urged the "better element" among Negroes to fight against the "women bars" and close them up, an avowed Christian joined the chorus of alarm against the downfall of the women of the race who frequented Decatur Street: "Just see them with glasses and quarts of beer! Hear the language that they use! See them almost beastly drunk! It is a shame. It is a disgrace to the race. It is a scandal on moral and civil men."[71] Various groups of preachers and "colored citizens" petitioned the city council before and after prohibition to "break up places where women congregate and drink."[72]

   The outrage expressed against women who drank was part of a larger discourse on the virtues of subordinate women in an urban setting. The sheer number of black women in cities like Atlanta magnified their visibility on the street and reinforced the perception that they were out of control—beyond the grip of black men as well as white authorities. Women's behavior became a trope for the race, their public deportment and carriage the basis by which some assumed the entire race would be judged. The journalist E. B. Barco was among the most consistent critics of female indulgence in a variety of urban amusements. His descriptions of women strolling the streets in the red-light district evoked images of seasoned sexual predators and pubescent hormones run amok: this "class," he wrote, "can be seen prowling around on the streets seemingly seeking whom they may or can devour, instead of being in their homes, helping their poor mothers to earn bread." Barco explained their delinquency as a racial deficiency: "Self pride in white women is natural instinct, but in the great majority of negro women self pride is much needed." His solution was disciplinary and blunt: "Let the city authorities enact an ordinance forcing this class of women off the streets after a certain hour, or lock them up."[73]

   WORKING-CLASS women and men largely refused to abide by the simplistic polarities between "wholesome" and "hurtful" amusements. Although women like Alice Adams and Mary Morton displayed some ambivalence about reconciling parental admonitions with youthful curiosity, they ultimately found respite in a wide range of recreational activities in small, private circles in their homes and neighborhoods and also in mass, popular events in the burgeoning red-light district. The division between decency and indecency that dominated the middle-class discourse on leisure reflected the tenor of debate throughout urban America as popular culture modernized. But the anxieties manifest everywhere about crowds of strangers indiscriminately engaging in festive social intercourse were magnified in the Jim Crow South, where whiteness was literally reinscribed through play— in grandiose landscaped gardens, mechanical amusement parks, shopping promenades, and in the theaters on stage and off. Decatur Street, the richest and most contested terrain, staunchly upheld the color line and at the same time openly defied it. Consumers, performers, and small entrepreneurs were multiracial and often engaged in interracial social, cultural, and material transactions. But middle-class reformers refused to abandon the sights, sounds, and visceral experiences of revelry to the whims of consumer preferences and demands.[74] The irony of this situation was that playing was hard work for everyone—for the officials and reformers, who worked hard to control, contain, and impose order on leisure time and space, and for working-class people, who worked hard at having fun.[75]

CHAPTER EIGHT

"Dancing and Carousing the Night Away"

ighttime leisure on Atlanta's Decatur Street was incomplete without a stop in the popular dance halls. Domestic workers were conspicuous among the dedicated dancers in the city who sought pleasure in the "jook joints"—night clubs devoted to dance and music. They contributed to the moment in American history in the 1910s when urban America "danced like mad." But public dance halls were among the most controversial popular amusement sites; they were often associated with crime, drinking, and illicit sex. When Lugenia Burns Hope and Henry Hugh Proctor constructed "wholesome" recreational programs to compete with Decatur Street entertainment, they singled out public dancing as the most egregious activity contributing to the moral decay of the black race. White reformers and city officials were also strong critics of public dancing and dance halls. The contests that ensued between the opponents of public dancing and the resilient devotees reveal broader tensions and anxieties about race, class, and sexuality.

A central issue at stake was control over black women's and men's bodies. Employers insisted it was their prerogative to limit the physical exertions of black women's bodies to domestic service. Black middle-class reformers tried to mollify white animosity and racial prejudice, especially in the post-riot era, by insisting that blacks conform to the standards of a chaste, disciplined, servile labor force—on and off the job. African-American wage-earners, however, asserted their own right to recuperate their bodies from exploitation. Their defiance exhibited more than creative release. The substance, style, and form of black vernacular dancing were profound expressions of a cultural aesthetic grounded in an emerging musical form, the blues.

The blues represented the music of post-slavery generations that bore the signs of a historical consciousness, as seen in its borrowings from plebeian art forms such as work songs, spirituals, and field hollers, and in its use of such traditional African-American devices as polyrhythm, falsetto, improvisation, and call and response. The blues also reflected the changing conditions of black life in its marked departure from the past. The centrality of the singer's individual persona, the highly personalized subject matter of songs, the thematic shifts toward the material world and the pursuit of pleasure were all characteristic of an emergent modern ethos. The philosophical underpinnings of the blues informed and reflected broader African-American working-class self-understandings in the modern world. This is revealed most poignantly in the ongoing battles over dancing.

THE POPULARITY and controversy of black dance have a long history. Slaves incorporated dance into their everyday lives to diminish the harsh realities of forced labor. They turned events like corn-shuckings into festive occasions, performing dances that mimicked their routine labor activities such as pitching hay, hoisting cotton bales, and hoeing corn. They also danced for pleasure on Saturdays and holidays and to express sadness in funeral rituals. Slaveholders tolerated dancing, and even enjoyed watching it, as long as it pacified bound labor, enhanced morale, and stayed within the boundaries of acceptable behavior. But dancing sometimes threatened the social order, as when slaves ridiculed masters through song lyrics and dance movement, when slaves defied orders by organizing clandestine dances, or when group solidarity was transformed into insurrections.[1]

Following emancipation, dancing continued to be an important expression of black culture and a source of conflict with white authorities. In the 1870s, African Americans in Atlanta danced in public places near the railroad depot downtown, in halls, bars, and in the privacy of their homes, much to the chagrin of the police. By the 1890s, public officials called for "Negro dance halls" to be outlawed because they were "crime breeders and a disgrace to the city."[2] The ties between drinking, dancing, and the sex trade led moral reformers throughout urban America to advocate regulations or prohibitions against public dance halls as eager working-class patrons flocked to them in droves.

Though there were critics who continued to point out the links between vice and public dance, other reformers sought to grant dance a new sense of respectability and legitimacy at the turn of the century. Although public dance halls of the past had been considered the domain of men and female prostitutes, modern dance halls permitted more social mingling between men and women of good repute. The growing acceptance of heterosexual socializing was also evident in changing attitudes about proper dance etiquette. Previously, dancing had stayed within strict boundaries of patterned movements, disciplined gestures, and formal distance to minimize the possibility of intimacy. In the early 1900s, however, dancing became more inventive, less rigid in style and bodily movement, and encouraged lingering physical contact.[3] Black migration to urban areas (and white "slumming") played a large role in contributing to the sudden popularity of dance in the dominant society in the 1910s and transformed social dancing itself.

The battles heated up between dancers and public officials in Atlanta in 1903 when the City Council imposed an exorbitant tax on black dance halls to force them out of business. But when proprietors and patrons circumvented the $200 assessment fee and kept dancing alive, the council moved to abolish these establishments that it blamed for producing a "carnival of crime." Dancing and dance halls continued unabated as the moral preachments of the elites fell on deaf ears among the black majority. Henry Hugh Proctor and other members of the black elite were among the most vocal critics of dancing and dance halls. They were supported by white ministers and businessmen. Working-class people themselves were rarely granted public platforms to air their opinions, but the lack of extant records that bear their oral or written testimony is compensated for in part by evidence of their vigorous efforts to sustain dancing in defiance of middle-class edicts. No laws, no taxes could stop their dancing; when necessary, they moved their quarters into the woods on the outskirts of the city to evade detection.[4] Controversies over dance during this period reveal the power of dancing as a cultural form and the way it embodied (literally and figuratively) racial, class, and sexual tensions in the urban South.

D OMESTIC laborers and others escaped from their workaday worries through dance in "jook joints" and settings also referred to as "dives." These were among the most important (re)creative sites of black working-class amusements at the turn of the century, where old and new cultural forms, exhibiting both African and European influences, were syncretized. The music and the movements invented there became cultural wares that traveled back and forth via migrants and itinerant entertainers moving from country to town to city and from South to North, forming common ties with people of African descent all over the nation.[5]

"The 'dive' is their evening mecca when they have a few dimes to spend and wish to dance and frolic and give themselves up to hours of uncontrolled pleasure and sport," one source reported.[6] These were places usually located in the basements of storefronts on Decatur, Peters, and Harris Streets. Some dance halls continued to share quarters with saloons, though they were mostly makeshift rooms devoted primarily to music and dance. As Thomas Dorsey said about the dance joints he frequented as a pianist, "Blues would sound better late at night when the lights were low, so low you couldn't recognize a person ten feet away, when the smoke was so thick you could put a hand full of it into your pocket." He described the characteristic odors that lingered in the air as "tired sweat, bootleg booze, Piedmont cigarettes, and Hoyettes Cologne."[7] Dorsey would play, improvising as he went along, for hours on end as the dancers moved gracefully to his music. He prided himself on his ability to play soft but perceptible sounds, in order to keep the police away. But the heat in Atlanta, especially during the summer, would often require windows to be opened, which meant that sounds could be heard on the streets.[8]

The dance halls where Dorsey played were autonomous places, where the patrons refused to be subjected to any rules but their own. Other dance halls were more regulated, however. These establishments often existed with the forbearance of police officers, who tolerated them in exchange for proprietors' cooperation in occasional roundups of wanted criminals. Henry Beattie, a white owner, ran one such dance hall on Decatur Street like an ironfisted "czar" in the early 1900s. He commenced the dancing early in the evening and stopped at 11:00 P.M. sharp. Though the music was continuous, a floor manager, with a billy club in hand to keep order, directed patrons to the floor with the ringing of a bell and collected a nickel per couple for each set. Prior to prohibition, as the couples danced they smoked and drank beer. But Beattie refused to let his patrons drink excessively. He would seize "a person who is over tipsy and shove him from the room and bid him be gone." If a fight broke out, he would lock the doors to hold the culprits hostage until the police could come in and arrest them.[9]

As working-class women and men danced the night away in dark, dingy, public, and, sometimes, shady places, the black elite danced to a different beat in more immaculate surroundings, demonstrating the class privileges they openly embraced. Their gala, private, and formal affairs purposely rejected the African influences conspicuous in the "snake hips" and "buzzard lope" in favor of more European-inspired polkas, waltzes, quadrilles, and pinafore lancers.[10] A white journalist in the conventional mocking tone used to deride the "pompous ethics" of the black bourgeoisie described these elite dances as events where "etiquette and decorum are painfully emphatic . . . [and] a grotesque exaggeration of politeness, and affectation [run] riot."[11] In less burlesque fashion, Perry Bradford recalled well-to-do black Atlantans doing set-dancing. As a youth, around 1905, he had attended dancing school on Wednesday afternoons. For ten cents he received lessons in Euro-American dance and a glass of lemonade.[12] This is not to say, however, that the black elite blindly aped white culture. Despite their statements to the contrary, black elites often incorporated distinctive African-American elements in their dancing, giving novel twists to quadrilles and polkas with improvised breaks, solos, and varied tempos.[13]

It was not dancing per se that the black elites rejected; rather, as their own balls indicated, they disdained dancing of a certain type: they criticized the physical surroundings and social atmosphere of public dance halls, and they condemned the character of working-class body language. In 1905, Proctor distinguished between the virtues of private dance and the sins of public dance. He argued: "A public dance hall [is a place] where anyone may go in and take part for a price," whereas private dancing took place among invited guests who were "socially responsible." The public dance hall was "a stumbling block to the weak and the immature of both sexes," he added; "such a place becomes a center of evil influences, and is a vestibule to the house of shame."[14]

Leaders of the Odd Fellows fraternal order also criticized dance halls. In 1915 they stated: "A dance hall is defined or understood to be a place frequented by the lower classes of people, where they dance all kinds of vulgar motions and expressions for the purpose of arousing that which is animal in the man." The litany of pejoratives continued, associating dance halls with "thugs" and "bums." These were places where women "dance and prance for pay," drinks, and for the entertainment of men, they argued. Ironically, the Odd Fellows were defending their own Roof Garden establishment from attacks by Proctor. The Roof Garden, which provided entertainment that included live music and dancing, opened with much fanfare and controversy in 1915. The Odd Fellows tried to exclude their unsullied facility from the taint of other popular dance halls.[15]

For middle-class blacks throughout the South dedicated to racial uplift, dance halls presented some of their greatest challenges to instilling the virtues that would lead the masses out of the spiral of so-called degradation. Proctor and other elite blacks summed up their position in a petition to the City Council in 1905 in which they denied their support of dance halls: "We resent the statement that there is a demand on the part of the better element of our people for those places." Stating their class biases more bluntly, they added: "The better element does not want them, and the worst element should not be permitted to have them."[16] The self-described elites persistently framed their pejorative descriptions of dancing and dance halls in the language of class. They disparaged people who made scanty livings through wage work as they sought to construct their own identity above the common fray. How one moved one's body constituted one's rank in society.

But despite this evidence of class-based attitudes and social institutions in Atlanta, there is also evidence of cross-over efforts in both directions. Perry Bradford grew up in a working-class family and neighborhoods, yet he gained access to some aspects of bourgeois culture, probably through his high school education at Atlanta University.[17] The dance schools reinforced the view that middle-class status was not hermetically sealed. One could aspire to its stature and achieve its privileges, in part, through proper training and education in the rules of correct bodily carriage.

Despite the rhetoric of race uplift that made insistent criticisms of dance halls patronized by the masses, many middle-class blacks, whether clandestinely or openly, enjoyed working-class amusements. The Whitman Sisters, for example, grew up in a privileged middle-class family, yet they dedicated their careers to entertaining the masses and borrowed liberally from the culture of working-class people, especially in their dances. The mixing across classes was noticeable on Decatur Street in places such as the Eighty One Theater.[18] African-American vernacular dance was nothing if not infectious—an element that worried some members of the elite. As one sociologist stated bluntly, the "anti-social" form of dance that originated among the "lower" class was dangerous because it could "spread upwards into and engross the so-called higher classes." The bulwarks of class stratification, in this estimation, were insufficient to protect the elite from contamination by the masses.[19]

The seamy reputation of Decatur Street in general and the close proximity of legal and illegal merriment were undoubtedly factors that tainted the reputation of dance halls in the minds of the most vocal members of the black elite. For the patrons of some dance halls, dancing was not the main attraction. The combination of gambling, alcoholic drinks, and excited bodies moving in time to the music was intoxicating, and sometimes the misunderstandings that could occur in festive crowds on any occasion would lead to petty skirmishes or mushroom into spirited melees.[20] Police records in Atlanta are replete with examples of lively partying gone awry, and fights that included women domestic workers were commonplace. Pinkie Chandler, for example, was injured by a beer glass thrown in her face by Helen Henry when she accidentally brushed up against Henry's partner while dancing; Delia Mitchell created trouble when she tried to squeeze onto an already crowded dance floor and another woman pushed her out of the way. The action outside the dance halls could generate a theater of its own as couples necked or said their farewells and youths gathered for the last brouhaha. Light-hearted fraternizing on the way home could turn sour as well, embroiling women in fights with each other or with men. Emma Pitts jumped through the window of a streetcar after leaving a dance hall and was arrested with two other women for disorderly conduct.[21] Fun and reprieve from hard work may have awaited working-class women and men in dance halls and on the streets, but not without a price; the police made few distinctions in culpability in their indiscriminate raids on "jook joints" and often subjected people to harsh punishments for alleged petty crimes.[22]

BLACK vernacular dance also generated controversy because of its distinctive physical characteristics, which challenged Euro-American conceptions of proper bodily etiquette. African-American dance emphasized the movement of body parts, often asymmetrically and independent of one another, whereas Euro-American dance demanded rigidity to mitigate its amorous implications. Black dance generally exploded outward from the hips; it was performed from a crouching position with the knees flexed and the body bent at the waist, which allowed a fluidity of movement in a propulsive rhythmic fashion. The facial gestures, clapping, shouting, and yelling of provocative phrases reinforced the sense of the dancer's glee. A woman might shout, for example, "C'mon Papa grab me!" as she danced.

It was these characteristics that the black elite found most objectionable. "In the name of Anglo-Saxon civilization," Proctor had urged in 1903, "remove these things that are ruining the character of our young men and stealing away the virtue of our young women."[23] Proctor's condemnation, though based on narrow cultural standards, recognized the sexual connotations that permeated black working-class dance. The sultry settings, dimmed lights, and prolonged musical renditions invited intimacy as couples swayed together. The "slow drag," one of the most popular dances in the 1910s, was described by one observer this way: "couples would hang onto each other and just grind back and forth in one spot all night." The Itch was described as "a spasmodic placing of the hands all over the body in an agony of perfect rhythm." The Fish Tail put the emphasis on the rear end, as the name suggested; the "buttocks weave out, back, and up in a variety of figure eights." The names of other dances had erotic overtones as well: the Grind, Mooche, Shimmy, Fanny Bump, Ballin' the Jack, and the Funky Butt. Skirt lifting, body caressing, and thrusting pelvic movements all conveyed amorous messages that offended moral reformers.[24]

Vernacular dance assumed these characteristics in large part from the inspiration of the music, reflecting the fact that in black culture, music and dance were virtually inseparable. African-American music is an engaging social practice where audience and performers are expected to respond to one another with oral and physical gestures. The complex rhythmic patterns of voice and instruments prompt the desire to mimic the emotions they evoke through bodily movement such as foot stomping, hand clapping, and leaping around. African-American music acknowledges the power of the body to be moved.[25]

The music that couples enjoyed in the dance halls was varied and fluid, typically characterized as ragtime or "lowdown" blues, performed live before the advent of records and the radio. The blues, which arose toward the end of the nineteenth century, grew to maturity in dance halls, rent parties, and vaudeville theaters and became more formalized in the 1910s and 1920s. In some clubs, the blues were generated by a pianist, a fiddler, or by one or more individuals "patting juba"—a practice dating back to slavery that involved clapping hands, snapping fingers, and patting limbs and armpits rhythmically. In other instances, a piano was the sole instrument driving the rhythmic beat. The dancers themselves would shout and yell as they moved.[26]

The blues and popular dance reflected a new aesthetic that was beginning to emerge in black cultural life. Like its ancestors, the blues inspired active movement rather than passive reception, and dance provided the mechanism for the audience to engage the performer in a ritual communal ceremony. Despite the connotations of its name, the blues was "good-time" music that generated a positive rhythmic impulse to divert and drive away depression and resignation among workers whose everyday lives were filled with adversity. The blues served as the call and dance as the response in a symbiotic performance in which ecstatic bodily movements mocked the lyrics and instrumentation that signified pain and lamentation.[27]

The close relationship between the blues and dance was especially evident in Atlanta, where musicians and vernacular dancers had a long-lasting influence on both art forms. "Didn't no dance go on without the blues," Dorsey recalled.[28] This close association was further reinforced by songs that originated in the city with lyrics describing particular steps. Perry Bradford composed tunes with detailed dance instructions, such as "Ballin' the Jack" and "the Original Black Bottom Dance."[29]

This close link between the blues and dance was disconcerting to middle-class and religious people as African Americans renegotiated the relationship between sacred and secular culture. The latter assumed a larger significance as blacks faced the exigencies of a new material, modern, industrial world. The tensions that resulted were most pronounced in the evolution of music and dance and their relationship to religion and the church. The shared pedigree of sacred and secular music and dance complicated matters for the pious, who emphasized the differences between shouting for the Lord and shouting for the Devil. The similarities in the ritual, cathartic, communal, and expressive purposes of secular and sacred music and dance threatened the province once occupied primarily by religion in African-American life. For middle-class Christians like Proctor, this close resemblance between raucous secular dancing and ecstatic religious worship made the former doubly objectionable. The most elite black religious denominations and individual churches consciously sought to divorce themselves from traditional styles of worship, preaching, and singing that were considered "heathen" or reminiscent of Africa and the plantation South.[30]

Dancing was ubiquitous in Atlanta throughout the black neighborhoods, in dance halls, picnics, house parties, and "in the churches, most of all," stated Bradford. "Every prayer meeting of the African Methodist Church ends in a sort of Black Bottom circle dance, with the dancers clapping their hands and crooning, and the preachers calling the steps," he explained further.[31] The circle dance Bradford described was probably very similar to the "ring shout." Dancers formed a circle and shuffled in a counterclockwise direction; they swung their bodies, clapped their hands, and shouted for joy as they became possessed with the Holy Ghost.[32] Some of the most fervent practitioners of the ring shout in Atlanta were members of the Sanctified Churches, derisively called the "Holy Rollers." They were held in nearly as much contempt by middle-class critics as the devotees of secular dance in the "dives." Neighbors and businesses in the vicinity of storefront houses of worship would call the police to arrest the "Holy Rollers" for disorderly conduct and disturbing the peace. The Neighborhood Union helped to remove a group from one area, after circulating a petition.[33]

When hauled into court, the Holy Rollers became spectacles, either through involuntary enactments of their religious fervor or through demonstrations requested by judges. White observers remarked on their failure to comprehend the difference between these sacred shouts and profane gestures such as those used in the "buck dance." Though ignorant of the complex cultural meaning of the "ring shout," these critics were aware of the shifting connotations of black dance, which differed more by its social context than its physical movements. The sacred shout, as musical sound and bodily movement, was indeed a variation of the "lowdown" blues that filled the airwaves of the night clubs and dance halls.[34]

The masses of black worshippers who continued to practice ecstatic religious expression disagreed with middle-class criticisms, though they opposed the sacrilegious uses of dance and music. Black worshippers objected less to the percussive beat of the music and the paroxysmic movements of vernacular dancers, which generated merriment and exhilaration, and more to the fact that secular performances paid homage to the Devil rather than to the Holy Ghost.

Reconciling worldly pleasure and spiritual reverence, however, was not always as simple as choosing right over wrong, or God over the Devil, even for devout church people. In 1916, delegates at the annual Georgia Conference of the AME Church railed against the evils of the card table, the theater, and the modern dance.[35] Yet individuals who engaged in popular amusements on Saturday night were among those who attended church on Sunday morning. Even as the gap between the sacred and the secular widened, the boundaries between these domains remained permeable and fluid. Despite the pronouncements by the AME Church, local congregants in Atlanta openly embraced popular amusements even in church sanctuaries. Henry McNeal Turner, himself an AME bishop, hosted vaudeville and minstrel shows in his well-regarded Tabernacle. Several other churches from various denominations followed suit.[36] Even Proctor's church sponsored an annual secular music festival, though it clearly intended Negro jubilee and European classical music to provide a moral alternative to those "places in this city that tend to drag down the colored servant."[37]

The masses of black women and men embraced dancing because it met needs not completely satisfied by the church or other institutions; it countered the debilitating impact of wage labor. As free people, African Americans could pursue entertainment at will—an important distinction from slavery, in which masters largely, though not entirely, controlled and orchestrated both work and leisure. In the unregulated and secluded "jook joints," and even in regulated dance halls such as Beattie's "dive," blacks could reclaim their bodies from appropriation as instruments of physical toil and redirect their energies toward other diversions.[38]

BLACK women domestic workers were singled out in these attacks against dancing in public halls. The black bourgeoisie lamented the shame and disgrace that befell the entire race when workers failed to live up to the highest expectations of dutiful service. White employers opposed the violation of what they considered their rightful claim to restrict black women's exertions to manual work. Dance halls were a menace, declared Proctor, because "the servant class tried to work all day and dance all night."[39] He warned employers that household laborers would not perform well if they used their leisure unproductively— dancing instead of resting in preparation for the next day of work.[40] Not missing the lesson of subservience proposed in Proctor's counsel, the white newspaper seized the opportunity to offer a reform: "Let the dance halls and places of low resort for the negro give way to schools for the domestic training of the race—schools for cooking and housework." It continued, "instead of dancing and carousing the night away, he (and especially she) will learn to become proficient in the task [for which] he is employed."[41]

White employers also objected to dancing by black domestic workers because they feared that the dance halls bred social contagions that would infect their homes. Some child-nurses were accused of sneaking into the "dives" with white children during the day, exposing the little ones to immorality and vice.[42] According to one clergyman: "The servants of the white people of the city were enticed into [dance halls] and corrupted by them. So the white people of the city were also affected by their presence."[43] It was believed that dancing encouraged sexual promiscuity among black women, who would then taint the white households through their illicit activity. The sexual connotations of black dance exacerbated these anxieties about women's behavior among the black and white middle classes.

Anthony Binga, a black minister in Virginia, wrote a detailed treatise against dancing and other urban vices. He criticized the "unholy passions" provoked by dancing and the aggressive behavior of women: "Look at the young girl or some one's wife borne around the room in the arms of a man; his arms are drawn around her waist; her swelling bosom rests against his; her limbs are tangled with his; her head rests against his face; her bare neck reflecting the soft mellow light of the chandelier, while the passions are raging like a furnace of fire." Women, he noted, were careless and carefree in their dancing and choice of dance partners. "But who is the individual with whom she is brought into such close contact? She does not know; neither does she care. The most she cares to know just now is that he is a graceful dancer."[44]

This image of women as socially dangerous and capable of arousing men's passions for evil purposes has a long legacy dating back to Adam and Eve. The particular association of black women dancing and illicit sex is evident in European perceptions of Africans and their descendants in the Americas dating back centuries.[45] Binga believed that women's corrupting power as demonstrated on the dance floor required measures to suppress and contain it, or society would face the consequence of mayhem. His critique of unrestrained female sexuality in the dance halls may have been encouraged by the perception that certain dances, with erotic overtones, were feminine and performed mostly by women. The "shake" and the "shimmy," also referred to as the "shimmy-she-wobble," were dances that were associated with women.[46] These were dances that may have been transformed from solo to couple dances, however, with their eroticism intact. Another version of the "shimmy" was depicted as very similar to the "slow drag." As Thomas Dorsey described it: "You couldn't do no shimmy alone, by yourself. They danced all night. You look around and nobody be moving. They'd just be shimmying."[47]

Ironically, the castigating remarks made by middle-class blacks and whites had something in common with the meaning conferred by the working class itself. Both sides understood that dancing interfered with wage work, though clearly from antithetical perspectives. The elite saw dancing as a hindrance to the creation of a chaste, disciplined, submissive, and hard-driving labor force—the hallmarks of the Protestant work ethic. Workers saw it as a respite from the deadening sensation of long hours of poorly compensated labor—critical to the task of claiming one's life as one's own.

Black dance itself embodied a resistance to the confinement of the body solely to wage work. The transformation of physical gestures in black dance from slavery to freedom demonstrates the rejection of wage work as the only outlet for physical exertion. Ex-slaves tended to abandon the references and gestures mimicking labor routines in their dances that they had practiced during slavery (such as "pitchin' hay" or "shuckin' corn") as urban freedom gave more meaning to making a living beyond the needs of subsistence alone. Consumption, entertainment, and personal gratification were also vital to working-class livelihoods and essential to an emergent modern ethos or blues aesthetic.[48]

Though dancing was seen as interfering with wage labor, the connotation of "work" in black culture had multiple meanings. Work not only meant physical labor, it also meant dancing. In addition, it meant engaging in sex. Dancing enabled a momentary escape from wage work, even as dance itself was considered work—of a different order. The ethics of drive, achievement, and perseverance took on a different meaning when removed from the context of wage relations. Dancers put a high value on mastery of technique and style, and they also competed with one another in jest and formal contests in which "working hard" became the criterion of a good performance. The proof could be found in the zeal and agility of body movements or in the perspiration that seeped through one's clothes. James P. Johnson, a pianist, suggested another way: "I saw many actually wear right through a pair of shoes in one night. They danced hard."[49]

The value placed on dancing as hard work resonated in particular with African-American women workers in a society in which the highest valorization of womanhood was largely defined by non-work. The ideal woman did not engage in wage work, and the ideal woman's vocation in the home was not considered work. Leola B. Wilson (Coot Grant) remembered her childhood in Birmingham, Alabama, at the turn of the century. Her aspirations to become an entertainer were nourished by her furtive glimpses through a peephole she drilled in a wall of her father's honky-tonk in order to observe adult entertainment. Wilson's recollections years later demonstrate how black women could reconstruct notions of womanhood through dance. "I remember a tall, powerful woman who worked in the mills pulling coke from a furnace— a man's job," she added. "It was Sue, and she loved men. When Sue arrived at my father's honky-tonk, people would yell: 'Here come Big Sue! Do the Funky Butt, Baby!' As soon as she got high and happy, that's what she'd do, pulling up her skirts and grinding her rear end like an alligator crawling up a bank."[50] Sue worked hard, like a man, during the day, but she shed her industrial pants and worked hard as a woman at night, as she danced in a setting in which femininity was appreciated for its compatibility with work of several different orders.

Further evidence of black women creating an alternative ethos can be seen in their dress. Domestic workers wore uniforms to work, or other plain outfits that signified poverty and low social status. But when they put away the wash tubs or left the kitchen stoves and sinks, they shed the sartorial symbols of servility for garments that reflected personal style and self-worth. This new mode of dressing emerged in the transition from slavery to freedom. In the antebellum era, African-American clothing was designed to be suitable for physical labor or to be reverent for religious worship. But when blacks became free people, their changing status could be seen in their adornment for leisure activities, unhindered by the requirements for either the practicality of work or the appropriate exhibition of piety for church.

As Alice Adams remarked: "I would always go to work neat and clean. But my dress up clothes, I didn't wear 'em to work. Because when I went out I wanted to change and I wanted to look different."[51] For Adams, demarcating the line between work and play was an important part of claiming her dignity, and changing her dress was a clear way to draw that line. Dressing in itself was fun and pleasurable. Willie Mae Cartwright had a very good relationship with a generous, fashionable employer. "She was always awful nice to me, would sell me good clothes cheap and let me use things of hers," Cartwright remembered. "I'd pick out two or three things—rings, pins, ear bobs, or a watch or bracelet—and she'd show me how to match them up pretty. She'd tell me which ones would look good together, and she'd let me wear all that stuff when I was going out and wanting to put on the dog." Unfortunately, Cartwright had an unpleasant encounter with the police as a result. When she walked down the street in her borrowed finery, a police officer stopped her and called her employer to make sure the jewelry was not stolen.[52]

The emphasis on dress was one more reason some critics of public amusements objected to dance halls. The increasing emphasis on conspicuous consumption and personal adornment was seen as immoral. But the particular dress of some women in dance halls provoked the most criticism. As Anthony Binga stated: "The fashionable dress, which is too thin and scantily cut to sleep in—even in a tropical clime—is worn through the cold night air to and from this [dance] room, where the temperature is sometimes in the nineties." He concluded: "The child of vanity will scarcely allow wrapping to touch her body for fear of disarranging her toilette."[53]

No doubt, women were increasingly wearing clothing that was less modest and restrictive than former fashions. But a few rare photographs of black women and men in dance halls show them "dressed up" in clothing typically associated with the middle class. They used this opportunity to construct their own notions of masculinity and femininity. The men donned hats, vests, jackets, and trousers held up by suspenders. The women wore flat-top or wide-brimmed hats, full-length skirts that hugged the hips and flared out at the bottom, blouses with pouter pigeon bodices and sleeves that were puffed out near the shoulders and fitted around the forearms.[54] The women gave careful attention to their dress style from their hairdos down to their underwear—the disclosure of pretty petticoats made of fine linen and crocheted edges was incorporated into certain dances such as the Funky Butt. Moreover, the emphasis and glorification of body parts such as the buttocks subverted dominant standards of beauty.[55] Black women were endlessly caricatured as grotesque and ugly in popular representations in the dominant culture. But in dance halls, black beauty could be highlighted and celebrated. The anthropologist Zora Neale Hurston summed up one alternative criterion of good looks in a color-phobic society: "Even if she were as black as the hinges of hell the question was 'Can she jook?'"[56]

IN SHORT, women participated in a wide variety of leisure endeavors. In particular, they helped to inscribe social dancing as a distinctive, transgressive cultural form. Their transgressions are best understood as an elaborate ethos that informed the ambitions, daily struggles, and consciousness of the black majority—a blues aesthetic. The major underlying principles that informed this aesthetic and that were embodied in vernacular dance were irreverence, transcendence, social realism, self-empowerment, and collective individualism.[57]

The blues and dance were developed with a fierce sense of irreverence—the will to be unencumbered by any artistic, moral, or social obligations, demands, or interests external to the community which blues and dance were created to serve. While the blues and vernacular dance forms borrowed from traditions of both Euro-America and Afro-America, they ultimately paid homage only to their own interpretations. Despite protests by white authorities or black reformers, black workers persisted in their public dancing to "lowdown" music, continually reaffirming the value that they placed on upholding a collective culture.

The feelings of self-empowerment and transcendence emanating from the blues and dance were evident in the power African Americans invested in sound and bodily movement and in the particular ways in which they generated these forces, especially through the use of polyrhythms. In Euro-American music and dance, the basic pulse was dependent on an evenly partitioned beat. In contrast, the dancer and musician in Afro-American culture were challenged to play and move around the beat, to subvert linear notions of time by playing against it. The complex rhythmic structure and driving propulsive action endowed participants with the feeling of metaphysical transcendence, of being able to overcome or alter the obstacles of daily life. If the sung word was more powerful than the spoken or written word, then the danced song was even more mighty than singing alone.[58] It was the symbiotic relationship between music and dance that made their combination a complex and rich cultural form. Workers used them for personal gratification, to reclaim their bodies from drudgery and exploitation, and actually changed, momentarily, their existential condition.

The blues and dance marked a new departure in the assertion of individualism, as well as a redefinition of the conventional Western meaning of that term. Slavery had largely denied this concept among African Americans, but as free people they reclaimed the importance of the self without diminishing the imperatives of the collective. In slavery, blacks were denied ownership of their bodies. In freedom, they reclaimed their right to use their bodies beyond their needs for subsistence alone. But their assertion of their individual rights did not preclude the expression of a collective sensibility. Blues was personal music; dance was a reclamation of one's individual body; yet both allowed and demanded an integral link between the person and the group. Some of the salient characteristics of the blues and of black music and dance in general, such as polyrhythm, improvisation, and antiphony, reinforced this notion of the simultaneity of the individual and the collective—of various elements going their own way, but still being held together by their relationship to each other.[59]

Call and response were generated within the music, as well as executed at the level of performance—the blues was seldom performed without dance, at least not prior to the advent of the radio and records. The mimetic power of the music inspired the gestures of the dancers, and the dancers themselves were like musical instruments—stomping, clapping, shouting, and patting juba. And finally, the blues and dance were striking in their candor and social realism. The dancer, musician, and singer responded to what they saw and experienced in the material world and expressed the horror and the beauty of those feelings in terms uncensored by middle-class decorum and propriety. They openly flaunted and confronted the world of the flesh, of "body-reality," and articulated joy and pain with emotional and kinetic intensity.[60]

The blues aesthetic is the key to understanding why African-American vernacular dance was such a contested terrain in Atlanta and the urban South and how it generated conflict over the black body. As an object of discipline and liberation, the body is a site where a society's ideas about race, class, gender, and sexuality are constructed to give the appearance of being mandates of nature while actually conforming to cultural ideologies. The body is the vehicle through which labor produces wealth, although the powerful usually resist acknowledging and rewarding the centrality of labor in the production of wealth. The importance of laboring bodies in the political economy is revealed, however, in the obsession of employers to repress and contain the autonomy of workers in order to reap the maximum benefits of their exertions. The mere sight of African Americans, especially domestic workers, deriving pleasure and expressing symbolic liberation in dance halls by posing alternative meanings of bodily exertion seemed threatening to employers.[61]

The threat was real, since white employers were denied unmitigated control over black labor. Unlike other commercialized recreation, such as the new amusement parks, where one encountered replicas of industrial life in the mechanized, standardized forms of play, dance halls still allowed for a great deal of creativity, imagination, improvisation, and, thereby, change.[62] Dance halls contained a strong element of impulsiveness and unpredictability, as dancers and musicians inspired one another to enact infinite permutations of gestures and sounds. Reformers' efforts to regulate the dance halls or to introduce tame, patterned movements were designed to counteract the forms of free expression that were difficult to suppress when patrons were left to their own devices.

Yet despite the tirades of incensed critics, dancing did have the effect of renewal and recovery, even if on the workers' own terms. It reinvigorated them for the next day of work and enabled them to persevere. It helped to maintain the social order by providing an outlet for workers to release their tensions, to purge their bodies of their travails on the dance floor. Dancing hard, like laboring hard, was consistent with the work ethic of capitalism. Black working-class dance, like the blues, looked back to vernacular roots and forward to the modern world. Black women had played a pivotal role in asserting this expressive practice, replicating dimensions of the social order around them.

Much was at stake for the black middle class in this struggle to contain and eradicate vernacular dance. The controversy over dancing occurred as a modern black bourgeoisie asserted its claim to define and direct racial progress. The black elite sought to impose its own values and standards on the masses, to obliterate plebeian cultural expressions that, in its view, prolonged the degradation of the race. While the black elite asserted its paternalism through the language of morality, law and order, and the Protestant work ethic, the white elite exercised its powerful and repressive will through the mechanisms of state power as well as through language. White Southerners had even more at stake in controlling black leisure and dancing, since they continued to make claims for reaping the benefits of black labor power long after African Americans had been divested as literal commodities. White fears of the bodily excesses perceived in dance were also rooted in their fears of sex, and especially anxieties about interracial sex. This paranoia was nurtured by the context in which much of the dancing occurred, in the subterranean world of the red light district on Decatur Street, "the melting pot of Dixie," where urban dwellers crossed over the color line more freely than elsewhere in the city. Yet the contest over the black body did not take place in the dance halls alone; fears of the social contagion of black women would reach their peak in "public health" campaigns.

CHAPTER NINE

Tuberculosis as the "Negro Servants' Disease"

At a health conference in Dallas, Texas, in 1915, a white physician described the menace that black health problems posed for white Southerners by branding African-American domestics as the culprits responsible for infecting their employers with disease. W. Willis, a writer in a black periodical, defended domestic workers, challenging the racist assumptions that informed popular medical and lay opinions about how disease spread. "It seems very strange that doctors are beginning to charge Negro servants up with white folks' disease," Willis stated.[1]

Although tuberculosis (TB) was an endemic disease with a long legacy, not an epidemic disease that suddenly appeared and multiplied, causing a catastrophe of deaths, the racial traits that white Southerners attached to it made it appear cataclysmic. Despite the predictions of Armageddon generated by these attributions, the accusing rhetoric was never matched by genuine public policies for dealing with the problem. The peculiarly subtle and ephemeral nature of TB as it silently and patiently attacked, sickened, and killed its human hosts over prolonged periods made the disease difficult to diagnose, which exacerbated fear and paranoia.[2]

Tuberculosis signified more than a purely physiological condition. The disease became a medium for "framing" tensions in labor and race relations, with the rhetoric cloaked in scientific and medical legitimacy. White Southerners used it to sanction racial inequalities, to reaffirm their assumption that nature had ordained the relegation of African

Americans to the mudsills of Southern society, as it had also judged them to reside at the bottom of the Western hierarchy of Man.

African-American women bore the brunt of the racist conjectures that undergirded the discourse on tuberculosis. As domestic workers, they transgressed the boundaries of racial segregation in their movement across the color line. In the early 1900s, middle-class and upper-class whites were increasingly moving away from the perils of urban living into the suburbs. Yet the incursions of black domestics who were indispensable to their preferred life-styles violated the preservation of these exclusive retreats. Like the controversy about working-class women's leisure, the discourse on disease precipitated another attack on the autonomy of black working-class women. But this time the white Southern assaults assumed a more virulent form, calling for systematic physical subjugation of black women's bodies. In the Jim Crow era, tuberculosis offered a persuasive vehicle for justifying and rationalizing harsh solutions in the name of public health.

The cultural logic that explains why and how white Southerners framed TB in these ways fits within a narrative structure that has accompanied public health panics throughout history. As a social phenomenon, TB can be seen as a "dramaturgical event" played out in sequential enactments. The drama opened in the wake of the naming of the crisis in the postwar period, reached its climax at the point of ritual and corporal condemnation of the perceived malefactors after the turn of the century, and subsided during World War I and the Great Migration.[3]

To UNDERSTAND how the Dallas physician's statement stigmatizing black domestics as carriers of TB became accepted as common knowledge, it is necessary to understand earlier conceptions of TB and how they changed over time. There were three significant turning points in the social drama in the late nineteenth century: the abolition of slavery in 1865, the validation of the germ theory, and the discovery of the tubercle bacillus in 1882.

Emancipation ignited passionate debates about the place of ex-slaves in American society, and the expertise of science and medicine was summoned to explain and resolve "the Negro problem" that freedom introduced. Physicians, public health reformers, politicians, planters, and urban employers concurred that there was a marked difference in the health status of African Americans between the antebellum and postbellum periods, and that the abolition of slavery offered the only credible explanation for the disparity. The diseases that blacks were succumbing to so readily as free people, it was argued, they had rarely, if ever, contracted when they were slaves. Accordingly, since the Civil War, the race had shown a marked predilection for insanity, typhoid fever, syphilis, alcoholism, bodily deformities, idiocy, and, especially, tuberculosis.[4]

Many scientists and laypersons believed that TB was rare among antebellum blacks because of the ameliorative conditions of slavery. According to Theophilus Powell, a Georgia physician: "Up to 1865 it was to the interest of the owners not to allow them to violate the laws of health; therefore, their hygiene surroundings were carefully guarded from their youth. Their lives were regular and systematic, and they were absolutely restrained from all dissipation and excesses."[5] Financial interests motivated masters to provide slaves with well-balanced diets of nutritious food, to expose them to fresh air and robust exercise, to offer protective clothing and sanitary shelter, Powell believed. Some postbellum commentators argued that slaveowners secured medical care for their slaves that exceeded the attention they gave to their own families. As L. C. Allen, another Georgia physician, stated succinctly, in slavery "a sickly negro was of very little value—a dead negro none."[6]

Then suddenly, the "bucolic" life of the plantation was breached by Northern soldiers storming the Mason-Dixon line, prying open the floodgates that had kept the "sickly Negro" at bay. A complete reversal in black health resulted that could only be explained by the removal of the "quarantine" effect of slavery. According to the physician E. T. Easley, the "suddenly altered status [of the Negro] in the body politic has brought upon him many evils, and he has shown himself notoriously incompetent to meet the issues of his new social relations."[7]

Many of the negative comments that white Southerners made about postbellum black health were, not coincidentally, also criticisms of urban life. It was not just that the social system of slavery had protected blacks from the ravages of disease; it was presumed that the rural ecology of plantations, the "natural" habitat of blacks, had also mitigated illnesses. The fact that tuberculosis was primarily an urban disorder fueled the correlations between disease, emancipation, and rural-to-urban migration.[8]

Another reason urban blacks were considered more susceptible to TB than rural blacks was that they could more easily avoid white surveillance. Typical indulgences in urban pleasures propelled their downward mobility on the evolutionary scale even further.[9] L. C. Allen highlighted the propensity of urban blacks to stay up late at night and "frolic" in the streets. Their attendance at picnics, dance halls, and theaters deprived them of the rest and sleep needed to revitalize their energy in order to engage in gainful work and seduced them into "licentious debaucheries of the most disgusting character."[10] Even seemingly innocent activities such as attending church did not escape reproach as high-risk behavior. Unsanitary church buildings and the germs of fellow parishioners were said to increase the spread of TB, and the ring shout was perceived by some medical professionals as "a frequent precursor if not a cause of insanity."[11] Other critics referred to injurious aesthetics and the violation of sumptuary laws. Urban blacks, especially working-class women, were criticized for "frivolously" spending money on fancy clothing, which prevented the use of their scarce resources for the preservation of health.[12] Anthony Binga's judgment of women's adoption of modern clothing takes on new meaning in this context: it could be life-threatening.

The consequences of black diversions were dire not only for black health, it was argued, but also for the body politic. Some whites articulated their fear in explicitly political terms, positing that blacks would Africanize the South through the imposition of deadly germs. Even after the presumed threat of black political power was thoroughly suppressed by disfranchisement, some physicians castigated the mental health implications of black political ambitions dating back to "Negro rule" during Reconstruction. "His friends rashly gave him the ballot before he was sufficiently intelligent to use it properly," L. C. Allen argued. "All this was bad for Cuffy—dreadfully bad. Hurtful ideas got into his head. He became unreliable. Criminal tendencies grew upon him, and evil ways overcame him."[13]

These ideas about post-slavery susceptibility to disease dovetailed with other perceived signposts of racial inferiority: woolly hair, black skin, small brains, dark blood, small lungs, large penises, obtuse face angles, and flat and thin labias.[14] Lest anyone should attribute these symptoms of disease and degeneracy to class and poverty rather than to race, upper-class African Americans were singled out for rebuke. According to the physician Thomas McKie, "the most elegant, the most refined, well-to-do families supplied by far the greatest number of insane and tuberculosis subjects." Race handicapped affluent blacks because they could not withstand the excessive "mental strain" necessary to emulate the "higher degree of civilization" and good health of "the better class of their white neighbors."[15]

THE CLAIM that antebellum slaves did not suffer from tuberculosis and other illnesses does not hold up under historical scrutiny. Nor does the notion that there was a catastrophic rise in disease after emancipation because slavery was good for the physical and mental health of its captives. Slaves contracted a variety of illnesses, including pneumonia, rheumatism, ulcers, typhoid fever, dropsy, scrofula, dysentery, diphtheria, influenza, scarlet fever, and whooping cough.[16] Some physicians even identified uniquely Negro diseases, such as Drapetomania (a so-called mental disorder caused by running away from slavery).[17] But tuberculosis was above all other diseases the leading cause of death for both blacks and whites in the nineteenth century.

This medical heritage was not denied by all white physicians, however. A Dr. Campbell of Knoxville, Tennessee, took issue with his colleague Theophilus Powell's paper read at the Annual Meeting of the American Medical Association held in Atlanta in 1896. "I have no doubt there has been a large increase [since slavery], but I must question his statement that the negro race was comparatively immune before emancipation. I have personal recollection that it was not so." Slaves often suffered and died from the most fatal form of the illness that was labeled "Negro Consumption," "Negro Poisoning," or "Struma Africana."[18] Unlike the typical pulmonary variety, "Negro Consumption" struck several organs simultaneously, taxing the body's natural capacity to fight off the disease. Antebellum Southern physicians interested in this acute form of the disease began studying it in the 1830s, reporting their findings in medical journals.[19] In at least one study, a physician identified filthy slave cabins and the miasmas they bred as a cause of the disease and urged the relocation of slaves to uninfected quarters.[20]

The idea that unsanitary slave cabins were associated with the spread of tuberculosis challenges the postbellum assertions that plantations were prophylactic resorts. Financial self-interest did not necessarily lead slaveholders to maintain optimal health and living conditions for their chattel, though some no doubt took care of their slaves for this reason. Slave diets were typically restricted to a few foods deficient in vitamins and animal protein; their clothes were often insufficient to protect them from the elements; and their quarters were often make-shift and overcrowded. And self-interest did not prompt planters to provide professional medical care for slaves; most owners relied on their own limited knowledge to administer remedies.[21]

If antebellum evidence overturns dominant postbellum assumptions, how and why did physicians later conclude that TB was rare or nonexistent among slaves? Physicians were neither neutral observers nor objective practitioners of infallible scientific methods. Though they often acknowledged the lack of dependable quantitative data to substantiate their claims, they openly relied on childhood memories and second-hand testimony from unnamed sources to support far-ranging speculations about "race." Even a physician like Campbell, who disagreed with some of his colleagues' conclusions, countered them with personal, anecdotal testimony of his own. Voluminous medical writings on the "Negro problem" in the age of Social Darwinism provide ample testimony that physicians unabashedly framed black health issues to rationalize Anglo-Saxon domination.[22]

African-American physicians did not permit the popular views of their white colleagues to go uncontested. Though they often agreed that blacks suffered disproportionately from diseases like tuberculosis compared to whites, they insisted that the differences were not rooted in innate racial traits but in social, political, and economic conditions. As the physician E. Mayfield Boyle stated, there is something wrong with the assertion that "the mere prevalence of tuberculosis among American negroes and its less prevalence among American whites need no further explanation than that the Negro's body is inferior." He continued: "One may also infer that the prevalence of, and almost exclusive tendency toward, suicidal tendency in the white race and its scarcity among American Negroes is indicative of inferior brain structure or mental endurance in whites and the reverse in Negroes."[23] Boyle insisted that the tendentious standards that were used to posit deficiencies in the black race would never be applied to the white race.

In hindsight, one might argue that white physicians deliberately tried to deceive (and sway) the public by denying the antebellum black experience with TB. But white physicians did not breach or subvert the standards of professional research protocol to write Negrophobic medical theories. The cultural logic that informed their opinions was consistent with acceptable scientific methods and beliefs of the time, and this cultural logic was constantly in flux. What physicians called TB in the postbellum period was different from what they called TB earlier in the century. Medical practitioners did not agree on a unified construct of the disease even within the same period. Tuberculosis was defined by symptoms that were arbitrarily grouped together on the basis of cultural assumptions rather than clinical diagnoses.[24] The imprecise, inconsistent, and negligent methods of diagnosing TB produced faulty statistics, which were used to bolster specious medical opinion. Discerning black physicians like Rebecca Cole questioned these methods. "Hosts of the poor are attended by young, inexperienced white physicians," she noted. "They have inherited the traits of their elders, and let a black patient cough, they immediately have visions of tuberculosis. Let him die, and though in the case there may be good reason for a difference of opinion, he writes 'tuberculosis,' and heaves a great sigh of relief that one more source of contagion is removed."[25]

Insensitive, unenlightened physicians could certainly make incorrect diagnoses, but even the most objective, fastidious clinician did not have the knowledge later developed to identify TB properly. This was a disease that could not be discerned on the basis of outward appearances alone, since symptoms usually did not become visible until victims were on the brink of death—if ever. The diagnosis was also complicated because TB sometimes mimicked other diseases like scrofula.[26] In the postbellum South, physicians did not suffer from willful amnesia about the disease's prior history; rather they reconfigured the "symptoms" and redefined the meaning of the disease. In the context of a post-slavery society still anxious about race relations, TB acquired a fresh genealogy: it was defined as an antebellum white disease that had become a postbellum black disease when the "quarantine" effect of slavery was removed.

The South was not unique in framing TB in images that bore little resemblance to its etiology. In nineteenth-century Northern societies, artists afflicted with TB were venerated. It was believed that the disease induced creativity by consuming the physical body down to its hidden spiritual core, revealing the deeper, purer qualities of the soul. Similarly, upper-class victims were considered chic; their pale, drained, thin figures were mimicked by others aspiring to achieve status. The literal wasting of the body was regarded as a mark of privilege and wealth. This image of TB became increasingly associated with white femininity as some of the ideals that were perceived to characterize TB, such as vulnerability and gentility, coincided with ideas about the weaker constitutions of upper-class ladies.[27] After the 1880s, however, images of virtue, spirituality, and refinement were replaced with derogatory attributions as TB became increasingly associated with poor and immigrant populations in the North and blacks in the South.

Two pivotal moments in medical history—the discovery of the tubercle bacillus and the acceptance of the germ theory—expedited the reconstruction of TB as a black disease in the South. Though TB was a centuries-old disease, its etiology was a mystery. In 1865 Jean-Antoine Villemin, a French army surgeon, began experimenting with inoculation, which added scientific credibility to the idea that diseases were contagious. The germ theory entered public debate, but most scientists remained skeptical. The idea that microbes were causative agents of diseases was new, but the concept of contagion was already widely accepted among laypeople long before it was validated by scientists searching for empirical evidence. It was not until Robert Koch, a German scientist, discovered and substantiated the tubercle bacillus in 1882 that the germ theory gained scientific legitimacy. Still, Koch's discovery was followed by two decades of controversy and then only gradual acceptance of his conclusions.[28]

In the pre–germ theory era, consumption was largely believed to be a disease that was inherited or one that spontaneously erupted as a result of a weak physical constitution. In the post–germ theory era, tuberculosis was discovered to be, as we know today, an infectious disease that could be transmitted from person to person as the bacillus was coughed up or spit out in the sputum of a victim. Once it became airborne, the bacillus could be passed on to other human beings who inhaled the infected droplets or touched objects or particles of dust that contained dried expectorate. This new knowledge may have settled age-old questions, but it also generated new misgivings. Many people now feared contamination from engaging in daily routines or entering public sites that had once seemed benign.[29] The germ theory also began to change dramatically the perception of TB as it sustained the hope that infectious diseases could be prevented and cured, which implied volition and responsibility on the part of the diseased person.

Issues of volition increasingly implicated African Americans as the agents of contamination, coinciding with the compelling developments in medical and lay understandings about the disparities between the races with regard to sickness and health and the impact of emancipation. By the end of the nineteenth century the "Negro problem" had become thoroughly medicalized, thanks to the persistence and transformation of pro-slavery arguments and to new discoveries in epidemiology that bolstered white Southern attitudes. As tuberculosis metamorphosed from a "white folks' disease" to a "Negro disease," the "Negro problem" became firmly established in scientific and medical thought.

ONCE blackness was thought to embody tuberculosis, the social drama moved into its second act by the first decade of the twentieth century. White Southerners could not ignore the fact that they also suffered from TB. The emergence of an anti-tuberculosis movement in the early twentieth century called attention to white, as well as black, TB sufferers. Whites were likely to be seen as victims, however, blacks as perpetrators. The distinction is striking in the contrasts between images of poor black and white women. White working-class women were more likely to be treated as worthy of public sympathy and their struggle against disease seen as noble. Black women, on the other hand, were more often treated with contempt. They were viewed as pathological agents of contamination as a result of innate racial inferiority.[30]

These differences notwithstanding, the problem remained of explaining how whites contracted a disease that they increasingly constructed as a black disease. As the racial paradigm for TB emerged during Reconstruction, there were already hints that black domestic workers would play a distinct role in the social drama. The physician Thomas McKie, for example, traced the origins of TB in the western part of South Carolina to a male and a female servant.[31] In the second act of the TB drama, whites transformed TB from a black disease to, more specifically, a "Negro servant's disease."

In the segregated South, black women became identified with TB and with infecting their white employers with the disease as a result of their frequent trips across the color line in their daily work. As an Atlanta physician stated bluntly, "a vast majority of our epidemic diseases are brought into our families through our servants."[32] Domestic workers were also perceived as carriers of syphilis, gonorrhea, diphtheria, and smallpox. But TB, the most widespread disease, was singled out most.[33] "We are ever subject to the death-dealing micro-organism at their hands," another physician commented. "They daily traverse our every pathway, enter every department of our homes as servants, directly, if you please, from the contaminated and polluted huts, cabins, hovels, slums, and dives, handling every vestige of linen, clothing, furniture, bric-a-brac, books, etc., in our living apartments, dining rooms, pantries, kitchens, and dairies," he continued.[34]

Child-nurses responsible for the care of white children were often named as the source of contagion when the youngsters fell ill. If the women themselves were not diseased, it was presumed that they were the conveyors of germs picked up from sick family members. "Not that they want to do harm," said William J. Northen, the governor of Georgia, "but purely from their affection for our little ones, they kiss them over and over again and sow the abundant seeds of disease and death."[35] Similarly, contaminated foods and utensils, whether real or imagined, were traced to cooks: "they expectorate when and where they please and we inhale the sputum; they prepare all that we eat, tasting as often as they like, and we taste what they leave; they drink from all our kitchen utensils and we do not know whether the vessels have been properly cleansed."[36]

The washerwomen above all others sparked the greatest fears of feculence and contagion. The ubiquity of black washerwomen and their contact with whites across the class spectrum made them appear culpable of infecting the entire white populace. "In negro communities in every section of the city washing for the white families is being done in the same room where lie victims in the last stages of tuberculosis," stated a typical news report in Atlanta.[37] Another commentator ascribed the blame unequivocally: "there seems little doubt that much of the spreading of diseases is due to this source alone."[38] The standard description portrayed these women washing and drying clothing using dirty equipment in unsanitary yards and homes. Once the clothes were dried, it was assumed that the clean garments were further contaminated as the laundresses ironed the items, occasionally spitting on their fingers to test the heat and stopping for periodic breaks to cough up sputum that would land on the linen.[39] The line of transmission continued as washerwomen carelessly threw the clothes on the floor to mingle with dust containing dried sputum or placed the finished items on the beds of TB victims.[40]

A Richmond physician imagined a more Byzantine route for the scourge that moved from home to the office to public accommodations: "Of course, we cannot assume that there is any unfortunate who arises in the morning from a bed whose linen was washed by a tuberculous laundress and goes down to a breakfast delivered at his back door by a tuberculous negro boy, prepared by a tuberculous cook, and served by a tuberculous maid." Even when the "innocent" victim went off to work, he was still haunted by the "tuberculous scrubwoman [who cleans his office] and later mops his fevered brow with a handkerchief laundered by the same tuberculous laundress, and perhaps lunches at a hotel where a tuberculous cook and waiter serve him!"[41] A broad spectrum of service workers outside private households were implicated in this and other scenarios, including cooks, chambermaids, waiters, street sweepers, porters, drivers, office boys, butlers, draymen, and candy factory workers.[42]

While black men did not escape unscathed in the scapegoating of TB carriers, black women were vilified not only because of their preponderance in white households, but also because of the stereotypes of libidinous women and the connotations of TB. As one white Southern physician stated: "Their girls early learn evil ways."[43] Whites considered African-American women as promiscuous by nature and saw their bodies as receptacles for dangerous, unspeakable germs. This stigma heightened anxieties among whites, who feared that sexual abandon could induce TB, not to mention VD (venereal disease).[44] "Many negro women have gonorrhea, and pay little attention to it. This is a very real menace to our white boys, and through them, after marriage, to our innocent daughters also. For, despite our best efforts, many boys are going to sow wild oats," stated a physician.[45] Despite the fact that white men sexually exploited black women, these women, the very objects of their scorn, were depicted as the seducers of innocent white boys in the VD-induces-TB narrative. Images of the black female servant as a sexually illicit contaminator were not unique to the white South, however. They are present throughout Western art and literature—from

William Hogarth's eighteenth-century paintings to Georges Cuvier's nineteenth-century medical descriptions and illustrations of the "Hottentot Venus."[46]

Two CARICATURES that were published in the *Atlanta Constitution* to warn the white public about the danger that lurked in the clothes baskets returned by their laundresses and about the germs embedded in the bodies of servants who entered their homes graphically captured the popular stereotypes of black women. In the post–germ theory era, the tubercle bacilli were often represented as demons that could fly through the air over great distances to defile unsuspecting persons.[47] The depiction of the domestic in one of the caricatures as a witch flying across the urban landscape followed by a swarm of pestilence demonstrates how this supernatural power was transferred to the domestic interloper. The figure is shown approaching a pristine columned mansion, labeled "average white home," having ascended out of a filthy, ramshackle bungalow—the average black home, by contrast. The message to the readers is unmistakable: the metaphorical wall of segregation demarcating white neighborhoods, no matter how immaculate, could not provide sufficient protection from the black female menace.

The second caricature was clearly designed to appeal to the instinct of self-preservation among white readers, by personalizing the characters. The cartoon shows the living quarters of "your washerwoman," as she administers medicine to a person lying in bed sick with a "contagious disease." The patient is cared for in a room filled with friends and neighbors, including "your cook," "your maid," and "your butler." The room is depicted with the signs of careless hygiene: an open slop bucket, a broken window that serves as a portal of entry and exit for disease, the cook's basket held on the contaminated bed, and the fraternizing between the sick patient and presumably healthy people. The washerwoman is the only character shown touching the convalescent, which she apparently did before and after washing the clothes of her patrons, which hang across the wall of her abode. Though the predominant image of domestics in the cartoons is decidedly pejorative, the shrewd reader is offered a subtle critique of the city's culpability in exacerbating disease—the presence of the city dump in the first illustration and the rejected application for hospital care in the second.

This ambivalent portrayal of TB that demonized black women but acknowledged underlying social conditions was more enlightened than the unequivocally pejorative depictions. This tension dominated the white anti-TB movement. When the Atlanta Anti-Tuberculosis Association, founded in 1907, began allowing blacks to visit its dispensary on alternate days in 1909, they compiled case histories of some of their new patients. The visiting nurses, led by Rosa Lowe, a former settlement house worker in the Atlanta Fulton Bag and Cotton Mill community, compiled a scrapbook with photographs and narrative descriptions of mostly African-American women who suffered from tuberculosis.

Armed with pen, paper, and camera, the anti-TB workers documented the abysmal conditions of black life in the city in order to warn the white public about the dangers it faced through its contact with black domestic workers. The camera's gaze caught the women and their houses in some of the same poses depicted in the cartoons: washerwomen hovering over sick persons and clothes hanging in diseased surroundings. The photographs of Sally Pride, Lula Cartwright, and Mary McIntosh were regarded as incriminating evidence, showing the women inside their cramped quarters that housed sick and dying TB victims as well as outside their houses with their unkempt yards and streets. These were all women who made their living as domestics or laundresses, a fact that was highlighted in the accompanying texts. The descriptions emphasized the overcrowded conditions: several sick and healthy people all sleeping in the same room, if not in the same bed, and women washing, drying, and hanging the clothes in the same rooms covered with excretions of the sick patients. The texts also told stories about the women's hardships. Maria Greer nursed a dying son and a sick husband while struggling to earn a living, while Nettie Williams was incapacitated and forced to rely on her young daughter, who worked as a child-nurse. Johnny Weeks, however, did not have anyone to take care of her and died alone.[48]

None of the cases collected by the anti-TB association aroused as much public attention as did that of Minnie Freeman, a twenty-two-year-old washerwoman and TB victim who lived with her mother and sister, also laundresses. Freeman achieved infamy because she "lived in the rear of a house on one of the most pretentious and popular residence streets in the whole city of Atlanta," the newspaper stated. "Her house was barely 300 feet from some of the most comfortable and attractive homes in the city." Freeman's story was singled out as "the most dangerous case on the records of the tuberculosis clinic." The alarm was justified, it was argued, because Freeman "threw off the germs of a terrible disease—enough to infect the whole city." Invoking hysteria similar to that which surrounded New York's infamous "Typhoid Mary," an Irish-American cook, Minnie Freeman was labeled "a walking germ factory" and criticized by the press at her death for having imperiled the lives of some 100,000 whites.[49]

IN REALITY, African-American women domestic workers did not contaminate white employers with tuberculosis. TB requires close, repeated contact with someone who has the active disease, and casual encounters with germ-laden clouds of droplets or dried expectorate, even when inhaled, were not sufficient to guarantee infection. As bacteriologists noted in the post–germ theory era, the healthy body has natural defenses to fight off the bacilli, which makes it difficult for hearty individuals living with sick persons to get the disease. Though most household servants in Atlanta did not live with employers, ironically, the minority who did were considered safer than those who returned to their own homes at night. Laundresses, the women who had the least contact with whites, were perceived as the principal sources of contagion, but TB could not be transmitted via clothes. The sun, heat, and open air would have killed the germs on garments hanging outdoors upon exposure.

In spite of the stigma that blamed domestic workers for spreading TB, virtually everyone in the United States had already been exposed to the bacillus, yet not everyone became sick or died from it. The body may harbor bacilli for decades and never manifest a discernible illness. Scientists, in fact, had been puzzled by this seeming randomness of the disease, which made them doubt the simplicity of the idea that germs were the causative agents.[50] The gradual acceptance of the germ theory, however, may have overemphasized the role that microorganisms played in TB, reinforcing fears that the bacilli were omnipresent—on streetcars, furniture, clothing, dust, and food. The greater emphasis given to volition and individual shortcomings by the germ theory also drew attention away from the fact that the bacilli became most viable under conditions that were determined by capitalist accumulation and racial oppression.

Money and power gave one access to the material resources necessary for good health, whereas poverty and racial oppression made it more difficult to work in a safe, well-ventilated environment, to earn decent wages, to buy the proper foods for a healthy diet, to live in properly constructed houses with suitable plumbing on well-maintained streets.[51]

Nonetheless, it is important to distinguish the racist rhetoric that named black women as the primary, even the sole, carriers of TB from the fact that African Americans suffered disproportionately because of poverty and Jim Crow. Though mortality and morbidity statistics for the period are unreliable, most scientists today believe that blacks and poor whites suffered from TB at a higher rate than more well-off whites. The politics of city governance in Atlanta gave greater priority to businesses and wealthy residents in the distribution of public resources, which exacerbated the risks of disease for the laboring poor at work and at home. The lack of running water and sanitary conveniences, the existence of dirty and unpaved streets, and the use of black neighborhoods as places to drain the sewage and dump the garbage of white residents living on the hills were optimal conditions for fostering sickness and death. The unwillingness of a city in which most residents rented their homes to force neglectful landlords to abide by housing codes aggravated the possibilities of disease.[52]

When poverty and occupational hazards were added to these factors of the physical environment, the opportunities for disease multiplied. Household workers' low wages deprived them of good-quality food, clothing, and shelter that would have helped to protect their families from the ravages of illness. But despite the generally poor health of domestics, rather than imperiling the lives of employers they helped to safeguard white families by performing the elaborate domestic chores of cleanliness and sanitation necessary for good health. Privileged people who could afford to hire servants reaped the benefits of well-being by having someone else perform their "dirty" work. Particularly during severe epidemics that necessitated extreme caution, hired help became more imperative.[53] Far from contaminating innocent white children, black women vigilantly attended to their needs.[54]

At least some observers identified TB as a "house disease," which meant that housework itself (prolonged working indoors in houses that were poorly ventilated) may have put women at risk of contracting TB, whether they were white housewives or black domestic workers.[55] If white employers could be contaminated by black domestics, a similar logic would hold that black women could become infected from white housewives and homes. The idea of the democracy of microbes or that "disease knows no color line" was a motto for public health campaigns and calls for public action in the 1910s. Yet most white Southerners seem to have failed to understand the full implications of this phrase. Although some emphasized the democracy of germs to urge that it was in the self-interest of whites to deal with the issue of black health, many also believed that "democracy" could not be reciprocated, that the germ could cross the color line in one direction only, from blacks to whites.[56]

The power of the stigma of black women household workers as carriers of TB was that it provided a crucial missing link in framing TB as a racial disease in the formative age of segregation. By casting TB, the number one health problem in the nation, as the "Negro servants' disease," the white South was able to shift attention away from itself as the region's high morbidity and mortality rates for all races increasingly came under attack by Northerners in debates about "Southern distinctiveness." In the early nineteenth century, many of the attributes of Southernness were considered quaint curiosities or peculiarities that were ephemeral and written about in good humor. By the end of the century, however, the persistence of disproportionately high rates of malaria, yellow fever, hookworm, infant mortality, and illiteracy plagued the South's reputation as fundamental indicators of aberrant regional characteristics. Hookworm, yellow fever, and malaria were perceived as "diseases of laziness," which coincided with stereotypes of the "lazy South." White Southerners were increasingly considered a backward and inferior breed of Anglo-Saxons, which discouraged immigration and forestalled financial investments in the region.[57]

White Southerners were often defensive in responding to negative stereotypes and displaced the blame for regional disparities onto certain groups. As C. E. Terry, a physician from Jacksonville, Florida, explained, "the excessive negro mortality, exerts a definite, harmful influence upon our growth and leads those, unacquainted with the facts, to erroneous impressions as to our sanitary standing."[58] Though African Americans were scapegoated most often, recent immigrants from the North were blamed for the high rates of yellow fever (the "strangers' disease"), and poor whites were most often identified with hookworm and pellagra ("diseases of poverty"). White Southerners initially resisted acknowledging these diseases, which clearly struck whites more often than African Americans. Hookworm was not diagnosed in the South until the 1890s when debates about Southern distinctiveness enlisted physicians in the search for explanations of why Southerners suffered from the disease more. Poor whites once perceived as romantic and picaresque in earlier periods became "crackers" and "dirt eaters"—social problems for the region. The problem of Southern distinctiveness was defined as a problem of a certain segment of the white population, the descendants of the lowest among the Anglo-Saxon race.[59]

The tendency to minimize or ignore health problems in the region that presumably afflicted whites more often than blacks was magnified in Atlanta, which valued its reputation of progressive hospitality to capitalist investment and attributed it to a favorable climate and good health. In the 1870s and 1880s, for example, Atlanta escaped the severe yellow fever epidemic that severely damaged rival port cities and benefited from the cotton merchants who brought their business to the Gate City in search of a better climate. City boosters, in the interest of business development, lost no opportunities to stress the moderate temperatures and mountain breezes that they claimed helped to prevent epidemics like yellow fever and poor health generally. In reality, Atlanta's distance from ports and the sea, rather than its proximity to the mountains, had spared it from certain epidemics, though the city had an annual death rate far in excess of the national average as a result of dysentery, typhoid fever, pneumonia, and TB.[60]

The discourse on TB portrayed African-American domestic workers as contaminants disrupting an otherwise healthy regional ecology. If disease constituted a metaphor for evil, dread, and pollution, the black female servant was a metaphor for disease. Disease meant more than ill health, however; it also literally meant dis-ease, or social disorder. As efforts to isolate the perceived diseased carriers and to arrive at new solutions would reveal, there was more at stake in the debate than public health. Employers were finding ever more sophisticated ways to deal with their racial fears.

As the drama moved into its penultimate act, the discourse on tuberculosis shifted from defining the problem to proposing solutions.

Several of the measures were draconian attempts to exert more control over black female bodies in order to eliminate the scourges threatening Anglo-Saxon domination. Yet ironically, in the end, many of the measures proposed by health reform advocates and politicians in Atlanta were initially presented with great fanfare, but then faded away without ever being implemented. A compelling feature of this drama was the ritual quality of these public negotiations. Regardless of whether or not the proposals were codified, the mere performance of public lamentations exorcised pestilence from the body politic and reassured the worried public that social order and hierarchy could be maintained. This response, however, existed in tension with other ways of framing the problems and the solutions for preventing the spread of TB without persecuting victims. African Americans and a small group of whites offered an alternative critique of the social and economic conditions that produced disease and instituted reforms consistent with their views.

The proposals to prevent the spread of TB that sustained the most interest and attention in Atlanta focused on regulating washerwomen. In 1904 the city of Macon, Georgia, passed a law to require washerwomen to buy badges that "resemble those kept on hand for the city's canines." Health reformers and politicians in Macon initiated the licensing system in response to complaints made to the police about "missing washerwomen and missing clothes." The badges were designed to keep tabs on washerwomen and to prevent stealing. Sanitary inspections of the homes of washerwomen were also included in the provision. The criminal justice and public health objectives of registration clearly overlapped. Atlantans took note.[61]

Following the Macon example, the police board in Atlanta proposed that the city council adopt a similar license requirement in 1905. African-American women were alarmed by the adverse effects they anticipated. "Nearly every day negro women inquire about the law, many believing they will be arrested if they take in washing without a permit and a license," it was reported.[62] Upon its first hearing by the ordinance committee of the city council, however, the measure was rejected. A few months later the idea was revived by a councilman at the urging of his constituents from the fashionable West End neighborhood in order to "give protection to the housekeepers of the city from irresponsible negro women who are making their living by washing clothes, but who are not as careful about returning garments as they are about taking them away."[63]

The prevention of theft was foregrounded in the rationale behind the revised legislation; public health concerns followed thereafter. The ordinance would require women to register their names and addresses and pay an annual fee of fifty cents in exchange for a license to wash. The licensee would then be required to report all incidents of contagious or infectious diseases within her home to the board of health within twenty-four hours of discovery. Failure to register, to report changes in residence, or to report incidences of disease could result in fines of up to ten dollars and/or compulsory work on a city public works project. The punitive emphasis given to disciplining and scrutinizing disease victims was consistent with the tenor of the broader public health movement in the nation. Police forces became integral to nascent public health infrastructures and to the enforcement of standards of purity, sobriety, and health.[64] Black citizens in particular were subjected to police intrusions in their homes in search of germs. Where the police left off, public health nurses and social workers took over in the surveillance of victims of TB. Both black and white poor women were subjected to invasions of their privacy under the pretext of health care. The Atlanta Anti-TB Association required home visits and inspections prior to admitting patients for treatment at its clinics. The clinics themselves literally exposed women's bodies to public view during medical examinations unobscured from the gaze of people in the waiting rooms.[65] The punitive provisions of the Atlanta ordinance were consistent with these practices, but the proposed law met the same fate as the previous one: it was rejected.[66] No explanations were offered in the newspaper or in the minutes of the city council meetings about why these measures failed, which was the beginning of a seemingly enigmatic pattern.

In 1910, similar proposals reemerged. This time Mrs. Victor Kriegshaber, the head of the health committee of the Atlanta Women's Club, contacted the city council and urged the adoption of an ordinance that would require a bimonthly physical examination of laundresses by ward physicians and sanitation inspection of their homes at the city's expense in order to verify the absence of contagious diseases. Those who were certified to be safe could obtain a license to wash from the city clerk, and those who refused to be examined or defied doctors' orders would be liable to fines and imprisonment.[67] A special committee was formed that included physicians who sat on the council and the appointed health officer of the city. In endorsing the measure, the *Atlanta Journal* paid dubious homage to the awe-inspiring washerwoman and the essential role of her labor to the well-being of white Atlanta. "Her failure to arrive on Saturday night would prove to the majority of the race a disaster as painful to contemplate as the failure of the sun to rise on the Sabbath morning," the newspaper editorialized. "To our sartorial existence she is, as it were, a mighty lung through which society's stream of shirts et cetera pours every week to be refreshed and purified. If her house is unsanitary or infected with germs, she becomes one of the most prolific sources of disease and contagion imagined."[68]

The *Atlanta Independent* quickly castigated the unfairness of the proposed law, although it supported the basic premise that health certification was an appropriate measure to safeguard public health. "We believe that the ordinance ought to entail or surround the washerwomen with the same protection from disease that it seeks to protect the employer from disease," the editors wrote. "Disease knows no class and follows no color line . . . To provide that the black man or poor class must walk into the rich man's house with a certificate of health and on the contrary, allow the rich man's soiled linens to go into the house of the poor, pregnant with germs of deadly disease, in the end will prove neither protection nor prevention to either class."[69] The black newspaper vowed to protest the ordinance if city officials insisted on passing a law that neglected to enforce equal sanitary standards among white and black residents alike.

Nellie Peters Black, a member of the Atlanta Anti-Tuberculosis Association, surprised the audience at the city council meeting when she put forth a critique similar to the black newspaper's: "What about protecting negro washerwomen from contagious disease in the home of white people who send out soiled clothes?" she asked.[70] She was also worried that the ordinance might cause undue hardship on black women who were trying to earn an honest living. This was a rare instance of a white person in the city openly acknowledging that diseases could be spread reciprocally between the races, and it was followed by an editorial in the *Atlanta Constitution* expressing similar sentiments. The city physician, J. P. Kennedy, tried to reassure the public that the ordinance would not impose hardships on black women because a TB hospital would be built for black patients—a hollow promise, because no such institution would be built for seventeen years.[71]

The one-sided character of the ordinance that singled out washerwomen caught the attention of skeptics who questioned the underlying motives of its proponents. Carlton M. Tanner, the pastor of Big Bethel African Methodist Episcopal Church, called attention to a "snake" lurking in the grass of the law. "Why confine this examination to the women who do the washing and not examine those who have the washing done?" Tanner queried. "Why should not the bakers and the cooks who prepared the food, the nurse girls who often prepare the children's food and sometimes even eat and sleep with them, be examined also?" he asked further. Not only did the ordinance have the potential for burdening and discouraging women from working as laundresses, Tanner suggested, but it would have a more sinister effect: the ordinance advanced the ambitions of industrialists committed to building commercial laundries and putting independent laundresses out of business. "I conscientiously believe that influences interested in the [steam] laundries are behind the whole thing," Tanner stated emphatically. He warned unsuspecting supporters of this underlying agenda that "they may find that unconsciously they are increasing the number of unemployed and have aided in building up a monopoly, right in our midst."[72]

The history of conflict that marked the development of entrepreneurial laundry businesses in competition with the independent washerwomen substantiates Tanner's astute comments. The technology of commercial laundries was still relatively primitive in the early twentieth century. Businesses in the South were organized as small shops that used a combination of manual labor, steam, and power equipment. The major difference between independent washerwomen and the commercial facilities was the workers' autonomy and control. Black women controlled the labor process in their own homes and neighborhoods, but in the age of scientific management, authority on the shop floor was delegated to professional managers. Though the number of independent laundry workers tended to decline as commercial facilities began to dominate in urban centers elsewhere by the early twentieth century, these businesses did not achieve prominence in the

South until after World War II, by which time home-operated machines would become more important in making washerwomen obsolete.[73] Industrial underdevelopment, however, did not dampen the resolve or enthusiasm of boosters in the 1910s.

Public controversies involving commercial laundries and independent black washerwomen dated back to the 1881 strike, when steam laundries tried to capitalize on the incident by lobbying the city for discounts on water consumption to lower costs for white consumers.[74] In later years, steam laundries continued to attack washerwomen directly or to use damaging innuendo to undercut their long-standing rivals. One newspaper ad warned: "It is worse than unwise to sleep on a sheet or pillow case that comes from any washerwoman's house."[75] In the "up-to-date establishment," by contrast, "every known precaution is taken to keep dirt and disease from getting a foothold," another advertisement stated.[76]

Champions of the industrialization of laundry work were not confined to the white elite. At least a few black-owned laundry firms existed in Atlanta by 1900, such as the Model Laundry, the Eagle Steam Laundry, and the Gate City Laundry. In the 1910s these businesses were given the endorsement of the black newspaper, itself a successful example of black enterprise, in the name of race pride. It welcomed the jobs created, as well as the services these firms provided for black communities.[77] In actuality, however, the benefits of small, privately owned businesses remained elusive for the masses.

Similarly, the Atlanta Federation of Trades, the umbrella institution of mostly white organized labor, fully endorsed laundry businesses that were sympathetic to their unions, in the hope that they could create new jobs and new recruits for labor unions. "For centuries back the washerwoman has been a delusion if not a scarecrow to housewives," the labor newspaper noted.[78] But washerwomen were not their only rivals; Chinese men had been operating laundry shops since the late nineteenth century in Atlanta, and the white labor activists resented the competition and used racist and xenophobic appeals to keep their constituents loyal. "Do you know the conditions under which your laundry is done by the slant-eyed Celestial? Are you satisfied to have this sojourner within our gates give your intimate linen a 'lick and a promise,' hiding his imperfect ablutions with nasty wax and hot irons?" the labor newspaper asked. The labor unionists criticized Chinese proprietors for undercutting competition with lower prices and urged white consumers to spend their dollars "with your American brother and not with the Celestial whose habits preclude sanitation in the handling of laundry work."[79]

No one could fully guarantee public health, despite insistent arguments to the contrary. Nor does the concern for public health fully explain the attention given to regulating black washerwomen. In the continual struggle to reestablish quasi-slavery, to enforce docility, laundry workers faced enormous hostility because they were the most independent domestic workers and the most difficult to subjugate. Just as the 1905 ordinance was ultimately rejected, so was the 1910 law. White reformers in Atlanta would continue to propose harsh regulatory measures for several more years. But in contrast to the vituperative rhetoric that framed TB as a disease spread by domestic workers, white Southerners demonstrated, as they had in previous efforts to regulate washerwomen, that they had a stake in the persistence of individualized, manual, low-wage household labor. Despite the obvious benefits of regulation, employers refused to surrender their traditional power to municipal authorities. The turn of the discourse toward reciprocal obligations for upholding cleanliness and sanitation may also have discouraged the idea of regulation, since whites could be judged by the same standards used to scrutinize black women.[80] But the debate would not end there.

A more comprehensive proposition to exert control over household workers emerged during the Atlanta mayoral campaign in 1912. George Brown, a physician, ran for office on a platform promising a healthy city. Supporters enthusiastically endorsed his candidacy by boasting of his previous record of standing "like a wall for Caucasian labor against incompetent negro labor" in the railroad industry and for his pro bono care of the white poor.[81] Brown promised pure drinking water, free bathing facilities, improved sanitary provisions at railroad stations, better streets, and a disease-free citizenry. He declared that the interests of business and industry should hold secondary consideration in municipal leadership: "We should build a city of homes first; that should be the keynote—healthy, happy homes, well protected, well policed, well lighted and well ventilated."[82]

Brown's proposal to create healthy, happy homes reflected the reform spirit of the period. The central feature of Brown's public health platform was a servants' bureau to be administered by the city on behalf of distressed white housewives. "You will have absolute control of the servants in this town," Brown promised. "Many a poor woman who is at present doing her own work would have the proper servant to do it had she the proper protection," he argued.[83] If the city would invest the bureau with "in a limited way, the powers of a court" to enforce regulations, Brown suggested that white employers could be sufficiently safeguarded from this scourge. The bureau would prohibit black women from working as domestics unless they submitted to a rigorous medical examination. Detailed records would be kept of employment history, work habits, and personal character, based on evaluations from employers. Direct intervention would be provided by the police to assist employers with "trouble" workers. Quitting work for reasons an employer deemed "wrongful," harboring infectious disease, or stealing could result in the worker being "immediately judged as a vagrant and ordered out of town or put to work under the supervision of the proper authorities."[84]

Brown stressed the advantages of this system in weeding out domestics responsible for spreading tuberculosis as well as "a filthy blood disease," implying that domestic workers had VD. He related instances of "how immoral servants handle and fondle your children during the day and frequent the lowest dives at night."[85] This reinforced the accusations that some child-nurses carried their white charges into the "dives." The cleansing mission of the servants' bureau would extend its reach beyond the scope of preventing the spread of pathogens to controlling the behavior of domestic workers after work hours—behaviors that challenged employers' claim to the benefits of their servants' physical exertions.

In the spirit of this broad sanitizing mission, Brown proposed another provision to control black women's work and leisure. "Today, if you discharge your cook, every one of that number belong to a negro secret society," Brown explained to white husbands. "They immediately go to the next meeting of that society and black list you and what is the result? You will find in a month that your wife will be possibly unable to secure a servant under any consideration." Brown promised to eradicate clandestine union activities among black secret societies, reasoning that while black workers were organized for self-protection, no one guarded the interests of "helpless" white housewives. "Our little women are made to suffer and worry and fret their souls out trying to handle incompetent, worthless, diseased and irresponsible negroes because no one has lifted his voice to help them [out] of their difficulty."[86] To provide further legitimacy to his platform, Brown cited endorsements from two black leaders, Henry Hugh Proctor and Richard Stinson, principal of the Atlanta Industrial School.[87]

Proctor and Stinson represented a minority opinion within the black community, as the opposition articulated by the Atlanta Baptist Ministers' Union indicated. The Brown campaign coincided with yet another round of proposed ordinances similar to previous efforts by the board of health to license washerwomen, which the ministers' union opposed.[88] In an open letter in the black newspaper addressed to "our white friends," the ministers affirmed their interest in upholding law and order and punishing criminal activity. "But we cannot persuade ourselves to believe that you will remain passive or stand silently by and allow your faithful, courteous, patient and uncomplaining working people to be subjected to such humiliation, discrimination, hardship and inconvenience in order to reach and control a very few unsatisfactory or dishonest servants." They offered commonsense business practices to prevent theft of clothing sent out to laundry workers, such as counting pieces and keeping records, and urged the use of references from community leaders to vouch for reliable employees. The ministers charged landlords with the responsibility of providing adequate sanitary facilities in tenement housing to prevent disease-breeding conditions, and encouraged the city to enforce its own sanitation laws. They warned that if the measure were passed, the city would face "the loss of some of our best working-women who could not allow themselves to be thus humiliated."[89]

With or without condemnation from blacks in the city, Brown's campaign and the concurrent ordinance generated by the board of health failed. Although fewer than eight percent of the total voters in the primary election supported Brown, his campaign acknowledged the importance of wage household labor in civic debates about municipal growth and the direction of economic development.[90] But Brown's attempt to make the preservation of white domesticity equal, if not superior, to the production of wealth and industry could not overcome the competition. By participating in the construction of the black female worker as a metaphor for disease, Brown had nonetheless helped to define the moral parameters of the healthy, model citizen as its antithesis.

Brown's servants' bureau plan and the proposed city ordinances were designed to enlist municipal authority in forcing black women to conform to the will of employers by subjecting the workers to the mercy of purity squads that would scrutinize their personal lives, physical bodies, and homes. Other white Southerners, however, advocated even more extreme measures to deal with the problem of the spread of TB. If the emancipation of slaves was the precipitating event leading to the "epidemic" of TB as a "Negro servants' disease," it would seem logical that a return to slavery, or slave-like arrangements, would provide the only real solution to the vexing problem. As J. H. McHatton, an Atlanta physician, suggested, whites should "encourage our servant to resume to a certain extent his former relations with us; to live in our house and on our premises, and let us assume as far as possible under existing circumstances our old supervision of his physical condition and material welfare."[91] McHatton's proposal of living-in to replicate slavery was precisely what black women feared most when they defended their right to live independent of white surveillance.

The efforts to eradicate the "Negro servants' disease" as proposed by McHatton, Brown, the Atlanta Women's Club, and others were either ineffectual or rejected by municipal officials and the voting populace, but the power of the ideas themselves was not diminished by their failure to become institutionalized. The mere act of repeatedly depicting black women as bearers of filth and contagion, and the mere proposal of harsh measures to regulate the culprits, were important public moments of ritual relief. These articulations allowed the employing class to measure itself against and unify in opposition to a despised Other, to reaffirm the moral values on which its authority rested—as much as for its own reassurance as for impressing subordinates with claims of its right to rule.

The criminalization of a wide range of social behaviors framed as public health issues betrayed the frustrations of employers constantly foiled by intractable workers. The persistent efforts of employers to make domestic workers' actions on and off the job an important part of civic debates is a testament to the resilient community infrastructure, autonomous spaces, and everyday resistance that were created by working-class women. Employers were constantly trying to reinvent ways of minimizing workers' dissent and limiting their autonomy with new mechanisms of control and punishment like the municipal ordinances and the servants' bureau. At the peak of the tuberculosis panic, the tensions between domination by employers and resistance by workers were articulated in terms of public health. But despite the urgent tone of the discourse claiming the need for prompt and systemic action by the state, in the end employers refused to permit any curtailment of their customary rights. Even when domestic labor relations seemed unstable and uncertain, employers preferred to exercise the prerogatives of personal power in controlling unruly workers rather than relying on abstract laws.

Yet as often happened in the daily exercise of racism in the South, an official servants' bureau or explicit repressive regulations were not necessary to bolster white rule. Police officers were already vested with the authority to carry out the function envisioned by Brown and other reformers and exacted punishments against domestic workers any time a complaint was made by an employer or at their own discretion. As a result, the homes of laundresses were raided, and the bodies of domestics were examined, in search of evidence of disorder or disease.[92]

THE POPULAR proposals for regulating and punishing black women who were stigmatized as disease carriers were countered by progressive black and white Southerners in public health campaigns. African Americans themselves took the lead in identifying the threat of TB to black life and trying to eliminate it. The Neighborhood Union (NU) provided the core leadership in the grass-roots anti-tuberculosis campaign and the development of community clinics. In a marked departure from the white Southern discourse that associated disease with innate racial inferiority, the NU attacked the problem from the perspective of poverty and inequality. Alice Carey, a teacher at Morris Brown College and a leader in the movement, dispelled racial stereotypes that stigmatized domestic workers. "It is the impulse of the intelligent negro to keep his home however small and humble, clean, and the whitest beds and cleanest floors are found in many a cabin home where the man is the day laborer, and the woman spends her day over the wash tub." Intelligence regarding sanitation was not a racial or even class trait, she suggested: "the idea of cleanliness and the meaning of ventilation is easily impressed, but among all people there are those who have to be taught."[93]

From the moment of the NU's inception, the reformers began informing themselves and their constituents about the causes and prevention of diseases. In the spirit of the social settlement house movement, they conducted research in the neighborhoods to discover the people's needs and the prevalence of health problems, and this became the basis of classes and demonstrations in personal and home hygiene, nursing, bathing the sick, and prenatal and postnatal care. They distributed information and sponsored lectures on the detection and treatment of tuberculosis, as well as typhoid, pellagra, and hookworm. They visited sick neighbors. They sponsored mothers' meetings to help develop and improve parenting skills to ensure good infant and child health. To counter the city's failure to provide adequate health care facilities, they opened a clinic with the support of volunteer black physicians and nurses. The community's response to these programs was overwhelmingly favorable, which taxed the capacity of the ambitious organization to meet the growing demand for its services.

The Neighborhood Union attacked the problem by developing self-help programs and garnering all the available resources and knowledge within the community, but the activists understood that there were externally imposed structures that impeded good health. Armed with detailed information culled from investigations of schools, neighborhoods, houses, churches, recreational facilities, and businesses, the activists lobbied the city government to correct public health hazards. Their research bolstered demands for the improvement of unpaved, neglected, swampy, and dark streets; the removal of garbage dumped in black neighborhoods; the repair of open sewers; the elimination of foul privies; the revamping and expansion of poorly ventilated and overcrowded schools. The group criticized irresponsible landlords for charging exorbitant rents for ramshackle housing and urged the city to enforce housing codes as well as to pass stricter sanitary regulations.[94]

The Neighborhood Union was one among many black organizations throughout the country that had taken the lead in the public health movement. Women's organizations and clubs, like the National Association of Colored Women and its affiliates, were especially active in this movement. In New Orleans, the Colored Teachers Association donated money for anti-TB work, and in Birmingham club women organized clinics. The Neighborhood Union, however, had developed a unique program based on its distinctive organizational structure and its strategy of dividing the city into zones for research and dispersal of services, which other groups outside the city tried to emulate.[95]

Despite the profuse verbal and written condemnations of blacks as the source of infectious disease, white Atlantans, in contrast, responded slowly to improving the health of African Americans. Though predictions of black extinction no doubt slowed the investment of resources for black health care, some whites began to take a different tack. Rosa Lowe, the secretary of the Atlanta Anti-Tuberculosis Association (AATBA), became the leading spokesperson among the latter group, although her initial views about African Americans were consistent with predominant attitudes. Black people "have no idea of cleanliness, either of body or soul," she remarked in one of her first reports in 1908. "They are naturally prone to disease by heredity (i.e. those born within the last twenty years) and by reason of their prevalent mode of life," she continued. "They are so markedly subject to certain special diseases, which may almost be called racial." Though she also focused on the poor conditions of overcrowded housing in contributing to black health problems like TB, she, like many whites in the city, stressed the danger that black washerwomen posed in infecting white patrons, as she did in the scrapbook of case histories and photographs. But even holding these views, Lowe stood apart from mainstream white thought in urging the training of more black nurses and the building of a hospital for black patients, which she hoped would not only improve health but also engender better race relations.[96]

In the course of her investigations about black health care Lowe discovered that African Americans, like the women in the Neighborhood Union, were already addressing the problem of poor health. Lowe began to meet with black women like Alice Carey, Anna Tate, Mary Floyd, Emma Rish, Minnie Ogletree, and Jimmie Smith as early as 1909.[97] Months later when the Atlanta Anti-TB Association began to open its clinic to blacks on alternate days and received a decidedly lackluster response, Lowe was encouraged to turn to the black activists for advice on how to reach their constituents. This experience and her growing awareness of an extensive network of black organizational activity helped to expand Lowe's views on racial and health issues. In 1914, she initiated the formation of a black branch of the AATBA by "selecting the most influential men and women in the community for co-workers in this line." By this time, blacks had already formed at least two anti-TB leagues, the Third Ward Relief Club and the Fourth Ward Anti-Tuberculosis League.[98]

Lowe's plan for gathering "the best" and most influential members of both races to work together to deal with health issues was an important step in developing sustained interracial cooperation in the city. "It remains to [the] hygienist to establish a friendly relation between these two races living in one community, upon both of whom the responsibility rests for a healthful city," she wrote. Lowe acknowledged the existence of racial discrimination in politics and social life and its impact on the health of African Americans. She envisioned an interracial alliance among elites, who would work to attack the problem of poor health as part of this broader context. "This program should not be confined to tuberculosis alone," she argued, "but should include educational, social, and recreational subjects." In contrast to her earlier views, Lowe seemed impatient with atavistic solutions offered by other whites. "It was recommended that housewives invite their cooks into family prayers and a mission be conducted among Negroes," she wrote. "I could but deplore the lack of vision in this group of good men and women for though the spirit is commendable, such a program does not meet present day requirements—it does not provide for citizenship, for cooperation work nor does it provide for education or recreation."[99]

African-American ministers, teachers, insurance agents, physicians, and nurses joined the black branch of the AATBA, as well as continuing to work within their own professional and social service organizations to improve black health. But they had to fight an uphill battle. The city of Atlanta had largely ignored the health problems not only of blacks but also of whites. There was no special facility available for the treatment of tuberculosis until 1911, when the Battle Hill Sanitorium was opened with the capacity of caring for sixty white patients—and this was the first in the state. A year later, the sanitorium expanded its facilities and opened a separate building for blacks. But it was not until 1927 that substantial provisions were made for black victims of TB.[100] In the meantime, the black branch of the AATBA, following the Neighborhood Union model, organized blacks in the city block by block. It sponsored clean-up campaigns, clinics, lectures, and classes. It investigated the conditions of private homes and businesses and pressured the city council to enforce sanitary laws and health regulations, to improve school buildings, and to provide playgrounds and swimming pools.[101]

African Americans and the most progressive whites did much to counter dominant racist notions linking disease to black servants. In the end, they were not always successful in implementing public health measures that benefited the people who were hit hardest by tuberculosis and other diseases, because they lacked sufficient financial resources to correct the fundamental social, economic, and political conditions that produced infectious diseases. The available medical facilities were mostly limited in scope and designed to train physicians and nurses more than to provide preventive care for patients. The continued intransigence of the white medical and public health establishment also burdened the self-help movement.[102] But progressive blacks and whites moved the discourse in new directions. Though the familiar arguments of the public debate regarding blacks and TB would live on for several more decades, the more complex views which leading reformers held regarding the issues would come to predominate nationally as the South underwent its most significant social transformation since emancipation.

THE CLOSING act of the TB drama constituted an anticlimactic transition and subsidence, occasioned by one of the most dramatic social transformations since the Civil War—the Great Migration. As the perceived disease carriers shifted geographically, the discourse on TB shifted rhetorically toward more complex frameworks for explaining the social implications of infectious diseases. Though white Southerners had dominated the medicalization of the "Negro problem," the scope of this discourse would broaden as blacks began to move to the North during and after World War I. The dire predictions of black extinction no longer seemed tenable in the face of demographic evidence that showed that the race was on the ascendancy in birth and survival rates, not on the brink of death. Increased contacts between African Americans and the medical establishment outside the South provided mounting clinical data to counter the decades of assertions made by Southern elites. Descriptions of inherent race traits did not disappear from the professional and lay literature or from debates about the causes of TB and other diseases, however, and domestic workers would continue to be seen as unique players in these scripts. Indeed, the black exodus itself and the shifting relationships it produced between North and South became the focus of intense medical debates about race. But the paradigm that predominated in the South was challenged by physicians and health activists like those in Atlanta who attributed racial disparities in the susceptibility to TB and other diseases to a variety of social, environmental, and economic factors.[103]

As the drama faded into the final act, relief appeared to be near for black women who had been subjected to disciplinary efforts to mold them into a quiescent work force. But at the very moment when economic opportunities began to widen for black women as a result of wartime expansion, white Southerners would deploy yet another round of strategies to constrict them. This time, however, black women would simply pack their bags and leave.

CHAPTER TEN

"Looking for a Free State to Live In"

lack women in Atlanta had traveled far and wide, literally and figuratively, since they entered the city in large numbers during and after the Civil War. Fifty years later, another war would precipitate a watershed moment in their struggle for freedom. Decades of thwarted dreams and the immediate repression of the First World War era led many black women and men to take to the road again to secure their liberties, this time outside the South.

The intensification of racial oppression in the South that prompted their departure is symbolized by the debut of what would become the most popular Hollywood film of all time. During the fifty-year anniversary of Appomattox, erstwhile Confederates witnessed a sterling rendition of their vision of the "War between the States" come to life. D. W. Griffith's *Birth of a Nation* opened to record-breaking and elated crowds in Atlanta theaters in December 1915.

The film portrayed the Civil War and Reconstruction as an ill-conceived Northern plot that stripped white Southern men of their rightful power and unleashed incompetent "Negro domination." With all the pageantry and fanfare of an exciting new medium, the feature-length epic treated theatergoers to the consoling archetypes of Old South legend: obsequious black Mammies upbraiding bad Negroes; an uppity mulatto Jezebel seducing white men; insolent black Union troops wreaking havoc; and ignorant, barefooted, and drunken black politicians unraveling centuries of polity and civility in hallowed legislative halls. The film reached its climax when the heroic Ku Klux Klan (KKK) rode in to save white civilization from debauchery by black brutes. To the cheers of the audience, as art imitated life, the Klan castrated and lynched a would-be black assailant in the name of protecting innocent white womanhood. As the local newspaper reported after the film's opening: "Never before, perhaps, has an Atlanta audience so freely given vent to its emotions and appreciation as last night. Spasmodic at first, the plaudits of the great spectacle at length became altogether unrestrained."[1]

The Birth of a Nation was not just lauded in Atlanta and throughout the South; it also garnered the critical praise of politicians, clergy, businessmen, and philanthropists from California to New York. President Woodrow Wilson, a professional historian, extolled the historical accuracy of the film's portrayal of a "tragic era." African Americans were not impressed, however. They were horrified by the perpetuation of myths and stereotypes that had become so deeply ingrained in American culture that they were taken at face value, even by those who identified themselves as enlightened liberals. The National Association for the Advancement of Colored People (NAACP) launched a nationwide protest campaign against the film, urging boycotts and the formation of a black film company to counter racial slander. In Atlanta and elsewhere the NAACP sought to have the film censored, but to no avail. Black war veterans carried picket signs in Washington, D.C., that stated: "We represented America in France. Why should 'The Birth of a Nation' misrepresent us here?"[2]

The opening of *Birth of a Nation* marked a banner year for bigotry in Atlanta. In a malicious atmosphere of anti-Semitism, Leo Frank, a Jew and the owner of a pencil factory, was convicted of raping and murdering Mary Phagan, a white girl employed by him. A mob of white men pulled Frank out of his jail cell and lynched him. In the wake of this event and just weeks before the debut of *The Birth of a Nation*, William J. Simmons, a former Southern Methodist Episcopal itinerant preacher and local organizer of the Woodmen of the World (a fraternal society), gathered a group of like-minded men at Stone Mountain to reinvigorate the Ku Klux Klan. The KKK had subsided after it had disrupted Reconstruction, but it inspired many other similar groups to continue its legacy throughout the nineteenth-century South. The KKK began to reemerge after the turn of the century. In the shadow of the larger-than-life granite carvings of Confederate heroes, the men pledged their unwavering loyalty to white supremacy, patriarchy, Christianity, and fraternalism. With this auspicious inauguration, Atlanta became the national headquarters of the KKK. The Klan erected its majestic Imperial Palace on the fashionable Peachtree Road.[3]

Advertisements for the hooded order and *The Birth of a Nation* appeared side by side in local newspapers. The film resonated with the resurrection of the KKK because it embodied many of the contradictory characteristics of progress and nostalgia that the Jim Crow era symbolized. Griffith's technical virtuosity, captivating artistry, and box office success place him among the nation's most innovative filmmakers. Like the modern qualities of Jim Crow itself, Griffith's medium was a product of technological advancement that was used to celebrate a yearning for a real and an imagined South of yore. And like important watersheds in the history of segregation, such as the Supreme Court ruling in *Plessy v. Ferguson*, the enthusiastic reception of the film nationwide reinforced the truce between North and South among those who sought to secure Anglo-Saxon domination.

The rebirth of the KKK and the showcasing of the film that lionized it also occurred within a year of the outbreak of the First World War. The officially sanctioned repression of civil rights and civil liberties during the war may have momentarily lessened the appeal of the Klan to the white masses. In the name of patriotism, as well as increasing anti-communism, local, state, and federal governments permitted encroachments on the civil liberties of American citizens. Wartime hysteria offered a pretext for vigilante violence by white men, who did not need to hide behind the masks, hoods, and robes of the KKK. "One hundred percent American" campaigns often coincided with white supremacist assaults on the freedom of blacks.

After the war ended, however, with the assistance of professional organizers and public relations experts, the KKK mushroomed from a few thousand to one hundred thousand by the end of 1920. Ministers, civic leaders, politicians, businessmen, and ordinary men joined the KKK in droves. The Atlanta branch, which was the most popular "fraternal order" and the most generous charitable organization in the city, included a mayor, a superior court judge, and a district attorney on its roster.[4]

For African Americans, these were "the dark days of bondage."[5]

Long-term oppression, wartime hysteria, and increased intimidation and physical assaults by the KKK challenged the tenacity of African Americans to defend their bodies, property, and civil rights. Dismayed by unrelenting racial oppression, many began turning to the alternative of last resort. A "willen workin woman" voiced this sentiment in a letter to the Chicago *Defender:* "We are in a land of starvaten," she explained. "I hope that you will healp me as I want to get out of this land of sufring."6 African Americans had come to Atlanta as recently freed slaves in the 1860s optimistic about their future, but after nearly fifty years of struggle, many were beginning the journey anew, "looking for a free state to live in."7

THE ERA of the First World War was marked not only by intensified political repression, but also by heightened political and labor unrest across the nation. The destruction of international commerce at the onset of the war in 1914 initially devastated the American economy, sending it into a sudden recession. But just as the Civil War stimulated growth and development of the Southern urban economy, World War I brought about an expansion of the American industrial complex. As manufacturers and businesses responded to European demands for war-related products and European immigrants traveled across the Atlantic to fight for their countries of origin, the demand for workers increased at an unprecedented rate.

When the United States officially entered the war in 1917, this need for workers accelerated and taxed the capability of businesses to fill vacated and newly created jobs. The federal government sought to neutralize the advantage to industry and to workers, eliciting a promise from Samuel Gompers, the president of the American Federation of Labor (AFL), to discourage his membership from using the occasion to "change existing standards." But the exceptional strike activity during the war effectively repudiated Gompers's word.8 African-American women household laborers also refused to yield to this compromise with capital and the state. As some blacks departed in large numbers to jobs in Northern industries to escape Jim Crow, others remained in the South and wielded the leverage at their disposal to alter the existing standards of racism and poverty.

African-American household workers who stayed in Atlanta relied on many of their familiar tactics, such as clandestine union organizing, which became an issue in another political campaign. Just as George Brown had proposed to restore order and health to Atlanta by exerting control over the servant population and outlawing secret societies, a member of the other infamous Brown family offered a similar solution two years later. Joseph M. Brown, son of the Civil War governor Joseph E. Brown, ran for the U.S. Senate against the incumbent, Hoke Smith, in 1914. "There is abundant circumstantial evidence to support the opinion among white people that in these secret societies the negroes discuss and try to regulate the price of cooking, nursing, chopping cotton, cotton picking, etc.," the younger Brown claimed.[9]

Brown was most perturbed by domestic workers who used the "blacklist" through their fraternal orders to identify unfair employers. Decades of incipient social unrest and occasional outbreaks like the 1881 washerwomen's strike were still palpable. Brown regarded the threat of uprisings to be the highest insult to white supremacy. "Every white lady in whose home negro servants are hired then becomes subservient to these negroes," he warned.[10] Yet by devoting such energy to assailing household workers and their organizations, Brown inadvertently revealed the power of organized societies to challenge unfair labor practices.

To stir up the racial fears of the white electorate, Brown raised the specter of interracial labor solidarity between black secret societies and white labor unions. "I have often wondered whether there was any connection between these negro secret societies and the white union leaders of the cities," Brown speculated.[11] Brown hoped to sully the reputation of his opponent, an ally of the white labor movement, by accusing him of currying favor with blacks. He identified the Georgia Federation of Labor and the Southern Labor Congress as the culprits organizing black workers to promote social equality—a charge that white labor activists in Atlanta vehemently denied.

The white trade unionists defended themselves against Brown's accusations by reminding the public that "the 'nigger' question is generally the last and most desperate resort of demagogues to win votes." They admitted the importance of black workers organizing in separate unions to prevent the undercutting of white workers, but they opposed any semblance of racial equality. "'Little Joe' knows that there is not a single white labor unionist in Georgia, or the South, who would stand for that sort of thing," they insisted. Though Joe Brown stirred up trouble by making such an insinuation, he lost the campaign.[12]

Clandestine labor organizing among household workers was evident throughout the South during the war. Underground unionization was afoot in Gainesville, Georgia, and employers took note. "The negro women in their lodges or in some other organization established for that purpose had formed an agreement as to the amount of work, number of hours, and the wage which they would agree upon with the whites," reported one investigator. Black women adopted the motto W.W.T.K. (White Women To the Kitchen) and instructed their members to abandon service altogether.[13] A secret society may have been responsible for a surreptitious strike among domestics in Rock Hill, South Carolina, in 1919. The workers identified their affiliation in a euphemistic "Fold-the-Arms Club." Perhaps not coincidentally, this was reminiscent of an Industrial Workers of the World slogan. Employers were puzzled by the action and could not identify the source of discontent. "More difficulty is experienced by Colored labor now than ever before in the history of the city and no one seems to be able to learn just what the trouble is," a reporter commented.[14]

This subtle strategy and the countless examples of quotidian struggles throughout this book are a reminder that strikes and formal unions were not the only tools of working-class resistance. Conventional strikes and trade unions, nonetheless, had their place. Black women in Houston established the Women's Domestic Union in 1916 and affiliated with the AFL. In Norfolk, Virginia, domestics, waitresses, oyster shuckers, and tobacco stemmers formed a branch of the Women Wage-Earners' Association and organized strikes in the fall of 1917 for higher wages. City officials considered this insurgency as tantamount to treason and apprehended the strikers as if they were vagrants. "The police department was not sent out to round up and arrest as slackers and loafers the three thousand white men who quit work in the navy yard because an increase in pay was denied them," the local black newspaper argued. "The women are asking for BREAD, why give them STONE?" But the counter-assault effectively ended the strike, and shortly thereafter the union disappeared.[15] In New Orleans, Ella Pete organized the Domestic Servants' Union with more than a thousand members and attempted to demand fair wages and hours without the open confrontation used in Norfolk. But even mild-mannered resistance during the war provoked allegations of outside agitators and German propaganda.[16]

The series of repressive retaliations against household workers' resistance is itself a measure of black women's effectiveness in foiling the best-laid plans of Jim Crow employers. Employers in Atlanta rallied to forestall the topsy-turvy world Brown had warned against in his Senate campaign. The World War I era resembled the Civil War period not only in the racist parallels provoked by the revival of the KKK and the popularity of *The Birth of a Nation*, but also in the resurgence of tactics used by disgruntled former slaveowners. The class actions of planters reverberated in the "collectives" that urban employers formed to regulate the wages of household workers and stymie competition. White housekeepers in Atlanta formed an organization for "mutual protection against the exactions which come from the inefficient servant."[17] This spirit of organization reached Savannah also, as one employer explained: "The women of Georgia have organized in nearly everything under the sun except to help one another in the matter of regulating domestic service." The employers proposed "pledge cards," with connotations of wartime loyalty oaths, to guarantee that the signers would abide by the agreed wages.

Outside Georgia, Montgomery employers discussed forming the Housewives' Union to avenge what they derisively referred to as the "sussieties" of domestic workers.[18] A group of women in Columbia organized the House Keepers' Association, and in Washington, D.C., the Housekeeper's Alliance was formed. "They can not compel 'good servants' to stay with them for the term of their natural lives," one report stated of the latter group's grievances. The Washington caucus planned to stop "runaways" with a blacklist system of its own.[19] Subversive actions, of course, were not the exclusive prerogative of workers. The employers' groups recast well-known workers' instruments by imitating the language of "union," "collective," and "mutual protection." They declared their entitlements to power and domination on the basis of the same principles of justice that endowed the protests of the oppressed.

Employers looked for other ways to minimize dissent among domestic workers. Some who had previously defended pan-toting as a benevolent gesture began attacking it as an outdated system that encouraged idleness among the spouses of household laborers and deprived the economy of able-bodied men.[20] They called for legislation to formally eradicate the tradition. A song attributed to black men captured the attitude that employers resented:

> I doan has to work so ha'd
> I's got a gal in a white man's ya'd;
> Ebery night 'bout half pas' eight
> I goes 'round to the white man's gate:
> She brings me butter and she brings me la'd—
> I doan has to work so ha'd![21]

A newspaper cartoon captured a similar sentiment in its headline: "It's the Late Birds that Get the Worm." A domestic worker is portrayed as a crow carrying a food basket (including a duped white man in miniature) to feed her jolly but hungry partner, who lounges serenely in a nest on "the family tree."[22] The message emphasized the victimization of white families, especially hard-working men whose earnings were pilfered by undeserving servants.

Though some employers advocated eliminating pan-toting to reduce compensation given to black domestics, thus coercing both black women and men to accept the prevailing terms of labor, not everyone agreed. Some feared that ending the tradition would alienate black women and encourage them to quit. Black women in Thomasville, Georgia, threatened to do exactly that when their city passed regulations to monitor pan-toting, proclaiming that they would rather go hungry than submit. The town's newspaper cautioned officials "to exercise a little discretion as to who they tackle," in light of the workers' responses.[23]

Other employers recognized that criminalizing customary rights would be perceived as insulting to domestic workers. "The cook's dignity is a factor in all domestic service contracts. That dignity is immediately offended if the housewife questions her about the rations she totes off after supper," a Montgomery newspaper editorialized. "Even under the most favorable relations between servant and housewife the servant, especially the cook, goes and comes more or less independently," it was added.[24] A self-proclaimed "Old Time Southerner" from the same city stated her objections to regulating pan-toting: "If I consent to my servant taking a little food home that is my business."[25] Just as employers had balked at supporting state intervention on their home turf in regulating household workers regarding the spread of disease, they continued to betray their ambivalence toward state regulations. They preferred to preserve their personalized relations with domestic workers even when they seemed most distressed about recalcitrant workers who challenged their authority.

This preference by employers to maintain the personalized character of domestic work gave them an advantage over other employers during the war. Most workers in industries and on farms raised their incomes between 1914 and 1919 through the prodding of protests, government contracts, and urgent military demands. By 1920, the wages of most Georgia workers, black and white, had hit an all-time high.[26] Because domestic labor in private homes stood outside the purview of government regulation, their wages were less subject to official pressure. But domestic workers were sometimes able to raise their wages by making it difficult for employers to retain them any other way. The continual difficulties employers experienced led some to pay higher wages to avoid the problems of the constant revolving door.[27] Despite such concessions, the wages of most domestics did not increase. Household workers, however, continued to express their opposition to work conditions that deprived them of a decent standard of living by drawing on decades of experience with creative resistance. Employers, in turn, worked individually and collectively to undermine the workers' agency in order to maintain an abundance of cheap labor. Their efforts would reach a hostile climax as tensions on the home front worsened.

IN MAY 1918, Enoch Crowder, the Selective Service Director, issued a "work or fight" order to conscript unemployed men into the armed forces. Trade unionists, alarmed by the persecutions that British workers on strike suffered under similar laws, immediately criticized the promulgation. Newton D. Baker, the Secretary of War, assured them of protection, but striking machinists in Bridgeport, Connecticut, were threatened with the order the next year.[28] Southern legislatures and city councils, however, never displayed this two-faced attitude. They deliberately designed their own "work or fight" laws to break the will of black workers. They also abandoned the original intention of the federal measure to fill the army with able-bodied *men* by prosecuting *women* and forcing them to work in domestic labor, jobs that were unrelated to the business of war.[29]

Conscripting household labor, however, appealed to employers facing their first substantial competition from industries seeking to hire black women. Between 1910 and 1920, the proportion of wage-earning black women in household work dropped from 84 percent to 75 percent.[30] Occupational choices for black women continued to follow the trend of previous decades, but some new options were opening as men joined the military and the demand for labor increased. Even before the war broke out, the Atlanta Woolen Mills and small women's clothing manufacturing plants began hiring black women. The Fulton Bag and Cotton Mill employed 121 black women by early 1914, this time without precipitating a walkout by white workers. Mill managers put black women in segregated groups in the handbag, printing, carding, spinning, and weaving departments. Black women also worked with black men as scrubbers and sweepers in the yards and waste house and performed domestic labor in the cafeteria and nursery. After the war began, cottonseed oil, furniture, lumber, box, pencil, metal, casket, candy, and garment factories hired black women. Only a minority of firms in Atlanta followed suit, however, and the overall number of black women in industries remained small.[31] Still, employers of domestic labor resented even mild constraints on their unfettered access to black women's labor.

Patriotism was used to justify the containment of this new mobility. Officials and employers labeled black women who refused to work as domestics as "idlers" even if they were gainfully employed in other fields. A group in nearby Macon, calling itself "friends" of the Negro, sent a warning to black women "slackers" who failed to follow the example of selfless white women who were taking jobs even when they did not need the earnings. All black women, regardless of their economic circumstances or personal preferences, were expected to fulfill their civic duty by engaging in "the labor [for] which they are specially trained and otherwise adapted." Black servants facilitated the entry of white women into war production by releasing them "from the routine of housework in order that they may do the work which negro women cannot do," it was stated. But the Macon group also contended that black women were obligated to serve their country in this way because they owed a special debt to society: the "liberality of the government

they are asked to defend has already placed them beyond want." The
Macon group concluded its advice with a thinly veiled warning: "We
prefer to appeal to the patriotism and the public duty of those who are
idle to accept the employment offered them by their white friends." But
if necessary, they vowed to enforce allegiance to the U.S. flag "more
energetically."[32]

Local "work or fight" laws reflected this "energetic" approach to
eliciting black women's loyalty. They intensified both extralegal violence and legal coercion to force black women into domestic work. A
vigilante group in Vicksburg, Mississippi, initiated a crusade to make its
community "one hundred per cent American" by ridding the streets of
"idle" black workers. The group tarred and feathered Ethel Barrett and
Ella Brooks. While the vigilantes escaped punishment, the physically
scarred and humiliated victims were forced to substantiate their employment as washerwomen in court. Meanwhile, Barrett's husband was
fighting in France to make the world safe for democracy, when neither
he nor his wife was guaranteed the protection of fundamental human
rights at home.[33]

Black women were attacked in this patriotic campaign all over the
South. Maria Parker, in Wetumpka, Alabama, was arrested because her
chosen occupation as a hairdresser did not meet the appropriate criteria
of servility. The town marshal arrested Parker and a washerwoman
working on her lot for "vagrancy." This same officer routinely moni-
tored black women's labor output by counting the clothes hanging in
their yards and arrested women who fell short of his quotas. Just a few
miles away in Montgomery, the police arrested Clare Williams and
sentenced her to ninety days in the stockade because she worked as a
domestic for a black family. It was not enough to work as a servant if
one did not labor for whites. Black housewives suffered the worst
harassment by this logic.[34]

Atlanta blacks began to organize an assault on "work or fight" persecutions through the NAACP. O. A. Toomer, the secretary of the
Atlanta branch, contacted the national office for advice and support.
John R. Shillady, the national secretary, responded to Toomer by
cautioning him against attacking the laws prematurely. "Many of our
northern and eastern cities are passing such laws and they are being
sustained by public opinion owing to the war," Shillady wrote. "It may,
therefore be dangerous to fight these laws lest the organization be

characterized as disloyal in so doing."[35] He urged the Atlanta branch to emphasize eliminating racial discrimination in the application of the laws rather than openly denouncing the measures themselves.

A couple of months later, however, the national NAACP office dispatched Walter F. White to investigate Southern conditions, which changed its perspective. "You will remember that when we were discussing the advisability of my making this investigation or study, that there was some doubt in both your mind and in mine as to whether the practice of conscripting Negro labor was extensive as yet," White reported to Shillady. "You will also remember that I said that if the condition was not actual, at present, it was potential and might develop, if not checked at the outset," he continued. "Well, since being here in the South I have learned the condition is not a potential one but rather a full grown development."[36]

Armed with substantial evidence of widespread abuse, the NAACP began an exhaustive campaign to abolish and preempt "work or fight" laws. The exploitation of black women household workers thus became the impetus for an expansion of the presence of the NAACP below the Mason-Dixon line. The material resources and moral support committed to this issue bolstered black resistance and increased the NAACP's Southern membership. Local organizations in the South that were formed expressly to fight wartime repression were inspired to reconstitute as branches of the NAACP.[37]

Buoyed by this esprit de corps, Atlanta blacks protested the inclusion of women in "work or fight" legislation before the state legislature and Governor Hugh Dorsey. African Americans politely but firmly reminded the governor of the negative ramifications of racist and sexist discrimination for the state's economy in light of the dramatic black migration that was under way. The law passed both houses of the legislature, but the governor vetoed the bill.

When the Atlanta City Council entertained a similar "work or fight" law, the NAACP was able to defeat it as well. Peter James Bryant, a minister and member of the NAACP, summarized the group's strategy: "We went up before His Honor, the Mayor, looked him squarely in the face and told him that the bill meant simply humiliation to black women and that black men had the same respect for their women as white men had for theirs." Bryant and other black men were outraged by the prosecution of gainfully employed women and especially by the harassment of housewives. They called the law unconstitutional "class legislation" because it was punitive toward mostly working-class women and would not be applied to white women.[38] An NAACP member from Bainbridge, Georgia, delivered this blunt message to his town's officials: "any attempt on the part of the City officers to force our wives, women who had husbands that were working for them . . . would bring about a race riot, and that we Colored men would fight them as long as we could get hold of a piece of them."[39]

African Americans throughout the South attempted to duplicate the Atlanta success, but the results were mixed. Though trade unions won a victory in New Orleans for black women, other cities were not so fortunate. Valdosta and Wrightsville, Georgia; Birmingham and Montgomery, Alabama; and Jackson, Mississippi, passed ordinances specifically requiring black women to carry work verification cards, despite determined resistance.[40] Regardless of whether or not localities mandated the inclusion of women in "work or fight" provisions, women were routinely subjected to harassment. Seventeen-year-old Nellie Atkins and Ruth Warf were arrested in Atlanta for refusing to work as household servants. "You can not make us work," they proclaimed to the police. They proceeded to break windows to vent their anger over the injustice of their arrest, which led the judge to double their sentences to sixty days each in the prison laundry.[41]

The manipulation of household workers during the war revealed another variation on a familiar theme. The South had a long and tarnished history of unabashed disdain for the principles of free labor, especially when the workers were black. White Southerners sought recourse in legal and physical coercion to achieve black female subservience because they could not achieve this in any other way during a period of unusual mobility. Beneath the rhetoric of "vagrancy," "idleness," and "patriotism," employers were distressed by black women's agency, just as they had been since Reconstruction. Investigations by the NAACP and others confirm that when workers quit or took time out of the labor market temporarily, demanded higher wages, or expressed discontent in any way, employers summoned "work or fight" laws to retaliate against them. More than a half-century after the Jackson washerwomen's strike, household workers in that city organized again and established a six-day workweek, with Sundays off. Their employers joined forces to counter the uprising and forced the workers to choose between working every day of the week or not at all. The latter choice would have subjected them to prosecution under the city's "work or fight" laws.[42] But if "work or fight" laws were designed to contain black mobility and force women to work under oppressive conditions, this strategy backfired. Black women and men were fed up with endless degradation and sought relief by leaving the region en masse.

BETWEEN 1914 and 1920 at least a half million black Southerners migrated to Northern industrial cities. African Americans picked up stakes from the land of their forebears to escape intolerable conditions in Atlanta and throughout the region. The movement accelerated in 1915 and 1916 as the KKK was reconstituted, vigilante violence and lynchings increased, and Northern industries began actively recruiting workers from the South. Migration increased again after the United States entered the war.[43] The timing of the Great Migration also coincided with the increase in white rural workers moving into urban areas, which increased competition for jobs and exacerbated racial tensions. The difficulty that cities had in containing these anxieties was demonstrated in events like the Atlanta Riot of 1906.[44]

The exodus during the war period followed a history of black relocations by people in search of the economic, political, and social dreams that had repeatedly been thwarted. Blacks considered expatriation to Africa, and their interest in this option rose and fell as the prospects for opportunities in the United States contracted and expanded. Working-class women had always been among the eager supporters of emigration. Between 1890 and 1910, Atlanta's own Henry McNeal Turner led a black nationalist movement with plans for returning to Africa.[45]

In 1903, Georgia Anderson and two hundred other domestics and women wage-earners from Savannah, after years of contemplation, petitioned the state legislature for a $2,000 appropriation so "that we may go home to our fathers land Africa." They articulated the same motivations that women and men expressed years later en route north: "Our wages are low: our chancis are bad we toile all the day long for our bread. then we dont have a nuf for us, and our childrens," they explained. They described their condition as "servatude." "Our husbands can not help us as they want too on account of low wages," they added. The women looked to Africa as the promised land for their families. "Our fathers land [is] waher we can have time to tend to our childrens, and raise them up in the fear of God. that they may have a chance to tast of slavation while it tis pasing by."[46] The state legislature never funded this project, but the petition poignantly expressed working-class women's aspirations that would be revived closer to home.

At the turn of the century a thousand African Americans moved to Liberia, founded by ex-slaves in 1822, and thousands more joined emigration clubs, subscribed to pro-emigration newspapers, or attended rallies in support of expatriation. In the end, most blacks stayed in the United States. Prior to World War I, African Americans moved incrementally from the country to towns to bigger cities within the South, sometimes temporarily in between agricultural seasons.[47] If blacks left their home states at all, they usually relocated to contiguous states. Those born in Georgia went to Alabama, Florida, the Carolinas, and Tennessee. But by the 1890s African Americans began to travel further away, surely a sign of their disillusion with de jure segregation and political disfranchisement. Georgia-born blacks journeyed to Illinois, New York, and Oklahoma. Gradually, Ohio, Pennsylvania, and New Jersey were added to the list. Before 1910, the top five states preferred by Georgia blacks were all located within the South. Between 1910 and 1920, however, Pennsylvania and Ohio ranked high on the list of preferred destinations. Since movement north was practically synonymous with movement to large urban centers, many Southerners made their mark in large industrial cities during the latter decade.[48]

The distinctiveness of the movement during World War I attracted wide attention. Blacks had never moved in such large numbers in previous migrations. And, of course, their movement to the North meant that they had abandoned the post–Civil War dreams of owning rural land. Although contemporary accounts depicted migrants as primarily agricultural peasants, more blacks left moderate-size Southern cities than those leaving the countryside. Unlike previous migrations in which women had outnumbered men, this time the sex ratio was reversed, largely because Northern industries recruited men.[49] Men often moved first while the women stayed behind, saving their wage earnings for a later departure of the remaining family members.

Once black women moved, they usually worked in the same occupations in the North as they had in the South. As white women abandoned domestic labor for industrial work, black women took their places. Domestic workers' jobs in the North paid in a day what was customarily a week's wage in the South. More factories opened their doors to black women after 1920, leading to a return of the earlier pattern of women leaving the South at a higher rate than men.[50]

Women explained the motivations behind their departures in letters to Northern black newspapers. Economic deprivations and injustices were foremost in their minds. "When you read this you will think it very strange that being only my self to support that it is so hard, but it is so," warned a widow from New Orleans. "Every thing is gone up but the poor colored people wages." This woman was aware of the structural limitations imposed on black economic mobility that limited not only her life chances, but those of all African Americans regardless of skill and education. "I have very pore learning altho it would not make much different if I would be througly edacated for I could not get any better work to do, such as house work, washing and ironing." Yet, she explained further, house work "pay so little for so hard work that it is just enough to pay room rent and a little some thing to eat." Her low wages compounded the problem of her poor health, making it difficult to earn the money she needed for proper medical care. Desperate for help, she reiterated the urgency for leaving: "the time is getting worse evry day."[51]

Young household workers in their teens and twenties wrote letters expressing concerns and hopes for their families. A seventeen-year-old from Alexandria, Louisiana, explained why migration was important to her: "A child with any respect about her self or his self wouldnt like to see there mother and father work so hard and earn nothing I feel it my duty to help." Another described herself as a "fatherless girl" looking for work for her mother, "a good laundress," and her sister, a nurse. A teenager from New Orleans described her family frustrations in greater detail: "i have ben looking for work here for three month and cand find any i once found a place 1$ a week for a 15 year old girl and i did not take that." This teen needed the money to assist her mother, who was struggling to provide for four other children. She offered to work hard in exchange for a job anywhere in the North: "i am not a lazy girl i am smart i have [not] got very much learning but i can do any work that come to my hand to do."[52]

While economic conditions were the main factor prompting migration, lynchings, police brutality, rape, inferior education, and political disfranchisement all contributed to black flight as well. African Americans drew on all the resources available to them to make informed decisions about whether or not they should leave, where they should go, and how to get there. Labor agents sent out by Northern employers offered free passes for train travel or promises of jobs. Black pullman porters, dining car waiters, and other railroad workers gathered news on their journeys regarding conditions in the North. Northern black newspapers, especially the Chicago *Defender*, provided advertisements for jobs and news about what life was like for blacks already living there. The newspapers also became advocates of using the movement as a tool of race advancement, highlighting the migration's political significance as an expression of discontent. Southerners bought the newspaper in churches, grocery stores, and barber shops. They read articles aloud to one another and passed them around until the newsprint was unreadable or worn to shreds. Migrants in the vanguard of the movement offered other conduits of information through the letters they wrote to family and friends and their occasional visits. They facilitated and encouraged further migration by offering advice and support in finding jobs and housing for more recent arrivals.[53]

Once the decision to leave was made, some left as individuals, but whole families and groups of friends often moved en masse, sometimes after months of careful preparation and planning through migration clubs. Women played an important role from the inception of the idea to resettlement in the North. The social networks they had built over the years in their daily activities as neighbors, fraternal members, churchgoers, and wage workers proved indispensable to mobilizing their communities once again.[54]

For many, however, migration never materialized beyond the stage of dreams and yearnings. Individual and family savings ran out before entire families could relocate. Labor agents reneged on promises, leaving workers stranded. The poorest people in the South often faced the hardest obstacles. As one observer noted: "In Atlanta I met a woman who told me that she was in domestic service where she had been employed for four years, that she wanted to get away. I asked her why she did not go and she replied that she could not afford it; that she could not get the railroad fare to go elsewhere."[55]

The blues reflected much of the promise and the pitfalls that awaited neophyte Northerners and affected those left behind in the South. The female blues singer personified the possibilities of movement for women. The commercialization of the singer and her song circulated an imaginative repertoire of potential destinations and savvy role models.[56] Blues lyrics also reflected some of the internal tensions and complications for women and men's relationships that migration engendered. The difficulties of saving enough money to send back home could challenge the purses of men sent ahead, and the lure of city life could sidetrack them. When W. C. Handy sang "St. Louis Blues," he may have captured the feelings of women whose partners found more glamorous love interests. As one stanza in the song goes:

> St. Louis woman wid her diamon' rings
> Pulls dat man aroun' by her apron strings
> 'Twant for powder an' for store-bought hair
> De man I love would not gone nowhere.[57]

The song suggests that there were a variety of considerations beyond economics that motivated African Americans to move, including romantic love and fascination with vibrant urban cultures.

Black flight from white oppression was not the only impetus for the grass-roots movement, but African Americans identified with runaway slaves escaping bondage. They invested migration with the hope that it would bring about all the imaginable pleasures of human life. They prayed that their dramatic departure would force the South to change its heart, and indeed it did. White Southerners responded by making life both better and worse for blacks who remained.

For a fleeting moment, many white Southerners openly welcomed the Great Migration, hoping that the "race problem" would be solved by ridding the region of blacks. But this fervor soon waned in the face of the harsh reality of the region's dependence on black labor. An Atlanta real estate agent summed up the sobering impact of the migration: "The somewhat large exodus of negroes to the North and East and to the seaboard which has been going on for the past eighteen months, has largely depleted our negro population," he wrote. This "has created a decided scarcity of common labor in this vicinity."[58] In a move reminiscent of planters' efforts following the Civil War, some cities and towns passed anti-enticement acts and assessed high license fees on labor agents to prevent them from recruiting workers away. They confiscated black Northern newspapers in the mail and drove them underground to diminish the black information network. They used the power of the press or individual persuasion to convince blacks that they could not withstand Northern winters or to disabuse them of notions of better life in the North. When all else failed, police arrested migrants at train stations who were preparing to depart.[59]

African Americans who stayed in the region and used the leverage that accompanied the labor shortage to demand better wages and conditions exacerbated the problem of scarcity. Employers' decreasing ability to find laborers did not merely reflect a declining market in absolute numbers, given that most blacks remained in the South; it also reflected black workers' determined efforts to deprive employers of the kind of labor that depended on compliant and submissive workers.[60] The struggle that ensued between domestic workers and employers was a familiar variation of this persistent dialectic. As workers asserted themselves, employers retaliated, devising new ways to keep the remaining workers deferential, and this in turn prompted more migration as well as more recalcitrance.

Governor Dorsey spoke of the alarming economic consequences of the Great Migration in his inaugural address in 1917. He began to take a more moderate approach to racial reform than his predecessors and made conciliatory promises of improving education to encourage blacks to stay in the South. Other white moderates in Atlanta joined in the chorus for greater racial tolerance and fairness.[61] Calls for improving race relations, however, were made with little intention of altering the fundamental inequities, and they came too late.

AFRICAN-AMERICAN ex-slaves had entered Atlanta in the 1860s hopeful about their future as free people. By 1920, however, hundreds of thousands had left the South en masse. The rise of the KKK and the popularity of *The Birth of a Nation* were dramatic events during the decade of the First World War that exposed the madness that propelled the Great Migration. Black frustrations had been building for decades, however, tempered only by politically optimistic moments that could not be sustained and the persistent pursuit of social justice that could not be guaranteed. Employers of domestic workers in Atlanta repeatedly singled out black women in some of the most insidious efforts to eliminate obstacles to Anglo-Saxon domination. Yet African-American women were resilient and creative, if not always successful in thwarting oppression, in their use of a variety of survival strategies—the establishment of strong community infrastructures and the use of countless other tactics to achieve liberty and justice. The story of the dialectic of repression and resistance would not end in 1920. Those who migrated to the North and those who stayed in the South, each in her own way, left a legacy of hope and determination as the struggle continued for many decades more.

Tables

Table 1 Atlanta population statistics by race and sex, 1860–1920

	1860	1870	1880	1890	1900	1910	1920
Total	9,554	21,789	37,409	65,533	89,872	154,763	200,581
Blacks	1,939	9,929	16,330	28,117	35,727	51,902	62,796
%	20	46	44	43	40	33	31
Female	—	5,560	9,008	15,777	20,921	28,683	33,803
%	—	56	55	59	56	55	54
Male	—	4,369	7,322	12,400	14,806	23,219	28,993
Whites	7,615	11,860	21,079	37,416	54,090	102,861	137,785
Female	—	5,693	10,257	18,465	27,567	51,650	70,350
%	—	48	49	49	51	50	51
Male	—	6,167	10,819	18,951	26,523	51,211	67,435

Sources: Ninth Census: Population (1872), vol. 1, p. 102; *Tenth Census: Population* (1883), vol. 1, p. 417; *Eleventh Census: Population* (1895), pt. 1, p. 527; *Twelfth Census: Population* (1901), vol. 1, pt. 2, p. 650; *Thirteenth Census: Population* (1913), vol. 2, p. 403; and *Fourteenth Census: Population* (1923), vol. 3, p. 222.

Note: The published census reports do not provide sex statistics for city populations until 1890. The sex figures for 1870 are estimates based on the 1874 city directory. See William Harris, "Work and Family in Atlanta," *Journal of Social History* 9 (Spring 1976): 323. Figures for 1880 are based on the manuscript census calculated by Gretchen Ehrmann Maclachlan, "Women's Work: Atlanta's Industrialization and Urbanization, 1879–1929" (Ph.D. diss., Emory University, 1992), p. 376.

Table 2 Wage-earning population in Atlanta (ages 10 and over), 1870–1920

	1870	1880	1890	1900	1910	1920
Total	—	17,078	29,478	40,790	76,108	99,024
Female	—	5,960	9,238	14,929	25,712	32,247
%	—	35	31	37	34	32
Black wage-earners	4,675	8,402	14,773	19,638	32,752	37,891
% of all wage-earners	—	49	50	48	43	38
Female	1,686	4,230	6,857	10,548	16,348	16,743
%	36	50	46	71	64	44
Black female domestics	1,628	4,165	6,296	9,713	13,794	12,606
% of all black female workers	97	98	92	92	84	75
% of all black wage-earners	35	50	43	49	42	33
Laundresses	759	1,837	2,986	4,817	7,430	5,522
% black	—	—	98	98	98	99
Servants	869	2,328	3,310	4,261	5,687	6,426
% black	—	—	95	97	95	96
Nurses/midwives	—	—	—	635	677	520
% black	—	—	—	83	87	73
Charwomen	—	—	—	—	—	141
% black	—	—	—	—	—	98

Sources: Jerry Thornbery, "The Development of Black Atlanta: 1865–1885" (Ph.D. diss., University of Maryland, 1977), pp. 196, 197, 214, 322; *Tenth Census: Population* (1883), vol. 1, p. 862; *Eleventh Census: Population* (1897), pt. 2, pp. 634–635; *Special Reports: Occupations, Twelfth Census* (1904), pp. 486–489; *Thirteenth Census: Population, Occupations* (1914), vol. 4, pp. 536–537; *Fourteenth Census: Population, Occupations* (1923), vol. 4, pp. 1053–1056.

Note: The 1870 published census does not provide occupational statistics for Atlanta, and the 1880 census does not list occupations by race. Figures compiled by Thornbery (for workers of ages 15 and over) from the manuscript censuses of 1870 and 1880 have been used instead. The "servant" category includes all domestic workers except laundresses, unless indicated otherwise (for example, nurses, charwomen).

Table 3 Ratio of female household workers per 1,000 families (ages 10 and over) for selected cities and states, 1880, 1900, and 1920[a]

	Domestics per 1,000 families[b]			Laundresses per 1,000 families			Domestics and laundresses per 1,000 families		
	1880	1900	1920	1880	1900	1920	1880	1900	1920
South									
Atlanta	331	214	136	233	238	113	564	452	249
Rest of Georgia	85	67	53	—	60	54	—	127	107
Nashville	310	196	110	135	193	116	445	389	226
New Orleans	206	157	121	80	101	86	286	258	207
Rest of Louisiana	65	59	56	—	34	32	—	93	88
Richmond	324	226	137	120	141	71	444	367	208
Washington, D.C.	299	269	152	87	127	63	386	396	215
North									
Boston	219	167	74	20	25	8	239	192	82
Rest of Massachusetts	109	104	46	—	12	4	—	116	50
Hartford	200	160	59	20	21	6	220	181	65
New York City	188	141	66	29	22	8	217	163	74
Rest of New York	113	87	43	—	11	8	—	98	51
Philadelphia	183	138	70	20	16	11	203	154	81

Sources: David M. Katzman, *Seven Days a Week: Women and Domestic Service in Industrializing America* (New York: Oxford University Press, 1978), pp. 61, 286; *Tenth Census: Population* (1883), vol. 1, passim; *Twelfth Census: Population* (1902), vol. 2, pt. 2, pp. clx–clxiv; *Special Reports: Occupations, Twelfth Census* (1904), passim; *Fourteenth Census: Population* (1923), vol. 3, *Occupations*, vol. 4, passim.

a. Note that black and white families are included in these ratios, which means that the number of domestics per family is actually higher, since very few blacks hired them.

b. Domestics represent all household workers except laundresses (for example, cooks, child-nurses, and maids).

Notes

Prologue

1. *American Missionary*, March 1866, p. 65. Details in the prologue are embellished, based on a composite of typical stories.

2. Entry of 22 July 1870, Abbie M. Brooks Diary, Atlanta History Center.

1. "Answering Bells Is Played Out": Slavery and the Civil War

1. As quoted in Armstead L. Robinson, "'Worser dan Jeff Davis': The Coming of Free Labor during the Civil War, 1861–1865," in *Essays on the Postbellum Southern Economy*, ed. Thavolia Glymph and John J. Kushma (College Station, Tex.: Texas A&M University Press, 1985), p. 37.

2. Entries for 5 May 1862, 2 May 1863, and 13 September 1863, Samuel P. Richards Diary, Atlanta History Center (hereafter cited as AHC). Details of the Ellen incident embellished. In an effort to preserve the historical integrity of the documents, I have quoted from sources exactly as they were written, as much as is consistent with clarity. Irregular and erroneous grammar, syntax, spelling, capitalization, and punctuation have been retained. Readers should assume that quotations throughout this book follow the original sources.

3. On this perspective see for example, Ira Berlin et al., *Slaves No More: Three Essays on Emancipation and the Civil War* (Cambridge: Cambridge University Press, 1992); Eric Foner, *Reconstruction: America's Unfinished Business, 1863–1877* (New York: Harper & Row, 1988), pp. 1–76; Leon F. Litwack, *Been in the Storm So Long: The Aftermath of Slavery* (New York: Alfred A. Knopf, 1979).

4. [Louisa F. Gilmer] to my dear father [Adam L. Alexander], 17 November 1861, Alexander-Hillhouse Family Papers, Southern Historical Collection, University of North Carolina, Chapel Hill (hereafter cited as SHC).

5. Louis Manigault, as quoted in Edmund L. Drago, *Black Politicians and Reconstruction in Georgia: A Splendid Failure* (Baton Rouge: Louisiana State University Press, 1982), p. 3.

6. Entry of 14 January 1862, Laura Beecher Comer Diary, SHC. See Robinson, "'Worser dan Jeff Davis,'" pp. 34–37.

7. On the impact of the war on Atlanta and the urbanization of the South, see James Michael Russell, *Atlanta, 1847–1890: City Building in the Old South and the New* (Baton Rouge: Louisiana State University Press, 1988), pp. 91–116; Clarence L. Mohr, *On the Threshold of Freedom: Masters and Slaves in Civil War Georgia* (Athens: University of Georgia Press, 1986), pp. 190–209; and Don H. Doyle, *New Men, New Cities, New South: Atlanta, Nashville, Charleston, Mobile, 1860–1910* (Chapel Hill: University of North Carolina Press, 1990), pp. 31–36.

8. See Richard C. Wade, *Slavery in the Cities: The South 1820–1860* (New York, 1964), pp. 4–16.

9. See Jonathan W. McLeod, *Workers and Workplace Dynamics in Reconstruction-Era Atlanta* (Los Angeles: Center for Afro-American Studies, University of California, 1989), pp. 5–6.

10. Russell, *Atlanta*, pp. 91–116; Mohr, *Threshold of Freedom*, pp. 190–209; and Doyle, *New Men*, pp. 31–36.

11. Russell, *Atlanta*, pp. 99–100; Atlanta *Southern Confederacy*, 16 April 1863, quoted in Steven Hahn, *The Roots of Southern Populism: Yeoman Farmers and the Transformation of the Georgia Upcountry, 1850–1890* (New York: Oxford University Press, 1983), p. 129; Drew Gilpin Faust, "Altars of Sacrifice: Confederate Women and Narratives of War," *Journal of American History* 76 (March 1990): 1224–1227; George C. Rable, *Civil Wars: Women and the Crisis of Southern Nationalism* (Urbana: University of Illinois Press, 1989), pp. 108–110; Victoria E. Bynum, *Unruly Women: The Politics of Social and Sexual Control in the Old South* (Chapel Hill: University of North Carolina Press, 1992), pp. 112, 120–129, 145–146.

12. Russell, *Atlanta*, pp. 72–74, 91–116; Mohr, *Threshold of Freedom*, pp. 190–209; Doyle, *New Men*, pp. 31–36; McLeod, *Workers and Workplace*, p. 6.

13. Russell, *Atlanta*, pp. 70–71; Wade, *Slavery in the Cities*, pp. 20–23.

14. Entry of 27 December 1862, Richards Diary, AHC.

15. Ibid., entry of 2 May 1863.

16. Ro. Cornilius Robson to Colonel David Barrow, 15 October 1863, David Barrow Papers, Hargrett Library, University of Georgia.

17. Atlanta *Daily Intelligencer*, 14 July 1863.

18. See Wade, *Slavery in the Cities*, pp. 32–33.

19. Samuel Stout to Isabel Harmon, 22 September 1863, Samuel H. Stout Papers, Robert W. Woodruff Library, Emory University.

20. Mohr, *On the Threshold of Freedom*, p. 133.

21. Wade, *Slavery in the Cities*, pp. 38–54. For examples of hiring out see entries of 15 July and 4 August 1864, William H. King Diary, SHC; entry of 29 October 1862, Laura Beecher Comer Diary, SHC.

22. George P. Rawick, ed., *The American Slave: A Composite Autobiography* (Westport, Conn.: Greenwood Press, 1941; 1972); *Georgia Narratives*, vol. 13, pt. 4, pp. 222 (hereafter cited as WPA Ga. Narr.). See also testimony of Sallie Blakley, WPA Ga. Narr., suppl., ser. 1, vol. 4, pt. 1.

23. T. C. Howard to [James] Gardener, 15 September 1860, James Gardener Papers, Georgia Department of Archives and History.

24. Wade, *Slavery in the Cities*, p. 43.

25. Jennie to Maria, 2 December 1862, in Amelia Akehurst Lines, *To Raise Myself a Little: The Diaries and Letters of Jennie, a Georgia Teacher 1851–1886*, ed. Thomas Dyer (Athens: University of Georgia Press, 1982), p. 193.

26. Ibid., entry of 24 July 1863, p. 204.

27. Ibid., entry of 2 December 1862, pp. 193–194.

28. As quoted in Herbert G. Gutman, *The Black Family in Slavery and Freedom, 1750–1925* (New York: Pantheon Books, 1977), p. 80. For other examples of sexual abuse of slave women see testimony of Aunt Carrie Mason, WPA Ga. Narr., vol. 13, pt. 3, pp. 112–113; testimony of Mollie Kinsey, WPA Ga. Narr., suppl. ser. 1, vol. 4, pt. 2, p. 373; and testimony of Tunis G. Campbell, 31 October 1871, in 42nd Congress, 2nd Session, House Report no. 22, pt. 6, *Testimony taken by the Joint Select Committee to Inquire into the Condition of Affairs in the Late Insurrectionary States* (Washington, D.C.: Government Printing Office, 1872), vol. 2, p. 862. Also see Deborah Gray White, *Ar'n't I a Woman? Female Slaves in the Plantation South* (New York: W. W. Norton, 1985), p. 78; Jacqueline Jones, *Labor of Love, Labor of Sorrow: Black Women, Work, and the Family from Slavery to Freedom* (New York: Basic Books, 1985), pp. 20, 27–28, 37–38; Elizabeth Fox-Genovese, *Within the Plantation Household: Black and White Women of the Old South* (Chapel Hill: University of North Carolina Press, 1988), pp. 189, 315, 323–326, 374; Thelma Jennings, "'Us Colored Women Had to Go Through A Plenty': Sexual Exploitation of African-American Slave Women," *Journal of Women's History* 1 (Winter 1990): 60–63.

29. Gutman, *Black Family*, p. 386.

30. "Sixty-Five Years a 'Washer & Ironer,'" in *God Struck Me Dead: Religious Conversion Experiences and Autobiographies of Negro Ex-Slaves,* ed. A. Watson, Paul Radin, and Charles S. Johnson (Nashville, 1945; reprint ed. Westport, Conn.: Greenwood Press, 1972), p. 186; see also Emma J. S. Prescott, "Reminiscences of the War," typescript, p. 53, AHC.

31. Wade, *Slavery in the Cities*, pp. 30–31.

32. "'Washer & Ironer,'" pp. 185–186.

33. Entry of 30 April 1862, in Lines, *Diaries and Letters*, p. 188.

34. Ibid., entry of 14 February 1863, p. 198.

35. See Wade, *Slavery in the Cities*, pp. 55–79, 143–179; Mohr, *Threshold of Freedom*, pp. 190–209.

36. As quoted in Mohr, *Threshold of Freedom*, pp. 202, 198–199; Russell, *Atlanta*, pp. 71–71, 110–111.

37. Mohr, *Threshold of Freedom*, pp. 201–209.

38. Russell, *Atlanta*, pp. 110–111.

39. Entries of 8 February and 24 July 1863, in Lines, *Diaries and Letters*, pp. 197, 204.

40. See Mohr, *Threshold of Freedom*, p. 206.

41. Mary A. H. Gay, *Life in Dixie After the War* (Atlanta: C. P. Byrd, 1897), p. 162.

42. Benjamin Quarles, *Negro in the Civil War* (Boston: Little, Brown, 1953; 1969), pp. 49–51; Drago, *Black Politicians*, pp. 4, 8.

43. Entry of 24 May 1865, Grace Elmore Diary, SHC.

44. See Rable, *Civil Wars*, p. 158.

45. For example, see A Richmond Lady [Sally A. Brock Putnam], *Richmond During the War; Four Years of Personal Observation* (Richmond: G. W. Carlton, 1867), pp. 264–266.

46. Entry of 22 January 1862, Comer Diary, SHC. See also entries of 5 May 1862 and 9 September 1864, Richards Diary, AHC.

47. Entry of 1 July 1863, in Lines, *Diaries and Letters*, p. 203. See also ibid., entry of 7 February 1863, p. 197.

48. Entries of 12 and 22 January 1862, Comer Diary, SHC.

49. Quoted in John T. Trowbridge, *The South: A Tour of Its Battle-Fields and Ruined Cities* (Hartford, 1866; reprint ed., New York: Arno, 1969), p. 171.

50. WPA Ga. Narr., vol. 12, pt. 1, p. 257.

51. Entry of 28 February 1863, Richards Diary, AHC; Sidney Root, "Autobiography," typescript, p. 16, AHC. On the general problem of domestic "crime," see, for example, entry of 29 July 1864, King Diary, SHC; Imogene Hoyle to Amaryllis Bomar, 28 November 1864, Bomar-Killian Papers, SHC; entry of 13 September 1863, Richards Diary, AHC; and entry of 29 July 1862, Comer Diary, SHC.

52. As quoted in Robinson, "'Worser dan Jeff Davis,'" p. 36. See also Rable, *Civil Wars*, pp. 118–119.

53. Prescott, "Reminiscences of the War," p. 43, AHC.

54. Entry of 15 July 1864, King Diary, SHC.

55. A. Hayne to Jefferson Davis, 8 August 1863 [1861], in *Freedom: A Documentary History of Emancipation, 1861–1867*, ser. 1, vol. 1, *The Destruction of Slavery*, ed. Ira Berlin et al. (Cambridge: Cambridge University Press, 1985), p. 695.

56. George C. Lawson, "Reminiscences of the March Through Georgia and the Carolinas: From Letters and Journal Written by George C. Lawson of the 45th Illinois Volunteers," 2 March 1865, pp. 73–74, Lawson Correspondence, AHC.

57. See Bynum, *Unruly Women*, pp. 112–114; Mohr, *Threshold of Freedom*, pp. 44–51.

58. "Petition from 95 Females in Jonesboro, Georgia" to Governor Joseph E. Brown, 26 May 1864, Telamon Cuyler Papers, AHC.

59. As quoted in Drago, *Black Politicians*, p. 4.

60. Ibid., pp. 7–12; Franklin M. Garrett, *Yesterday's Atlanta* (Miami: E. A. Seeman, 1974), pp. 23–40; Elise Reid Boylston, *Atlanta: Its Lore, Legends and Laughter* (Doraville, Ga.: Foote & Davies, 1968), pp. 87–90.

61. Prescott, "Reminiscences of the War," p. 63, AHC. See also entry of 26 December 1864, Grace B. Elmore Diary, SHC; and testimony of Mrs. Ward, 15 November 1883, in U.S. Congress, Senate, Committee on Education and Labor, *Report Upon the Relations Between Labor and Capital* (Washington, D.C.: Government Printing Office, 1885), vol. 4, p. 329.

62. Elizabeth H. Botume, *First Days Amongst the Contrabands* (Boston: Lee and Shepard, 1893), p. 140.

63. Prescott, "Reminiscences of the War," pp. 59–60, AHC; Mohr, *Threshold of Freedom*, p. 103.

64. Drago, *Black Politicians*, pp. 10–15; Gutman, *Black Family*, p. 386; Mohr, *Threshold of Freedom*, pp. 90–95; Berlin et al., *Slaves No More*, pp. 68, 175.

65. Russell, *Atlanta*, pp. 113–115; Doyle, *New Men*, pp. 31–33.

66. Imogene Hoyle to Amaryllis Bomar, 28 November 1864, Bomar-Killian Papers, AHC. See also John Richard Dennett, *The South As It Is: 1865–1866*, ed. Henry M. Christman (New York: Viking, 1965), p. 269.

2. Reconstruction and the Meanings of Freedom

1. See Table 1 at the back of the book; Franklin M. Garrett, *Yesterday's Atlanta* (Miami: E. A. Seeman, 1974), p. 38; Eric Foner, *Reconstruction: America's Unfinished*

Revolution, 1863–1877 (New York: Harper & Row, 1988), pp. 81–82; Leon F. Litwack, *Been in the Storm So Long: The Aftermath of Slavery* (New York: Knopf, 1979), pp. 310–316; U.S. Department of the Treasury, Register of Signatures of Depositors in the Branches of the Freedman's Savings and Trust Company, Atlanta Branch, 1870–1874 (Microfilm Publication, M-544), National Archives (hereafter cited as Freedman's Bank Records). Frederick Ayer to George Whipple, 15 February 1866 (Georgia microfilm reels), American Missionary Association Archives, Amistad Research Center, Tulane University (hereafter cited as AMA Papers).

2. John Richard Dennett, *The South As It Is: 1865–1866,* ed. Henry M. Christman (New York: Viking, 1965), pp. 267–271; Sidney Andrews, *The South Since the War: As Shown by Fourteen Weeks of Travel and Observation in Georgia and the Carolinas* (Boston, 1866; reprint ed., New York: Arno, 1970), pp. 339–340; Don H. Doyle, *New Men, New Cities, New South: Atlanta, Nashville, Charleston, Mobile, 1860–1910* (Chapel Hill: University of North Carolina Press, 1990), p. 31.

3. Rebecca Craighead to [Samuel] Grant, 15 January 1866, Georgia, AMA Papers; Andrews, *South Since the War,* p. 340; Whitelaw Reid, *After the War: A Tour of the Southern States, 1865–1866* (London, 1866; reprint ed., New York: Harper & Row, 1965), p. 355; Doyle, *New Men,* pp. 34–35; Howard N. Rabinowitz, *Race Relations in the Urban South 1865–1890* (New York: Oxford University Press, 1978), pp. 5–17.

4. See James Michael Russell, *Atlanta, 1847–1890: City Building in the Old South and the New* (Baton Rouge: Louisiana State University Press, 1988), pp. 117–128.

5. Frederick Ayers to Rev. George Whipple, 15 February 1866, Georgia, AMA Papers.

6. See Rebecca Craighead to Rev. Samuel Hunt, 30 April 1866, Georgia, AMA Papers; E. T. Ayer to Rev. Samuel Grant, 3 February 1866, Georgia, AMA Papers; Harriet M. Phillips to Rev. Samuel Grant, 15 January 1866, Georgia, AMA Papers; *American Missionary* 13 (January 1869): 4; John T. Trowbridge, *The South: A Tour of Its Battle-Fields and Ruined Cities* (Hartford, 1866; reprint ed., New York: Arno, 1969), p. 453.

7. Rebecca Craighead to Rev. Samuel Grant, 15 January 1866, Georgia, AMA Papers.

8. Frederick Ayers to Rev. George Whipple, 15 February 1866, Georgia, AMA Papers.

9. See Table 1 at the back of the book.

10. Gretchen Ehrmann Maclachlan, "Women's Work: Atlanta's Industrialization and Urbanization, 1879–1929" (Ph.D. diss., Emory University, 1992), p. 29.

11. H. A. Buck to General [Davis Tillson], 2 October 1865, Letters Recd., ser. 732, Atlanta, Ga. Subasst. Comr., Record Group 105: Bureau of Refugees, Freedmen, and Abandoned Lands (hereafter cited as BRFAL), National Archives (hereafter cited as NA), [FSSP A-5153]; Franklin Brown to Gen. Tillson, 30 July 1866, Unregistered Letters Recd., ser. 632, Ga. Asst. Comr., BRFAL, NA, [FSSP A-5327]; clipping from *Augusta Constitutionalist,* 16 February 1866, filed with Lt. Col. D. O. Poole to Brig. Gen. Davis Tillson, 19 February 1866, Unregistered Letters Recd., ser. 632, Ga. Asst. Comr., BRFAL, NA, [FSSP A-5447]. Citations for photocopied documents from the National Archives that were consulted at the Freedmen and Southern Society Project, University of Maryland, conclude with

the designation "FSSP" and the project's document control number in square brackets: for example, [FSSP A-5447].

12. Quoted in Trowbridge, *South Tour*, pp. 453–454.

13. Jerry Thornbery, "The Development of Black Atlanta, 1865–1885" (Ph.D. diss., University of Maryland, 1977), pp. 48–53; Edmund L. Drago, *Black Politicians and Reconstruction in Georgia: A Splendid Failure* (Baton Rouge: Louisiana State University Press, 1982), pp. 113–116.

14. Brig. Genl. Davis Tillson to Captain George R. Walbridge, 12 March 1866, Letters Recd., ser. 732, Ga. Subasst. Comr., BRFAL, NA, [FSSP A-5153]; Capt. Geo. R. Walbridge to Brig. Genl. David Tillson, 1 March 1866, vol. 98, pp. 80–81, Letters Recd., ser. 729, Atlanta, Ga. Subasst. Comr., BRFAL, NA, [FSSP A-5153].

15. Rebecca Craighead to Rev. Samuel Hunt, 15 February 1866, Georgia, AMA Papers; see also F. Ayers to Rev. George Whipple, 15 February 1866, Georgia, AMA Papers.

16. Rebecca Craighead to Rev. Samuel Hunt, 15 February 1866, Georgia, AMA Papers.

17. Thornbery, "Black Atlanta," pp. 63–64.

18. Harriet M. Phillips to Reverend Samuel Grant, 15 January 1866, Georgia, AMA Papers.

19. Atlanta *Daily Intelligencer*, 10 August 1866.

20. Testimony of Abram Colby, 28 October 1871, in 42nd Congress, 2nd Session, House Report no. 22, pt. 6, *Testimony taken by the Joint Select Committee to Inquire into the Condition of Affairs in the Late Insurrectionary States* (Washington, D.C., 1872), vol. 2, p. 700 (hereafter cited as KKK Hearings). See also testimony of Alfred Richardson, 7 July 1871, KKK Hearings, vol. 1, p. 12.

21. Doyle, *New Men*, pp. 38–48, 151; Jonathan W. McLeod, *Workers and Workplace Dynamics in Reconstruction Era Atlanta* (Los Angeles: Center for Afro-American Studies, University of California), pp. 10–16.

22. McLeod, *Workers and Workplace*, pp. 24–31, 45, 61, 75, 81, 91, 94.

23. Ibid., pp. 77–92, 100–103; Thornbery, "Black Atlanta," pp. 191–225.

24. Entry of 27 May 1865, Ella Gertrude Clanton Thomas Journal, William R. Perkins Library, Duke University (hereafter cited as DU).

25. See entries for May 1865, Thomas Journal, DU.

26. Quoted in Charles Stearns, *Black Man of the South and the Rebels; or, the Characteristics of the Former, and the Recent Outrages of the Latter* (New York: American News Co., 1872), pp. 44–45. See Elizabeth Fox-Genovese, *Within the Plantation Household: Black and White Women of the Old South* (Chapel Hill: University of North Carolina Press, 1988), pp. 37–99.

27. Atlanta *Daily Intelligencer*, 25 October 1865.

28. Myrta Lockett Avary, *Dixie After the War: An Exposition of Social Conditions Existing in the South during the Twelve Years Succeeding the Fall of Richmond* (Boston: Doubleday, 1906), p. 192; entries for 17 June through 2 December 1866, Samuel P. Richards Diary, Atlanta History Center (hereafter cited as AHC); entries for May 1865, Thomas Journal, DU; Emma J. S. Prescott, "Reminiscences of the War," typescript, pp. 49–55, AHC.

29. Entry of 18 July 1865, John H. Cornish Diary, Southern Historical Collection, University of North Carolina, Chapel Hill (hereafter cited as SHC).

30. Entry of 17 June 1866, Richards Diary, AHC.

31. Prescott, "Reminiscences of the War," pp. 49–50, 55, AHC.

32. Atlanta *Daily New Era*, 27 February 1868.

33. Mr. J. T. Ball to Maj. Knox, 19 March 1866, Unregistered Letters Recd., ser. 2250, Meridian, Miss. Subasst. Comr., BRFAL, NA, [FSSP A-9423].

34. Alexa Wynell Benson, "Race Relations in Atlanta, As Seen in a Critical Analysis of the City Council Proceedings and Other Related Works, 1865–1877" (M.A. thesis, Atlanta University, 1966), pp. 43–44; Foner, *Reconstruction*, pp. 199–202; Theodore Brantner Wilson, *The Black Codes of the South* (University, Ala.: University of Alabama Press, 1965); Rabinowitz, *Race Relations*, pp. 34–35; Atlanta *Daily New Era*, 27 February 1868.

35. Entry of 29 May 1865, Thomas Journal, DU.

36. D. H. Campbell to Sister, 25 June 1866, Campbell Family Papers, DU. For another example see George Y. Bradley to Maj. R. H. Graves, 10 January 1868, George Y. Bradley Papers, DU.

37. Virginia Shelton to William Shelton, 20 August 1866, Campbell Family Papers, DU. See also Ellen Chisholm to Laura Perry, 27 July 1867, Perry Family Papers, AHC.

38. Affidavit of Mary Long, 6 August 1866, ser. 248, Jacksonsport, Ark. Supt., BRFAL, NA, [FSSP A-2505].

39. Affidavit of Samuel Ellison, 16 January 1867, T-22 1867, Registered Letters Recd., ser. 3570, Nashville, Tenn. Subasst. Comr., BRFAL, NA, [FSSP A-6406].

40. Foner, *Reconstruction*, pp. 425–444; see testimony of Abram Colby, 28 October 1871, KKK Hearings, vol. 2, pp. 699–702.

41. Testimony of Alfred Richardson, 7 July 1871, KKK Hearings, vol. 1, pp. 12, 18.

42. Foner, *Reconstruction*, pp. 87, 290–291; Elsa Barkley Brown, "Negotiating and Transforming the Public Sphere: African American Political Life in the Transition from Slavery to Freedom," *Public Culture* 7 (Fall 1994): 107–126; Thomas C. Holt, *Black Over White: Negro Political Leadership in South Carolina during Reconstruction* (Urbana: University of Illinois Press, 1977), pp. 34–35.

43. Macon *Georgia Weekly Telegraph*, 8 October 1872, as quoted in Edmund L. Drago, "Militancy and Black Women in Reconstruction Georgia," *Journal of American Culture* 1 (Winter 1978): 841.

44. Testimony of Hannah Flournoy, 24 October 1871, KKK Hearings, vol. 1, p. 533. On Ashburn's death see Drago, *Black Politicians*, pp. 145, 153.

45. Testimony of Joe Brown, 24 October 1871, KKK Hearings, vol. 1, p. 502.

46. Rhoda Ann Childs, "Affadavit of the Wife of a Discharged Georgia Black Soldier," 25 September 1866, in *Freedom: A Documentary History of Emancipation 1861–1867*, ser. 2, vol. 2, *The Black Military Experience*, ed. Ira Berlin et al. (Cambridge: Cambridge University Press, 1982), p. 807.

47. Henry McNeal Turner's emancipation speech, 1 January 1866, Augusta, as quoted in Herbert G. Gutman, *The Black Family in Slavery and Freedom, 1750–1925* (New York: Pantheon Books, 1977), p. 388. See also Catherine Clinton, "Bloody Terrain: Freedwomen, Sexuality and Violence During Reconstruction," *Georgia Historical Quarterly* 76 (Summer 1992): 318; Atlanta *Weekly Defiance*, 24 February 1883.

48. Eliza Frances Andrews, *The War-Time Journal of a Georgia Girl, 1864–1865*, ed. Spencer Bidwell King, Jr. (Macon, Ga.: Arvidian Press, 1960), p. 349.

49. Gutman, *Black Family*, pp. 387–388.

50. Testimony of Z. B. Hargrove, 13 July 1871, KKK Hearings, vol. 1, p. 83. See also testimony of George B. Burnett, 2 November 1871, KKK Hearings, vol. 2, p. 949. See Jacquelyn Dowd Hall, *Revolt Against Chivalry: Jesse Daniel Ames and the Women's Campaign Against Lynching* (New York: Columbia University Press, 1974).

51. Bvt. Maj. John Leonard to Capt. W. W. Deane, 30 July 1866, Unregistered Letters, ser. 632, Ga. Asst. Comr., BRFAL, NA, [FSSP A-5411]; Lt. Col. Geo. Curkendall to Brig. Gen. Davis Tillson, 26 December 1865, G-18 1866, Letters Recd., ser. 15, Comr., BRFAL, NA, [FSSP A-5189]; A. Ramsey Nininger to Bvt. Maj. Genl. Davis Tillson, 8 July 1866, Letters Sent, ser. 4389, vol. 226/583 DS, p. 60, Dept. of the South, U.S. Army Continental Commands, Record Group: 393, NA, [FSSP C-1557].

52. Affidavit of Barbara Price, 15 May 1867, Misc. Court Records, ser. 737, Atlanta, Ga. Subasst. Comr., BRFAL; Bvt. Maj. Fred. Mosebach to Mayor and City Council of Atlanta, 15 May 1867, and Bvt. Maj. Fred. Mosebach to Col. C. C. Sibley, 21 May 1867, vol. 99, pp. 49 and 53–54, Letters Sent, ser. 729, Atlanta, Ga. Subasst. Comr., BRFAL, NA, [FSSP A-5709]. See also James M. Russell and Jerry Thornbery, "William Finch of Atlanta: The Black Politician as Civic Leader," in Howard N. Rabinowitz, ed. *Southern Black Leaders of the Reconstruction Era* (Urbana: University of Illinois Press, 1982), pp. 317, 332.

53. The apprenticeship system was not entirely limited to the conscription of minors; young adults actively providing for themselves were also apprenticed. For example, a turpentine worker with a wife and child was defined as an orphan in North Carolina. See Foner, *Reconstruction*, p. 201.

54. Martin Lee to Mr. Tillson, 7 December 1866, in Ira Berlin et al., "Afro-American Families in the Transition from Slavery to Freedom," *Radical History Review* 42 (Fall 1988): 102–103.

55. Entry of 27 May 1865, Thomas Journal, DU. Evidence from ex-slave narratives suggests a pattern of exploitation of child laborers; they received little or no cash wages. See testimony of Nancy Smith, in George P. Rawick, ed., *The American Slave: A Composite Autobiography* (Westport, Conn.: Greenwood Press, 1941; 1972), *Georgia Narratives*, vol. 13, pt. 3, p. 302 (hereafter cited as WPA Ga. Narr.); testimony of Georgia Telfair, WPA Ga. Narr., vol. 13, pt. 4, p. 5.

56. Rebecca M. Craighead to Rev. E. Smith, 5 May and 25 April 1867, Georgia, AMA Papers.

57. See Jacqueline Jones, *Soldiers of Light and Love: Northern Teachers and Georgia Blacks, 1865–1873* (Chapel Hill: University of North Carolina Press, 1980), pp. 152–153.

58. Rebecca M. Craighead to Bvt. Brig. Gen. J. H. Lewis, 11 May 1866, Ga. Asst. Comr., C-69, 1867, Letters Recd., ser. 631, Ga. Asst. Comr., BRFAL, NA, [FSSP A-415].

59. F. Ayers to Rev. George Whipple, 15 February 1866, Georgia, AMA Papers.

60. *American Missionary* 15 (September 1871): 200–201.

61. Prescott, "Reminiscences of the War," p. 56, AHC. Prescott goes on to reveal that Silvey died penniless, without the help of former owners.

62. Freedman's Bank Records.

63. See Gutman, *Black Family*, pp. 185–256.

64. Freedman's Bank Records.

65. Gutman, *Black Family*, pp. 9–23; Berlin et al., "Afro-American Families," pp. 92–93.

66. Corporal Murray, as quoted in J. R. Johnson to Col. S. Lee, 1 June 1866, in Berlin et al., "Afro-American Families," p. 97.

67. For examples of these efforts see Wm. H. Sinclair to Freedmen's Bureau agent at Savannah, Ga., 12 September 1866, Unregistered Letters, ser. 1013, Savannah, Ga. Subasst. Comr., BRFAL, NA, [FSSP A-5762]; R. F. Patterson to Col. D. C. Poole, Letters Recd., ser. 732, Atlanta, Ga. Subasst. Comr., BRFAL, NA, [FSSP A-5704].

68. Gutman, *Black Family*, pp. 418–425.

69. 1st Lt. F. E. Grossmann to the Acting Assistant Adjutant General, 1 October 1866, in Berlin et al., "Afro-American Families," pp. 97–98. Gutman, *Black Family*, pp. 418–425.

70. Affidavit of Rosa Freeman, 24 July 1866, in Berlin et al., "Afro-American Families," pp. 99–100.

71. James D. Anderson, *The Education of Blacks in the South, 1860–1935* (Chapel Hill: University of North Carolina Press, 1988), pp. 4–9, 16; Herbert G. Gutman, "Schools for Freedom: The Post-Emancipation Origins of Afro-American Education," in Herbert G. Gutman, *Power and Culture: Essays on the American Working-Class*, ed. Ira Berlin (New York: Pantheon, 1987), p. 294; Jones, *Soldiers of Light and Love*, p. 59.

72. Gutman, "Schools for Freedom," pp. 286, 294; Jones, *Soldiers of Light and Love*, p. 62; Anderson, *Education of Blacks in the South*, pp. 4–32.

73. Drago, *Black Politicians*, pp. 27–28.

74. Ibid., pp. 27–28, 35–54.

75. Russell and Thornbery, "William Finch of Atlanta," pp. 319, 322; Russell, *Atlanta*, p. 181.

76. Mrs. E. T. Ayers to Rev. Samuel Hunt, 1 September 1866, Georgia, AMA Papers.

77. Jennies Barium to Rev. Samuel Grant, 27 January 1866, Georgia, AMA Papers; Andrews, *South Since the War*, p. 338.

78. Sarah J. Thomas to Mr. [Edmund A.] Ware, 11 October 1869, Edmund A. Ware Papers, Robert W. Woodruff Library, Clarke Atlanta University.

3. Working-Class Neighborhoods and Everyday Life

1. Jerry Thornbery, "The Development of Black Atlanta, 1865–1885" (Ph.D. diss., University of Maryland, 1977), pp. 7–12; Dana F. White, "The Black Sides of Atlanta: A Geography of Expansion and Containment, 1970–1870," *Atlanta Historical Journal* 26 (Summer-Fall 1982): 199–225; James M. Russell, "Politics, Municipal Services, and the Working Class in Atlanta, 1865–1890," *Georgia Historical Quarterly* 66 (Winter 1982): 467–491.

2. Richard J. Hopkins, "Public Health in Atlanta: The Formative Years, 1865–1879," *Georgia Historical Quarterly* 53 (September 1969): 299.

3. Howard L. Preston, *Automobile Age Atlanta: The Making of a Southern*

Metropolis 1900–1935 (Athens: University of Georgia Press, 1979), pp. 7–12; Russell, "Politics, Municipal Services," pp. 467–491; Thornbery, "Black Atlanta," pp. 7–12; White, "Black Sides of Atlanta," pp. 199–225; John H. Ellis, "Businessmen and Public Health in the Urban South During the Nineteenth Century: New Orleans, Memphis, and Atlanta," *Bulletin of the History of Medicine* 44 (May-June 1970): 197–371; John H. Ellis and Stuart Galishoff, "Atlanta's Water Supply, 1865–1918," *Maryland Historian* 8 (Spring 1977): 5–22; Hopkins, "Public Health in Atlanta," pp. 287–304.

4. See Ellis, "Businessmen and Public Health," p. 200; Russell, "Politics, Municipal Services," pp. 487–488.

5. See for example, entries for 1 September 1877 and 1 June 1878, Samuel P. Richards Diary, Atlanta History Center (hereafter cited as AHC); Russell, "Politics, Municipal Services," pp. 480–491; Howard N. Rabinowitz, *Race Relations in the Urban South, 1865–1890* (New York: Oxford University Press, 1978), pp. 114–120; Ellis and Galishoff, "Atlanta's Water Supply," pp. 6–22. Even city officials acknowledged that limited potable water bred disease. See "Report of the President [George Hillyer]," in Atlanta, Board of Water Commissioners, "Twenty-Fourth Annual Report of the Board of Water Commissioners to the General Council of the City of Atlanta, for the Year Ending December 31, 1898," pp. 6–7, AHC.

6. Preston, *Automobile Age Atlanta*, pp. 7–12; Don L. Klima, "Breaking Out: Streetcars and Suburban Development, 1872–1900," *Atlanta Historical Journal* 30 (Summer-Fall 1982): 67–82.

7. Timothy J. Crimmins, "West End: Metamorphosis from Suburban Town to Intown Neighborhood," *Atlanta Historical Journal* 30 (Summer-Fall 1982): 33–50.

8. For a contemporary description of the Ponce de Leon Spring see Ernest Ingersoll, "The City of Atlanta," *Harper's New Monthly Magazine*, December 1879, p. 39; Klima, "Streetcars and Suburban Development," pp. 70–71; Stephen W. Grable, "The Other Side of the Tracks: Cabbagetown—A Working-Class Neighborhood in Transit During the Early Twentieth Century," *Atlanta Historical Journal* 26 (Summer-Fall 1982–1983): 54–65; Jonathan W. McLeod, *Workers and Workplace Dynamics in Reconstruction Era Atlanta* (Los Angeles: Center for Afro-American Studies, University of California, 1989), p. 11; Jacquelyn Dowd Hall, "Private Eyes and Public Women," in *Work Engendered: Towards a New History of American Labor*, ed. Ava Baron (Ithaca, N.Y.: Cornell University Press, 1991), p. 246; Gary M. Fink, *The Fulton Bag and Cotton Mills Strike of 1914–1915: Espionage, Labor Conflict, and New South Industrial Relations* (Ithaca, N.Y.: Industrial Labor Relations Press, 1993), pp. 7, 26, 160.

9. On black residential enclaves see *Atlanta Constitution*, 20 July 1881; F. Ayers to Rev. E. Smith, 22 July 1867, Georgia, AMA Papers; Thornbery, "Black Atlanta," pp. 16–43; John Dittmer, *Black Georgia in the Progressive Era 1900–1920* (Urbana: University of Illinois Press, 1977), pp. 12–14; White, "Black Sides of Atlanta," pp. 199–225; Eugene M. Mitchell, "Queer Place Names in Old Atlanta," *The Atlanta Historical Bulletin* 1 (April 1931): 29; Annie S. Barnes, *The Black Middle-Class Family: A Study of Black Subsociety, Neighborhood, and Home in Interaction* (Bristol, Ind.: Wyndham Hall Press, 1985), pp. 27–30; Mildred Warner, "Community Building: The History of Atlanta University Neighborhoods" (Atlanta, 1978), in Neighborhood File, AHC; Alexa Henderson and Eugene Walker, "Sweet Auburn: The Thriving Hub of Black Atlanta" (unpublished paper prepared for the Martin

Luther King, Jr., National Historic Site and Preservation District), Neighborhood File, AHC.

10. Ingersoll, "City of Atlanta," pp. 41–43.

11. See Richard R. Wright, *A Brief Historical Sketch of Negro Education in Georgia* (Savannah: Robinson Printing House, 1894); Willard Range, *The Rise and Progress of Negro Colleges in Georgia* (Athens: University of Georgia Press, 1951).

12. Thornbery, "Black Atlanta," pp. 33–35.

13. See Tables 1 and 2 at the back of the book. The figures for 1870 were probably small partly as a result of census under-counting, a typical problem for women workers and blacks generally.

14. In 1870 and 1880, Southern black women were three times more likely to participate in the labor force than Southern white women, and married black women were nearly six times more likely to participate than married white women. See Claudia Goldin, "Female Labor Force Participation: The Origin of Black and White Differences, 1870 and 1880," *Journal of Economic History* 37 (March 1977): 94; William Harris, "Work and the Family in Black Atlanta, 1880," *Journal of Social History* 9 (Spring 1976): 319–330; Janice L. Reiff et al., "Rural Push and Urban Pull: Work and Family Experiences of Older Black Women in Southern Cities, 1880–1900," *Journal of Social History* 16 (Summer 1983): 39–48; Thornbery, "Black Atlanta," p. 34; Jacqueline Jones, *Labor of Love, Labor of Sorrow: Black Women, Work, and the Family from Slavery to Freedom* (New York: Basic Books, 1985), p. 113; Herbert G. Gutman, *The Black Family in Slavery and Freedom, 1750–1925* (New York: Pantheon Books, 1977), pp. 442–450, 624–642.

15. "Washer and Ironer," pp. 187–188.

16. *Atlanta Medical and Surgery Journal* 1 (October 1884): 427; Thornbery, "Black Atlanta," pp. 34, 35, 37, 41; Gretchen Ehrmann Maclachlan, "Women's Work: Atlanta's Industrialization and Urbanization, 1879–1929" (Ph.D. diss., Emory University, 1992), pp. 162–170.

17. See Table 2 at the back of the book for statistics related to household laborers.

18. Dorothy Bolden, interview by Bernard E. West, 7 December 1978, typescript, Living Atlanta Collection, AHC. Sarah Hill, "Bea the Washerwoman," Federal Writers Project Papers, Southern Historical Collection, University of North Carolina, Chapel Hill (hereafter cited as FWP, SHC).

19. Testimony of Georgia Telfair, in George P. Rawick, ed., *The American Slave: A Composite Autobiography* (Westport, Conn.: Greenwood Press, 1941; 1972), Georgia Narratives, vol. 13, pt. 4, p. 8 (hereafter cited as WPA Ga. Narr.); Elizabeth Kytle, *Willie Mae* (New York: Alfred A. Knopf, 1958), p. 26; Gutman, *The Black Family*, pp. 630–631; David M. Katzman, *Seven Days a Week: Women and Domestic Service in Industrializing America* (New York: Oxford University Press, 1978), pp. 79–82.

20. Testimony of Carrie Nancy Fryer, WPA Ga. Narr., vol. 12, pt. 1, p. 341; see also "The Three Sisters," p. 9.

21. For insightful readings of the meaning of ex-slave women's presumed withdrawal from wage labor to "play the lady" see Thavolia Glymph, "'I'se Mrs. Tatom Now': Freedom and Black Women's Reconstruction," paper presented at the Annual Meeting of the Southern Historical Association, November 1992 (in Tera W. Hunter's possession), and Leslie Schwalm, "'In Their Own Way and At

Such Times as They Think Fit': Work and Family in Former Slave Women's Definitions of Freedom," paper presented at the Annual Meeting of the Southern Historical Association, November 1992 (in Tera W. Hunter's possession). See also Jones, *Labor of Love*, pp. 58–59; Gutman, *Black Family*, pp. 167–168; Litwack, *Aftermath of Slavery*, pp. 244–245; Foner, *Reconstruction*, pp. 84–87.

22. Edward Bacon, "I Don't Know What's the Matter," FWP, SHC.

23. Testimony of Susan Castle, WPA Ga. Narr., vol. 12, pt. 1, p. 182; Lucille Smith Hughs, "My Pot Pourri of Ninety Years," vol. 1, p. 165 in Sussana M. Hughs Papers, AHC; entry of 7 August 1876, Evelyn Harden Jackson Diaries, Hargrett Library, University of Georgia (hereafter cited as UG).

24. Katzman, *Seven Days a Week*, pp. 117–118; Daniel E. Sutherland, *Americans and Their Servants: Domestic Service in the United States from 1800 to 1920* (Baton Rouge: Louisiana State University Press, 1981), pp. 82–94.

25. For a trenchant critique of how scholars have erroneously calculated domestic workers' wages see Bettina Berch, "'The Sphinx in the Household': A New Look at the History of Household Workers," *Review of Radical Political Economics* 16 (Spring 1984): 105–121. For secondary literature that discusses wages see Katzman, *Seven Days a Week*, pp. 273, 304–305; Sutherland, *Americans and Their Servants*, pp. 107, 110; Faye E. Dudden, *Serving Women: Household Service in Nineteenth Century America* (Middletown, Conn.: Wesleyan University Press, 1983), pp. 219–225, 325; Jones, *Labor of Love*, pp. 128, 132, 206–207; Elizabeth Ross Haynes, "Negroes in Domestic Service in the United States," *Journal of Negro History* 8 (October 1923): 413–426. Wage rates cited in this study have been determined by primary sources that follow:

Employers' diaries and account books: Account Books of Martha Thomas Wingfield Reid and Sarah F. Reid Grant, 1879–1882, Inman-Grant-Slaton Papers, AHC; Household Account Books, 1871–1877, Joseph E. Brown Papers, AHC; Daily Account Books, 1884–1887, Crumley Family Papers, AHC; Account Book 1875, John Emory Bryant Collection, William R. Perkins Library, Duke University (hereafter cited as DU); 15 February 1872, J. E. to wife [Emma], John Emory Bryant Collection, DU; Valeria Burroughs Commonplace Books, 1865–1881, SHC; 10 July 1865, Mrs. Harriett V. [Alexander] Cummings to Miss Emma M. Barnett, Alexander-Hillhouse Family Papers, SHC; Entry of 15 October 1865, Richards Diary, AHC; 1866–1869, Receipts, 1866–1869, DuBose Family Papers, UG; Account Book, 1872, Milligan Family Papers, SHC; Entry for 29 December 1866, Samuel Andrew Agnew Diary, SHC; Entry for 16 September 1868, Mary Elizabeth (Carter) Rives Diary, SHC; Mary Susan Ker Diaries, 1891–1899, SHC; Margaret R. Benning Account Books, 1892–1910, AHC; Louisa Porter Minis Diaries, 1899–1900, Minis Family Papers, SHC; Fannie Harling Account Books, 1902–1916, AHC; Mary Fries Patterson Diaries, 1911, SHC.

Domestic workers' reports: Kytle, *Willie Mae*, pp. 116–117; A Negro Nurse, "More Slavery at the South," *Independent* 25 (January 1912): 196–197; Daisy Johnson, "All I do is Just Heads," FWP, SHC; Hill, "Bea the Washerwoman," FWP, SHC; testimony of Annie Jackson, FWP, SHC; testimony of Lizzie Mercer, FWP, SHC; testimony of Elvic L. Robinson, FWP, SHC; Odelia Lester Anderson, "I Maids for the Coeds," FWP, SHC; Ruby Owens, Interview by Bernard E. West, 23 January 1979, tape recording, Living Atlanta Collection, AHC; Alice Adams, Interview by Bernard E. West, 20 November 1978, transcript, Living Atlanta Collection, AHC; Annie Alexander, Interview by Bernard E. West, 29 May 1979, transcript, Living Atlanta Collection, AHC; Dorothy Bolden, Interview.

Other studies and reports: testimony of Robert B. Kyle, 12 November 1883, in U.S. Department of Labor, Committee on Education and Labor, *Report Upon the Relations Between Labor and Capital* (Washington, D.C.: Government Printing Office, 1885), vol. 4, p. 26 (hereafter cited as *Labor and Capital*); testimony of Mrs. Ward, 15 November 1883, *Labor and Capital*, vol. 4, p. 345; "Condition of the Negro in Various Cities," *Bulletin of the Department of Labor* 2 (May 1897): 257–359; W. P. Burrell, "Report of the Committee on Business and Labor Conditions in Richmond, Virginia," *Proceedings of the Hampton Negro Conference* 6 (July 1902): 42–43; Katherine Tillman, "The Paying Professions for Colored Girls," *The Voice of the Negro*, 4 (January-February 1907): 54–56; *Savannah Tribune*, 27 January 1900; *Southern Workman* 35 (July 1906): 415; W. E. B. Du Bois, "The Negroes of Farmville, Virginia: A Social Study," *Bulletin of the Department of Labor* 14 (January 1898): 22; W. E. B. Du Bois, *Mortality Among Negroes in Cities* (Atlanta: Atlanta University, 1896); Ruth Reed, *Negro Women of Gainesville, Georgia* (Athens: University of Georgia, 1921); "Minutes of the Joint Meeting held on July 27th, 1917," Atlanta Lung Association Collection, AHC; T. J. Woofter, "The Negroes of Athens, Georgia," *Bulletin of the University of Georgia* 14 (December 1913): 42, 47; British Board of Trade, *Cost of Living in American Towns* (London: His Majesty's Stationery Office, 1911).

26. See entries for 1866, Burroughs Commonplace Books, 1865–1881, SHC.

27. See entries for 1880–1899, Edwin Edmunds Account Books, 1838–1892, SHC.

28. See Woofter, "The Negroes of Athens," p. 48.

29. Ker Diaries, 1891–1899, SHC; Burroughs Commonplace Books, 1865–1881, SHC; Robert Harding Towels Account Books, 1866–1869, Calvin Henderson Wiley Papers, SHC. See also Patterson Diaries, 1911, SHC; Mrs. W. S. Chisholm Day Book, SHC.

30. Susan Strasser, *Never Done: The History of American Housework* (New York: Pantheon, 1982), passim.

31. See "The Daily Routine of Work," n.d., Grimball Family Papers, SHC; A Negro Nurse, "More Slavery at the South," p. 196.

32. A Negro Nurse, "More Slavery at the South," p. 196; Kytle, *Willie Mae*, p. 62.

33. Dorothy Bolden, Interview.

34. Strasser, *Never Done*, pp. 36–46.

35. As quoted in Haynes, "Negroes in Domestic Service in the United States," p. 411.

36. See Polly Stone Buck, *The Blessed Town: Oxford, Georgia, at the Turn of the Century* (Chapel Hill: University of North Carolina Press, 1986), pp. 15–16; and Kathleen Ann Smallzried, *The Everlasting Pleasure: Influences on America's Kitchens, Cooks and Cookery, From 1565 to the Year 2000* (New York: Appleton-Century-Crofts, 1956), pp. 93–102.

37. Buck, *Blessed Town*, p. 16.

38. Kytle, *Willie Mae*, p. 25; Reed, *The Negro Women of Gainesville*, p. 16.

39. Strasser, *Never Done*, pp. 105–121; Ruth Schwartz Cowan, *More Work for Mother: The Ironies of Household Technology from the Open Hearth to the Microwave* (New York: Basic Books, 1983), pp. 65, 98.

40. See Katzman, *Seven Days a Week*, pp. 185–187; British Board of Trade, *Cost*

of Living, p. 52; Atlanta *Journal of Labor*, 20 November 1903; Ray Stannard Baker, *Following the Color Line: American Negro Citizenship in the Progressive Era* (New York, 1908; reprint ed., New York: Harper and Row, 1964), p. 53; Kytle, *Willie Mae*, pp. 118–119; Walter L. Fleming, "The Servant Problem in a Black Belt Village," *Sewanee Review* 8 (January 1905): 14; Du Bois, "Negroes of Farmville," p. 21; Timothy J. Crimmins, "Bungalow Suburbs: East and West," *Atlanta Historical Journal* 30 (Summer-Fall 1982): 84–86; Clifford M. Kuhn et al., *Living Atlanta: An Oral History of the City, 1914–1948* (Athens: University of Georgia Press, 1990), pp. 38, 113; Dolores E. Janiewski, *Sisterhood Denied: Race, Gender, and Class in a New South Community* (Philadelphia: Temple University Press, 1985), pp. 43–44, 127–129; Victoria Byerly, *Hard Times Cotton Mill Girls: Personal Histories of Womanhood and Poverty in the South* (Ithaca, N.Y.: Cornell University Press, 1986), pp. 99, 125, 132, 147, 152.

41. Strasser, *Never Done*, p. 109. For examples of a washerwoman working in employers' homes see Mary Raoul Millis, *The Family of Raoul: A Memoir* (Asheville, N.C.: The Miller Printing Co., 1943), pp. 109–110; and Minis Diary, Minis Family Papers, vol. 12, n.d., SHC.

42. Ingersoll, "City of Atlanta," pp. 33–34.

43. Hill, "Bea the Washerwoman," pp. 4, 13–15; Jasper Battle, "Wash Day in Slavery," in WPA Ga. Narr., vol. 2, pt. 1, p. 70; testimony of Rias Body, WPA Ga. Narr., vol. 12, pt. 1, p. 87; Ruby Lorraine Radford, "Slavery: Compilation Made from Interviews with 30 Slaves," in WPA Ga. Narr., vol. 13, pt. 4, p. 352; Buck, *Blessed Town*, pp. 116–120; testimony of Paul Smith, WPA Ga. Narr. vol. 13, pt. 3, p. 321; Millis, *Family of Raoul*, pp. 109–110; Botume, *First Days Amongst the Contrabands*, pp. 50, 52; Reed, *Negro Women in Gainesville*, pp. 15–16, 32; Katzman, *Seven Days a Week*, pp. 72, 82, 124; Sutherland, *Americans and Their Servants*, p. 92; Dudden, Serving Women, pp. 224–225; Patricia E. Malcolmson, *English Laundresses: A Social History, 1850–1930* (Urbana: University of Illinois Press, 1986), pp. 11–43; Strasser, *Never Done*, pp. 105–121.

44. Hill, "Bea the Washerwoman," p. 14.

45. See Buck, *Blessed Town*, p. 115; Battle, "Wash Day in Slavery," p. 70; Botume, *First Days Amongst the Contrabands*, p. 52.

46. See Table 2 at the back of the book; and Thornbery, "Black Atlanta," p. 222.

47. See Table 2 at the back of the book.

48. McLeod, *Workers and Workplace*, p. 102.

49. Katzman, *Seven Days a Week*, pp. 60–62; see Table 3 at the back of the book.

50. On similar trends in Baltimore and Washington, D.C., see Paul A. Groves and Edward K. Muller, "The Evolution of Black Residential Areas in Late Nineteenth Centuries," *Journal of Historical Geography* 1 (1975): 186–190.

51. Joseph A. Hill, *Women in Gainful Occupations 1870 to 1920* (Washington, D.C., 1929), pp. 334–336; Katzman, *Seven Days a Week*, pp. 87–91.

52. Testimony of Albert C. Danner, 13 November 1883, *Labor and Capital*, vol. 4, p. 105.

53. *Atlanta Journal*, 3 March 1883.

54. Testimony of Mrs. Ward, 15 November 1883, *Labor and Capital*, vol. 4, p. 343.

55. On incipient strikes see Katzman, *Seven Days a Week*, pp. 195–197. For more examples of domestics quitting constantly see entries for 2 and 21 October

1883, 28 September and 16 October 1884, Richards Diary, AHC; entries for 1886 through 1902, Ker Diaries, SHC; "Your affectionate mother" [Elizabeth A. D. Van Dyke] to Jodie [Van Dyke Inman], 18 November 1889, Inman-Grant-Slaton Family Papers, AHC; entries for September, October, and November 1880 and February and March 1884, Emily J. W. Bealer Diary, Georgia Department of Archives and History (hereafter cited as GAH).

56. Testimony of Mrs. Ward, 15 November 1883, *Labor and Capital*, vol. 4, p. 328.

57. This helps to explain the undercount of black women wage-earners in the census reports. A surprising number were listed as "at home," as non-wage-earners, at the time of the census. These figures are perhaps best understood as an indication of the number of black women withdrawn from the labor market at any given time, as opposed to an absolute number of non-wage-earners.

58. E. P. Thompson, "The Moral Economy of the English Crowd," *Past and Present* 50 (February 1971): 76–135. For an insightful discussion of a similar practice involving "social wages" see Marcus Rediker, *Between the Devil and the Deep Blue Sea: Merchant Seamen, Pirates, and the Anglo-American Maritime World, 1700–1750* (Cambridge: Cambridge University Press, 1987), pp. 116–152. For comparison of "vails" and customary rights in seventeenth- and eighteenth-century London see Peter Linebaugh, *The London Hanged: Crime and Civil Society in the Eighteenth Century* (Cambridge: Cambridge University Press, 1992), pp. 250–255.

59. Meta Morris Grimball to J. Berkeley Grimball, 18 December 1865; Kytle, *Willie Mae*, pp. 116–117.

60. Entry for 4 May 1879, Richards Diary, AHC.

61. Testimony of Mrs. Ward, 15 November 1883, *Labor and Capital*, vol. 4, p. 343; 22 May 1883, Robert [Murphy] to Georgia [Russell Murphy], J. Eagan Papers, AHC; 6 November 1885, [Mary Owens Campbell Kelley] to "old friend," Campbell Family Papers, DU.

62. Buck, *The Blessed Town*, pp. 114–115; *Savannah Tribune*, 27 July 1912.

63. See, for example, *Atlanta Constitution*, 25 September 1875. A newborn mulatto baby was abandoned and a black woman living nearby assumed care for the infant; Hill, "Bea the Washerwoman," p. 4; Julia Campbell Buggs et al., "The Three Sisters," pp. 5, 9, FWP, SHC; *Atlanta Constitution*, 25 September 1875.

64. Buggs et al., "The Three Sisters," pp. 5, 9.

65. Testimony of Anna Parks, WPA Ga. Narr., vol. 13, pt. 1, p. 163; see also Hill, "Bea the Washerwoman," pp. 4, 5.

66. *Atlanta Constitution*, 20 July 1881.

67. More people were arrested for disorderly conduct than any other offense. Atlanta, *Annual Reports*, of the City Officers, 1884–1914, AHC; Reed, *Negro Women of Gainesville*, p. 38; testimony of Mrs. Ward, 15 November 1883, in *Labor and Capital*, vol. 4, p. 326.

68. Ingersoll, "City of Atlanta," p. 34.

69. Ibid.; *American Missionary* 13 (April 1869): 75.

70. See Thornbery, "Black Atlanta," p. 210; Strasser, *Never Done*, pp. 16–31.

71. Black consumers provided a thriving business for Jewish street peddlers, who invested the profits in grocery stores, clothing and dry goods stores, saloons, and pawnshops. See Steven Hertzberg, *Strangers Within the Gate City: The Jews of*

Atlanta, 1845–1915 (Philadelphia: The Jewish Publication Society of America, 1978), pp. 183–184.

72. *Atlanta Constitution*, 21 August 1875; U.S. Department of the Treasury, Register of Signatures of Depositors in the Branches of the Freedman's Savings and Trust Company, Atlanta Branch, 1870–1874 (Microfilm Publication, M-544), National Archives (hereafter cited as Freedman's Bank Records); Thornbery, "Black Atlanta," pp. 204, 324.

73. U.S. Manuscript Population Census, Fulton County, 1880; Thornbery, "Black Atlanta," p. 329.

74. See, for example, testimony of Anna Parks, WPA Ga. Narr., p. 163, and Buggs et al., "The Three Sisters," p. 12.

75. McLeod, *Workers and Workplace*, pp. 41, 100.

76. Gay, *Life in Dixie After the War*, p. 288.

77. *Atlanta Constitution*, 28 July 1880 and 20 July 1881.

78. Ingersoll, "City of Atlanta," p. 43.

79. See Henry T. Sampson, *Blacks in Blackface: A Source Book on Early Black Musical Shows* (Metuchen, N.J.: The Scarecrow Press, 1980), p. 4; Tom Fletcher, *100 Years of the Negro in Show Business* (New York: Da Capo Press, 1984), pp. v–vi; Robert C. Toll, *Blacking Up: The Minstrel Show in Nineteenth-Century America* (New York: Oxford University Press, 1974); Michael Rogin, "Black Masks, White Skin: Consciousness of Class and American National Culture," *Radical History Review* 54 (Fall 1992): 141–152; Eric Lott, *Love and Theft: Blackface Minstrelsy and the American Working Class* (New York: Oxford University Press, 1993); William Barlow, *Looking Up at Down: The Emergence of Blues Culture* (Philadelphia: Temple University Press, 1989), p. 119. For local coverage of the Rabbit's Foot Co. see *Atlanta Independent*, 25 October 1908.

80. *Atlanta Constitution*, 20 July 1881.

81. Ibid., 20 July 1881, 3 February 1882, and 10 August 1879.

82. James Michael Russell, "Atlanta, Gate City of the South, 1847 to 1885" (Ph.D. diss., Princeton University, 1971), p. 310; Thornbery, "Black Atlanta," p. 229.

83. City of Atlanta, *Annual Reports*, 1884–1886, 1902–1903, AHC. For state crimes see Georgia Prison Commission Report, Principal Keepers Report, 1873–1897, GAH.

84. British Board of Trade, *Cost of Living*, p. 51; *The Gospel Trumpet*, April 1877, in Georgia, AMA Papers; Georgia, House of Representatives Special Committee, "Joint Committee of the Senate and House to Investigate the Convict Lease System of Georgia," 1908, vol. 3, pp. 169–177, GAH; Susan Tucker, *Telling Memories Among Southern Women: Domestic Workers and Their Employers in the Segregated South* (Baton Rouge: Louisiana State University Press, 1988), p. 87; *Atlanta Constitution*, 9 September 1881.

85. On women's neighborhood networks and survival strategies see Christine Stansell, *City of Women: Sex and Class in New York 1789–1860* (New York: Alfred A. Knopf, 1986), pp. 41–62; Ellen Ross, "Survival Networks: Women's Neighborhood Sharing in London Before World War I," *History Workshop* 15 (Spring 1983): 4–27; Jeanne Boydston, "To Earn Her Daily Bread: Housework and Antebellum Working-Class Subsistence," *Radical History Review* 35 (April 1986): 7–25.

86. *Atlanta City Directory*, 1881; F[rederic] Ayers to Rev. E. P. Smith, 22 July 1867, Georgia, AMA Papers; Thornbery, "Black Atlanta," pp. 138, 147–148, 158–159.

87. See Henderson and Walker, "Sweet Auburn," pp. 19–25; "Background Research on Auburn Avenue," Living Atlanta Collection, AHC; Homer C. McEwen, "First Congregational Church, Atlanta: 'For the Good of Man and the Glory of God,'" *The Atlanta Historical Bulletin* 21 (Spring 1977): 131–132.

88. *Atlanta Constitution*, 29 May 1878; *American Missionary* 19 (January 1875): 17–18; Elizabeth Johnson Harris, "Memoirs," p. 13, DU.

89. Thornbery, "Black Atlanta," pp. 147–169.

90. See *Minutes of the Annual Session of the Atlanta Baptist District B.Y.P.U. and Sunday School Convention*, 1916–1920, Interdenominational Theological Center Collection, Robert W. Woodruff Library, Clarke Atlanta University; and *Minutes of the Third Annual Session of the Atlanta Missionary Baptist Association*, 1906, Georgia Baptist Collection, Mercer University Library (hereafter cited as GBC, MU).

91. See, for example, *Minutes of the Annual Session of the Antioch Primitive Baptist Association*, 1879–1913, GBC, MU; Clarence M. Wagner, *Profiles of Black Georgia Baptists* (Gainesville, Ga.: Wagner, 1980); Evelyn Brooks Higginbotham, *Righteous Discontent: The Women's Movement in the Black Baptist Church, 1880–1920* (Cambridge, Mass.: Harvard University Press, 1993), pp. 47–80.

92. First Congregational Church Records, microfilm, GAH.

93. See, for example, Isaiah 14:32 (Revised Standard Version); Bruce M. Metzger and Michael D. Coogan, *Oxford Companion to the Bible* (New York: Oxford University Press, 1993), p. 830.

94. All information on secret societies in Atlanta is taken from the following sources: Freedman's Bank Records; U.S. Manuscript Population Census, Fulton County, 1870; *Atlanta City Directory*, 1870–1872, 1874; E. R. Carter, *The Black Side: A Partial History of the Business, Religious and Educational Side of the Negro in Atlanta, Ga.* (Atlanta, 1894; reprint ed., Freeport, N.Y.: Books for Libraries Press, 1971), pp. 24–27; W. E. B. Du Bois, ed., *Some Efforts of American Negroes for their Own Social Betterment* (Atlanta: Atlanta University Press, 1898), pp. 12–20; W. E. B. Du Bois, ed., *Efforts for Social Betterment Among Negro Americans* (Atlanta: Atlanta University Press, 1909); *American Missionary* (October 1889): 292; Southern Regional Office Records, National Urban League Papers, Library of Congress; *Atlanta Constitution*, 23 October 1912.

95. *Southern Recorder*, 20 April 1888.

96. *Atlanta Constitution*, May 1877, 9 January 1879. Thornbery, "Black Atlanta," p. 255. See also Chapter 4.

97. See Peter J. Rachleff, *Black Labor in the South: Richmond, Virginia, 1865–1890* (Philadelphia: Temple University Press, 1984), pp. 30–31.

98. Freedman's Bank Records; Carter, *Black Side*, p. 26.

99. See Freedman's Bank Records; U.S. Manuscript Population Census, Fulton County, 1870 and 1880; *Atlanta City Directory*, 1870–1872.

100. Dittmer, *Black Georgia*, p. 45.

101. Claude F. Jacobs, "Benevolent Societies of New Orleans Blacks During the Late Nineteenth and Early Twentieth Centuries," *Louisiana History* 29 (Winter 1988): 21–33.

102. Ibid. Some white health care professionals objected to this function and accused secret societies of spreading disease. See, for example, Oscar Dowling, "The Negro and Public Health," in *The Call of the New South: Addresses Delivered at*

the Southern Sociological Congress, Nashville, Tennessee, May 7 to 10, 1992, ed. James E. McCulloch (Nashville: Southern Sociological Congress, 1912), p. 213.

103. See Betty M. Kuyk, "The African Derivation of Black Fraternal Orders in the United States," *Comparative Studies in Society and History* 25 (October 1983): 559–592; Carter G. Woodson, "Insurance Business Among Negroes," *Journal of Negro History* 14 (April 1929): 202–226; Monroe N. Work, "Secret Societies as Factors in the Social and Economic Life of the Negro," in *Democracy in Earnest: Southern Sociological Congress 1916–1918*, ed. James E. McCulloch (Washington, D.C.: Southern Sociological Congress, 1918), pp. 342–350.

104. Kuyk, "African Derivation of Black Fraternal Orders," passim.

105. Rachleff, *Black Labor in the South*, pp. 13–33. Sarah Jane Early estimated that women's mutual aid societies for the entire South numbered more than five thousand, with at least 250,000 total members. See Early, "The Organized Effort of the Colored Women of the South to Improve Their Condition," *National WCTU Annual Report* (1894), in *The Three Sarahs: Documents of Antebellum Black College Women*, ed. Ellen NicKenzie Lawson (New York: E. Mellen Press, 1984), pp. 718–724; Kathleen C. Berkeley, "'Like a Plague of Locust': Immigration and Social Change in Memphis, Tennessee" (Ph.D. diss., University of California, Los Angeles, 1980), pp. 165–223; Armstead L. Robinson, "Plans Dat Comed from God: Institution Building and the Emergence of Black Leadership in Reconstruction Memphis," in *Toward a New South? Studies in Post-Civil War Southern Communities*, ed. Robert McMath and Orville Burton (Westport, Conn.: Greenwood Press, 1982), pp. 71–102; Elsa Barkley Brown, "Womanist Consciousness: Maggie Lena Walker and the Independent Order of Saint Luke," *Signs* 14 (Spring): 610–633.

106. Testimony of Mrs. Ward, 15 November 1883, *Labor and Capital*, vol. 4, p. 344; Ma [Margaret Cronly] to darling Rob [Cronly], 29 June 1881, Cronly Family Papers, DU.

4. "Washing Amazons" and Organized Protests

1. *Jackson Daily Clarion*, 24 June 1866, in *The Black Worker: A Documentary History from Colonial Times to the Present*, 8 vols., ed. Philip S. Foner and Ronald L. Lewis (Philadelphia: Temple University Press, 1978–1984), vol. 2, p. 345; see also Dorothy Sterling, ed., *We Are Your Sisters: Black Women in the Nineteenth Century* (New York: Norton Press, 1984), p. 356.

2. *Jackson Daily Clarion*, 24 June 1866, in Foner and Lewis, *Black Worker*, vol. 2, pp. 344–345.

3. Ibid.

4. Leon F. Litwack, *Been in the Storm So Long: The Aftermath of Slavery* (New York: Knopf, 1979), p. 441; Philip S. Foner, *Organized Labor and the Black Worker 1619–1973* (New York: International Publishers, 1974), pp. 17–22; Eric Arneson, *Waterfront Workers of New Orleans: Race, Class and Politics 1863–1923* (New York: Oxford University Press, 1991), pp. 21–25, 28–32, 53–59; Peter J. Rachleff, *Black Labor in the South: Richmond, Virginia, 1865–1890* (Philadelphia: Temple University Press, 1984), pp. 42–44, 73, 81.

5. Philip S. Foner, *The Great Labor Uprising of 1877* (New York: Monad Press, 1977), pp. 7–9.

6. Ibid., pp. 197–199; *Galveston Daily News*, 31 July 1877.

7. *Galveston Daily News*, 1–7 August 1877.

8. Ibid., 1 August 1877.

9. Ibid.; Sterling, *We Are Your Sisters*, pp. 356–357; Foner and Lewis, *Black Worker*, vol. 2, p. 167.

10. *Galveston Daily News*, 7 August 1877.

11. Ibid., 1 August 1877.

12. Ibid.

13. Ronald Takaki, *Strangers from a Different Shore: A History of Asian Americans* (New York: Little, Brown, 1989; reprint ed., New York: Penguin Books, 1990), pp. 92–95; Suecheng Chan, *Asian Americans: An Interpretive History* (Boston: Twayne, 1991), pp. 33–34; Paul C. P. Siu, *The Chinese Laundryman: A Study of Social Isolation*, ed. John Kuo Wei Tchen (New York: New York University Press, 1987), pp. 45–54.

14. *Galveston Daily News*, 1 August 1877.

15. Ibid., 5 August 1877.

16. Maud Cuney-Hare, *Norris Wright Cuney: A Tribune of the Black People*, ed. Tera W. Hunter (Austin: Steck-Vaughn, 1913; reprint ed., New York: G. K. Hall, 1995); Lawrence D. Rice, *The Negro in Texas: 1874–1890* (Baton Rouge: Louisiana State University Press, 1971), pp. 35–37, 78, 82, 95, 189–190.

17. *Galveston Daily News*, 1 August 1877. See the biography of Cuney written by his daughter, Maud Cuney-Hare, which praises Cuney and condemns the strikers' grievances as "not important enough to demand public sympathy." Cuney-Hare, *Norris Wright Cuney*, p. 24.

18. For a discussion of the variety and forms of black political leadership in this era, see Nell Irvin Painter, *Exodusters: Black Migration to Kansas after Reconstruction* (New York: Knopf, 1976), pp. 14–16, 65, 71–137, 243–255; Thomas C. Holt, *Black Over White: Negro Political Leadership in South Carolina during Reconstruction* (Urbana: University of Illinois Press, 1977).

19. *Galveston Daily News*, 1 August 1877.

20. Ibid., 5 August 1871.

21. Ibid., 7 August 1877.

22. Ibid., 2 August 1877.

23. Ibid., 16 August 1877.

24. On women's protest styles and the use of public space see Temma Kaplan, "Female Consciousness and Collective Action: The Case of Barcelona, 1910–1918," *Signs* 7 (Spring 1982): 552–564; Jacquelyn Dowd Hall, "Disorderly Women: Gender and Labor Militancy in the Appalachian South," *Journal of American History* 73 (September 1986): 366, 372–375.

25. Mary Roberts Davis, "The Planning of the Industrial Expositions of 1881 and 1895: Expressions of the Philosophy of the New South" (M.A. thesis, Emory University, 1952), provides a splendid critique of the Atlanta Expositions and the New South movement unmatched by other accounts. See also Augusta Wylie King, "International Cotton Exposition: October 5th to December 31, 1881, Atlanta, Georgia," *Atlanta Historical Bulletin* 4 (July 1939): 181–198; C. Vann Woodward, *Origins of the New South, 1877–1913* (Baton Rouge: Louisiana State University Press, 1951), p. 124; James Michael Russell, *Atlanta, 1847–1890: City Building in the Old South and the New* (Baton Rouge: Louisiana State University Press, 1988),

pp. 234–235; Don H. Doyle, *New Men, New Cities, New South: Atlanta, Nashville, Charleston, Mobile, 1860–1910* (Chapel Hill: University of North Carolina Press, 1990), pp. 152–158.

26. Ibid.

27. On this painting, see King, "International Cotton Exposition," p. 191; Davis, "Industrial Expositions," p. 9.

28. For a similar interpretation of Southern fairs that followed the 1881 exposition, as well as other fairs throughout the nation, see Robert W. Rydell, *All the World's a Fair: Visions of Empire at American International Expositions, 1876–1916* (Chicago: University of Chicago Press, 1984), pp. 2–8, 72–104.

29. As quoted in Davis, "Industrial Expositions," p. 20; see also Doyle, *New Men*, p. 155.

30. Davis, "Industrial Expositions," pp. 143–148.

31. Ibid.; *Marietta Journal*, 15 and 20 September 1881 (emphasis added).

32. *Atlanta Constitution*, 10 September and 12 December 1880, as quoted in Davis, "Industrial Expositions," p. 142.

33. James Michael Russell, "Atlanta, Gate City of the South, 1847–1885" (Ph.D. diss., Princeton University, 1971), p. 243.

34. Jerry Thornbery, "The Development of Black Atlanta, 1865–1885" (Ph.D. diss., University of Maryland, College Park, 1977), p. 211; *Atlanta Constitution*, 6 September 1881.

35. On this point see Elsa Barkley Brown, "Negotiating and Transforming the Public Sphere: African American Political Life in the Transition from Slavery to Freedom," *Public Culture* 7 (Fall 1994): 123; James C. Scott, *Domination and the Arts of Resistance: Hidden Transcripts* (New Haven: Yale University Press, 1990), pp. 108–135; Kaplan, "Female Consciousness," pp. 545–566.

36. *Atlanta Constitution*, 29 May 1877.

37. Ibid., 9 January 1879 and 29 July 1881.

38. Ibid., 29 July 1881.

39. Thornbery, "Black Atlanta," pp. 226–265; Eugene J. Watts, "Black Political Progress in Atlanta, 1868–1895," *Journal of Negro History* 59 (July 1974): 272–275.

40. Thornbery, "Black Atlanta," p. 245; Watts, "Black Political Progress," pp. 272–275; James Michael Russell and Jerry Thornbery, "William Finch of Atlanta: The Black Politician as Civic Leader," in *Southern Black Leaders of the Reconstruction Era*, ed. Howard N. Rabinowitz (Urbana: University of Illinois Press, 1982), pp. 312–329.

41. See Ruth Currie McDaniel, "Black Power in Georgia: William A. Pledger and the Takeover of the Republican Party," *The Georgia Historical Quarterly* 62 (Fall 1978): 225–239; Olive Hall Shadgett, *The Republican Party in Georgia: From Redemption through 1900* (Athens: University of Georgia Press, 1964), pp. 76–89; Russell and Thornbery, "William Finch of Atlanta," p. 328.

42. *Atlanta Constitution*, 3 August 1880. On other political meetings see *Atlanta Constitution*, 18 September 1880; Thornbery, "Black Atlanta," p. 329; Watts, "Black Political Progress," p. 275.

43. *Atlanta Constitution*, 3 August 1880.

44. See Chapter 2.

45. For the best analysis of women and politics during this period see Brown, "Negotiating and Transforming the Public Sphere," pp. 107–146.

46. *Atlanta Constitution*, 20 and 29 July 1881.

47. The following historians have treated the washerwomen's strike. They all borrow from Howard N. Rabinowitz's account, which emphasizes black inefficacy in the face of white power. Rabinowitz's haste in minimizing the significance of the event led him to ignore important evidence to the contrary and to overstate the reprisals made against the women. See Howard N. Rabinowitz, *Race Relations in the Urban South, 1865–1890* (New York: Oxford University Press, 1978), pp. 74–76; David M. Katzman, *Seven Days a Week: Women and Domestic Service in Industrializing America* (New York: Oxford University Press, 1978), pp. 196–197; William H. Harris, *The Harder We Run: Black Workers Since the Civil War* (New York: Oxford University Press, 1982), p. 37; Faye E. Dudden, *Serving Women: Household Service in Nineteenth Century America* (Middletown, Conn.: Wesleyan University Press, 1983), p. 232; Sterling, *We Are Your Sisters*, pp. 357–358; Jacqueline Jones, *Labor of Love, Labor of Sorrow: Black Women, Work, and the Family from Slavery to the Present* (New York: Basic Books, 1980), pp. 148–149; Donna Van Raaphorst, *Union Maids Not Wanted: Organizing Domestic Workers 1870–1940* (New York: Praeger, 1988), p. 200. My own interpretation is closest to the only other study that has considered most of the available evidence: Thornbery, "Black Atlanta," pp. 215–220.

48. Thornbery, "Black Atlanta," pp. 219–220.

49. *Atlanta Constitution*, 21 July 1881. For notices of the strike in newspapers in the vicinity, see Athens *Weekly Banner*, 2 August 1881, and *Marietta Journal*, 11 August 1881.

50. According to Susan Levine, local papers in the nineteenth century often called women trade unionists "amazons" instead of "ladies" to undermine their femininity. Despite the intention to insult the women's character, however, the language acknowledged the political potency of their actions. See "Labor's True Women: Domesticity and Equal Rights in the Knights of Labor," *Journal of American History* 70 (September 1983): 323–339.

51. See Christine Stansell, *City of Women: Sex and Class in New York, 1789–1860* (New York: Alfred A. Knopf, 1986), pp. 58–62, 82–83; Kaplan, "Female Consciousness," pp. 558, 565.

52. *Atlanta Constitution*, 29 July 1881.

53. Ibid.

54. See Rabinowitz, *Race Relations in the Urban South*, p. 112; Gretchen Ehrmann Maclachlan, "Women's Work: Atlanta's Industrialization and Urbanization, 1879–1929" (Ph.D. diss., Emory University, 1992), p. 271.

55. *Atlanta Constitution*, 29 July 1881.

56. It is possible that Sam Gardner was punished along with the women, but the newspaper report of the court proceedings did not mention any action taken against him. See *Atlanta Constitution*, 30 July 1881.

57. See U.S. Manuscript Population Census, Fulton County, 1880. The census lists a "Carrie Jones," age twenty-nine, as a live-in cook with an eight-year-old son. It is possible that Jones could have worked as a washerwoman the next year. There were two Sallie Bells listed. The other was identified as a thirty-seven-year-old washerwoman living on Grady's Row in Summer Hill. She was married to Thomas, a fifty-two-year-old hotel porter who was sometimes unemployed. Other occupants in the Thomases' home included their three-year-old daughter and Sallie's eighteen-year-old brother, a barroom worker. A family of seven was also listed as sharing

the same dwelling: Malinda Hill, a thirty-year-old washerwoman, with five children and a husband.

58. *Atlanta Constitution*, 21 and 29 July 1881.

59. Ibid., 29 July 1881. Dora Watts, a live-in domestic worker on Jones Street near Summer Hill, was the alleged informant.

60. *Atlanta Constitution*, 24 July 1881.

61. See Table 3 at the back of the book.

62. See Susan Strasser, *Never Done: A History of American Housework* (New York: Pantheon Books, 1982), pp. 116–121; Katzman, *Seven Days a Week*, pp. 130–134. Gretchen Maclachlan argues that the washerwomen's predominance was "challenged" by steam laundries beginning in the 1880s; however, the evidence does not support this claim. See "Women's Work," p. 229.

63. *Atlanta Constitution*, 20 July 1881.

64. Thornbery, "Black Atlanta," pp. 212–213.

65. See, for example, *Atlanta Constitution*, 20 February 1975.

66. *Atlanta Constitution*, 3 August 1881 (emphasis added); Atlanta City Council Minutes, 1 and 15 August 1881, vol. 9, Atlanta History Center (hereafter cited as AHC).

67. *Atlanta Constitution*, 3 August 1881.

68. Ibid.

69. Ibid.

70. Ibid.

71. Ibid., 21 and 26 July 1881.

72. Ibid., 29 July 1881. See also Rabinowitz, *Race Relations in the Urban South*, p. 73; Thornbery, "Black Atlanta," pp. 218–219.

73. Atlanta City Council Minutes, 15 August 1881, AHC; *Atlanta Constitution*, 16 August 1881.

74. The paper reported early that at least one employer yielded to her laundry workers' demands. But no other information was printed on how many employers relented or refused to raise wages. See *Atlanta Constitution*, 26 July 1881.

75. Ibid., 6 September 1881.

76. *New York Times*, 4 August 1881.

77. Hannibal I. Kimball, *International Cotton Exposition (Atlanta, Georgia 1881): Report of the Director-General* (New York: D. Appleton, 1882), pp. 584–585. See also Woodward, *Origins of the New South*, p. 124.

78. For an excellent discussion of the evolution of boarding practices in Atlanta see Maclachlan, "Working Women," pp. 163–168, 174–177.

79. Athens *Weekly Banner*, 17 May and 28 June 1881.

80. For an original reading of black working-class self-activity see Robin D. G. Kelley, "'We are Not What We Seem': Rethinking Black Working-Class Opposition in the Jim Crow South," *Journal of American History* 80 (June 1993): 75–112. See also James C. Scott, *Weapons of the Weak: Everyday Forms of Peasant Resistance* (New Haven: Yale University Press, 1985), especially chaps. 2, 7, 8. On women's ability to transform everyday cultural traditions into mass mobilizations against their oppressors see Kaplan, "Female Consciousness."

81. On the dialectical relationship between domination and resistance see Kelley, "'We are Not What We Seem'"; Scott, *Domination and the Arts of Resistance*, especially chaps. 1, 3, 4; Rosalind O'Hanlon, "Recovering the Subject *Subaltern*

Studies and Histories of Resistance in Colonial South Asia," *Modern Asian Studies* 22 (1988): 189–224; and Lila Abu-Lughod, "The Romance of Resistance: Tracing Transformations of Power through Bedouin Women," *American Ethnologist* 17 (February 1990): 41–55.

5. The "Color Line" Gives Way to the "Color Wall"

1. The language of the law, as quoted in August Meier and Elliott Rudwick, "The Boycott Movement against Jim Crow Streetcars in the South, 1900–1906," in Meier and Rudwick, *Along the Color Line: Explorations in the Black Experience* (Urbana: University of Illinois Press, 1976), p. 268.

2. *Savannah Tribune*, 29 August 1896.

3. *Savannah Tribune*, 5 November 1892, 15 September 1896; *Atlanta Constitution*, 25–26 July 1896, 3 and 14 August 1896; *Atlanta Independent*, 6 February 1906; Meier and Rudwick, "Boycott Movement," pp. 267–289; John Dittmer, *Black Georgia in the Progressive Era, 1900–1920* (Urbana: University of Illinois Press, 1977), pp. 16–19; Clarence A. Bacote, "Negro Proscriptions, Protests, and Proposed Georgia Solutions, 1880–1908," *Journal of Southern History* 25 (November 1959): 476–478; Robin D. G. Kelley, "'We are Not What We Seem': Rethinking Black Working-Class Opposition in the Jim Crow South," *Journal of American History* 80 (June 1993): 103–110; Howard N. Rabinowitz, *Race Relations in the Urban South, 1865–1890* (New York: Oxford University Press, 1978), pp. 190–194.

4. See Earl Lewis, *In Their Own Interests: Race, Class, and Power in Twentieth Century Norfolk, Virginia* (Berkeley: University of California Press, 1991), pp. 90–109.

5. *Atlanta Journal and Constitution*, 26 December 1991; *Atlanta Constitution*, 21 August 1904; Dana F. White, "The Black Sides of Atlanta: A Geography of Expansion and Containment, 1970–1870," *Atlanta Historical Journal* 30 (Summer-Fall 1982): 208–209.

6. Lee Fuse Wood, *The Bedford Pine Neighborhood (Atlanta, GA), 1871–1987* (College Park, Ga.: Ditto Press, 1988); Timothy J. Crimmins, "Atlanta Palimpsest: Stripping Away the Layers of the Past," *Atlanta Historical Journal* 30 (Summer-Fall 1982): 31; Michael Leroy Porter, "Black Atlanta: An Interdisciplinary Study of Blacks on the East Side of Atlanta, 1890–1930" (Ph.D. diss., Emory University, 1974), pp. 92–93, 104.

7. Porter, "Black Atlanta," pp. 178–189; Kathleen Adams, Interview by Bernard E. West, 11 March 1979, transcript, Living Atlanta Collection, Atlanta History Center (hereafter cited as AHC).

8. Alexa Henderson and Eugene Walker, "Sweet Auburn: The Thriving Hub of Black Atlanta, 1900–1960" (unpublished paper prepared for the Martin Luther King, Jr., National Historic Site), AHC; Porter, "Black Atlanta," pp. 118–151; Kathleen Adams, Interview.

9. Mildred Warner, *Community Building: The History of Atlanta University Neighborhoods* (n.p., 1978), AHC; Ann D. Byrne and Dana F. White, "Atlanta University's 'Northeast Lot': Community Building for Black Atlanta's Talented Tenth," *Atlanta Historical Journal* 30 (Summer-Fall 1982): 156–173.

10. Timothy J. Crimmins, "West End: Metamorphosis from Suburban Town

to Intown Neighborhood," *Atlanta Historical Journal* 30 (Summer-Fall 1982): 47; Don L. Klima, "Breaking Out: Streetcars and Suburban Development, 1872–1900," *Atlanta Historical Journal* 30 (Summer-Fall 1982): 74–81; Dana F. White, "Landscaped Atlanta: The Romantic Tradition in Cemetery, Park, and Suburban Development," *Atlanta Historical Journal* 30 (Summer-Fall 1982): 102–105; Rick Beard, "From Suburb to Defended Neighborhood: The Evolution of Inman Park and Ansley Park, 1890–1980," *Atlanta Historical Journal* 30 (Summer-Fall 1982): 113–123.

11. "A Community History of the Johnsontown Neighborhood" (unpublished paper prepared for the Division of Planning and Marketing Department of Planning and Public Affairs, Metropolitan Atlanta Rapid Transit Authority), 1981, AHC; Porter, "Black Atlanta," pp. 105–108; Great Britain, Board of Trade, *Cost of Living in American Towns* (London: Her Majesty's Stationery Office, 1911), p. 56.

12. *Atlanta Journal and Constitution*, 26 December 1991; Stephen W. Grable, "The Other Side of the Tracks: Cabbagetown—A Working-Class Neighborhood in Transition During the Early Twentieth Century," *Atlanta Historical Journal* 30 (Summer-Fall 1982): 51–67; Gary M. Fink, *The Fulton Bag and Cotton Mills Strike of 1914–1915: Espionage, Labor Conflict, and New South Industrial Relations* (Ithaca, N.Y.: ILR Press, 1993), pp. 17–18, 26–30, 39; Gretchen Ehrmann Maclachlan, "Women's Work: Atlanta's Industrialization and Urbanization, 1879–1929" (Ph.D. diss., Emory University, 1992), pp. 39–41, 60–65; Porter, "Black Atlanta," pp. 106–107, 110.

13. *Atlanta Independent*, 25 July 1908; Atlanta *Journal of Labor*, 10 February 1905; Howard L. Preston, *Automobile Age Atlanta: The Making of a Southern Metropolis 1900–1935* (Athens: University of Georgia Press, 1979), pp. 12–15.

14. W. E. B. Du Bois, "The Problem of Housing the Negro: V. The Southern City Negro of the Lower Class," in *Du Bois: Writings in Periodicals Edited by Others*, ed. Herbert Aptheker (Millwood, N.Y.: Kraus-Thomson, 1982), pp. 131–134; W. E. B. Du Bois, ed., *The Negro American Family* (Atlanta: Atlanta University, 1908), pp. 73–74; British Board of Trade, *Cost of Living*, p. 57.

15. Atlanta *Journal of Labor*, 24 April 1911. On rental prices see Du Bois, "The Problem of Housing," p. 133; Lucy Laney, "Causes of Excessive Mortality: Poverty," in *Mortality Among Negroes in Cities*, ed. Thomas N. Chase (Atlanta: Atlanta University, 1896), p. 19; "Condition of the Negro in Various Cities," *Bulletin of the Department of Labor* 2 (May 1897): 291–294; Atlanta *Journal of Labor*, 24 March 1916, 12 September 1919.

16. Lugenia Burns Hope, Draft Speech, 1908 or 1909, Neighborhood Union Papers, Robert W. Woodruff Library, Clarke Atlanta University (hereafter cited as NU, AU). See also H. R. Butler, "Causes of Excessive Mortality: Neglect," in Chase, *Mortality Among Negroes in Cities*, p. 17.

17. Dittmer, *Black Georgia*, pp. 13–14; *Atlanta Constitution*, 14 June 1913.

18. Maclachlan, "Women's Work," pp. 180–188.

19. *Savannah Tribune*, 27 May 1893. See also Alice Adams, Interview, by Bernard E. West, 20 November 1979, transcript, Living Atlanta Collection, AHC; A Negro Nurse, "More Slavery at the South," *Independent* (25 January 1912): 198–199.

20. Maclachlan, "Women's Work," pp. 172, 183, 188.

21. Nurse, "More Slavery at the South," pp. 196–197.

22. Ibid., pp. 197–198; W. E. B. Du Bois, "The Negroes of Farmville, Virginia: A Social Study," *Bulletin of the Department of Labor* 3 (January 1898): 22.

23. Sarah Hill, "Bea the Washerwoman," p. 4, Federal Writers Project Papers, Southern Historical Collection, University of North Carolina, Chapel Hill (hereafter cited as FWP, SHC). See also Du Bois, "Negroes of Farmville," p. 22; David M. Katzman, *Seven Days a Week: Women and Domestic Service in Industrializing America* (New York: Oxford University Press, 1978), pp. 216–217; Elizabeth Clark-Lewis, *Living In, Living Out: African American Domestics in Washington, D.C., 1910–1940* (Washington, D.C.: Smithsonian Institution Press, 1994), pp. 48–49.

24. Elizabeth Kytle, *Willie Mae* (New York: Knopf, 1958), p. 116.

25. Alice Adams, Interview.

26. Daisy Johnson, "All I do is Just Heads," FWP, SHC.

27. A Negro Nurse, "More Slavery at the South," p. 197.

28. For complaints about poor service and character flaws see *Atlanta Constitution*, 4 November 1900, 7 and 9 August 1901, 5 June 1904; see, for example, T. J. Woofter, "Negroes of Athens, Georgia," *Bulletin of the University of Georgia* 14 (December 1913): 45–47.

29. For an insightful comparison see Peter Linebaugh, *The London Hanged: Crime and Civil Society in the Eighteenth Century* (Cambridge: Cambridge University Press, 1992), pp. 329–330.

30. Ray Stannard Baker, *Following the Color Line: An Account of Negro Citizenship in the American Democracy* (1908; reprint ed., New York: Harper and Row, 1964), p. 58.

31. On white working-class employers see Ruby Owens, Interview by Bernard E. West, 23 January 1979, tape recording, Living Atlanta Collection, AHC; British Board of Trade, *Cost of Living*, p. 52; Laura Julia Campbell Buggs et al., "The Three Sisters," FWP, SHC; *Journal of Labor*, 20 November and 11 December 1903, 29 May 1908; Baker, *Following the Color Line*, p. 53; Kytle, *Willie Mae*, pp. 118–119; Walter L. Fleming, "The Servant Problem in a Black Belt Village," *Sewanee Review* 8 (January 1905): 14; Du Bois, "Negroes of Farmville," p. 21; Katzman, *Seven Days a Week*, pp. 185–187; interviews with Mrs. Boyd, Cecilia Trommerhauser, and Annie Green, Home Visit Schedules (Georgia), Record Group 86: U.S. Department of Labor, Women's Bureau, National Archives; Susan Tucker, *Telling Memories Among Southern Women: Domestic Workers and Their Employers in the Segregated South* (Baton Rouge: Louisiana State University Press, 1988), pp. 116, 117–118, 161, 227–228; Susan Strasser, *Never Done: The History of American Housework* (New York: Pantheon, 1982), pp. 105–121; Timothy J. Crimmins, "Bungalow Suburbs: East and West," *Atlanta Historical Journal* 30 (Summer-Fall 1982): 84–86; Clifford M. Kuhn et al., *Living Atlanta: An Oral History of the City, 1914–1918* (Athens: University of Georgia Press, 1990), p. 113; Steven Hertzberg, *Strangers Within the Gate City: The Jews of Atlanta, 1845–1915* (Philadelphia: Jewish Publication Society of America, 1978), p. 182; Dolores Janiewski, *Sisterhood Denied: Race, Gender, and Class in a New South Community* (Philadelphia: Temple University Press, 1985), pp. 43–44, 127–129; Victoria Byerly, *Hard Times Cotton Mill Girls: Personal Histories of Womanhood and Poverty in the South* (Ithaca, N.Y.: Cornell University Press, 1986), pp. 99, 125, 132, 147, 152. For a comparison of white South African miners hiring black servants and laundrymen see Charles van Onselen, *Studies in the Social and Economic History of the Witwatersrand, 1886–1914*, vol. 1: *New Babylon*, pp. 7–8, vol. 2: *New Nineveh*, pp. 3–7, 22 (New York: Longman, 1982).

32. Entries of 28 July and 14 September 1885, Emily J. W. Bealer Diary, Georgia Department of Archives and History (hereafter cited as GAH).

33. See entries for September 1880, Bealer Diary, GAH.

34. Polly Stone Buck, *The Blessed Town: Oxford, Georgia, at the Turn of the Century* (Chapel Hill: University of North Carolina Press, 1986), p. 115.

35. Glenn Rainey, Interview by Clifford M. Kuhn, 14 February 1979, transcript, Living Atlanta Collection, AHC.

36. Baker, *Following the Color Line*, p. 53. See also Sarah Myers, FWP, SHC.

37. Aside from the evidence of the high ratio of domestics per employing families (see Table 3 at the back of the book), which substantiates the widespread availability of domestic work for hire, there are no statistics available for this period of study to verify the extent to which white wage-earners hired domestic workers. There are estimates on the 1930s that confirm the common practice of working-class whites hiring black servants, however. See C. Arnold Anderson and Mary Jean Bowman, "The Vanishing Servant and the Contemporary Status System of the American South," *American Journal of Sociology* 59 (November 1953): 223–224; Phyllis Palmer, *Domesticity and Dirt: Housewives and Domestic Servants in the United States, 1920–1945* (Philadelphia: Temple University Press, 1989), pp. 7–13. See also Catherine L. Woods to "Your Excellency" [Franklin D. Roosevelt], 20 October 1933, Record Group 86: Women's Bureau, Correspondence, Household (Domestic File), National Archives.

38. Buggs, "The Three Sisters," p. 10, FWP, SHC. For examples of the complexities of these relationships, see Byerly, *Hard Times Cotton Mill Girls*, pp. 99, 125, 132, 147, 152.

39. See Kytle, *Willie Mae*, pp. 118–119.

40. Du Bois, "Negroes of Farmville," p. 21; Anderson and Bowman, "Vanishing Servant," p. 225; Annie Alexander, Interview by Bernard E. West, 29 May 1979, transcript, Living Atlanta Collection, AHC; "Condition of the Negro in Various Cities," p. 287; *Atlanta Constitution*, 22 July 1899; Justice R. H. Terrell, "The Negro in Domestic Service," *The Colored American Magazine* 9 (November 1905): 631–633; Willard B. Gatewood, *Aristocrats of Color: The Black Elite, 1880–1920* (Bloomington: Indiana University Press, 1993), p. 196; Alexa Benson Henderson, *Atlanta Life Insurance Company: Guardian of Black Economic Dignity* (Athens: University of Georgia Press, 1990), pp. 30–31.

41. Ruth Reed, *Negro Women of Gainesville, Georgia* (Athens: University of Georgia Press, 1921), p. 17.

42. *Atlanta Constitution*, 5 May 1891.

43. W. E. B. Du Bois, ed., *The Negro Artisan* (Atlanta: Atlanta University, 1902), p. 90; W. E. B. Du Bois, ed., *The Negro American Artisan* (Atlanta: Atlanta University, 1912), p. 46; see Table 2 at the back of the book.

44. On dressmakers see Eileen Boris, "Black Women and Paid Labor in the Home: Industrial Homework in Chicago in the 1920s," in *Homework: Historical and Contemporary Perspectives on Paid Labor at Home*, ed. Eileen Boris and Cynthia R. Daniels (Urbana: University of Illinois Press, 1989), pp. 33–38; Joan M. Jensen, "Needlework as Art, Craft, and Livelihood Before 1900," *A Needle, A Bobbin, A Strike: Women Needleworkers in America*, ed. Joan M. Jensen and Sue Davidson (Philadelphia: Temple University Press, 1984), pp. 13–16; Ava Baron and Susan E. Kelp, "'If I Didn't Have My Sewing Machine': Women and Sewing-Machine Technology," in Jensen and Davidson, *Needle*, pp. 47, 50; Maclachlan, "Women's Work," pp. 33–34, 52.

45. *Atlanta Independent*, 23 January 1904; Atlanta *Weekly Defiance*, 24 February 1883; *Atlanta Independent*, 7 October 1905, 27 January 1906, 28 April 1906.

46. Du Bois, *Negro Artisan* (1902), p. 28.

47. See Atlanta *Weekly Defiance*, 24 February 1883; *Atlanta Independent*, 26 March 1904, 3 March 1906, 1 August 1906; *Atlanta Constitution*, 5 August 1903, 15 March 1907; Table 2 at the back of the book; Maclachlan, "Women's Work," pp. 19–93. On Laura Ryals see *Atlanta Constitution*, 18 October 1904.

48. For example, see *Atlanta Constitution*, 17 September 1895; 3 July 1899; 2 February 1909; 8 February 1912.

49. *Atlanta Constitution*, 5 July 1889, 17 September 1895, 26 March, 15 May, 18 and 19 June 1900; 30 November 1902; *Atlanta Journal*, 12 April and 12 August 1901; *Atlanta Independent*, 28 October 1905, 22 September 1906; "Condition of the Negro in Various Cities," pp. 257–359; "Reports of the Martha Home," 1913–1915, Christian Council Papers, AHC; Minute Book, 1908–1918, NU, AU; *Report of the Vice Commission to the Mayor and Council of the City of Atlanta, Ga.* (Atlanta, 1912); Maclachlan, "Women's Work," pp. 203–225; Ruth Rosen, *The Lost Sisterhood: Prostitution in America, 1900–1918* (Baltimore: Johns Hopkins University Press, 1982).

50. Ruby Owens, Interview.

51. Ibid.

52. Ibid.

53. *Atlanta Constitution*, 5 August 1897; Maclachlan, "Women's Work," pp. 77–86; Mercer Griffin Evans, "The History of the Organized Labor Movement in Georgia" (Ph.D. diss., University of Chicago, 1929), pp. 84–85.

54. *Atlanta Constitution*, 5 August 1897. See Jacquelyn Dowd Hall et al., *Like a Family: The Making of a Southern Cotton Mill World* (Chapel Hill: University of North Carolina Press, 1987), p. 66; Maclachlan, "Women's Work," p. 82.

55. Hall, *Like a Family*, p. 36.

56. *Atlanta Constitution*, 5 August 1897.

57. Ibid., 5 August 1897.

58. Ibid., 6 August 1897.

59. Ibid., 6 August 1897.

60. Ibid., 8 and 9 August 1897; Fink, *Fulton Bag and Cotton Mill Strike*, p. 40; Hall, *Like a Family*, p. 101; Maclachlan, "Women's Work," p. 84; Eugene J. Watts, *Social Basis of City Politics: Atlanta, 1865–1903* (Westport, Conn.: Greenwood Press, 1978), pp. 30, 73–74, 102, 117, 156; Thomas Mashburn Deaton, "Atlanta During the Progressive Era" (Ph.D. diss., University of Georgia, 1969), pp. 303–354. For reports on the growth of white labor unions and women's involvement see *Atlanta Journal*, 30 March 1901, and *Atlanta Constitution*, 17 and 19 July 1901.

61. *Atlanta Constitution*, 7, 8, and 15 December 1897.

62. Ibid., 16 December 1897.

63. John Michael Mathews, "Studies in Race Relations in Georgia" (Ph.D. diss., Duke University, 1970), p. 218.

64. For comparison see Elsa Barkley Brown and Gregg D. Kimball, "Mapping the Terrain of Black Richmond," *Journal of Urban History* 21 (March 1995): 325–328.

65. See Maclachlan, "Women's Work," pp. 52–68; Jacquelyn Dowd Hall, "Private Eyes, Public Women: Images of Class and Sex in the Urban South,

Atlanta, Georgia, 1913–1915," in *Work Engendered: Toward a New History of American Labor*, ed. Ava Baron (Ithaca, N.Y.: Cornell University Press, 1991), pp. 260–261.

66. Atlanta *Weekly Defiance*, 28 October 1881, as quoted in Eugene J. Watts, "The Police in Atlanta, 1890–1905," *Journal of Southern History* 39 (May 1973): 172. See also Howard N. Rabinowitz, "The Conflict between Blacks and the Police in the Urban South, 1865–1900," *The Historian* 39 (November 1976): 62–76; Dittmer, *Black Georgia*, pp. 138–139.

67. For examples of conflicts between blacks and white policemen see *Atlanta Constitution*, 18 February 1880; 14 July 1881; 28 September 1881; 2 May 1882; 17 August 1883; 25 August 1883; 2 April 1885; 9 March 1887; 1–3 August 1888; 13 October 1888; 22 October 1888; 5 July 1889; 27 July 1896; 14 January 1896; 7 August 1897; 8 April 1901; 31 July 1901; 26 March 1909; 14 March 1909; 18 March 1909; 7 May 1911.

68. *Atlanta Constitution*, 27 September 1881.

69. Gertrude is an invented name; only her surname was identified in the newspaper.

70. *Atlanta Constitution*, 27 September 1881. There were several other incidents where African Americans contested police arrests in other parts of the city on the same day.

71. For examples, see *Atlanta Constitution*, 16 March 1880; 31 July 1887; 28 December 1901.

72. Atlanta *Weekly Defiance*, 29 October 1881, as quoted in Rabinowitz, "Conflict between Blacks and the Police," p. 72.

73. *Atlanta Constitution*, 7 October 1903.

74. Ibid., 26 August 1883.

75. Ibid., 26 August 1883.

76. Ibid., 24 June 1892.

77. Ibid., 25 March 1895, as quoted in Watts, "The Police in Atlanta," p. 176; Rabinowitz, "Conflict between Blacks and the Police," p. 74.

78. Watts, *Social Basis of City Politics*, pp. 21–31; Eugene J. Watts, "Black Political Progress in Atlanta, 1868–1895," *Journal of Negro History* 59 (July 1974): 268–296; Rabinowitz, *Race Relations*, pp. 315–318; John Hammond Moore, "The Negro and Prohibition in Atlanta, 1885–1887," *South Atlantic Quarterly* 69 (Winter 1970): 38–57.

79. The account of the riot is based on the following: *Atlanta Constitution*, 23–28 September 1906; J. Max Barber, "The Atlanta Tragedy," *The Voice* 3 (November 1906): 473–479; Charles Crowe, "Racial Violence and Social Reform: Origins of the Atlanta Riot of 1906," *Journal of Negro History* 53 (July 1968): 234–256; Dittmer, *Black Georgia*, pp. 97–101; Gregory L. Mixon, "The Atlanta Riot of 1906" (Ph.D. diss., University of Cincinnati, 1989), chaps. 11–16; David Fort Godshalk, "In the Wake of the Riot: Atlanta's Struggle for Order, 1899–1919" (Ph.D. diss., Yale University, 1992), p. 8–77; C. Vann Woodward, *The Strange Career of Jim Crow*, 3rd ed. (New York: Oxford University Press, 1955; 1974), pp. 82–93.

80. Crowe, "Racial Violence and Social Reform," pp. 246–249; Dittmer, *Black Georgia*, 87–88.

81. Crowe, "Racial Violence and Social Reform," pp. 234–235; Dittmer, *Black Georgia*, pp. 111–114, 122.

82. Crowe, "Racial Violence and Social Reform," pp. 249–254; Barber, "Atlanta Tragedy," pp. 476–478.

83. Dittmer, *Black Georgia*, pp. 124–138; Crowe, "Racial Violence and Social Reform," pp. 251–254; Woodward, *Strange Career of Jim Crow*, pp. 86–87; Barber, "Atlanta Tragedy," pp. 473–479; Baker, *Following the Color Line*, pp. 3–25. See also Jacquelyn Dowd Hall, *Revolt Against Chivalry: Jessie Daniel Ames and the Women's Campaign Against Lynching* (New York: Columbia University Press, 1974), pp. 145–157.

84. As quoted in Crowe, "Racial Violence and Social Reform," p. 252. On Felton see LeeAnn Whites, "Rebecca Latimer Felton and the Problem of 'Protection' in the New South," in *Visible Women: New Essays on American Activism*, ed. Nancy A. Hewitt and Suzanne Lebsock (Urbana: University of Illinois Press, 1993), pp. 41–61.

85. Barber, "Atlanta Tragedy," pp. 473–474.

86. As quoted in Mary Roberts Davis, "The Planning of the Industrial Expositions of 1881 and 1895: Expressions of the Philosophy of the New South" (M.A. thesis, Emory University, 1952), p. 150.

87. Crowe, "Racial Violence and Social Reform," p. 254. On imperialism and racism see Michael Hunt, *Ideology and U.S. Foreign Policy* (New Haven, Conn.: Yale University Press, 1987), pp. 46–91.

88. Barber, "Atlanta Tragedy," p. 477; Dittmer, *Black Georgia*, pp. 127–130.

89. Ethel Waters, *His Eye is On the Sparrow* (New York: Doubleday, 1951; Bantam, 1959), p. 91.

90. Ibid., pp. 92–93.

6. Survival and Social Welfare in the Age of Jim Crow

1. For other studies of working-class women reformers and cross-class alliances in this era, see Evelyn Brooks Higginbotham, *Righteous Discontent: The Women's Movement in the Black Baptist Church, 1880–1920* (Cambridge, Mass.: Harvard University Press, 1993), pp. 153, 174–180, 204–207, 218–219; Jacquelyn Dowd Hall, "O. Delight Smith's Progressive Era, Labor, Feminism, and Reform in the Urban South," in *Visible Women: New Essays on American Activism*, ed. Nancy A. Hewitt and Suzanne Lebsock (Urbana: University of Illinois Press, 1993), pp. 166–198; Nancy A. Hewitt, "In Pursuit of Power: The Political Economy of Women's Activism in Twentieth Century Tampa," in Hewitt and Lebsock, *Visible Women*, pp. 208–209; Sarah Deustch, "Learning to Talk More Like a Man: Boston Women's Class-Bridging Organizations, 1870–1940," *American Historical Review* 97 (April 1992): 379–404.

2. *Atlanta Constitution*, 23 December 1891. There was a strike among domestic workers in Brunswick, Georgia, a few months before the washerwomen's strike, as well as a bootblacks' strike in Atlanta. See *Atlanta Constitution*, 19 September and 26 October 1891. Cooks in Columbus, Georgia, formed a union in 1906 and in response a prominent businessman organized white housewives in the city to counter the cooks. A year later, the washerwomen in Columbus went on strike to protest a city ordinance that prevented them from using rolling carts to transport the wash down the streets. See *Atlanta Constitution*, 10 September 1906; 17 September 1907.

3. *Atlanta Constitution*, 8 August 1904. This article was written by Henry

Rutherford Butler, a prominent African-American physician and businessman. It is difficult to discern, however, whether he was expressing his own anti-union sentiment or the actual thoughts and intentions of the members themselves.

4. *Atlanta Constitution,* 10 June 1905; *Atlanta City Directory,* 1902–1905. For another example of a workers' organization cooperating with employers, see W. P. Burrell, "Report of the Committee on Business and Labor Conditions in Richmond, Virginia," *Proceedings of the Hampton Negro Conference* (July 1902): 43–44.

5. A Negro Nurse, "More Slavery at the South," *Independent* (25 January 1912): 199; Elizabeth Ross Haynes, "Negroes in Domestic Service in the United States," *Journal of Negro History* 8 (October 1923): 412–413. For a perspective denying that pan-toting was a common practice see, for example, *Savannah Tribune,* 29 July 1911. For a deft analysis of similar customary rights among servants, shipwrights, tailors, dock workers, and other workers in eighteenth-century England, see Peter Linebaugh, *The London Hanged: Crime and Civil Society in the Eighteenth Century* (Cambridge: Cambridge University Press, 1992), pp. 246, 251–255, 329, 339, 375, 378–381, 394, 406–407.

6. *Montgomery Advertiser,* 25 February 1916, in Tuskegee Institute News Clip File, microfilm.

7. "The Negro Problem: How it Appeals to a Southern White Woman," *Independent* 54 (18 September 1912): 2227; Walter L. Fleming, "The Servant Problem in a Black Belt Village," *Sewanee Review* 13 (January 1905): 8.

8. As quoted in Polly Stone Buck, *The Blessed Town: Oxford, Georgia, at the Turn of the Century* (Chapel Hill: University of North Carolina Press, 1986), p. 115; Testimony of Mrs. Ward, 15 November 1883, in U.S. Senate Committee on Education and Labor, *Report Upon the Relation between Labor and Capital* (Washington, D.C.: Government Printing Office, 1885), vol. 4, p. 344.

9. *Atlanta Journal,* 27 July 1903; *Atlanta Journal,* 13 July 1903; *Atlanta Constitution,* 16 February 1892, 2 September 1902, 3 July 1903, 13 January 1904, 3 September 1911.

10. Laura Buggs et al., "The Three Sisters," pp. 10–12, Federal Writers Project Papers, Southern Historical Collection, University of North Carolina, Chapel Hill (hereafter cited as FWP, SHC). See also Sarah Hill, "Bea the Washerwoman," pp. 5, 14, FWP, SHC. For other examples of criminal charges made against household workers for theft, see *Atlanta Constitution,* 1 March 1884, 9 March 1887.

11. See *Atlanta Constitution,* 8 and 13 September 1881. For analysis of thefts as political and economic acts see Linebaugh, *London Hanged,* 407; and Alex Lichtenstein, "'That Disposition to Theft, With Which They Have Been Branded': Moral Economy, Slave Management, and the Law," *Journal of Social History* 21 (Spring 1988): 413–440.

12. For examples, see *Atlanta Constitution,* 14 April 1886, 2 September 1902, and 13 July 1903.

13. *Atlanta Constitution,* 13 July 1899; Atlanta *Journal of Labor,* 14 May 1915.

14. James Murphy Hill Business Records, Account Book, January 1910–November 1911, Georgia Department of Archives and History; *Atlanta City Directory,* 1909–1912.

15. Atlanta *Journal of Labor,* 27 November 1903. See also Atlanta *Journal of Labor,* 16 October 1903, 23 October 1912; *Atlanta Constitution,* 23 September 1916; W. P. Burrell, "Savings and Loan," in "Ninth Annual Report of the Hampton

Negro Conference," *The Hampton Bulletin* 1 (September 1905): 73–74; Atlanta Chamber of Commerce Minutes, 1 January 1904 to 28 November 1905, vol. 3, pp. 48–53, Atlanta Chamber of Commerce.

16. See *Fulton County Daily Reports*, 1895–1920, Atlanta History Center (hereafter cited as AHC).

17. *Atlanta Constitution*, 30 August 1903.

18. Ibid., 23 September 1916. See Ruth Reed, *The Negro Women of Gainesville, Georgia* (Athens: University of Georgia Press, 1921), p. 31.

19. Atlanta Chamber of Commerce Minutes, 1 January 1904–28 November 1905, vol. 3, pp. 48–53, Atlanta Chamber of Commerce; Burrell, "Savings and Loan," pp. 73–74; Atlanta *Journal of Labor*, 16 October and 27 November 1903, 23 October 1912; *Atlanta Constitution*, 4 September 1904.

20. See Jacqueline Ann Rouse, *Lugenia Burns Hope: Black Southern Reformer* (Athens: University of Georgia Press, 1989), pp. 1–56.

21. *Atlanta Constitution*, 27 March 1900, 4 November 1900, 22 and 23 December 1900, 13 January 1901.

22. "The Gate City Free Kindergarten," 1917, and "The Story of the Gate City Free Kindergarten Association," Neighborhood Union Papers, Robert W. Woodruff Library, Clarke Atlanta University (hereafter cited as NU, AU); *Atlanta Constitution*, 30 May 1911; *Spelman Messenger* 22 (February 1906); *Atlanta Independent*, 28 July 1917; Rouse, *Lugenia Burns Hope*, pp. 28–29, 43–45; Cynthia Neverdon-Morton, *Afro-American Women of the South and the Advancement of the Race, 1895–1925* (Knoxville: University of Tennessee Press, 1989), p. 142.

23. Louise Delphia Shivery, "The History of Organized Social Work Among Atlanta Negroes 1890–1935" (M.A. thesis, Atlanta University, 1936); Rouse, *Lugenia Burns Hope*, p. 65.

24. On Neighborhood Union program and activities, see Minute Book, 1908–1918, NU, AU; *Atlanta Constitution*, 31 January and 2 February 1911; Edward Franklin Frazier, "Neighborhood Union in Atlanta," *Southern Workman* 52 (September 1923): 437–442; Shivery, "History of Organized Social Work"; Rouse, *Lugenia Burns Hope*, pp. 57–90; Neverdon-Morton, *Afro-American Women of the South*, pp. 145–162; Gerda Lerner, "Early Community Work of Black Club Women," *Journal of Negro History* 59 (April 1974): 158–167; Elisabeth Lasch-Quinn, *Black Neighbors: Race and the Limits of Reform in the American Settlement House Movement, 1890–1945* (Chapel Hill: University of North Carolina Press, 1993), pp. 120–124; Dorothy Salem, *To Better Our World: Black Women in Organized Reform* (New York: Carlson, 1990), pp. 97–99, 112–13, 190, 239.

25. Mrs. J. B. Blayton, Interview by Bernard E. West, 15 March 1979, transcript, Living Atlanta Collection, AHC.

26. Neighborhood Union Charter, 1911, NU, AU.

27. See, for example, Letter to the Atlanta Board of Education, 1913, and "Survey of Atlanta Public Schools," 1913–1915, NU, AU; "Minutes of the Women's Social Improvement Committee," 1913, in Shivery, "History of Organized Social Work," pp. 458–461.

28. "Petitions Sent to City Hall," 1911–1913, and letter to Mayor [Keys], ca. 1920–1922, NU, AU; Shivery, "History of Organized Social Work," pp. 75–79.

29. Shivery, "History of Organized Social Work," pp. 79–89.

30. Neighborhood Union Charter, 1911, NU, AU.

31. Minute Book, 1908–1918, NU, AU; Rouse, *Lugenia Burns Hope*, pp. 70, 89–90.

32. See Deborah Gray White, "The Cost of Club Work, the Price of Black Feminism," in Hewitt and Lebsock, *Visible Women*, pp. 247–269; Linda Gordon, "Black and White Visions of Welfare: Women's Welfare Activism, 1890–1925," *Journal of American History* 78 (September 1991): 569–570; Rouse, *Lugenia Burns Hope*, pp. 89–90.

33. See Hallie Brooks, Interview by Bernard E. West, 27 February 1979, transcript, Living Atlanta Collection, AHC.

34. Minute Book, 1908–1918, NU, AU; Shivery, "The History of Organized Social Work"; Rouse, *Lugenia Burns Hope*, pp. 65–68; Lerner, "Early Community Work of Black Club Women," pp. 162–166.

35. The current literature on the Neighborhood Union depicts the organization's membership as college-educated, middle-class women. None has examined the role of working-class women. See Rouse, *Lugenia Burns Hope*, p. 89; Dittmer, *Black Georgia*, p. 64; Lerner, "Early Community Work of Black Club Women," pp. 163–167; Lasch-Quinn, *Black Neighbors*, p. 122; Salem, *To Better Our World*, p. 98; Neverdon-Morton, *Afro-American Women*, pp. 145–148.

36. On the role of the NU in founding the Atlanta School of Social Work, see Rouse, *Lugenia Burns Hope*, pp. 48, 83–85; Salem, *To Better Our World*, pp. 190, 239.

37. No one other than Hope was ever elected to the office of president during her active years into the 1930s, although there were periods when an "acting" president was elected to relieve her of some of the burdens of the heavy work load.

38. Biographies of activists and data on their participation in the NU are compiled from the following sources: Minute Book, 1908–1918, Lugenia Hope's "Time Book," 1913, Neighborhood Union Charter 1911, "Board of Management and Presidents of Neighborhoods," 1908–1909, "Zone Boundaries and Persons in Charge," 1914, NU, AU; "Directory of NU for 1912," "Tag Day Drive," 1919, "Report of Zone Chairmen," 1919, in Shivery, "History of Organized Social Work," pp. 453–455, 474, 475; *Atlanta City Directory*, 1908–1920; and U.S. Manuscript Population Census, Fulton County, 1910.

39. *Atlanta Constitution*, 28 June 1891; Neverdon-Morton, *Afro-American Women*, p. 143.

40. *Atlanta Constitution*, 4 June 1905; *Atlanta City Directory*, 1905–1913.

41. "Gate City Free Kindergarten," NU, AU; Gordon, "Black and White Visions of Welfare," p. 561; *Atlanta Constitution*, 28 July 1917.

42. *Atlanta Constitution*, 30 October 1912; *Atlanta Journal*, 22 March 1901. On institutional churches see Ralph E. Luker, *The Social Gospel in Black and White: American Racial Reform, 1885–1912* (Chapel Hill: University of North Carolina Press, 1991), pp. 170–190.

43. As quoted in Luker, *Social Gospel in Black and White*, p. 190.

44. On the First Congregational Church see *Atlanta Independent*, 4 February 1911; *Atlanta Constitution*, 30 October 1912; H[enry] H[ugh] Proctor to Atty. Chapin Brinsmade, 11 December 1913, Group 1, Series L, Addendum, National Association for the Advancement of Colored People Papers, Library of Congress; Luker, *Social Gospel in Black and White*, pp. 184–190; Dittmer, *Black Georgia*, pp. 63–64; Homer C. McEwen, Sr., "First Congregational Church, Atlanta: 'For

the Good of Man and the Glory of God,'" *Atlanta Historical Bulletin* 21 (Spring 1977): 129–142.

7. *"Wholesome" and "Hurtful" Amusements*

1. Alice Adams, Interview by Bernard E. West, 20 November 1979, tape recording, Living Atlanta Collection, Atlanta History Center (hereafter cited as AHC); Mary Morton, Interview by Bernard E. West, 11 February 1980, transcript, Living Atlanta Collection, AHC.

2. Georgina Susan Hickey, "Visibility, Politics, and Urban Development: Working-Class Women in Early Twentieth Century Atlanta" (Ph.D. diss., University of Michigan, 1995), pp. 246–250.

3. As quoted in Dana F. White, "Landscaped Atlanta: The Romantic Tradition in Cemetery, Park, and Suburban Development," *Atlanta Historical Journal* 30 (Summer-Fall 1982): 102–103; Clifford M. Kuhn et al., *Living Atlanta: An Oral History of the City, 1914–1948* (Athens: University of Georgia Press, 1990), p. 265; David Nasaw, *Going Out: The Rise and Fall of Public Amusements* (New York: Basic Books, 1993), pp. 2–4.

4. *Atlanta Constitution*, 2 August 1903.

5. Charles Crowe, "Racial Violence and Social Reform—Origins of the Atlanta Riot of 1906," *Journal of Negro History* 53 (July 1968): 245.

6. Hickey, "Visibility, Politics, and Urban Development," pp. 272–275.

7. Alice Adams, Interview.

8. Information on clubs was found in the following sources: *Atlanta Independent*, 1905–1910; *Atlanta Constitution*, 2 January 1892, 2 December 1893, 10 May and 7 July 1894, 10 September 1895; Kathleen Adams, Interview by Bernard E. West, 11 March 1980, typescript, Living Atlanta Collection, AHC. See also August Meier and David Lewis, "History of the Negro Upper Class in Atlanta, Georgia, 1890–1958," *Journal of Negro Education* 28 (Spring 1959): 128–139; John Dittmer, *Black Georgia in the Progressive Era, 1900–1920* (Urbana: University of Illinois Press, 1977), pp. 59–61; Herman "Skip" Mason, Jr., *Going Against the Wind: A Pictorial History of African-Americans in Atlanta* (Atlanta: Longstreet Press, 1992), pp. 43, 54. The photograph referred to in the text, taken in 1913, is located in the Long-Aikeen-Rucker Papers, AHC.

9. Ruby Owens, Interview by Bernard E. West, 23 January 1979, tape recording, Living Atlanta Collection, AHC; Dittmer, *Black Georgia*, pp. 68–69. See also *Atlanta Journal*, 15 June 1900; *Atlanta Constitution*, 5 July 1904.

10. Dittmer, *Black Georgia*, pp. 69–70; Minutes of the Atlanta Chamber of Commerce, 6 July 1910, p. 17, Atlanta Chamber of Commerce.

11. *Atlanta Constitution*, 6 July 1902.

12. Ibid., 29 June 1904.

13. *Atlanta Journal*, 4 July 1901.

14. *Atlanta Independent*, 6 August 1904; Dittmer, *Black Georgia*, p. 66; Perry Bradford, *Born with the Blues: Perry Bradford's Own Story, The True Story of the Pioneering Blues Singers and Musicians in the Early Days of Jazz* (New York: Oak Publications, 1956), p. 19; Howard N. Rabinowitz, *Race Relations in the Urban South, 1865–1890* (New York: Oxford University Press, 1977), pp. 229–230; Earl Lewis,

In Their Own Interests: Race, Class, and Power in Twentieth Century Norfolk, Virginia (Berkeley: University of California Press, 1991), pp. 102–106.

15. Atlanta *Weekly Defiance*, 24 October 1882.

16. *Atlanta Constitution*, 2 and 15 July, September 1891; Lee Fuse Wood, *The Bedford Pine Neighborhood* (College Park, Ga.: Ditto Press, 1988), p. 8.

17. See John F. Kasson, *Amusing the Million: Coney Island at the Turn of the Century* (New York: Hill and Wang, 1978), pp. 17–28, 61–86.

18. *Journal Magazine*, 18 May 1913, in Franklin M. Garrett, *Atlanta and Environs: A Chronicle of its People and Events* (Athens: University of Georgia Press, 1969), vol. 2, pp. 607–609.

19. Ibid.; *Atlanta City Directory*, 1910; Atlanta City Council Minutes, 6 July 1910, vol. 22, p. 438, AHC.

20. "Preliminary Outline for Sweet Auburn Historical-Cultural Study," Living Atlanta Collection, AHC.

21. Alice Adams, Interview; Kathleen Adams, Interview.

22. *Atlanta Constitution*, 22 January 1906; James E. McCulloch, *The Call of the New South: Addresses Delivered at the Southern Sociological Congress, May 7–10, 1912* (Nashville: Southern Sociological Congress, 1912), p. 112; *Atlanta Constitution*, 31 July 1911.

23. Lary May, *Screening Out the Past: The Birth of Mass Culture and the Motion Picture Industry* (New York: Oxford University Press, 1980), pp. 16–18.

24. See Kathy Peiss, *Cheap Amusements: Working Women and Leisure in Turn-of-the-Century New York* (Philadelphia: Temple University Press, 1986), pp. 56–114, 186–189; Joanne J. Meyerowitz, *Women Adrift: Independent Wage Earners in Chicago, 1880–1930* (Chicago: University of Chicago Press, 1988), pp. 117–139.

25. Hickey, "Visibility, Politics, and Urban Development," pp. 244–293. See, for example, *Atlanta Constitution*, 13 October 1910; 12 and 14 June, 26 and 27 September 1912.

26. William Barlow, *Looking Up at Down: The Emergence of Blues Culture* (Philadelphia: Temple University Press, 1989), pp. 121, 180.

27. Henry T. Sampson, *Blacks in Blackface: A Source Book on Early Black Musical Shows* (Metuchen, N.J.: Scarecrow Press, 1980), pp. 4–9; Tom Fletcher, *100 Years of the Negro in Show Business* (New York: Da Capo Press, 1984), pp. v–xvii.

28. See Robert C. Toll, *Blacking Up: The Minstrel Show in Nineteenth Century America* (New York: Oxford University Press, 1974), pp. 270–274.

29. Barlow, *Looking Up at Down*, p. 121.

30. Sampson, *Blacks in Blackface*, pp. 11–19.

31. Okeh and Columbia record companies both had race labels and were active in searching for talent and producing in Atlanta at this time. See Barlow, *Looking Up at Down*, p. 194; Sampson, *Blacks in Blackface*, pp. 11–19; New York *Freeman*, 12 December 1913, in Tuskegee Institute News Clip File, microfilm (hereafter cited as TINF).

32. *Atlanta Independent*, 16 May 1914; Sampson, *Blacks in Blackface*, p. 128; Mason, *Going Against the Wind*, p. 67.

33. Bailey also owned the Dixie Theater and the Arcade Theater. New York *Freeman*, 12 December 1913, in TINF; Barlow, *Looking Up at Down*, pp. 121, 192; Clifford M. Kuhn et al., *Living Atlanta: An Oral History of the City, 1914–1948* (Athens: University of Georgia Press, 1990), p. 301; Ethel Waters, *His Eye Is on the Sparrow* (New York: Doubleday, 1951; Bantam, 1959), pp. 88–89.

34. Chris Albertson, *Bessie* (New York: Stein and Day, 1972), pp. 28–32, 56; Barlow, *Looking Up at Down*, p. 166; Michael W. Harris, *The Rise of Gospel Blues: The Music of Thomas Andrew Dorsey in the Urban Church* (New York: Oxford University Press, 1992), pp. 30, 42.

35. Sampson, *Blacks in Blackface*, pp. 102–107; Marshall Stearns and Jean Stearns, *Jazz Dance: The Story of American Vernacular Dance* (New York: Macmillan, 1968), pp. 85–89; Marjorie Garber, *Vested Interests: Cross-Dressing and Cultural Anxiety* (New York: Harper Perennial, 1992), pp. 276–279.

36. See *Atlanta Independent*, 6 and 13 February and 11 and 18 September 1909.

37. *Atlanta Journal*, 16 July 1900.

38. See Clarence Muse and David Arlen, *Way Down South* (Hollywood: David Graham Fischer, 1932), pp. 66–67.

39. As quoted in Stearns, *Jazz Dance*, p. 88.

40. Stearns, *Jazz Dance*, p. 85; Bradford, *Born with the Blues*, p. 19; Muse and Arlen, *Way Down South*, pp. 66–67. Muse and Arlen claim that Albany Whitman disapproved of his daughters' careers and even disowned them. The evidence on the issue of parental approval, however, is conflicting. Their mother, for example, was their manager and chaperon when they first became professionals.

41. Stearns, *Jazz Dance*, pp. 85–91.

42. Bob Rusch, "Georgia Tom Dorsey Interview," *Cadence*, December 1978, p. 9; Harris, *The Rise of Gospel Blues*, pp. 19–20, 26–46.

43. Bradford, *Born with the Blues*, p. 16–18; Barlow, *Looking Up at Down*, pp. 125–128.

44. *Atlanta Independent*, 1904–1918.

45. Ibid., 6 February 1909.

46. See, for example, *Atlanta Independent*, 13 February 1909 and 18 September 1909; George A. Waller, "Another Audience: Black Moviegoing, 1907–16," *Cinema Journal* 31 (Winter 1992): 10–11.

47. *Atlanta Independent*, July 1908; Mason, *Going Against the Wind*, pp. 53, 63; George A. Waller, "Black Nickelodeon," *Black Film Review* 7 (1993): 32–34; Waller, "Another Audience," pp. 3–25.

48. Harris, *The Rise of Gospel Blues*, p. 30; Peiss, *Cheap Amusements*, pp. 148–149; Mary Carbine, "'The Finest Outside the Loop': Motion Picture Exhibition in Chicago's Black Metropolis, 1905–1928," *Camera Obscura* 23 (1990): 27–29.

49. Harris, *The Rise of Gospel Blues*, pp. 32–36, 42.

50. *Atlanta Independent*, 30 September 1905; see also 16 September and 21 October 1905 and 16 May 1914.

51. Dittmer, *Black Georgia*, pp. 66–67.

52. Sampson, *Blacks in Blackface*, pp. 20–23.

53. Bradford, *Born with the Blues*, p. 18; Barlow, *Looking Up At Down*, pp. 115–117.

54. *Atlanta Constitution*, 29 July 1904 and 4 August 1904. The sponsoring organization was not identified in the newspaper.

55. See Roy Rosenzweig, *Eight Hours for What We Will: Workers and Leisure in An Industrial City, 1870–1920* (Cambridge: Cambridge University Press, 1983), pp. 36–64; Peiss, *Cheap Amusements*, pp. 16–21.

56. Jim O'Neal and Amy O'Neal, "Living Blues Interview: Georgia Tom Dorsey," *Living Blues: A Journal of the Black American Blues Tradition* 20 (March-April 1975): 18.

57. *Atlanta Constitution,* 16 June 1908.

58. See Evelyn Brooks Higginbotham, *Righteous Discontent: The Women's Movement in the Black Baptist Church, 1880–1920* (Cambridge, Mass.: Harvard University Press, 1993), p. 38.

59. On working-class views on temperance, see Rosenzweig, *Eight Hours for What We Will,* pp. 94, 97–98, 103–117.

60. Jacqueline Jones, *Soldiers of Light and Love: Northern Teachers and Georgia Blacks, 1865–1873* (Chapel Hill: University of North Carolina Press, 1980), pp. 159–161; *Atlanta Independent,* 22 October 1910; *Atlanta Constitution,* 24 September 1891.

61. Ball, "Prohibition in Georgia," p. 701; Atlanta City Council Minutes, 20 June 1910, p. 422, AHC.

62. See, for example, *Atlanta Journal,* 15 May and 24 October 1900. See also Rabinowitz, *Race Relations in the Urban South,* p. 244. "Dago bar joints," presumably Italian saloons, are mentioned in *Atlanta Independent,* 22 September 1906. Spies hired by the management of the Fulton Bag and Cotton Mills company claimed the discovery of the interracial crime ring. See Jacquelyn Dowd Hall, "Private Eyes, Public Women: Images of Class and Sex in the Urban South, Atlanta, Georgia, 1913–1915," in *Work Engendered: Toward a New History of American Labor,* ed. Ava Baron (Ithaca: Cornell University Press, 1991), p. 252.

63. *Atlanta Constitution,* 30 September 1906; Rabinowitz, *Race Relations in the Urban South,* p. 188.

64. On prohibition see Rabinowitz, *Race Relations in the Urban South,* pp. 212, 314–315; Dittmer, *Black Georgia,* pp. 111–113; S. Mays Ball, "Prohibition in Georgia: Its Failure to Prevent Drinking in Atlanta and Other Cities," *Putnam's Magazine,* March 1909, pp. 694–701. Local prohibition efforts were further complicated by police practices which permitted "liquor limits"—designated areas of the city that could sell drinks with impunity. See Eugene J. Watts, "The Police in Atlanta, 1890–1905," *Journal of Southern History* 39 (May 1973): 173.

65. Ball, "Prohibition in Georgia," pp. 696–697.

66. R. R. Kinney to Members of the City Council, Atlanta, Ga., 20 June 1910, Aldine Chambers Papers, AHC. See also "Address by Mayor Robert F. Maddox" [To the League of American Municipalities, Annual Convention, Montreal, Canada], 26 August 1909, Maddox Papers, AHC. For examples of raids see *Atlanta Constitution,* 6 and 7 August 1895, 13 August 1897, 10 January 1898, 15 January 1907.

67. *Atlanta Constitution,* 23 March 1901; *Atlanta Journal,* 23 March 1901, 23 and 27 May 1903.

68. See Rabinowitz, *Race Relations in the Urban South,* p. 243; Hickey, "Visibility, Politics, and Urban Development," pp. 262–263. The *Nashville Banner* complained of an infamous drinking and gambling den in 1890 that had existed for twenty years and served "the lowest negroes of both sexes." In contrast see Peiss, *Cheap Amusements,* pp. 16–33.

69. See, for example, *Atlanta Constitution,* 15 May and 18 June 1900, 30 November 1902; *Atlanta Journal,* 12 April and 12 August 1901. For other evidence of women arrested for drinking, as well as prostitution, see "Reports of the Martha Home," 1913–1915, in Christian Council Papers, AHC.

70. *Atlanta Constitution,* 24 April 1904, 13 July 1903; *Atlanta Independent,* 22

September 1906. It should be noted that McHenry was among those who flip-flopped on the prohibition issue from wet to dry, from the 1885 to the 1887 campaign. See Rabinowitz, *Race Relations in the Urban South*, p. 315.

71. *Atlanta Independent*, 24 March 1906. On similar pronouncements in the northeast see Hazel V. Carby, "Policing the Black Woman's Body in an Urban Context," *Critical Inquiry* 18 (Summer 1992): 738–755.

72. Atlanta City Council Minutes, 2 May 1904, vol. 20, p. 290, AHC; *Atlanta Constitution*, 22 April and 16 June 1908, 12 June 1912.

73. *Atlanta Independent*, 28 October 1905. For comments on the issue by Henry Hugh Proctor and others, see *Atlanta Constitution*, 13 July 1903; *Atlanta Independent*, 22 September 1906; Waller, "Another Audience," p. 7.

74. Nasaw, *Going Out*, p. 5.

75. See Paul E. Willis, *Common Culture: Symbolic Work at Play in the Everyday Cultures of the Young* (Boulder: Westview Press, 1990), pp. 1–29.

8. "Dancing and Carousing the Night Away"

1. Katrina Hazzard-Gordon, *Jookin': The Rise of Social Dance Formations in African-American Culture* (Philadelphia: Temple University Press, 1990), pp. 3–47; Lawrence W. Levine, *Black Culture and Black Consciousness: Afro-American Folk Thought from Slavery to Freedom* (New York: Oxford University Press, 1977), pp. 15–17; Sterling Stuckey, *Slave Culture: Nationalist Theory and the Foundations of Black America* (New York: Oxford University Press, 1987), pp. 64–67.

2. *Atlanta Constitution*, 26 August 1877, 20 August 1897; Howard N. Rabinowitz, *Race Relations in the Urban South: 1865–1890* (New York: Oxford University Press, 1978), pp. 243–246.

3. Lewis A. Erenberg, *Steppin' Out: New York Nightlife and the Transformation of American Culture, 1890–1930* (Chicago: University of Chicago Press, 1981), pp. 20, 150–155; Hazzard-Gordon, *Jookin'*, p. 124.

4. See, for example, *Atlanta Constitution*, 18 March 1901.

5. Hazzard-Gordon, *Jookin'*, pp. 63–94; Zora Neale Hurston, "Characteristics of Negro Expression," in *Negro Anthology*, ed. Nancy Cunard (London, 1934; reprint ed., New York: Negro Universities Press, 1969), pp. 29–30.

6. *Atlanta Constitution*, 6 August 1900.

7. As quoted in Michael W. Harris, *The Rise of Gospel Blues: The Music of Thomas Andrew Dorsey in the Urban Church* (New York: Oxford University Press, 1992), p. 60.

8. Ibid., pp. 44–45.

9. *Atlanta Constitution*, 6 August 1900. See Eugene J. Watts, "The Police in Atlanta, 1890–1905," *Journal of Southern History* 39 (May 1973): 173; Rabinowitz, *Race Relations in the Urban South*, p. 46.

10. Hazzard-Gordon, *Jookin'*, p. 70; Richard W. Thomas, "Working-Class Origins of Black Culture: Class Formation and the Division of Black Cultural Labor," *Minority Voices* 1 (Fall 1977): 81–103.

11. *Atlanta Constitution*, 13 July 1902.

12. Marshall Stearns and Jean Stearns, *Jazz Dance: The Story of American Vernacular Dance* (New York: Macmillan, 1968; reprint ed., Da Capo Press, 1994), p. 23.

13. Ibid.

14. *Atlanta Independent,* 4 October 1915.

15. *Atlanta Independent,* 9 October 1915. For the full controversy on the opening of the Roof Garden see also *Atlanta Independent,* 16 and 19 June, 3 July, and 4 October 1915; John Dittmer, *Black Georgia During the Progressive Era, 1900–1920* (Urbana: University of Illinois Press, 1977), p. 57.

16. *Atlanta Constitution,* 20 February 1905. See also W. E. B. Du Bois, ed., *Morals and Manners Among Negro Americans* (Atlanta: Atlanta University, 1914), pp. 90–97; Dittmer, *Black Georgia,* p. 66; George A. Waller, "Another Audience: Black Moviegoing, 1907–19," *Cinema Journal* 31 (Winter 1992): 7.

17. Perry Bradford, *Born with the Blues: Perry Bradford's Own Story, The True Story of the Pioneering Blues Singers and Musicians in the Early Days of Jazz* (New York: Oak Publications, 1956), p. 18.

18. See Clifford M. Kuhn et al., *Atlanta: An Oral History of the City, 1914–1948* (Athens: University of Georgia Press, 1990), p. 301. See also Leroi Jones, *Blues People: Negro Music in White America* (New York: William Morrow, 1963), p. 128.

19. William H. Jones, *Recreation and Amusement among Negroes* (Washington, D.C., 1927; reprint ed., Westport, Conn.: Negro Universities Press, 1970), p. 122; Hazel V. Carby, "Policing the Black Woman's Body," *Critical Inquiry* 18 (Summer 1992): 750–751.

20. See comments by Henry Hugh Proctor and Monroe N. Work in W. E. B. Du Bois, ed., *Some Notes on Negro Crime* (Atlanta: Atlanta University, 1904), pp. 50–51.

21. *Atlanta Constitution,* 23 June 1900, 7 May 1904, 9 March 1905, 25 July 1905; *Atlanta Journal,* 19 and 23 June 1900, 12 September 1900; James E. McCulloch, ed., *The Call of the New South: Addresses of the Southern Sociological Congress* (Nashville: Southern Sociological Congress, 1912), p. 112; British Board of Trade, *Cost of Living in American Towns* (London: His Majesty's Stationery Office, 1911), p. 58; T. J. Woofter, *Negro Problems in Cities* (College Park, 1928; New York: AMS Press, 1969), pp. 269–279.

22. For figures showing the disproportionate numbers of blacks arrested for petty crimes see, for example, City of Atlanta, *Annual Reports,* 1884–1886, 1902–1903, Atlanta History Center.

23. *Atlanta Constitution,* 7 July 1903.

24. Quotations from Stearns, *Jazz Dance,* pp. 1–12, 21, 24, 27.

25. See Stuckey, *Slave Culture,* pp. 57–59; Levine, *Black Culture,* pp. 16, 203; Susan McClary, *Feminine Endings: Music, Gender, and Sexuality* (Minneapolis: University of Minnesota Press, 1991), pp. 8–25, 54–57, 153.

26. *Atlanta Constitution,* 6 August 1900, 13 July 1902. See Paul Oliver, *Blues Fell This Morning: Meaning in the Blues* (Cambridge: Cambridge University Press, 1960), pp. 1–11; Levine, *Black Culture,* pp. 221–239; Jones, *Blues People,* pp. 50–94; Roger D. Abrahams, *Singing the Master: The Emergence of African American Culture in the Plantation South* (New York: Pantheon Books, 1992), pp. 94–95.

27. Albert Murray's appropriately titled study makes the best argument for the relationship between blues and dance; see *Stomping the Blues* (New York: McGraw-Hill, 1976). See also Larry Neal, "The Ethos of the Blues," *Black Scholar* 3 (Summer 1972), in *Sacred Music of the Secular City: From Blues to Rap,* ed. Jon Michael Spencer (Durham: Duke University Press, 1992), pp. 36–46; Paul Oliver, *Songsters and Saints: Vocal Traditions on Race Records* (Cambridge: Cambridge University Press, 1984), pp. 18–46.

28. As quoted in Harris, *Rise of Gospel Blues*, p. 31.

29. Stearns, *Jazz Dance*, pp. 103–114.

30. Levine, *Black Culture*, pp. 136–297; Murray, *Stomping the Blues*, pp. 21–42; Jones, *Recreation and Amusements*, pp. 65–66; Evelyn Brooks Higginbotham, *Righteous Discontent: The Women's Movement in the Black Baptist Church, 1880–1920* (Cambridge, Mass.: Harvard University Press, 1993), pp. 44, 199–200.

31. As quoted in Harry T. Sampson, *Blacks in Blackface: A Source Book of Early Black Musical Shows* (Metuchen, N.J.: The Scarecrow Press, 1980), pp. 341–342.

32. Stuckey, *Slave Culture*, pp. 3–97; Levine, *Black Culture*, pp. 37–38, 141, 165–166; Hazzard-Gordon, *Jookin'*, p. 81; Abrahams, *Singing the Master*, pp. 44–45, 91–92, 141; Stearns, *Jazz Dance*, pp. 3, 29–31, 32, 47, 123, 129; Sterling Stuckey, "Christian Conversion and the Challenge of Dance," in *Choreographing History*, ed. Susan Leigh Foster (Bloomington: Indiana University Press, 1995), pp. 54–68.

33. Jacqueline Anne Rouse, *Lugenia Burns Hope: Black Southern Reformer* (Athens: University of Georgia Press, 1989), p. 70; Jerma A. Jackson, "Testifying at the Cross: Thomas Andrew Dorsey, Sister Rosetta Tharpe, and the Politics of African-American Sacred and Secular Music" (Ph.D. diss., Rutgers University, 1995), pp. 73–76.

34. See *Atlanta Constitution*, 10 November 1908, 13 August 1910, 14 August 1910. A group of white Holy Rollers were arrested on similar charges. See *Atlanta Constitution*, 13 October 1910.

35. Dittmer, *Black Georgia*, p. 53.

36. See *Atlanta Independent*, 1903–1910.

37. *Atlanta Constitution*, 29 and 15 June 1913, 4 July 1914. The festival began in 1909, and proceeds were donated to the church's social projects, including the Working Girls Home.

38. See Paul Gilroy, "One Nation Under a Groove: The Cultural Politics of 'Race' and Racism in Britain," in *Anatomy of Race*, ed. David Theo Goldberg (Minneapolis: University of Minnesota Press, 1990), p. 74.

39. *Atlanta Constitution*, 3 July 1903. Employers of domestics and other workers in the North also complained about "Blue Monday," the difficulty of getting workers to perform their duties after a weekend of festivities. See Kathy Peiss, *Cheap Amusements: Working Women and Leisure in Turn-of-the-Century New York* (Philadelphia: Temple University Press, 1986), p. 34.

40. *Atlanta Constitution*, 19 February 1905.

41. Ibid., 21 February 1905.

42. *Atlanta Journal*, 10 January 1900.

43. *Atlanta Constitution*, 20 February 1905.

44. Anthony Binga, *Binga's Address on Several Occasions: Should Church Members be Disciplined for Attending Balls or Theaters?* [Printed by Vote of the General Association of Virginia, ca. 1900], Schomburg Center for Black Culture, New York Public Library, p. 10.

45. See, for example, Phyllis Rose, *Jazz Cleopatra: Josephine Baker in Her Time* (New York: Doubleday, 1989), p. 27; Roger D. Abrahams and John F. Szwed, eds., *After Africa: Extracts from British Travel Accounts and Journals of the Seventeenth, Eighteenth, and Nineteenth Centuries Concerning the Slaves, Their Manners, and Customs, in the British West Indies* (New Haven: Yale University Press, 1983), pp. 290–291.

46. See Stearns, *Jazz Dance*, pp. 112, 235. See also Richard Leppert, *Music and Image* (Cambridge: Cambridge University Press, 1988), pp. 73–74.

47. As quoted in Harris, *Rise of Gospel Blues*, p. 53.

48. Hazzard-Gordon, *Jookin'*, p. 87.

49. As quoted in Stearns, *Jazz Dance*, p. 24; see also Paul Gilroy, *"There Ain't No Black in the Union Jack": The Cultural Politics of Race and Nation* (London, 1987; reprint ed., Chicago: University of Chicago Press, 1991), p. 203.

50. As quoted in Stearns, *Jazz Dance*, p. 24.

51. Alice Adams, Interview by Bernard E. West, 20 November 1979, tape recording, Living Atlanta Collection, AHC.

52. Elizabeth Kytle, *Willie Mae* (New York: Knopf, 1958; reprint ed., Athens: University of Georgia Press, 1993), pp. 140–141.

53. Binga, *Binga's Address*, p. 9.

54. *Atlanta Constitution*, 6 August 1900, 13 July 1902. For a range of dress during the period see Patricia K. Hunt, "Clothing as an Expression of African-American Women in Georgia, 1880–1915," *Georgia Historical Quarterly* 76 (Summer 1992): 459–471. See also Peiss, *Cheap Amusements*, pp. 57–65.

55. For recent examples see Tricia Rose, "'Never Trust a Big Butt and a Smile,'" *Camera Obscura*, no. 23 (May 1990): 109–131.

56. Hurston, "Characteristics of Negro Expression," p. 30. This is not to romanticize notions of beauty among African Americans. Hurston states that black women were disparaged in some black folklore and songs, some of which were sung in jook joints. In addition, advertisements for skin whiteners and hair straighteners appeared regularly in black newspapers.

57. My analysis of the blues aesthetic is informed by previously cited historical and cultural studies of the blues, but it has benefited especially from Dwight Andrews and Larry Neal. See Andrews, "From Black to Blues," in *Sacred Music of the Secular City*, pp. 47–54; and Neal, "The Ethos of the Blues." For a theoretical analysis of blues and literature see Houston A. Baker, Jr., *Blues, Ideology, and Afro-American Literature* (Chicago: University of Chicago Press, 1984).

58. Andrews, "From Black to Blues," p. 52.

59. On the relationship between the individual and the collective in music and feminist theory, see Elsa Barkley Brown, "'What Has Happened Here': The Politics of Difference in Women's History and Feminist Politics," *Feminist Studies* 18 (Summer 1992): 295–311; Levine, *Black Culture*, p. 133.

60. The term "body-reality" is taken from Neal, "The Ethos of the Blues," p. 38.

61. See John Fiske, *Understanding Popular Culture* (Boston: Unwin Hyman, 1989), pp. 49–95.

62. For insights into how amusement parks reinforced and challenged the social order of industrial life, see John F. Kasson, *Amusing the Million: Coney Island at the Turn of the Century* (New York: Hill and Wang, 1978).

9. Tuberculosis as the "Negro Servants' Disease"

1. *Christian Recorder*, 16 December 1915, in Tuskegee Institute News Clip File, microfilm (hereafter cited as TINF).

2. See Charles E. Rosenberg, *Explaining Epidemics and Other Studies in the History of Medicine* (Cambridge: Cambridge University Press, 1992), pp. 278–279, 301.

3. The conceptualization of this chapter is indebted to two critical motifs borrowed from Charles E. Rosenberg: the idea that diseases are culturally "framed" to reflect a society's values, and the idea that historically, epidemics as a social phenomenon have followed a narrative script that is similar in structure to "dramaturgical events." See *Explaining Epidemics*, pp. 278–317.

4. See for example, E. T. Easley, "The Sanitary Condition of the Negro," *The American Weekly* 3 (31 July 1875): 49–50; Theophilus Powell, "The Increase of Insanity and Tuberculosis in the Southern Negro Since 1860, and its Alliance, and Some of the Supposed Causes," *Journal of the American Medical Association* 27 (5 December 1896): 1185–1188; Thomas McKie, "A Brief History of Insanity and Tuberculosis in the Southern Negro," *Journal of the American Medical Association* 28 (20 March 1897): 537–538; Thomas J. Mays, "Human Slavery as a Prevention of Pulmonary Consumption" (1904), in *Germs Have No Color Line: Blacks and American Medicine 1900–1940*, ed. Vanessa Northington Gamble (New York: Garland, 1989), pp. 6–11; J. C. Patterson as quoted in Powell, "Increase of Insanity and Tuberculosis," p. 1187.

5. Powell, "Increase of Insanity and Tuberculosis," p. 1186.

6. L. C. Allen, "Negro Health Problem," *American Journal of Public Health* 5 (March 1915): 195; H. J. Archard, "Tuberculinization of the Negro," *Journal of the National Medical Association* 4 (1912): 225; Powell, "Increase of Insanity and Tuberculosis," p. 1186. See also Seale Harris, "Tuberculosis and the Negro," *Journal of the American Medical Association* 41 (1903): 834; J. F. Miller as quoted in Mays, "Human Slavery as a Prevention," p. 195.

7. Easley, "Sanitary Condition of the Negro," p. 49.

8. Katherine Ott, "Political Culture, Medical Culture: How Emancipation Shaped Gilded Age Tuberculosis" (paper presented at the Johns Hopkins University American History Seminar, 13 April 1994), pp. 19–20; Powell, "Increase of Insanity and Tuberculosis," p. 1186; Thomas D. Coleman, "Susceptibility of the Negro," *Transactions of the American Climatological Association* 19 (1903): 127; Allen, "Negro Health Problem," p. 194; H. R. Landis, "Tuberculosis Problem and the Negro," in *Sixteenth Annual Report of the Henry Phipps Institute* (Philadelphia: Phipps Institute, 1923), p. 4; Truman A. Parker, "The Negro as a Factor in the Spread of Tuberculosis," *Virginia Medical Semi-Monthly* 14 (8 October 1909): 292; Charles H. Smith, "Have American Negroes Too Much Liberty?" *The Forum* 16 (September 1893–February 1894): 176–183.

9. Allen, "Negro Health Problem," p. 195

10. Ibid., pp. 195–199.

11. McKie, "Brief History of Insanity and Tuberculosis," p. 538; Harris, "Tuberculosis in the Negro," p. 3.

12. Coleman, "Susceptibility of the Negro," p. 128; Smith, "Have American Negroes Too Much Liberty?" pp. 178–179.

13. Allen, "Negro Health Problem," p. 195.

14. Easley, "Sanitary Condition of the Negro," p. 49; Harris, "Tuberculosis in the Negro," pp. 2–3; Mays, "Human Slavery as a Prevention," pp. 193–194; "Discussion on the Paper of Dr. Jones" (1907), in Gamble, *Germs Have No Color Line*, p. 25; Coleman, "Susceptibility of the Negro," pp. 122–127; Edwin R. Baldwin as quoted in Coleman, "Susceptibility of the Negro," p. 131; John S. Haller, Jr., "The Physician Versus the Negro: Medical and Anthropological Concepts of Race in the

Late Nineteenth Century," *Bulletin of the History of Medicine* 44 (March-April 1970): 157–159; Stuart C. Gilman, "Degeneracy and Race in the Nineteenth Century: The Impact of Clinical Medicine," *Journal of Ethnic Studies* 10 (1983): 35–38.

15. McKie, "Brief History of Insanity and Tuberculosis," p. 453.

16. See Kenneth F. Kiple and Virginia Himmelsteib King, *Another Dimension to the Black Diaspora: Diet, Disease, and Racism* (Cambridge: Cambridge University Press, 1981), pp. 135–188; Todd L. Savitt, *Medicine and Slavery: The Disease and Health Care of Blacks in Antebellum Virginia* (Urbana: University of Illinois, 1978), pp. 27–243; John S. Haller, Jr., "The Negro and the Southern Physician: A Study of Medical and Racial Attitudes 1800–1860," *Medical History* 16 (July 1972): 242–249.

17. Samuel A. Cartwright, "Report on the Disease and Physical Peculiarities of the Negro Race," *New Orleans Medical and Surgical Journal* (May 1851): 691–715; Haller, "Negro and the Southern Physician," p. 249.

18. As quoted in Powell, "Increase of Insanity and Tuberculosis," p. 1188. For other dissenting views among white physicians emphasizing surroundings, occupations, and modes of life instead of innate racial traits as explanations for black susceptibility to TB, see Charles L. Minor from Asheville, N.C., and Sanger Brown from Chicago, both as quoted in Coleman, "Susceptibility of the Negro," p. 131.

19. Savitt, *Medicine and Slavery*, pp. 42–56; Kiple and King, *Another Dimension to the Black Diaspora*, pp. 135–188; Marion M. Torchia, "Tuberculosis among American Negroes: Medical Research on a Racial Disease, 1830–1950," *Journal of the History of Medicine and Allied Science* 32 (July 1977): 253–254, 259; Haller, "Negro and the Southern Physician," pp. 242–243.

20. Torchia, "Tuberculosis among Negroes," p. 259.

21. Savitt, *Medicine and Slavery*, pp. 57–73, 83–110; Kiple and King, *Another Dimension to the Black Diaspora*, pp. 146–188; Haller, "The Negro and the Southern Physician," pp. 245–246.

22. See Haller, "Physician Versus the Negro," pp. 155–157; Torchia, "Tuberculosis among American Negroes," pp. 258–261; Ott, "Political Culture, Medical Culture," pp. 2–33; David McBride, *From TB to AIDS: Epidemics among Urban Blacks since 1900* (Albany: State University of New York Press, 1991), pp. 9–30; Gamble, *Germs Have No Color Line*, Introduction.

23. E. Mayfield Boyle, "The Negro and Tuberculosis" (1912), in Gamble, *Germs Have No Color Line*, p. 45. See also Kelly Miller, "The Negro Anti-Tuberculosis Society of Washington," *Journal of Outdoor Life* 6 (May 1909): 129–130; H. Llewellyn Harris, Jr., "The Negro Health Problem," *Opportunity* 4 (September 1926): 291. John E. Hunter, a black physician from Lexington, Kentucky, was not as vigorously consistent in countering arguments made by white colleagues as Boyle and others. Hunter concurred in some of the most blatantly racist opinions in an article written by Seale Harris, although he emphasized socioeconomic inequities as the primary cause for TB among blacks. See Hunter, "Tuberculosis in the Negro: Causes and Treatment" (1905), in Gamble, *Germs Have No Color Line*, pp. 12–19; Harris, "Tuberculosis in the Negro," pp. 1–5; Archard, "Tuberculization of the Negro: A Letter," p. 43.

24. See Barbara Bates, *Bargaining for Life: A Social History of Tuberculosis, 1876–1938* (Philadelphia: University of Pennsylvania Press, 1992), pp. 11–24; Rene

Dubos and Jean Dubos, *The White Plague: Tuberculosis, Man, and Society* (Boston: Little, Brown, 1952), chaps. 6–9.

25. "First Meeting of the Women's Missionary Society of Philadelphia," *Woman's Era* (1896).

26. See Kiple and King, *Another Dimension of the African Diaspora*, pp. 135–146.

27. See Mark Caldwell, *The Last Crusade: The War on Consumption 1862–1954* (New York: Atheneum, 1988), p. 22; Nan Marie McMurry, "'And I? I Am in a Consumption': The Tuberculosis Patient, 1780–1930" (Ph.D. diss., Duke University, 1985), pp. 42–58; Barbara Ehrenreich and Deirdre English, *Complaints and Disorders: The Sexual Politics of Sickness* (Westbury, N.Y.: Feminist Press, 1973), pp. 11–44.

28. There were scientists before Koch, dating back to the sixteenth century, who theorized about the tuberculosis microbe and contagion. See Dubos and Dubos, *White Plague*, chaps. 6 and 8; Bates, *Bargaining for Life*, p. 16; Nancy Tomes, "The Private Side of Public Health: Sanitary Science, Domestic Hygiene, and the Germ Theory, 1870–1900," *Bulletin of the History of Medicine* 64 (1990): 509–539; Tomes, "Moralizing the Microbe: The Germ Theory and the Moral Construction of Behavior in the Late 19th Century T.B. Movement" (paper presented at the "Health and Morality" Meeting, MacArthur Foundation, 22–24 June 1992); Sheila M. Rothman, *Living in the Shadow of Death: Tuberculosis and the Social Experience of Illness in American History* (New York: Basic Books, 1994), pp. 179–193.

29. See Tomes, "Moralizing the Microbe," pp. 4–23; Rothman, *Living in the Shadow of Death*, pp. 179–193; Bates, *Bargaining for Life*, pp. 7–8, 11–24.

30. See Georgina Susan Hickey, "Visibility, Politics, and Urban Development: Working-Class Women in Early Twentieth Century Atlanta" (Ph.D. diss., University of Michigan, 1995), pp. 136–155.

31. McKie, "Brief History of Insanity and Tuberculosis," p. 537. For attributions made about domestics spreading disease during the antebellum period, see entry for 2 February 1863 in Amelia Akehurst Lines, *To Raise Myself a Little: The Diaries and Letters of Jennie, a Georgia Teacher, 1851–1866*, ed. Thomas Dyer (Athens: University of Georgia Press, 1982), p. 197; entry for 2 January 1862, Samuel P. Richards Diaries, vol. 9, 71, Atlanta History Center (hereafter cited as AHC); Savitt, *Medicine and Slavery*, pp. 56–57.

32. H. McHatton, "Our House and Our Servant," *Atlanta Journal-Record of Medicine* 5 (July 1903): 216–217.

33. See, for example, Allen, "The Negro Public Health Problem," p. 194; Lucille Smith Hughs, "My Pot Pourri of Ninety Years," 1965–1966, typescript, Susanna M. Hughs Papers, AHC.

34. E. H. Jones, "Tuberculosis in the Negro" (1907), in Gamble, *Germs Have No Color Line*, p. 20.

35. William J. Northen, "Tuberculosis among Negroes," *Journal of the Southern Medical Association* 6 (October 1909): 418; McHatton, "Our House and Our Servant," p. 216.

36. Northen, "Tuberculosis among Negroes," p. 418.

37. *Atlanta Constitution*, 19 December 1909.

38. Ruth Reed, *The Negro Women of Gainesville, Georgia* (Athens: University of Georgia, 1921), p. 18.

39. *Atlanta Constitution*, 19 December 1909 and 8 June 1913.

40. For other examples linking domestics to the spread of disease, see Wilson, N.C. *The Daily Times*, 7 September 1912, in TINF; H. L. Sutherland, "Health Conditions of the Negro in the South: with Special Reference to Tuberculosis," *Journal of the Southern Medical Association* 6 (October 1909): 399–407; Charles P. Wertenbaker to Surgeon General, 20 March 1909, book no. 6, p. 405, Charles P. Wertenbaker Papers, Alderman Library, University of Virginia; *Atlanta Constitution*, 24 March 1910; 7 January, 1, 2, and 13 September 1912; *Montgomery Advertiser*, 7 April 1913, in TINF; C. E. Terry, "The Negro: His Relation to Public Health in the South," *American Journal of Public Health in the South* 3 (April 1913): 304; "Report of the W. G. Raoul Foundation State Agents Profusely Illustrated with Comment and Suggestions on Treatment of Consumption" (Atlanta, 1914), copy in Atlanta Lung Association Collection, AHC (hereafter cited as ALAC, AHC); W. W. Tindall [Fulton County Children's Court Judge] to Rosa Lowe [Secretary of the Anti-Tuberculosis Association], 16 March 1914, ALAC, AHC; *Richmond Planet*, 21 November 1914, in TINF; Lawrence Lee, "The Negro as a Public Health Problem in Public Health Charity," *American Journal of Public Health* 5 (March 1915): 208; Mary Dickinson, "Tuberculosis Spread by Wash-Women," *Healthology* 1 (April 1919):72–75, copy in the ALAC, AHC; *The Mobile Forum*, 23 August 1919, in TINF; Algernon B. Jackson, "The Need of Health Education Among Negroes," *Opportunity* 2 (August 1924): 235.

41. Parker, "Negro as a Factor in the Spread of Tuberculosis," p. 290.

42. See, for example, *Atlanta Constitution*, 5 and 7 January 1912; *Richmond Planet*, 21 November 1914, in TINF; Jones, "Tuberculosis in the Negro," p. 20; Northen, "Tuberculosis in Negroes," p. 419.

43. Allen, "Negro Health Problem," p. 196.

44. See Ehrenreich and English, *Complaints and Disorders*, p. 30.

45. Allen, "The Negro Health Problem," p. 196; Thomas W. Murrell, "Syphilis and the American Negro—A Medico-Sociological Study," *Transactions of the Fortieth Annual Session of the Medical Society of Virginia* (October 1909): 168–174. For other views on VD and domestics see Lee, "The Negro as a Problem," pp. 207–208; McHatton, "Our House and Our Servant," p. 217.

46. See Sander L. Gilman, "Black Bodies, White Bodies: Toward an Iconography of Female Sexuality in Late Nineteenth-Century Art, Medicine, and Literature," *Critical Inquiry* 12 (Autumn 1985): 204–242.

47. Tomes, "Moralizing the Microbe," p. 21.

48. Scrapbook, 1909, pp. 28–50, ALAC, AHC.

49. Scrapbook, 1909, p. 21, ALAC, AHC; *Atlanta Constitution*, 19 December 1909; Ehrenreich and English, *Complaints and Disorders*, pp. 57–59.

50. Bates, *Bargaining for Life*, pp. 7–8; Tomes, "Private Side of Public Health," pp. 528–529; Tomes, "Moralizing the Microbe," pp. 8–16; Rothman, *Living in the Shadow of Death*, pp. 179–193; Caldwell, *Last Crusade*, p. 6.

51. See Dubos and Dubos, *White Plague*, pp. 199–207; Nancy Krieger and Mary Bassett, "The Health of Black Folk: Disease, Class, and Ideology in Science," in *The "Racial" Economy of Science: Toward a Democratic Future*, ed. Sandra Harding (Bloomington: Indiana University Press, 1993), pp. 161–169.

52. Stuart Galishoff, "Germs Know No Color Line: Black Health and Public Policy in Atlanta, 1900–1918," *Journal of the History of Medicine and Allied Sciences*

40 (January 1985): 23; McBride, *From TB to AIDS*, pp. 1–30; Gamble, *Germs Have No Color Line*, Introduction.

53. During yellow fever epidemics blacks were often hired as nurses, gravediggers, and policemen in the South, to compensate for the loss of white lives and the need for additional help. See Jo Ann Carrigan, "Yellow Fever: Scourge of the South," in *Disease and Distinctiveness in the American South*, ed. Todd Savitt and James Harvey Young (Knoxville: University of Tennessee Press, 1988), p. 62; Dennis C. Rousey, "Yellow Fever and Black Policemen in Memphis: A Post Reconstruction Anomaly," *Journal of Southern History* 60 (August 1985): 357–374.

54. See, for comparison, Richard J. Evans, *Death in Hamburg: Society and Politics in the Cholera Years 1830–1910* (New York: Oxford University Press, 1987), pp. 352, 409–412, 467.

55. Dickinson, "Tuberculosis Spread by Wash-Women," pp. 72–75. For reports identifying housewives showing a propensity for TB see "Statistical Report of Patients in Tuberculosis Clinic," April 1912 and September 1912, ALAC, AHC; and "Annual Report," Atlanta Anti-Tuberculosis Association, 1916, ALAC, AHC; Tomes, "Moralizing the Microbe," pp. 20–21.

56. *Atlanta Constitution*, 1 January 1914; Tomes, "Moralizing the Microbes," pp. 26–29; Galishoff, "Germs Know No Color Line," p. 29; Gamble, *Germs Have No Color Line*, Introduction.

57. James O. Breeden, "Disease as a Factor in Southern Distinctiveness," in Savitt and Young, *Disease and Distinctiveness*, pp. 1–28; Alan I. Marcus, "Hookworm and Southern Distinctiveness," in Savitt and Young, *Disease and Distinctiveness*, pp. 79–99.

58. Terry, "The Negro: His Relation to Public Health," p. 300; see also Dr. Saunders, as quoted in Terry, p. 309.

59. Marcus, "South's Native Foreigners," in Savitt and Young, *Disease and Distinctiveness*, pp. 79–99; Elizabeth Etheridge, "Pellagra: An Unappreciated Reminder of Southern Distinctiveness," in Savitt and Young, *Disease and Distinctiveness*, pp. 100–119.

60. Galishoff, "Germs Know No Color Line," pp. 31–33.

61. *Atlanta Constitution*, 25 and 30 January 1904.

62. *Atlanta Constitution*, 12 January 1905; Atlanta City Council Minutes, 19 December 1904, AHC.

63. *Atlanta Constitution*, 1 May 1905.

64. See Michel Foucault, *The Birth of the Clinic: An Archaeology of Medical Perception* (New York: Vintage, 1975), pp. 25–26; Ehrenreich and English, *Complaints and Disorders*, pp. 63–66.

65. See Hickey, "Visibility, Politics, and Urban Development," pp. 150–154.

66. Atlanta City Council Minutes, 1 and 15 May 1905, AHC.

67. *Atlanta Constitution*, 11 February, 11 and 12 March 1910; McHatton, "Our House and Our Servant," p. 419. Ruth Reed offered another solution—the creation of public wash houses run by the city and required for use by laundry workers, at a nominal fee. Similarly, the Methodist Episcopal Church South discussed building a "community laundry" for black women in Nashville. See Reed, "Negro Women of Gainesville," p. 18; *Savannah Tribune*, 31 May 1919.

68. *Atlanta Journal*, 12 February 1910; *Atlanta Journal*, 11 February 1910; *Atlanta Constitution*, 10–11 January 1910.

69. *Atlanta Independent*, 19 February 1910. See also *Savannah Tribune*, 26 March and 30 April 1910.

70. *Atlanta Constitution*, 11 March 1910.

71. Ibid., 11 and 12 March 1910, 2 October 1912.

72. Ibid., 25 March 1910.

73. David M. Katzman, *Seven Days a Week: Women and Domestic Service in Industrializing America* (New York: Oxford University Press, 1978), pp. 60–62, 72, 130; Ruth Schwartz Cowan, *More Work for Mother: The Ironies of Household Technology from the Open Hearth to the Microwave* (New York: Basic Books, 1983), pp. 105–107. For the classic study on workers' control see David Montgomery, *Workers' Control in America: Studies in the History of Work, Technology, and Labor Struggles* (Cambridge: Cambridge University Press, 1979).

74. See Atlanta, Minute Book, Board of Water Commissioners, 9 September 1908, April 1909, pp. 96, 203, AHC. Black washerwomen were not specifically mentioned in the minute book. The laundry firms wanted to receive the same discounts as large manufacturers and larger discounts than individual consumers.

75. As quoted from *Savannah Tribune*, 20 January 1912.

76. *Atlanta Constitution*, 23 October 1912 and 7 August 1910. See Atlanta *Journal of Labor*, 28 August 1908, for an article indicting commercial laundries, along with other industrial workshops, for fostering TB and other contagions through unsanitary practices.

77. *Atlanta City Directory*, 1900; *Atlanta Independent*, 1 August 1914, 6 October 1917.

78. Atlanta *Journal of Labor*, 30 August 1912; see also 20 September 1907 and 30 May 1913. The Federation was serious about increasing the ranks of organized labor. It threatened a consumer boycott if commercial laundry workers refused to affiliate themselves with the International Steam Laundry Worker's Union. See Atlanta *Journal of Labor*, 17 November 1911.

79. Atlanta *Journal of Labor*, 12 February 1915.

80. For comparisons on regulation of domestic workers elsewhere, see Sandra Lauderdale Graham, *House and Street: The Domestic World of Servants and Masters in Nineteenth Century Rio de Janeiro* (Cambridge: Cambridge University Press, 1988), pp. 91–136; Patricia E. Malcolmson, *English Laundresses: A Social History, 1850–1930* (Urbana, Ill.: University of Illinois Press, 1986), pp. 44–69; Karen Transberg Hansen, *Distant Companions: Servants and Employers in Zambia, 1900–1985* (Ithaca: Cornell University Press, 1989), pp. 74–75; Keletso E. Atkins, *The Moon is Dead! Give Us Our Money! The Cultural Origins of an African Work Ethic, Natal, South Africa, 1843–1900* (Portsmouth, N.H.: Heinemann, 1993), pp. 126–137; Charles van Onselen, *Studies in the Social and Economic History of the Witwatersrand, 1886–1914*, vol. 2, *New Nineveh* (New York: Longman, 1982), pp. 74–110. See also *Atlanta Constitution*, 19 March 1910; *Savannah Tribune*, 6 January 1912; *New York Age*, 27 November 1915; *Montgomery Advertiser*, 14–23 January 1914, in TINF.

81. *Atlanta Constitution*, 29 September 1912.

82. Ibid., 28 September 1912.

83. Ibid., 28 September 1912.

84. Ibid., 28 and 15 September 1912.

85. Ibid., 15 September 1912.

86. Ibid., 15 September 1912.

87. Stinson and Proctor were praised as "two wise negro leaders" for their expression of similar sentiments on other occasions. See *Atlanta Constitution*, 8 September 1912.

88. Ibid., 2 and 4 September, 2 and 5 October 1912.

89. *Atlanta Independent*, 5 October 1912.

90. *Atlanta Constitution*, 3 October 1912.

91. McHatton, "Our House and Our Servant," p. 218. See also J. H. Stanley as quoted in "Discussion on the Paper of Dr. Jones," p. 179; and Gamble, *Germs Have No Color Line*, Introduction.

92. See Scrapbook, 1912, ALAC, AHC.

93. *Atlanta Constitution*, 7 November 1909.

94. Minute Book, 1908–1918, Neighborhood Union Papers, Robert W. Woodruff Library, Clarke Atlanta University (hereafter cited as NU, AU); "Partial Report of the Work of the Neighborhood Union to the Atlanta Tuberculosis Association," 1917–1919, NU, AU; *Atlanta Constitution*, 31 January and 2 February 1911; Jacqueline Anne Rouse, *Lugenia Burns Hope: Black Southern Reformer* (Athens: University of Georgia Press, 1989), pp. 71–81; Dorothy Salem, *To Better Our World: Black Women in Organized Reform, 1890–1920* (Brooklyn, N.Y.: Carlson, 1990), pp. 108–109; Cynthia Neverdon-Morton, *Afro-American Women of the South and the Advancement of the Race, 1895–1925* (Knoxville: University of Tennessee Press, 1989), pp. 146–160; "Atlanta's Public Health Program," n.d., Southern Regional Office Records, National Urban League, Library of Congress.

95. See Salem, *To Better Our World*, pp. 107–109; Neverdon-Morton, *Afro-American Women in the South*, pp. 146–160.

96. Lowe, "The Negro, Present Conditions—Relief, A Hospital and District Nursing," 1908, ALAC, AHC; Alton Timothy Dial, "Public Health in Atlanta During the Progressive Era" (M.A. thesis, Georgia State University, 1970), p. 88; Galishoff, "Germs Know No Color Line," p. 28.

97. *Atlanta Constitution*, 16 May 1909. See also *Atlanta Constitution*, 19 May and 18 October 1910.

98. *Atlanta Constitution*, 21 June 1914.

99. Lowe, "City Tuberculosis Program for Negroes," 1914, ALAC, AHC.

100. Galishoff, "Germs Know No Color Line," pp. 26–28; Dial, "Public Health," pp. 62–65; Edward H. Beardsley, *A History of Neglect: Health Care for Blacks and Mill Workers in the Twentieth Century South* (Knoxville: University of Tennessee Press, 1987), pp. 24–25, 128–136.

101. "Summary of the Negro Work which the Association is Launching" [1915], ALAC, AHC; Rosa Lowe, "Notes on Work of Negro Race Committee," 1915, ALAC, AHC; H. H. Pace, "Report from Negro Anti-Tuberculosis Association," 20 April 1916, ALAC, AHC; Rosa Lowe, "Report of the Negro Work," 14 June 1917, ALAC, AHC; *Atlanta Constitution*, 19 April and 8 June 1914.

102. See McBride, *From TB to AIDS*, pp. 25–26.

103. McBride, *From TB to AIDS*, pp. 31–62; David McBride, *Integrating the City of Medicine: Blacks in Philadelphia Health Care, 1910–1965* (Philadelphia: Temple University Press, 1989), pp. 31–63; Keith Wailoo, "The Sickled Cell: Ideology and Technology in Twentieth Century Medicine" (paper presented at the Organization of American Historians Meeting, Atlanta, Georgia, April 1994).

10. *"Looking for a Free State to Live In"*

1. *Atlanta Constitution*, 7 and 9 December 1915; *Atlanta Journal*, 7 December 1915; Thomas Cripps, *Slow Fade to Black: The Negro in American Film, 1900–1942* (New York: Oxford University Press, 1993), pp. 41–57; Nancy MacLean, *Behind the Mask of Chivalry: The Making of the Second Ku Klux Klan* (New York: Oxford University Press, 1994), pp. 4–27; John Dittmer, *Black Georgia in the Progressive Era, 1900–1920* (Urbana: University of Illinois Press, 1977), pp. 185–186.

2. As quoted in Cripps, *Slow Fade to Black*, p. 143.

3. MacLean, *Behind the Mask of Chivalry*, pp. 4–27; Dittmer, *Black Georgia*, pp. 185–186; Clifford M. Kuhn et al., *Living Atlanta: An Oral History of the City, 1914–1948* (Athens: University of Georgia Press, 1990), pp. 12, 253.

4. For a cogent analysis of the timing of the KKK revival and its membership see MacLean, *Behind the Mask of Chivalry*, pp. 4–17. See also Kuhn et al., *Living Atlanta*, pp. 313–314; Dittmer, *Black Georgia*, p. 186.

5. As quoted in Kuhn et al., *Living Atlanta*, p. 9.

6. Letters from Migrants, 27 and 28 April 1917 (files from the Chicago *Defender*), Series 6, National Urban League Papers, Library of Congress (hereafter cited as NUL, LC).

7. Quotation and chapter title from Letters from Migrants, 24 March 1917 (files from the *New York Globe*), NUL, LC.

8. David Montgomery, *The Fall of the House of Labor: The Workplace, the State, and American Labor Activism, 1865–1925* (New York: Cambridge University Press, 1987), pp. 370–382.

9. 1914 campaign literature, Joseph M. Brown Papers, Atlanta History Center (hereafter cited as AHC).

10. 1914 campaign literature, Joseph M. Brown Papers, AHC; Dewey W. Grantham, Jr., *Hoke Smith and the Politics of the New South* (Baton Rouge: Louisiana State University Press, 1958), pp. 270–273.

11. 1914 campaign literature, Joseph M. Brown Papers, AHC. See also *Atlanta Constitution*, 31 March 1910. The owner of Crawford Coal and Ice Company reported that black men had boycotted his company as a result of their involvement in a secret society. He stated that other firms were facing a similar situation.

12. Atlanta *Journal of Labor*, 24 July 1914. See also Atlanta *Journal of Labor*, 1 May 1914.

13. Ruth Reed, *Negro Women of Gainesville, Georgia* (Athens: University of Georgia Press, 1921), p. 46.

14. *Savannah Tribune*, 31 May 1919.

15. *Houston Labor Journal*, 6 May 1916; Norfolk *Journal and Guide*, 29 September and 6 October 1917; Philip S. Foner, *Women and the American Labor Movement: From World War I to the Present* (New York: Free Press, 1980), vol. 2, pp. 66–67.

16. New Orleans *Louisiana States*, 23 July 1918, in Tuskegee Institute News Clip File (hereafter cited as TINF).

17. *Atlanta Constitution*, 8 October 1914.

18. *Montgomery Advertiser*, 21 February 1916, in TINF.

19. *Southern Recorder*, 29 March 1913; Atlanta *Journal of Labor*, 24 March 1911. There are also examples of employers forming organizations with workers to pursue a more amicable (and maternalistic) approach. See W. P. Burrell, "Report on the

Committee on Business and Labor Conditions," *Proceedings of the Hampton Negro Conference* 6 (July 1902): 43–44.

20. For other discussions of the controversy see T. J. Woofter, "The Negroes of Athens, Georgia," *Bulletin of the University of Georgia* 14 (December 1913): 46–47; Reed, *Negro Women of Gainesville*, p. 28.

21. As quoted in Ray Stannard Baker, *Following the Color Line: American Negro Citizenship in the Progressive Era* (New York, 1908; reprint ed., New York: Harper and Row, 1964), p. 61. See also *Montgomery Advertiser*, 30 August 1916, in TINF.

22. *Montgomery Advertiser*, 30 August 1916, in TINF. See also Henry Wrights Gibbs, *The Negro as an Economic Factor in Alabama* (Nashville, 1919), p. 61.

23. *Atlanta Constitution*, 20 August 1916.

24. *Montgomery Advertiser*, 21 February 1916, in TINF.

25. Ibid., 25 February 1916, in TINF.

26. Dittmer, *Black Georgia*, p. 191; James R. Grossman, *Land of Hope: Chicago, Black Southerners, and the Great Migration* (Chicago: University of Chicago Press, 1989), p. 52; MacLean, *Behind the Mask of Chivalry*, p. 25.

27. See Francis Taylor Long, "The Negroes of Clarke County, Georgia, During the Great War," *Bulletin of the University of Georgia* 19 (September 1919): 40–43.

28. David M. Kennedy, *Over Here: The First World War and American Society* (New York: Oxford University Press, 1980), p. 269.

29. Walter F. White, "'Work or Fight' in the South," *The New Republic* 18 (1 March 1919): 144–146; Cynthia Neverdon-Morton, *Afro-American Women of the South and the Advancement of the Race, 1895–1925* (Knoxville: University of Tennessee Press, 1989), p. 73.

30. See Table 2 at the back of the book.

31. Gretchen Ehrmann Maclachlan, "Women's Work: Atlanta's Industrialization, 1879–1929" (Ph.D. diss., Emory University, 1992), pp. 86–87, 90–98; George E. Haynes, *The Negro at Work during World War and Reconstruction: Statistics, Problems, and Policies Relating to the Greater Inclusion of Negro Wage Earners in American Industry and Agriculture* (Washington, D.C.: Government Printing Office, 1921), pp. 124–133.

32. Macon *News*, 18 October 1918, in TINF. The federal government also made similar appeals to black women through war propaganda. See, for example, the Portsmouth, Virginia, *Star*, 21 October 1918, in TINF.

33. Walter F. White, "Report of Conditions Found in Investigation of 'Work or Fight' Laws in Southern States," Group 1, Series C, Administrative Files, National Association for the Advancement of Colored People Papers, Library of Congress (hereafter cited as NAACP, LC).

34. White, "Report of Conditions Found in Investigation of 'Work or Fight' Laws in Southern States," Group 1, Series C, NAACP, LC.

35. John R. Shillady to O. A. Toomer, 5 October 1918, Group 1, Series G, Branch Files, NAACP, LC.

36. Walter F. White to Shillady, 26 October 1918, Group 1, Series C, Administrative Files, NAACP, LC.

37. See "Tenth Anniversary Conference of the National Association of Colored People: Reports of Branches," 28 June 1919, Group 1, Series B, Annual Conference Files, NAACP, LC; and A. B. Johnson to James Weldon Johnson, 16 December 1918, Group 1, Series G, Branch Files, NAACP, LC.

38. Rev. P. J. Bryant, Remarks to the 10th Annual Conference of the NAACP, 24 June 1919, Group 1, Series B, Annual Conference Files, NAACP, LC; *Atlanta Constitution*, 9 November 1918. See also *Atlanta Constitution*, 10 July–25 August, 9 November 1918; Dittmer, *Black Georgia*, p. 198.

39. G. R. Hutto to Walter F. White, 21 October 1918, Group 1, Series C, Administrative Files, NAACP, LC. See also P. J. Bryant's Tenth Annual Conference Address, 1919, Group 1, Series B, Annual Conference Files, NAACP, LC.

40. White, "'Work or Fight' in the South," pp. 144–146; Chicago *Defender*, 13 July 1918, in TINF; *New York Age*, 19 October and 16 November 1918, in TINF.

41. Quoted in *Baltimore Daily Herald*, 10 September 1918, Group 1, Series C, Administrative Files, NAACP, LC.

42. *New York Age*, 19 and 2 November 1918, in TINF.

43. See Carole Marks, *Farewell—We're Good and Gone: The Great Black Migration* (Bloomington: Indiana University Press, 1989); Gavin Wright, *Old South, New South: Revolutions in the Southern Economy Since the Civil War* (New York: Basic Books, 1986), pp. 157–207; Thomas Jackson Woofter, *Negro Migration: Changes in Rural Organization and Population of the Cotton Belt* (New York, 1920; reprint ed., New York: Negro Universities Press, 1969), pp. 105–122; Dittmer, *Black Georgia*, pp. 186–191.

44. Woofter, *Negro Migration*, pp. 123–132; Marks, *Farewell*, pp. 13–14, 49–79; Neil R. McMillen, *Dark Journey: Black Mississippians in the Age of Jim Crow* (Urbana: University of Illinois Press, 1989), pp. 258–270.

45. Dittmer, *Black Georgia*, pp. 175–178; Edwin S. Redkey, *Black Exodus: Black Nationalist Thought and Back-to-Africa Movements, 1890–1910* (New Haven: Yale University Press, 1969), pp. 19, 24; Grossman, *Land of Hope*, pp. 25–31.

46. *Atlanta Constitution*, 26 June 1903.

47. See Peter Gottlieb, *Making Their Own Way: Southern Blacks' Migration to Pittsburgh, 1916–1930* (Urbana: University of Illinois Press, 1987), pp. 23–30; Grossman, *Land of Hope*, pp. 25–31.

48. See Simon Kuznets, Dorothy Thomas Swaine et al., *Population Redistribution and Economic Growth, United States, 1870–1950*, 3 vols. (Philadelphia: American Philosophical Society, 1957–1964). For statistics on Georgia-born blacks, see vol. 3, p. 308, Table P-3.

49. Kuznets et al., *Population Redistribution*, vol. 1, pp. 129–131, Table P-1 and vol. 3, pp. 131, 151–152; Marks, *Farewell*, pp. 36–39.

50. See Darlene Clark Hine, "Black Migration to the Urban Midwest: The Gender Dimension, 1915–1945," in *The Great Migration in Historical Perspective*, ed. Joe William Trotter, Jr. (Bloomington: Indiana University Press, 1991), pp. 127–146; Maurine Weiner Greenwald, *Women, War, and Work: The Impact of World War I on Women Workers in the U.S.* (Westport, Conn.: Greenwood Press, 1980), pp. 20–27; Joanne J. Meyerowitz, *Women Adrift: Independent Wage Earners in Chicago, 1880–1930* (Chicago: University of Chicago Press, 1988), pp. 12–16; Jacqueline Jones, *Labor of Love, Labor of Sorrow: Black Women, Work, and the Family from Slavery to Freedom* (New York: Basic Books, 1985), pp. 152–195.

51. Letters from Migrants, 10 June 1917, Series 6 (files from the Chicago *Defender*), NUL, LC.

52. Letters from Migrants, 6 June, 19 May, 27 August 1917, Series 6 (files from the Chicago *Defender* and *New York Age*), NUL, LC.

53. Grossman, *Land of Hope*.

54. Joe William Trotter, Jr., "Introduction: Black Migration in Historical Perspective," in *The Great Migration in Historical Perspective*, p. 8.

55. George L. Vaugh, "The Negro in Labor and Industry," Address to the Tenth Anniversary Conference, June 1919, Group 1, Series B, Annual Conference Files, NAACP, LC.

56. See Hazel V. Carby, "'It Jus Be's Dat Way Sometime': The Sexual Politics of Women's Blues," *Radical America* 20 (June–July 1986): 9–22; Farah Jasmine Griffin, *"Who Set You Flowin'?": The African-American Migration Narrative* (New York: Oxford University Press, 1995), pp. 52–61.

57. Sterling Brown et al., eds., *The Negro Caravan* (New York: Dryden, 1941), pp. 472–473. (Paramount Series no. 20098, January 1922.)

58. Dan Carey (Atlanta Real Estate Board) to U.S. Housing Corporation, 27 September 1918, Atlanta Ga., Record Group 3: U.S. Housing Corporation Records, National Archives.

59. Dittmer, *Black Georgia*, pp. 188–189; Grossman, *Land of Hope*, pp. 44–47.

60. Grossman, *Land of Hope*, pp. 40–41. See also *Bessemer Weekly*, 16 November 1918.

61. Dittmer, *Black Georgia*, p. 189.

Acknowledgments

his book could not have been written without the generosity of many individuals and institutions. Several foundations have provided subventions for research, travel, and writing. Both the Carter G. Woodson Institute Predoctoral Fellowship at the University of Virginia and the Smithsonian Institution Postdoctoral Fellowship at the National Museum of American History made it possible for me to work on the manuscript full time and provided communities of scholars whose wide-ranging knowledge across disciplines inspired me at pivotal moments. I also wish to acknowledge the late Armstead L. Robinson and the staff of the Woodson Institute. Other foundations include the Ford Foundation Postdoctoral Fellowship, Duke University; American Association of University Women Educational Foundation Dissertation Fellowship; Lena Lake Forrest Fellowship/Business and Professional Women's Foundation Research Grant; American Philosophical Society Research Grant; American Council of Learned Societies Research Grant; Woodrow Wilson Dissertation Research Grant in Women's Studies; John F. Enders Research Fellowship, Yale University; Institute for the Arts and Humanities, University of North Carolina, Chapel Hill; Institute for Research in the Social Sciences, Summer Fellowship, University of North Carolina, Chapel Hill; and University Research Council Publication Grant, University of North Carolina, Chapel Hill.

Without the efficiency and knowledge of archivists and librarians, difficult research would have been impossible. I thank staff members at the following institutions who helped me wend my way through countless records: Yale University libraries; Atlanta History Center; Georgia Department of Archives and History; Robert W. Woodruff Library, Clark Atlanta University; Southern Historical Collection, University of North Carolina, Chapel Hill; the Library of Congress; the National Archives; William R. Perkins Library, Duke University; Robert W. Woodruff Library, Emory University; Alderman Library, University of Virginia; and Mercer University Library. Leslie Rowland and her staff at the Freedmen and Southern Society Project at the University of Maryland graciously allowed me to peruse their voluminous files and share their work space.

The ideas in this book have gone through many fruitful revisions thanks to the intellectual stimulation provided by colleagues across the country in seminars and conferences. Conversations following lectures given at the following institutions were very beneficial: Carnegie Mellon University, Department of History; National Museum of American History; George Mason University, Department of History; University of Maryland, College Park, Department of History; the German Historical Institute, Washington, D.C.; Comparative History of Blacks in the Diaspora Seminar, Michigan State University; Massachusetts Institute of Technology, Department of History; Princeton University, Women's Studies Program; University of Missouri, Kansas City, Department of History; Similarly, I have learned from audiences and commentators on panels at the following conferences: Organization of American Historians; Berkshire Conference on the History of Women; Southern Historical Association; Black Women in the Academy Conference at Massachusetts Institute of Technology; American Historical Association; Southern Labor Studies Conference.

My debts to individuals who have assisted me in this enterprise are immense. David Montgomery and Nancy Cott were steadfast readers throughout the painstaking creative process, providing cogent chapter-by-chapter critiques that always pushed me to new heights. Julius S. Scott, III, read and edited many drafts, with the acumen of a diligent critic and the patience of a friend.

Some of my favorite historians read the entire manuscript and provided extremely helpful comments. Jacquelyn Hall's scholarship has been a model and her collegiality refreshing. I have also been able to rely on Robin D. G. Kelley to inspire me to make intellectual connections I had not imagined before. Others provided insightful, detailed comments as well: Peter Rachleff, Joe W. Trotter, John W. Cell, Nancy A. Hewitt, David Roediger, Eric Arneson, Clifford M. Kuhn, and Julie Green. I am also grateful to John W. Blassingame and to Mario T. Garcia.

Other colleagues have been generous in commenting on selected chapters and sharing their ideas with me. Jerma Jackson and Saidiya Hartman have been there from the beginning, reading drafts and helping to keep my life in perspective. Evelynn Hammonds, Keith Wailoo, and Catherine Ott were especially valuable in contributing to my knowledge of the history of medicine and science. Elsa Barkley Brown, Deborah E. McDowell, Herman Bennett, Leslie Rowland, Waldo Martin, Eric Lott, and Jennifer Morgan have challenged me in our many talks about American history and culture and their readings of my work. Pete Daniel, Ronald M. Radano, Joseph P. Reidy, Alison Kibler, Armstead L. Robinson, Dagmar Herzog provided close readings at various stages also.

David Godshalk, Eric Arneson, Daniel Letwin, and Susan Porter Benson provided useful information from their own research notes. Mary Jane Aldrich-Moodie was a superb research assistant; she was tireless in reading reams of microfilm, ferreting out rich nuggets of material. Genna Rae McNeil's thoughtfulness as a colleague and friend has been enriching. Sibyl Wagner provided an anchor as I juggled matters of work and life.

I am grateful to Denise Stinson for her enthusiasm in finding the right press and for introducing me to Joyce Seltzer. Joyce, an outstanding editor, made many contributions during the process of crafting the book. I wish to thank others at Harvard University Press as well, including Maria Ascher for helping to tighten the narrative, Mary Ellen Geer for her patience and skill in the final copyediting, and Annamarie McMahon for the beautiful book design.

Finally, family and friends from Connecticut to Florida sustained me with their love and encouragement, providing me with warm places to sleep, good food, and other diversions during the seemingly never-ending process of research and writing; my thanks to Bruce Hunter, Eliza Hunter, Celestine Hunter, Hubert Hunter, Barbara Hunter, Janette Webster, Cynthia Glover, Ianthia Scott, Julius S. Scott, Jr., Clifford Charles, Valerie Mosley Diamond, and Hilda Hutto. My greatest thanks go to my parents, Inell Harper Hunter and Willie J. Hunter, for filling in the gaps when resources lagged and for their love and devotion throughout the years.

Index

Slaves, 2, 5–6, 15; runaway, 1, 8, 14, 15, 16,
    18, 20, 236; buying and selling of, 5, 9,
    11; prewar urban occupations, 8–9;
    mobility of, 9, 12–13, 16; Confederacy
    and, 14, 15, 18–19; loyalty to masters,
    17–18, 19; Union and, 20; medical care
    for, 189, 192
Slayton, Allen, 19
Slocum, Joe, 162
Smallpox epidemic, 24
Smith, Bessie, 156, 159, 161
Smith, Hoke, 124, 125, 223
Smith, Jimmie, 215
Social activities, 20, 60, 64, 65, 66;
    neighborhood networks, 67–68, 69, 75,
    114, 235; restricted by work demands,
    106; equality/autonomy in, 115–116,
    118, 120, 125, 126, 164, 223; black
    institutions of, 124; mobility in, 124,
    155. *See also* Community; Leisure
    activities, black
Social Darwinism, 192
Social reform, 7, 69, 124–125, 136. *See also*
    Progressivism/progressive reform
Social work, 140–141
Sojourners of Truth, 163
South: Civil War and postwar conditions,
    3, 4, 5, 6–7, 8, 17, 26; agricultural
    economy, 7, 8, 21; occupational structure
    of, 65; diseases in, 202–203; distinctive
    character of, 202–203; social
    transformation in, 217; racial causes of
    migration from, 219. *See also* New South
Southern Amusement Company, 156
Southern Labor Congress, 223
Spelman College, 49, 163
Starnes, William, 89, 90, 91
Star of Bethlehem society, 71
Stearnes, Etta, 27
Steele, Carrie, 142
Sterilization of black women, 127
Stewart, Emmie, 133
Stinson, Richard, 211
Storrs School, 49, 68
Stout, Samuel, 10
Streetcars, 99, 101, 118, 128
Strikes. *See* Galveston, Texas labor strike;
    Jackson, Mississippi labor strikes; Labor
    resistance; Laundresses/washerwomen:
    strikes and boycotts; Police: strike
    activities and; Textile industry strike
String Beans theater act, 156
Suburbanization, 188

Suffrage. *See* Voting
Summer Hill School, 48

Tanner, Carlton M., 207
Tate, Anna, 215
Tate, James, 49
Taxes, 76, 91, 92, 93–94, 104, 170
Teachers, 40, 62–63, 138; black, 26, 41, 43,
    85, 101, 112, 131–132, 136, 138, 142
Telfair, Georgia, 51
Telfair, Joe, 51
Temperance movement, 69, 125, 163
Terry, C. E., 202
Texas, 74. *See also* Galveston, Texas labor
    strike
Textile industry strike, 114–120
Textile Workers Protective Union, 114,
    116, 117
Theater Owners' Booking Association
    (TOBA), 155, 156, 157
Thomas, Gertrude, 28, 30
Thomas, Rebecca, 71
Thomas, Sarah J., 42–43
Thomasville, Georgia, 226
Tillory, Julie, 1, 2
Tillory, Paul, 1
Tillson, Davis, 41
Tolliver, Harriet, 71–72
Tom Baxter's theater club, Jacksonville,
    Florida, 155
Tom Golden's theater club, Savannah,
    Georgia, 155
Toomer, O. A., 229
Transportation industy, 92, 111, 112, 118.
    See also Railroad(s); Streetcars
Traveling tent shows, 100
True Sisters of Honor, 71–72
Tuberculosis: anti-tuberculosis movement,
    137, 195–200, 204–209, 213, 216;
    domestic workers and, 187–189,
    195–197, 198–199, 200–210, 213,
    217–218, 227; lay opinions of, 187, 189,
    194, 217; public policy, 187; racist
    rhetoric and, 187–188, 190–191, 192,
    193, 195, 198–200, 202, 206, 212–213;
    white physicians and, 187–193, 195, 196,
    202, 212; carriers, 188, 193, 196–197,
    201, 203, 213; class and, 188, 191, 194,
    201, 206; germ theory and, 188,
    194–195, 198, 200, 202; pre–Civil War,
    188, 189, 191–193, 195; black victims,
    189–190, 191, 195, 197, 199, 200–201,
    216; post–Civil War, 189, 191, 193;